A Character of its Own:
Ashbury College 1891 - 1991

Tony German

FOREWORD BY
THE HONOURABLE ROBERT L. STANFIELD
P.C., Q.C., L.L.D.

Published by Creative Bound Inc.
Box 424
151 Tansley Drive
Carp, Ontario, CANADA K0A 1L0
(613) 831-3641

ISBN 0-921165-15-3
Printed and bound in Canada
©1991 Tony German

Edited by Jenny Wilson
Book design by Wendelina O'Keefe
Cartoons are taken from past issues of the *Ashburian* and Ashbury College yearbooks

Canadian Cataloguing in Publication Data

German, Tony, 1924-

A character of its own: Ashbury College, 1891-1991

Includes bibliographical references and index
ISBN 0-921165-15-3

1. Ashbury College (Ottawa, Ont.)-History.
I. Title.

LE3.A83G37 1991   373.713'84   C91–090343–3

TABLE OF CONTENTS

DEDICATION

To those memorable and
specially dedicated teachers
who leave their imprint on our lives.

FOREWORD

The Ashbury I attended for three years following the stock market crash of 1929 was very much the creation of G.P. Woollcombe, the only Headmaster the school had ever known. I remember the school with affection, and I believe the same can be said of my older brother Charles, and my younger brother Pete who also went to Ashbury. The school then probably put too much emphasis on conformity, but at least I learned to accept rules without a sense of oppression. At the time I valued the school principally for its athletic programme, but as the years have gone by my appreciation has focused on Harry Wright, a truly great teacher who also brought to the classroom the prestige of an athlete.

Unfortunately the combination of Woollcombe and Wright could not last forever, and Wright failed as Headmaster when he took over from Dr. Woollcombe in the depths of the Great Depression. Ashbury entered years of adversity and struggle continuing through and beyond the Second World War. Readers of Tony German's history may wonder whether those responsible for directing and supporting the school (and, as an alumnus, I was one of the latter) deserve to have Ashbury survive. But it did survive and came to flourish as a result of new leadership and perhaps memories of what Ashbury had been when G.P. Woollcombe was Headmaster and Harry Wright was teaching.

Tony German tells the story frankly, warts and all. The story covers a century in the life of a Canadian institution founded with courage, established with determination, damaged and weakened by misfortune and neglect, but rising again to take its place among the best schools in the country. May Canada itself have the good fortune to get through its troubles so successfully!

Hon. Robert L Stanfield

PREFACE

The Board and the Headmaster of Ashbury College, right from the outset, agreed that this book was not to be an exercise in Centennial self-congratulation: a history should record the relevant facts and draw conclusions from the past so we can better face the future. Having rested confidence in me they in no way sought to influence or interfere. Thus the synthesis and analysis, the opinions and conclusions in this book are entirely my own and in my view there are indeed certain aspects of Ashbury's story that constitute a cautionary tale.

I didn't go to Ashbury but I was raised nearby and I have a number of friends to this day who went there when I went off to Trinity College School in Port Hope. Naturally I thought that mine was the best school going and just as naturally that Ashbury was rather second-rate. In point of fact, at that time – just before World War II – it was at a pretty low ebb. Like all such schools Ashbury has had its ups and downs.

As the school's first Director of Development from 1972 to 1978, I saw it from the inside during a period of major advance. The opportunity to develop The Forum for Young Canadians given me then by Headmaster Bill Joyce and a very active Board brought one of the happiest and most productive interludes of my life.

The five Headmasters from 1945 onwards, Ogden Glass, Ronald Perry, Bill Joyce, Tony Macoun and Roy Napier each gave me his frank and revealing insights. My sincere thanks. Captain George Woollcombe (1911-20) contributed notably to the parts concerning his father, the Founder. I owe special thanks to two alumni-authors for allowing me to include excerpts from their books: Robin MacNeil for *Wordstruck*; Daniel Farson for *Out of Step*. Over 150 others of all ages and stages – Board members, alumni, students, staff, administrators – from those who knew Ashbury as far back as 1910 right to the present day took the time and trouble to relate their experiences personally or on paper. I am most grateful to every one of them.

Before I started, Andrew Johnston (1972-80) had worked very effectively towards getting the school's archives in order and he completed a good deal of vital research on the early times in conjunction with the late Dr. R. Hubbard. Of my summer research assistants Rosanne Fyfe contributed well then Cullen Perry added energy, initiative and very useful work. As students, Antony Simpson, Alasdair Bell, Duncan Pound and Leigh Spotswood made important contributions. Antony and Alasdair continued after they graduated. The response of Ashbury's office arm to the extra load I put upon them all was typical of their ever-cheerful helpfulness. Vicky Wilgress and her Development Office gave me invaluable support. My editor, Jenny Wilson, carried out an extraordinarily difficult task (names, names, names!) as well as keeping me on track with fine judgement and consummate skill.

There's no doubt about the impact of Ashbury College on its people; and it is people of course that have made Ashbury College. From the high times and the low their memories have emerged, very largely affectionate, often wry, frequently hilarious, occasionally bitter, sometimes sad. With all this added to the files and minutes and tidbits in the school's archives and with the *Ashburian*'s columns going back 80 years, I was richly served with information and with personal impressions. Though I was able to specifically include only a fraction, all of it has added to the story.

Revisiting the school to write this book has been a fascinating experience. And what writer wouldn't be delighted to have had a most satisfying denouement and a happy ending delivered on a platter? Indeed, the passage of one hundred years turned Ashbury College into an institution of which its Founder would be proud.

Tony German
Kingsmere
Old Chelsea, Quebec

CHAPTER 1
A PRIVATE SCHOOL FOR BOYS

Mr. George P. Woollcombe B.A., graduate in honours of Christ Church, Oxford: assistant master at Trinity College School, Port Hope: and late assistant master at Bishop's College School, Lennoxville: intends next September to open in Ottawa a private school for a limited number of gentlemen's sons.

Boys will be received from the age of eight to fourteen and will be instructed in English, Classics, Mathematics and French. Ten boys have already been promised and an early application is desired. Apply to Geo. P. Woollcombe, B.A., T.C.S., Port Hope.

References kindly permitted to C.J.S. Bethune D.C.L. Headmaster of T.C.S., Port Hope; the Rev. T. Adams D.C.L. Rector of B.C.S., Lennoxville: the Hon. E. Dewdney, J.Gormully Esq.

The *Ottawa Journal*, Tuesday, May 19, 1891

George Penrose Woollcombe was a young man on the move. He had been born in the year of Confederation, 1867, in High Wycombe, Buckinghamshire, England, the son of an Anglican clergyman. After attending the Royal Grammar School and High Wycombe School, he took his BA at Christ Church College, Oxford. That October, 1888, he sailed for Canada and joined Bishop's College School (BCS), Lennoxville, Quebec, as fourth assistant master. The following fall he moved to Trinity College School (TCS), Port Hope.

Both were well-established private boarding schools for boys. Bishop's was founded in 1836 to serve the educational needs of "sons of English gentlemen"; TCS, started in 1865, was affiliated with Trinity College, Toronto, and the high Anglican Church. In each of them a solid career lay ahead. Woollcombe made a strong impression on two respected headmasters and on the parents of at least four Ottawa boys who were at Bishop's. Those parents, by the nature of things in Ottawa, were well placed in the huge lumbering industry, in the burgeoning civil service, and also in the Church of England laity. They sparked the notion of a school in Ottawa to meet the standards they wanted for their own children, different as they were from those of the public schools.

Upper Canada's Common Schools Act dated back to 1816. There were local elementary schools and grammar schools in the bigger towns; Ottawa had a grammar school from 1843. But private schools popped up. Bytown's first, the splendidly titled English Mercantile and Mathematical Academy, opened in 1827 on Rideau Street at

Mosgrove. Like many, it was run by a local teacher-entrepreneur and didn't last long.

But most of the substantial schools were started by religious groups. There was the ongoing fight by Roman Catholics to retain their own. There were Protestant interdenominational schools. Those founded by Anglicans, who by and large had the influence and money, were in the mould of the great English "public" schools which had grown to such influence through the Victorian era, and whose graduates – and this was certainly not lost on upper-crust Canadians – so completely dominated British social and political life.

The resolutions of 1864 leading to Confederation gave control of education to local legislatures. Canada today is rare among the advanced nations of the world in having no national educational policy. But reasons at the time were compelling enough and by late in the century Ontario's system had won international acclaim. At expositions in Philadelphia and Paris in the 1870s it was judged outstanding in the English-speaking world. In 1893 in Chicago it won 21 awards from kindergarten through high school and normal school, to mechanics' institutes and education for the deaf and blind.

School was compulsory for four months of the year for children aged seven to 12. The age limit wasn't raised to 16 until 1919. There were fees for high schools and collegiate institutes, and even at the turn of the century, while 85 percent of Ottawa children went to elementary school, only one in 10 went on from there.

Ottawa public schooling had had a major boost when the government moved from Quebec to the new Dominion's designated capital in 1866. The old grammar school was elevated to the Ottawa Collegiate Institute in 1871. It later divided into Lisgar and Glebe Collegiates and provided education for boys and girls aimed at university entrance. It fostered a very active Lyceum which promoted cultural activities, music, drama, lectures and debating. A quarter of the graduates went on to the universities, the professions and teachers' college. The Ottawa Normal School had been active since 1875. Elementary schools were particularly overcrowded, however, with one teacher to 50 students.

Canada was starting to pull out of a long depression. Ottawa had a population of 44,000 and was growing fast. Its mainstay was lumbering which had thrived throughout the Valley since Philemon Wright took his first raft of squared timber down to Quebec in 1806. By late-century sawn lumber had become the biggest part of the business. In spite of its ups and downs, lumbering was always basically robust and the hard-driving lumber barons who'd built it had piled up pretty tidy fortunes.

The richest Ottawans packed their boys off to boarding schools in Canada or abroad. Girls, too, though in fewer instances. The Ottawa Ladies' College had provided an answer for their girls for some time. In the English "public" schools of the Victorian era most headmasters were clergymen, and that pattern, plus staff imported from England, held in their equivalents like TCS and Bishop's. Woollcombe wasn't yet in holy orders – he was ordained in 1903 – and his school was non-denominational. But his church connections served him well.

Two men who were very active in the Anglican Synod backed him from the start: William H. Rowley, the Secretary-Treasurer of the giant E. B. Eddy's, and John Orde, a prominent lawyer. They gained the support of people like lumber barons Ward Hughson and John Gilmour and senior civil servant Fred White, and that got things started. In September 1891 "Mr. Woollcombe's School" opened in a single room in the Victoria Chambers fronting on Wellington Street on the east side of Metcalfe.

That fall the *Dominion Illustrated* published "a special number devoted to Ottawa and the Parliament of Canada" and remarked glowingly on the new school. It had been open a matter of weeks. The Principal was 24 years old with slight experience. His ads in the *Journal* had continued right through September and he wasn't overwhelmed by his 17 students. However, they were, according to the *Illustrated*, "certainly among the elite of this city," and that bore the hallmark of success.

Gushed the *Illustrated*, "The inestimable powers of personal influence, association, example and individual work are among the features of a first class private school that combine to make the boy a true man. . . . Mr. Woollcombe's school has satisfied the most fastidious and critical, its conduct reflecting on him the highest credit for energy, erudition and superior ability."

If the journalist was awed by the school's patrons, he was impressed too by the young man himself. Woollcombe hadn't come to Ottawa just to make a living running a small, albeit refined and well-connected, day school. He firmly intended to establish a permanent and much larger private boarding school with its prime aim the "general culture, the all-round development that promises the highest type of character...." His school already had "a life of its own, a character of its own and a civilization of its own which will combine to give a healthy tone to the school."

A trifle ponderous Victorian journalese may sound, but George Woollcombe's vision of his life's work was succinct and crystal clear. And his school, a hundred years on, would reflect his aims for it in every way.

Victoria Chambers was a sound choice – a prestigious, well-founded building, right across the road from Parliament Hill and in the same block as the Rideau Club where the gentlemen supporting the new school foregathered. It was also served by the streetcars of the brand new Ottawa Electric Railway.

Ottawa was still notorious for unpaved streets and uncertain sewers, but it had just stepped right into the van of North American public transportation. The key was abundant hydro-electric power and Thomas Ahearn was the pioneer. He'd been born down in the working-class stews of Le Breton Flats in 1855 and had started telephone services in Ottawa. He actually achieved a long distance call to Pembroke in 1879 and installed a switchboard in the Parliament Buildings in 1882. He and his partner, Warren J. Soper, then monopolized hydro-electric generation at the Chaudière Falls, provided the first street lighting and began distributing domestic electricity.

Their next major venture was the Ottawa Electric Street Railway Company. The revolutionary service, which swept away the horse-drawn streetcars, was inaugurated the summer Woollcombe arrived. Ahearn personally drove the first, and Soper the second, of five luxurious new cars up from the Albert Street car-barn, along Wellington and out Bank to the Exhibition Grounds. The Mayor sat up front and the band of the Governor General's Foot Guards played merrily in the rear.

Ambition and ability. From telegraph messenger to tycoon, Le Breton Flats to the Rideau Club, Tommy Ahearn's was a rags-to-riches story in the Horatio Alger style. Ahearn and Soper were both listed later among the Ashbury Founders and second and third generations of theirs were students. For the time being, their electricity powered the lights and electric bells in the up-to-the-minute Victoria Chambers. As well, so said the *Dominion Illustrated*, the building boasted steam heating, hot and cold water baths and an elevator, and was "one of the most desirable and convenient Chambers in Ottawa."

If Woollcombe – like Ahearn in his own field – was on the move, so was the city. Three telephone exchanges served it, though subscribers could only speak to parties on their own exchange until Bell Telephone pulled things together in 1899. The Ottawa Golf Club opened in 1891 with a nine-hole course in Sandy Hill on land that's now Strathcona Park. It moved across the Ottawa River five years later and in 1912 became the Royal Ottawa.

Only a few years earlier Ottawa had had the dubious name of the roughest, toughest town in North America. It was still a rough-and-tumble place: mill hands and rivermen on the tear; shantymen roaring into town with their winter's pay; farmers bringing in their produce to the Byward market with its lusty, brawling collection of taverns, mostly pretty seamy, and a floating population of shady characters that's changed proportionately little in a hundred years. These were early union – and union-busting – days. As the boys studied in their first term, the whole of the Ottawa police force turned out to hold back strikers at Booth's, Eddy's and Perley & Pattee's lumber mills at the Chaudière. Millowners huddled with police. Strikers jeered as tender-handed clerks loaded the barges for shipping out.

Sir John A. Macdonald had died in June 1891. Cyril Currier, who was 10 years old, lived on Wellington Street and he saw the funeral cortege from his Grandmother Slater's house right next door at number 186. He watched in fascination as a stately relative, Major Percy Sherwood, Commissioner of the North West Mounted Police, rode by on horseback. That splendid officer was, as all the family knew, in acute discomfort. Not only was it pouring rain, but he was suffering from a monumental boil on his backside.

Cyril joined Woollcombe's growing school in 1894. His was a lumbering line from the roots of Bytown, and he rode the great squared timber cribs down the Chaudière slide until they were no more. On his mother's side he went back through the Sparks and Slater families to Philemon Wright. On the other side, his grandfather, Joseph M. Currier, MP, had married Wright's granddaughter Hannah. So Cyril was the great-great-grandson twice over of the first settler. In 1868 grandfather Joseph had built the fine stone house on the cliff above Governor's Bay that's now the Prime Minister's residence, 24 Sussex Drive. Currier sold it to William Cameron Edwards of the next generation of lumber barons – and Ashbury patrons – in 1904. One way or another Ottawa was pretty intertwined.

Mr. Woollcombe's school flourished. French was taught by Monsieur Joseph-Marie Fleury, who had a language school in the Chambers. The Rev. Dr. McMeekin, a renowned speech expert, taught writing and elocution. He cut a dramatic figure in clerical attire, with flashing spectacles, a white mane and flowing beard. He revelled in recitation, one hand grasping the lapel of his gown, the other gesturing to the sky. Woe betide the boy who dropped a "g" or slurred an "r."

During the second spring term, McMeekin directed the boys, aged 10 to 12, in the trial scene from *The Merchant of Venice*. Casting was brisk. The Principal pronounced that Victor Heron, because of his red cheeks, would play Portia. He emphasized it, typically, with a firm pinch of the reluctant actor's ear. They staged their play in St. John's Church hall with young Heron agonizing through "the quality of mercy." Nerves and summer heat between them had him sweating like a horse under a heavy judicial wig. The rest of the cast: Bob Gormully as Shylock; Harry McLean, the Duke; Charlie Tupper, Bassiano; Billy Palmer, Antonio; Louis White, Gratiano. So began, right from the start, a hundred years' tradition of theatre at Ashbury.

There was no schoolyard so the "Woollcombe Boys," as they were quickly dubbed, played leapfrog at recess in front of the West Block, wearing their blue and white caps. Paths of new ventures are seldom smooth. Fred White was a strapping young fellow – he later played hockey for the famous Silver Seven – and family lore has it that on a certain occasion he squared off with the Principal and knocked him down the stairs. For this he was banished for a couple of terms to Bishop's.

In 1894, the year Cyril Currier moved from the Normal Model school to become a Woollcombe boy, the school ran out of space. Cyril's Grandmother Slater had died and Woollcombe moved half a block west to her house at 186 Wellington Street. Now he advertised for "resident and day boys" and called the school "Ashbury House School" after the Devonshire village and manor house which had been home to the Woollcombe family since the seventeenth century.

Woollcombe's roots were very much in England. The previous year he had gone back and had been married to Miss Julia Acres by his father, Rev. William Woollcombe, in Liverpool. Now, with his bride of a year, he moved into rooms over the school. There were born Philip and Maithol and, in April 1898, baby Phyllis. But the thriving young family was sadly blighted just five weeks later. Julia Woollcombe died.

The portrait by an old boy, artist Robert Hyndman, that hangs at Ashbury captured the Rev. Dr. G.P. Woollcombe, BA, MA, LLD, long after he had retired – dignified, keen of eye, but shrunk with age. The stained glass window on the north side of the Chapel projects his kindliness, the firm and fatherly teacher-priest well into middle age. Photographs of the day, however, show a keen-eyed and determined young man. He was lean, vigorous, well set-up, a good cricketer and quite athletic. No doubt he'd restrained himself in his bout with Fred White. His firm belief in the merits of sport and physical fitness put its stamp on the school from the start.

The small backyard at number 186 had barely enough room to squeeze in the 47 boys and five staff for the group photograph in 1896, much less space for calisthenics. The Principal (he wasn't known as "Headmaster" until 1907) sent the whole school off daily to run around Parliament Hill. They cheated, of course, particularly on wet days, ducking in the back door by the Parliamentary Library and taking a short cut through the Centre Block, dodging the minions of the Sergeant-at-Arms. Then Woollcombe found room for a hockey rink on a vacant lot behind the school on Sparks Street.

All this made a lasting impression on Cyril Currier. He already had a bicycle – a "penny-farthing" with one big wheel with direct drive pedals and a tiny rear wheel – and he took to racing. Throughout his life he always exercised – without cheating. Hockey, badminton, bicycling (on more advanced models than his first), canoeing, calisthenics, walking. Fit as a fiddle and alert until his last days, he saw his old school meet the challenges of its time for a further 90 years, until he died just shy of his 104th birthday.

Ottawa continued to grow. Asphalt came first to Sparks Street in 1895. R.J. Devlin, the Sparks Street clothier and another Ashbury Founder, who always spiced up his newspaper ads, proclaimed, "Yes the asphalt cometh, but it cometh through great tribulation. It looks as though the city council were getting ready for the Last Trump and were behind as usual." Ottawans have gnashed their teeth over potholes ever since.

In 1896 the tired Tory regime, barely propped up since Sir John A's death by four Prime Ministers (including Bassiano's father, Sir Charles Tupper), was swept away by Wilfrid Laurier. Elegant, stylish, white of hair, his trademark horseshoe stickpin agleam, he would be seen daily by the boys, going to and from Parliament Hill on the Sandy Hill streetcar.

Laurier's grace, style, magnetism, oratory and political skill captured Canadians' imagination. Prosperity was back. The country was on the go. The next year, 1897, was Queen Victoria's Diamond Jubilee. Pageantry, fireworks, parades, celebrations, elegant balls at Rideau Hall. Laurier, far from being carried away by the splendour of events, followed his belief in Canada's future independence and at the Colonial Conference in London stood firm against Britain's push to centralize the Empire. A new spirit was alight across the land.

The country flourished and grew; so did Ottawa, so did optimism, so did the demand for Ashbury places. In 1899, with the city population pushing over 68,000, Woollcombe took the plunge. He bought a substantial house and property on Argyle Avenue, west of Metcalfe Street, right by the present Canadian Museum of Nature, and laid his plans for a major move.

But momentous events were afoot. On the afternoon of October 25, 1899, the whole of Ashbury House School turned out to cheer Ottawa's soldiers heading off to the South African War. The 43rd Battalion's band led the parade along Wellington Street past the school, swinging along to "Soldiers of the Queen," as bracingly British a march as ever was written. The boys surged off in the throng of 15,000, cheering themselves hoarse. They followed down to the Union Station where Sir Wilfrid Laurier himself was submerged in the huge crush as the troop-train pulled out for Quebec. With the soldiers were three khaki-clad nursing sisters, Canada's first to go to war.

It wasn't a big unit. Just 12 days before, Sir Wilfrid had made the decision with his Cabinet to send 1000 men. He jumped onto the streetcar across from the East Block and lurched out along Sussex Street to Rideau Hall to tell the Governor General, the Earl of Minto. As soon as the news was out, the Governor General's Foot Guards and the 43rd Battalion filled Ottawa's quota of 125 men in an instant. They were to form D Company of the Royal Canadian Regiment. Allan Gilmour was the first Ashbury old boy to join the colours; William Ritchie was right on his heels. Both went over with the RCRs.

Britain dispatched a huge expeditionary force but by December was calling on the Dominions for more troops. Nicholas Slater went off with the Canadian Mounted Rifles. Strathcona's Horse, a new unit raised by Lord Strathcona of Canadian Pacific

Railway fame, camped at Lansdowne Park for a couple of weeks that winter en route to shipping out for the front. Splendid fellows all, they were mostly volunteers from the ranks, or ex-ranks, of the Mounted Police, heroic figures to the boys as they stalked along Sparks Street or hitched a foot on the brass rail of one of the many bars that lined it. Among them were old boys Douglas Vernon Ritchie and John F. Gilmour. The Strathconas were commanded by the hero of the northwest, the legendary Sam Steele. Everett Currier, Cyril's old boy brother, joined the South African Mounted Irregulars. By the war's end in 1902, Canada had sent 7300 troops to South Africa to fight the Boers.

Laurier walked a political tightrope. In London in 1897 he had declared roundly that he was "British to the core," at the same time working seriously for true independence for Canada within the Empire. He strove hard too for a bicultural country. But French Canada wanted no part of Britain's imperialist war against a dominated, cut-off colonial people who seemed to have so much in common with themselves. The English population of Canada, instinctively and instantly, was all for backing Britain.

Laurier's compromise was that only volunteers would go to fight and that Britain would pay for everything – the arms and equipment, the support, even the shilling a day pay for a trooper. There was a bonanza in it for at least one local firm. Lt. Col. James Woods manufactured canvas goods in a plant in Hull and supplied the lumbering industry. He developed a new light cotton tent and outfitted all the imperial forces in South Africa throughout the war. It formed the basis of a very substantial fortune.

In Ontario pro-British feeling ran high. People picked it up through their families, of course, though the large Irish population and the many ex-Americans would hardly have passed such sentiments on. An Englishman like George Woollcombe could be expected to reinforce the feelings that his boys would certainly get from home. From the early nineties all young Ontarians attending school were fed a strong diet of allegiance to Canada, the maple leaf, the beaver. The Ontario reader they used, the poetry they learned by heart, the history they were taught, the books and the magazines they read, all promoted loyalty and extended it without question to the Empire and the Crown.

By spring 1900, names like Paardeburg, Mafeking and Liliefontein and the initiative and exploits of the Canadians in this unorthodox war were ringing in everyone's ears. All seemed to be unfolding in the Mother Country's favour, but Laurier expressed Canada's growing confidence in the House of Commons, declaring to Britain, "If you want us to help you, call us to your councils."

Six weeks later, on a fine breezy April morning, a small house over in Hull caught fire. Nothing unusual about that – until it spread quickly through the town to Eddy's mill and caught the stacked-up timbers. The Ottawa Fire Department rushed to help Hull's. The situation was dangerous. Buglers called out the militia. The mayor telegraphed for help.

Then, with the rising westerly wind, the fire jumped across to Booth's and Bronson's giant lumber yards. The whole of the Chaudière area – mills, generating stations, houses – was ablaze by mid afternoon. From Ashbury House School huge smoke clouds could be seen billowing across the river. This was more than a routine fire. Many of the boys lived to the west towards the flames, along Sherwood Heights above Le Breton Flats, and at the Chaudière. The school closed. Jack Hughson rushed to his house on Bronson Avenue. His sisters and his young brother Hugh were on the roof watching the inferno approach, the flaming cinders flying in the wind. People by the thousands swarmed up the steep hill from the Flats, their belongings in barrows or on their backs. Refugees thronged the lawns of the big houses on the Heights.

By 5 p.m. Montreal fire fighters had arrived by rail with all their equipment. But fire raced through Le Breton Flats and devastated a half-mile swath to Carling Avenue. The whole city, the Hughson house included, barely escaped being consumed, saved by the cliff dividing Sherwood Heights from Le Breton Flats and the fact that the tearing wind dropped at dusk. The Hughson sawmill, by a stroke of luck, escaped.

The city turned itself into an instant refugee camp. Aid poured in from the rest of Canada, Britain, the USA, France. Miraculously only seven people died, but 15,000 were left homeless. That included such people as J.R. Booth and other leading citizens who had had fine big houses at the Chaudière. They built their next ones in Sandy Hill, Centretown or Rockcliffe. A lot of the relief money went to rebuilding houses for those who couldn't handle their loss.

Catastrophic as the Great Fire was, Ottawa bounced back quickly. The economy was strong. Lumbermen, from the top down, were a tough and resourceful lot. George Woollcombe was too, and he hardly missed a beat. His great expansion plan stood firm.

Chapter 2

Argyle

In June 1900, Ashbury College Company Limited was incorporated for carrying on the business, at or near the City of Ottawa, of "a day and boarding school for boys and girls." G.P. Woollcombe was never known to have entertained the idea of girls in his school, but for the time being the provision was there. His original backers were solidly behind him. Rowley was Chairman of the Board of Directors, Orde a Director and legal counsel. Woollcombe was a shareholder, Secretary-Treasurer and Managing Director.

The list of the first shareholders reads like "Who's Who." Sir Sanford Fleming, the great railway engineer and inventor of standard time; Hon. A.G. Blair, MP, ex-Premier of New Brunswick and Sir Wilfrid Laurier's Minister of Railways and Canals; H.F. McLachlin, Ward C. Hughson, John B. Fraser and W.H. Rowley, all major figures in lumbering; Mrs Mary Blackburn, widow of Robert Blackburn, MP, and Managing Director of New Edinburgh's Blackburn Woollen Mills; Warren Y. Soper, electrical engineer and Tommy Ahearn's partner in the Chaudière Hydro and Ottawa Electric Railway; Lt. Col. D.C.T. Irwin; and R.J. Devlin, the prominent and whimsical Sparks Street clothier.

It was as well-heeled, talented, experienced and interesting a group of influential turn-of-the-century Canadians as one could gather around a table at the Rideau Club – though Mrs Blackburn wouldn't have been allowed to set foot inside that male preserve. From 1906 the industrious and successful Lt. Col. James Woods took an active part, but most of the shareholders were quite content to leave things to Woollcombe, Rowley, Orde and Woods, who acted as Vice-Chairman of the Board.

The new company immediately bought the Argyle property for the $9750 Woollcombe had paid for it. They authorized $1700 for some improvements, including a gymnasium built for an extraordinarily modest $300. That fall Ashbury College opened in fine new quarters with steam heat, electric light, 45 day boys and 13 boarders. In their own quarters were the Principal and his family and three live-in masters.

In the midst of all the dealings and preparations for the move Woollcombe had married Miss Jessie Marian Mickle. She came from pioneer stock. Her grandfather had brought a large family out to the Huron Tract in 1832. Her father, Charles, built a thriving lumbering business in Bruce County and became a leading citizen of Guelph. He and his family, 13 children in all, had moved to Toronto and Jessie was teaching at Miss Harmon's School for Girls in Ottawa when she and Woollcombe met. He could have found no finer wife, mother for his children or partner for his own pioneering. She became as much a part of Ashbury College as her husband.

As the calendar for 1901 declared, the school's aim was to develop in each student a high standard of scholarship and an upright, manly and Christian character.

The Governor General, the Earl of Minto, was sufficiently impressed to send along his son and heir, Lord Victor Melgund. Minto's "reign" in Ottawa combined the ostrich-feathered opulence of the Victorian court with Edwardian raciness. With the death of the remarkable old Queen that year society shook off the old confines like an overtight corset.

Fees for a day boy in the top forms at Ashbury were $72 a year and for a boarder $316. There were extras like $4 for sports – football, hockey and cricket – $4 for gymnastics and calisthenics, $20 for German taught by Herr Boettger of Leipzig University and $10 for manual training. Ashbury was right up with the times. Manual training had been started at Woodstock College, a private school similar to Ashbury, and by the turn of the century had found its way into city schools across the province.

Ashbury College was a regular limited company set up for profit, and the Directors and Woollcombe between them ran a tight and orderly operation. The Head's salary was $1200 per year, with a gradual increase to $1500 by 1907-8. The scale for the Collegiate Institute Principal was $1800, rising at $100 a year to $2600. Woollcombe, though, did have bed and board. For some years Ashbury's books showed a modest return. But there were always improvements to be made; no dividends were declared, thus no added return for G.P.'s investment in money, energy and skill.

When Hugh Hughson joined his older brother Jack at Ashbury in 1904, two of the masters lived in the school. J.R. Montizambert, MA – robust, mustachioed, a first-rate schoolmaster and coach of hockey and football – had taught at TCS with Woollcombe before coming to join his old friend in Ottawa to teach mathematics. The other resident was Woollcombe's younger brother John with a BA from Cambridge. He taught English and junior mathematics. George Woollcombe himself taught classics and English.

The non-resident teachers still included the round-faced, affable M. Fleury and stately Dr. McMeekin. Miss A. Blanchet, BA, taught the small boys and instructed in German, though she never got into the school photos. Mr. P.W. Currie taught physical science. He had a BA from Toronto and a BSc from Owens. Mr. C. Emery, called "Professor," instructed in gymnastics and physical culture as part of his larger business in Ottawa. There was a regular manual training instructor, and two ladies and two gentlemen came in to teach music. One of them, J. Edgar Birch, was another friend from TCS. An Englishman and a fine musician, he had come to Ottawa in 1895 as an organist and choirmaster. He became a central figure in the musical community – a driving force in the Ottawa Choral Society from the start and organist at St. Andrew's for 21 years until his death. He and Woollcombe were fast friends. He taught music at Ashbury almost continually until he died. Woollcombe took his solemn part in his old friend's funeral service at St. Andrew's in 1931.

Woollcombe's staff, who of course earned less than he did, fared rather badly compared to the Collegiate staff. A male non-specialist there started at $900; a specialist's salary ran from $1200 to $1800. The problem of below-average salaries was to be a constant thread through Ashbury's history – indeed through that of all private schools – for a good 70 years. High regard wasn't matched by high return. Single masters lived in and got bed and board, but generally you took a cut to be a cut above.

The latter point was certainly true at this time for teachers in the public elementary schools. Women started at $324 a year. A male teacher in a rural area averaged $484. Compare that with a charwoman in the public service at $321, a street sweeper at $421 and a City Hall stenographer at $528.

Woollcombe had responsibilities. To his first family of Philip, Maithol and Phyllis, Jessie added Edward and George. Woollcombe studied theology, was ordained priest in the Anglican Church in 1903 and until 1909 was assistant at St. George's Church. That brought a small and welcome stipend. But money wasn't his driving force; achievement was. In 1906 he took his MA at Bishop's University. In 1908, modest income and all, he became a member of the Rideau Club. With that ultimate Ottawa accolade he had all the classic qualifications to head a major school in Canada's capital.

The *Ashburian,* Issue Number 1, was published in December 1906 – a bargain at 25 cents per copy, 75 cents a year for three issues, post-free to any part of the world. The first Editor was a master rejoicing in the name of W.W. Hartley-Stansfield of Christ's College, Cambridge, who arrived that fall by way of teaching at Inverness College, Scotland, Scarborough College, England, and Wei-Hei-Wei School in China.

Woollcombe must have caught him as he passed through Ottawa en route home. He published his own poem, "The Wail of the Exile," in that first *Ashburian.* It compared the rest of the world most unfavourably with his preferred "smoke and dirt of Leicester Square" and demolished Canada and his own meal ticket in one deathless stanza:

> *The Rockies may not be surpassed,*
> *Niagara may remove your breath,*
> *If through Canadian heat you last,*
> *Then winter freezes you to death.*

Hartley-Stansfield did not return the following year.

School news was a little sparse. The first issue was padded out with three colourful pages, again by the Editor, on "A Chinese Vice-Regal Reception" in Teintsin. The student Assistant Editor, Edmund F. "Nixie" Newcombe, wrote of "The Joys and Sorrows of a first Caribou Hunt." He urged old boys to send in stories of their own adventures and encouraged them with "CHB's" (surely Charlie Butterworth's) hair-raising account of canoeing wild river canyons in "Seven Months on the Alaskan Boundary."

There was enough in it, though, to show a school very much on the move. Jack Hughson, as Military Correspondent, reported on the cadet corps, one year old and attached to the Governor General's Foot Guards. Under the ministrations of Sergeant-Major Carwardine it was already rated best in the city. Mr. Carwardine was the postman along Elgin Street, but when he changed into his long-service Coldstream Guards uniform and brushed his moustache to its old ferocity, all quailed. That included Wilf Butterworth, who never forgot Carwardine's insistence on "rigid dis-SIP-lin."

A new school cap was in vogue, blue with the Ashbury arms worked in red on a shield of white. The coming hockey season augured well. The 1906 team had beaten the Collegiate Institute – not bad as the high school had four times the number of Ashbury boys – and swept the Carling Cup. The Cup, presented by the mother of two Old Ashburians of the Ottawa brewing family, was for competition between Ashbury, St. Alban's in Brockville and St. John's (later Lower Canada College) in Montreal.

Old boys' news was reported with the fond expectation that they were continuing the Ashbury principles of "Hard Work, Honour and Fidelity." Eleven were at McGill (where Gordon Raphael was Captain of Hockey); six were at the Royal Military College (RMC), Kingston, including Charles Read who'd passed in second out of 7000 applicants the previous May; one each attended Queen's, Bishop's and Toronto universities; and seven had permanent army commissions.

Handily, there was an old boy at the Ottawa branch of the Imperial Bank, the Royal Bank and the Bank of Commerce; and wilderness traveller Charlie Butterworth was starting his lifetime career at the Bank of Ottawa before moving on to the Bank of Montreal. After the war Charlie married J. Edgar Birch's daughter Hilda. Birch's other daughter Marjorie became the invaluable "office-everything" at Ashbury for years. Thus the Ashbury web began to be woven.

The *Ashburian* of December 1907 carried the "Head-Master's Report" of the previous spring *in toto*. It was a classic of its kind, in suitably florid style, delivered to a distinguished company including Governor General Earl Grey. Ashbury, said Woollcombe, was an old, established, permanent institution in the city's life. Graduates were most successful in the universities, though the aim "was not merely in the intellectual successes of its pupils, but chiefly in the successful development of such a character of those who sit within its class-rooms as shall cause them to grow up to be men who with hearts and soul fear God and honour their King."

Senior boys properly led the younger in "the true spirit of loyalty to authority," he said. Sport – football, hockey, cricket – and physical training and gymnastics under Professor Emery were most important for health and well-being, and everyone took part. They had a major place in the school but, bucking the current deplorable trend, at Ashbury it was playing the game and not the winning that was the proper end.

Woollcombe could well have been alluding to hockey. The Stanley Cup, the oldest trophy still competed for professionally in North America, had been donated by Governor General Lord Stanley in 1893. It was for amateur competition. Nominally. Ferocious rivalry had brought in some pretty questionable practices and play. Anathema to the amateur purist in Woollcombe they may have been, but the Ottawa Valley produced some of the finest and the toughest of players and Ashbury boys celebrated wildly when the Silver Seven won in 1903, 1904 and 1905 and the Senators in 1910 and 1911.

The Head singled out one school leaver, Nixie Newcombe. After nine Ashbury years he was off to McGill with abilities that "presage for him a brilliant future." Nixie's father was Deputy Minister of Justice and he too was headed for the law. Woollcombe and his school had struck a very deep chord of loyalty in Nixie. He was to become the longest-standing and most committed Governor in the school's history.

These were stimulating times. Sir Wilfrid Laurier led the mood of optimism. The twentieth century was the century of Canada. The West was opening up fast. The country was booming and Ottawa with it. By 1907 100,000 people lived within three miles of City Hall. Civic boosters lauded 108 miles of roads (though only 15 miles were paved) and 42 miles of electric tramways. Nine railway lines ran 110 trains per day into three stations.

Lumbering was still king, though these were the years of change. The last of the great squared timber rafts had been sent down the Ottawa River by J.R. Booth (another Ashbury shareholder) in 1904. Already sawn lumber was yielding pride of place to pulp and paper and hydro power. And government was moving up as an industry of its own. Its payroll in the city had reached an unheard-of $100,000 per month.

By 1907, with Ashbury bulging at the seams with 80 boys, it was clearly time for major expansion. The Ashbury calendar located the school "in one of the healthiest and most picturesque suburbs of Ottawa with the advantages of country air as well as those attaching to city life," but Woollcombe was looking for a proper country location. At the end of 1907, 10 of the faithful shareholders put up $8000 in return for preference shares and the company bought "the westerly 10 acres of block 10 of the McKay Estate" from Rockcliffe Property Company for $12,000. Building lots in Rockcliffe (spelled without the second "c" in those days) had been on the market since 1864.

At the end of 1908 Ottawa architects Weeks and Keefer were commissioned to draw up plans. Building costs were estimated at $50,000, including fees and the cost of bridge financing. Subscriptions to debentures to cover the cost were coming in nicely. Ward Hughson lent $7300 to pay off the Argyle mortgage before the property was put on the market. All bid fair for the opening of a splendid new school building in September 1909. And high time too, because enrolment had reached 97 boys, 22 of them boarders, and the demand was high.

But on April 29, George Woollcombe announced to the Board that he'd accepted the Headmastership of Bishop's College School. It was a bombshell. Everything stopped. Certainly it was an honour for Woollcombe, and justly earned. But Ashbury was a one-man show. Without Woollcombe, the absolute mainstay since it started, where would the confidence be found to go through with the whole bold plan? The Board decided on the spot to settle the architects' account, tell subscribers the plans were abandoned and seek a new Principal to carry on in the existing quarters.

Then the challenge of the whole new venture and the certainty that without him it wouldn't go ahead prevailed over the prestige and security of Bishop's. On June 24 Woollcombe presented the Board with $5035 in hand from the year's operations and his commitment to stay. What's more, he subscribed to 147 more common shares for himself. Things moved fast. The tender of Byers and Anglin of Montreal for the building was accepted and in November lumberman J.B. Fraser advanced the $7000 to complete the land purchase. Building went on apace.

There were extras, of course. Oddly, in light of the steady interest in physical training and fitness, there was no gymnasium in the original plans. It was added at the end of the rear wing for $3450. There was no provision for a Chapel either but that had to wait. Water came from the city main on Acacia Avenue, but there were no sewers in Rockcliffe so some $2800 was spent on a septic tank and tile bed with the inside plumbing changed to suit. There were minor changes for the ice-house – an essential of the times.

In the spring of 1910 the Argyle property went on the market and the boys returning that fall moved into their brand-new Rockcliffe quarters. Woollcombe moved his own family into the west wing, which was designed as the Headmaster's house. With some new arrivals after Christmas there were 67 day boys and 48 boarders for a total of 115 – the highest ever.

The original estimate for the whole new package – land included at $12,000 – had been $62,000. With the extras and contingencies the final bill was $87,567. Forty thousand dollars had been subscribed initially by shareholders and friends for 5 percent first mortgage bonds, and some $17,000 to preferred and common shares. The Argyle property, still unsold, was expected to realize at least $8000. Some $20,000 remained to be raised or carried as additional debt.

But that was a small matter compared to the achievement. In 19 years of working closely with his original mentors, Rowley and Orde, George Woollcombe had won the confidence of hard-headed, experienced Ottawa people. Now the objective he'd put on record in 1891 – a first-class private boarding school – was actually there. It had in its various moves realized the rhetoric of the *Dominion Illustrated* of 1891. It had a life and a character of its own. It already had a rich store of memories and traditions of its own. And there was no question of its healthy tone. In this fast-growing city in a seemingly ever-expanding country, George Penrose Woollcombe, aged 43, had realized his Canadian dream.

CHAPTER 3
ROCKCLIFFE

Returning to school in the fall of 1910 meant a total change of surroundings. No more the made-over and added-to house in residential Ottawa. Day boys could take the streetcar to the new-named Ashbury stop at the bottom of Park Road, 100 yards short of the end-of-the-line loop at Buena Vista. There were fewer than 60 houses and cottages in Rockcliffe (versus some 650 today) but the parkland had been bought by the city in 1893 and the streetcar did plenty of weekend custom with skiers and picnickers. From the streetcar stop it was an eight-minute walk past woods and fields with scattered houses to Ashbury's 10 acres.

The boarder getting off the train with trunk and baggage for the term had a substantial cab ride from the railway station to Rockcliffe. Turning off Mariposa the wheels would crunch on the D-shaped gravel driveway past some attractive shade trees. Spacious grounds spread off to the right and ahead was the splendid new school. Architect Allan Keefer, who had been at Ashbury in the 1890s, had designed it – as the calendar said in "Elizabethan style." Attached at the east end, on the right, solid and substantial, was the Headmaster's house.

Inside the main door on the right there were two large classrooms. On the left were the office, the Headmaster's study and more classrooms. The dining room projected back in the short leg of the "L," behind it were the kitchen and domestic offices, then the gymnasium. The basement housed a play room, bicycle room, chemistry lab, carpenter's shop and locker room. There was room for an indoor rifle range, and a passage led to the main lavatories and the gym.

The gym was a vast improvement on the facilities at Argyle. It did temporary duty as a chapel because the present Chapel – with assembly hall and classroom underneath – wasn't added until 1912. On the second floor in the front wing were another classroom, rooms for boys, masters, matron and nurse and an infirmary. The third floor had more rooms for boys and masters. The attached Headmaster's house had access to the main school on two floors.

Ottawa too was building fast to match the growth of government. The previous seven years had produced the Royal Observatory on Carling Avenue by the Experimental Farm, and on Sussex Street the Public Archives (now the War Museum) and the Mint. The Victoria Memorial Museum, the school's ex-neighbour on Argyle Avenue, was being completed. Stone and castle-like embellishments blended those latter buildings with the Gothic style of the Parliament Buildings.

Allan Keefer, though, had gone for a homier, warmer feel and had achieved it well. Construction was first-class – rock-solid brick and reinforced concrete. It was as near fireproof as a building could be, with firemain outlets on every floor. Steam heat and electric light with wiring in iron conduits put it right up with the best.

The Headmaster's house was far more palatial than anything the Woollcombes had ever had. With five children they needed some space. Maithol and Phyllis, aged 15 and 12, were at home. Philip, aged 16, was in his tenth and last year at the school.

Edward had started his 10-year stint in 1907. George, still too little, had to wait another year. There was still room on the top floor to house a few of the smallest boarders under warm, if strict, family care.

In December the Governor General, Earl Grey, inspected the new building and addressed the boys in the gymnasium. He urged them "above all things to cultivate that spirit of manly honour which has made the British Empire what it is today." In sports they should play in a straightforward way rather than seek to win at all costs. To top it all off, he announced that he'd present a medal for proficiency – the Governor General's Medal. The first recipient was L.E.L. Koelle in 1912.

Promotional copy in the calendar and the *Ashburian* glowed with the school's advantages. Justly, too. It had the plant, the location and the atmosphere for the private boarding school of Woollcombe's dreams. The city was close enough – and had developed enough – for the school to stress the educational advantages of the seat of Dominion government. Yet, in its rural setting, it was a great place for rambling. The grounds had all the space in the world for football and cricket; and in winter they boasted their own rinks and even a massive timber toboggan slide. Another shrewd bid for business was to point out to Senators and members of the Commons that they could keep in touch with sons who came to board.

But the essence of the school hadn't changed. G.P. Woollcombe was in his twentieth year as Headmaster. Without doubt he was the driving force. Policy was set and business conducted, as it had been from the start, almost entirely by President W.H. Rowley, John Orde and Woollcombe. The school itself revolved around him and his unclouded concept of educating boys. The annual calendar and the *Ashburian* lauded the merits of such long-term continuity in a Headmaster. Tried and solid methods, established traditions, conventional middle-class social values and morals, discipline, manners and deportment, rigid curriculum, hard work and physical fitness – these were the stuff of a first-rate school of the day.

From opening day the school was full. And it was full of life and activity, too. Games, of course. With the school's expanded facilities activity increased in every department. The cadet corps – every boy who was physically fit was a member – quivered and thrived under Sergeant-Major Carwardine's eagle-eyed "dis-SIP-lin." Shooting in the new gallery for the cup given by old boy Willis O'Connor sharpened skills for springtime sessions on the Rockcliffe Rifle Ranges. It was an easy walk. Outdoor matches were held there for the Bate Cup, and scores were entered in the Canadian Rifle League competitions.

Cadets and rifle shooting were very much a part of high school life across Canada, where the militia armouries were a part of the social fabric of every town. The Ashbury Corps in 1912 stood first in the Military District and was second in all Canada in rifle shooting. It was a regular source of pride. The following year the Corps got six brand-new Ross rifles. The Ross rifle was deadly accurate with the much improved peep-sights, but it was doomed to damnation when it wouldn't function in the Flanders mud.

On one memorable day of drilling on the school grounds, word came that the Keefer house was on fire. Off rushed the whole Ashbury Corps, moving at the double through Rockcliffe, the Sergeant-Major in charge. Sixty strong, they actually formed the classic bucket brigade and saved the house. This was the stuff of *Chums* and the *Boy's Own Paper,* and indeed of the Horatio Alger books and G.A. Henty adventures that had just been presented to the library by Mr. Gill.

Now Scouting opened up a whole new range of activity. The Boy Scouts had started in England just after the South African War and quickly developed into a major movement with huge membership and remarkable influence. Scouting captured the imagination, especially of city-bound boys who would never have thought of the outdoors except as a place to come from out of the rain. It inculcated a moral code and a set of values: honour, doing one's best, helping others, duty to God and the King.

A lot of Ashbury boys were used to the idea of going off into the bush with a tent and a canoe, and the Woollcombe code left no doubt about honour, duty and loyalty. But Scouting had a structure, a ritual, a uniform and a ready-made outdoor programme.

The Troop expanded, but field days and weekend camps tested the keenness of the day boy members. Fairy Lake, for instance, the site of an area Scout jamboree, was reached by hiking to the Rockcliffe boathouse, taking the ferry to Gatineau Point and hoofing it the rest of the way. In all this lay the beginnings of outdoor education at Ashbury College and the discovery of a classic route for later transgressors to the taverns on the Quebec side of the river.

There was plenty of work to be done on the grounds. To fashion a decent playing field with good turf thousands of rocks had to be dug out. Fred Oliver, who joined the school as general handyman that first year, shifted every one of them himself. Over the ensuing years he gradually built the hand-piled stone wall that runs in front of the school, along Mariposa and down Springfield and Glenwood. It is the personal monument to a most remarkable man.

Fred had come from England in 1906, settled in Ottawa and married. When Ashbury moved to Rockcliffe, he was working as a part-time gardener for a Mr. Howard, retired manager of the Royal Bank, who lived nearby. Ashbury needed a full-time man-of-all-work. Howard introduced him, and Mrs. Woollcombe, who was making domestic arrangements, hired him. Her realistic admonishment: it would be long hours, hard work and low wages. In 41 years of faithful and quite extraordinary service, not one of these conditions ever changed.

His day started at 4:45 a.m.: fire up the boilers and the hot water heater, start the fires in the kitchen stoves with kettles on and boiling for the cook by 6:30, clean the two offices, masters' common room and classrooms, milk the cow, and have breakfast at 7:00. Somewhere in there he closed the boys' windows, woke the masters with their tea trays and polished their boots. Later in the day he had to clean all the knives and forks – there was no stainless steel – bring in ice from the school's ice-house, clean it of sawdust and chip it, feed and tend the chickens and other livestock, cut the grass, attend to the grounds, shovel the snow in winter and flood the rinks. In the second year he laid out two grass tennis courts in front of the school. Like the multitude of other added chores Fred took it on with quiet competence and no complaint.

In the singles tournament that spring Mr. D.E. Cecil Wood and Melbourne O'Halloran met in the final. Two hard-fought sets went to Mr. Wood who then retired, leaving the first Ashbury tennis singles championship to O'Halloran. The next year popularity demanded a third court. Fred Oliver, as always, obliged.

There were outbuildings and an enclosure behind the school for livestock. The school had horses, and some boys rode their own. Charlie Billings, for one, rode his mare in every day from the old family home at Billings Bridge and loosed her in the paddock. The horses and Bossy, the highly productive Jersey cow, often got loose and Fred had to round them up. The Head's shout of "Oliver, horses!" meant bring the shovel and clean up the lawns. Bossy came in season and Fred walked her three miles to Cyrville to the appointed bull. On the way, though, she was assaulted by another suitor who smashed down a cedar rail fence in his enthusiasm. Fred had no choice but to hurdle the fence on the other side of the road and let nature take its course. The hard part was explaining to the Head. Soon after, when Bossy outwore her welcome by trampling over neighbours' gardens, she was disposed of – with calf.

Mowing and snow ploughing were done by horses. Delivery wagons were horse-drawn and converted to runners in winter. Cars didn't take kindly to Rockcliffe snow conditions, though, and Dr. George McCarthy, the school doctor, often had to leave his car near Rideau Hall and tramp in. A working party of boys, delighted with the task, would run off to dig the car out and point it in the right direction for his next call.

One of the real sparks of the school was David Verner. He played on the first football and hockey teams for three years, starting off little, wiry and quick, and gradually weighing in with the rest. In football, coached by Rough Rider Dave McCann, he was a fine tackle, and fast and dodgy carrying the ball. But he was a bit lazy turning out to practice – likely the reason he wasn't Captain. He was Captain of hockey, though, and the school's best, not too fast on his skates but a great playmaker. He had a good turn of speed on foot – in the spring of 1912 he was the first winner of the Fleming Cup for top points on sports day. The cup was presented that year by Mrs. Fleming, and the distinguished Sir Sandford was guest speaker.

Verner was an all-rounder. As the *Ashburian* staff artist he was a great hand with a sketching pen. He also hammered out rousing ragtime on the piano. He shone in the classroom mainly by entertaining Hugh Hughson, Alan Beddoe and others at the back, and confounding the masters, with his sleight of hand. Since childhood he'd been fascinated by string and card tricks, and had developed quite amazing skill.

A pretty insouciant type all round, but his family steered him towards more conventional pursuits and in 1913 he passed well into RMC. He wasn't amused by the hazing in his recruit year, especially being lined up to swim across a large hole cut in the ice. But he did amuse others with his magic. The colonel caught him once in the showers and challenged him with, "Let's see what you can conjure up now, Verner." The reply was a soggy joker flipped between his fingers.

After the air force – dull because with his sketching skills they kept him in the drawing office – Verner went off to New York and became a professional magician under the name of Dai Vernon. At one stage he was terribly injured in a fall and nearly lost both arms. He fought back, recouped his skills and became one of America's best-known magicians. He travelled the world performing and was a close friend of Houdini and Blackstone.

Until he died, aged 97, he could usually be found, spry and sparkling-eyed, at magicdom's palatial headquarters, The Magic Castle, in Los Angeles. He was born in 1894, only three years after the school was founded, and watched the great fire of 1900 wide-eyed from Parliament Hill. Of his time, young E.P. Taylor, who won the junior 100 yards on the same sports day as Dai won the Fleming Cup, became more widely known. But David Verner / Dai Vernon was, by just about any standard, the most colourful of the lot.

Old boys news was by now a feature in the *Ashburian*. Following Nixie Newcombe's exhortation in the first issue, they were quite good correspondents. Nixie himself was at McGill with the largest group of graduates. RMC attracted the second largest. Entry to RMC was a national plum. G.P. Woollcombe had always encouraged boys to go for it, and he pointed with pride to the school's record there and the numbers who by now held the King's commission.

G.P. had for some time been a good friend of Rockcliffe neighbour, Rear Admiral Charles Kingsmill, Canada's first Director of the Naval Service. His two sons, Walter and Grange, came to Ashbury in 1909 and 1911. G.P. was interested in the new navy too, and Trennick Bate joined as a cadet in 1910. Charlie Beard, who had left the school earlier to go to the British training ship "Conway", joined as well. The navy hadn't been officially inaugurated but Ottawa insiders, Sir Henry Bate among them, knew it was coming. Soon the Royal Naval College of Canada was founded in Halifax. Woollcombe encouraged more boys to apply. The *Ashburian* carried articles on the vigorous life at the new College and letters, solicited by the Head from Trennick Bate, with intriguing tales of a midshipman's adventures in the mighty HMS *Dreadnought*.

Off to the Naval College next went Rastus Reid and St. G. Lindsay, followed by Val Godfrey, Edson Sherwood and F.J. Adams ("Cruiser" because he had a fat stern). A little later went Ted Orde, second son of Ashbury's earliest supporter, L.H. Burpee, Jack Mitchell, the Kingsmills and G.P.'s own sons, Edward and George. Most were at sea in World War I. Many also fought in World War II.

The Royal Naval College of Canada closed in 1922 when the navy was starved for funds. Only 150 graduated, but those early cadets provided the core for the navy's gigantic expansion in World War II. Twelve of them were old Ashburians, plus Beard and Bate in the first class of seven. An extraordinary input into a Canadian institution by one small school.

In that first year in Rockcliffe the operating account was stable but there was a heavy debt load. Never again did the Company declare a dividend and that hit George Woollcombe, the biggest single holder of common shares, squarely in his expectations. His salary rose to $2500 all found by 1914, but in fact the days of the private school as a business venture were over. A new Ontario Assessment Act in 1910 had ruled that educational institutions paying dividends would be subject to taxation. The alternative was to reorganize as a foundation with shareholders surrendering their stock. St. Andrew's College, Toronto, for example, did so and the word got around, but Ashbury didn't follow suit until 1918.

The Argyle property still hung around the school's neck. There were no buyers. Even knowing the right people, the federal government wouldn't rent it. Ward Hughson, anxious to free up his money, was politely told he'd have to wait.

Then came another blow. In 1911 Ottawa suffered a major typhoid epidemic and that hit enrolment very hard. Water was the problem. Neither the Ottawa sewers nor the water mains were anything like perfect. Contents mixed, and the dread disease raced through the city. Ashbury had its own septic system which seemed quite innocent, but water came from city mains; kitchen staff were paid extra to boil it. The city's problem was finally fixed, but Ashbury took no chances and dug a 65-foot well. As the school calendars emphasized for some years, it provided pure water "for drinking, cooking and teeth cleaning through a Pasteur germ-proof filter, frequently analysed to ensure that its purity is maintained." However, it all made for a tough year, and at the 1911 Annual General Meeting interest payment on debentures was postponed. Fortunately debenture holders all had strong personal interest in the school.

In January 1912 the school had its first visit from the new neighbours at Government House, as Rideau Hall was known. His Royal Highness the Duke of Connaught with the Duchess toured the school, inspected and complimented the Scout Troop and spoke to the boys about duty to their school and the Empire. As with his predecessor, the Governor General neglected to mention Canada in between. Later the Duke invited the whole school for tea, tobogganing on the slide beloved by Ottawa socialites and a hockey game, Ashbury vs his staff. Ashbury won at a walk, 5-2.

On Sundays the school walked to St. Bartholomew's en masse, or went to the Cathedral or another church by streetcar. Sometimes the cadet corps had a church parade with the Foot Guards. The daily services were held in the gym, with music provided by two violins, a cornet and a piccolo. It all left a lot to be desired and in spite of the debt load Woollcombe went hard after something very close to his heart – a proper Chapel.

He was a formidable fund-raiser by now. By June 1912 he had commitments for $5000 in hand. His modern hard-nosed technique included printing in the *Ashburian* the names of the 127 cash donors and the 17 who gave furnishings, and pointing out on the next line that $1800 was still needed for an organ.

Confidence high again, the Board gave the go-ahead with any shortfall to be charged to the "capital funds account," that is, added to the growing tab. Donations ranged from $200 down (most directors and shareholders were in the top bracket) and finally reached a total of $6000. Allan Keefer designed a separate structure, just east of the main wing, with the Chapel above and the assembly hall and a classroom, dubbed Siberia that winter in spite of the touted steam heat, underneath.

The Chapel was a simple, warm little gem. Walls of brick and ash pews, with beams and pitched roof stained to match. The windows were glazed with saffron-coloured cathedral glass. Stained glass would come in due course. The sanctuary, behind a brass railing, contained a finely carved altar with dorsal hangings and handsomely carved episcopal chair and clergy stalls.

The first services took place on Sunday, January 19, 1913. Holy Communion at 8:00, Matins at 11:00 and at 7:00 an overflow crowd for the dedication. The distinguished group of clergy that nearly overflowed the chancel included the Archbishop and the Archdeacon of Ottawa, Rev. Dr. Rexford, Principal of the Montreal Diocesan Theological College, Rev. Dr. Voohris, Headmaster of the Cathedral Choir School of New York, who later came to teach at Ashbury, Rev. T. Garrett and, of course, Rev. George P. Woollcombe.

Previously, each day had started with prayers and scripture study. Now there were morning and evening prayer services every day and Holy Communion, Matins and Evensong on Sundays. There were moans, of course. Graduating boarders said they'd built up a church credit for life. But even rushing into it tugging the tie straight, smoothing the hair, hopping on one foot and polishing the other toe on the back of the calf, the Chapel was always a place to pause – if just in refuge – and surround oneself with a little peace. If only by osmosis, the rituals, the wisdoms, the richness and rhythms of King James English and the music, cadence and imagery of psalms and hymns filled a compartment of the mind with something of value that would be there right through life.

At Easter, on the heels of this historic occasion, the Head invited 20 old boys to dine at the school to talk about forming an association. There were 277 old Ashburians spread far and wide from the first 22 years. G.P., fresh from financing the Chapel, no doubt had future fund-raising very firmly in mind. But that wasn't mentioned. The stated objective was for old boys to keep in touch with each other and the school with them.

The "first annual" meeting and dinner of the Ashbury College Old Boys Association was held the following Easter. Louis White, diminutive beside his strapping brothers, was the Secretary. He had entered the old school on its first day in the Victoria Chambers. His whimsical notice mailed to members proclaimed the annual fee to be $1. Forty old boys, enticed as well by the new Old Boys Supplement in the *Ashburian,* boarded the Aylmer streetcar below the one-year-old Chateau Laurier for the ride out to the Royal Ottawa Golf Club.

The Head stepped down as President and Willis O'Connor was elected. Louis White continued as Secretary. Nixie Newcombe represented Montreal, where he was practising law. Alan Beddoe, the official artist, had illuminated the menus and toast lists. He'd also designed an old boys' lapel pin, noting the school colours had changed in 1911 from red and blue to cardinal, white and green.

A convivial evening, many toasts and speeches and a strong message from G.P.: proselytize, bring in new boys. The school was in great shape in every way but financially, and it couldn't break even without more boys. The problem: it was practically unknown outside Ottawa and the Valley. He repeated the plea, headed "My Dear Boys," in an open letter in the next *Ashburian.* He wasn't asking old boys for money, "at any rate not at present." But it was up to them to spread the Ashbury net.

G.P. had always understood public relations and there was no doubt about the school's name in the city. In April 1914, the physical training instructor, "Professor" W.H. Hewitt staged a complex gymnastics display with over 60 boys at St. Patrick's Hall. It attracted, according to the *Ottawa Journal,* "nearly four hundred of Ottawa's most distinguished people," including the Governor General, Princess Louise and the Archbishop. A disciplined programme of Swedish drill, parallel bars, vaulting horse and pyramids, to the accompaniment of Mr. Wiggins' piano, drew loud applause, vice-regal praise for Hewitt and a whole holiday for the boys.

Meanwhile, the Board of Directors pondered finance. There were 108 boys enrolled. Besides Woollcombe, who taught classics, divinity and English, there were seven on the regular teaching staff, plus J. Edgar Birch for music, "Professor" Hewitt for physical culture and gymnastics, the new Sergeant-Major Turner for cadets and the Matron, Mrs. Aylwin. Rising costs nudged boarders' fees up to $500 per year (laundry at 15 articles a week included), plus a sports fee of $8.

The 50 shareholders included just about every big name in Ottawa. W.H. Rowley was still President, and Orde, Woods and Woollcombe were now joined on the Board of Directors by J. Roberts Allan, F.A. Heney of the coal company, and lumberman J.B. Fraser. At Fraser's urging the debenture issue was increased by $20,000 to $60,000. He had a genuine interest in private schooling, and was the biggest debenture holder and creditor. Altogether Ashbury College Company Ltd. owed him and his company over $40,000, and he was very much aware that private schools weren't business ventures. He was closely connected with St. Andrew's College and had turned in his shares when the Directors decided to form a trust. With Ashbury he realized he could forfeit everything he'd put in, but he didn't turn a hair.

The City of Ottawa was growing steadily. In 1914 the population was over 108,000. Ashbury's tight financial position was in tune with the depressed economy of that year. Fraser accepted interest only on his loans. Board members Woods, Allan and Heney set out to dispose of the unsold mortgage bonds, sell the Argyle property and deal with Ward Hughson's loan. Again, the annual dividend was passed.

Now the Headmaster put his finger on a basic Ashbury problem. The new school was designed, equipped and geared to handle 62 boarders, plus the few youngsters in the Head's house. All the fixed overhead was there in the form of domestic space and staff, live-in masters, etc. But a day boy took a full share of classroom space and only paid a fraction of the boarder's fee. Reduce the number of day boys and more boarders could be taken for the cost of victuals only. As well, though, Woollcombe firmly believed in the value of a boarding school education. Ashbury, in his view, should be another BCS or TCS. More boarders could be fitted in and he was sure the demand was there.

But the financial agonizing behind the scenes never disturbed the lively tenor of the school. Tennis boomed. A fourth court was added by the faithful Fred Oliver, and he stacked more stones neatly on his fence. The three-way perpetual challenge went on in football, hockey and athletic sports with St. Alban's and Lower Canada College (LCC). LCC won the track meet in Brockville that spring. The standard must have been extraordinary. At Ashbury's own sports day – if the school's stopwatch is to be believed – Roy Maclaren won the 220 yards in 22 seconds and H.L. Holland took the 100 yards in 10.2. Academic prowess was confirmed too. P.E. Biggar won the Governor General's Medal for the second year and stood first in Canada for entry to RMC.

In that summer of 1914 G.P. convinced the Board that Ashbury should be solely a boarding school. The calendar for 1914-15 went out with no reference at all to day boys. In no time shareholders and parents were on the warpath. Ashbury had been built by Ottawa people. Boarding, they all agreed, was most important for boys from places like Pembroke, Arnprior, Fort Coulonge and Buckingham, where many of them came from. But the tail mustn't wag the dog.

Ottawa people had built the school, yet their sons and grandsons would be cut off from the best education in the area unless they chose to pay the price for boarding right on their own doorsteps. G.P. was a very determined man, stubborn to a fault where his own convictions were concerned and the storm raged on all summer. Letters flew between Ottawa and the favoured resorts of Murray Bay, Metis and St. Andrew's, and up the Gatineau to the substantial summer cottages at Thirty One Mile Lake and Blue Sea. Finally, for the first and only time in the recorded history of G.P. Woollcombe's headship, he was defeated. On September 1 the Board decided that day boys could return at the discretion of the Headmaster, with fees raised substantially to $40 per term, $160 a year. A day school with facilities for boarders or a boarding school with space for day students? It was a dichotomy that was to trouble Ashbury one way and another for many years.

That same summer, Canada looked inwards at her own problems. The economy was on the slide. It was the second year of a prairie drought. New railways, just finished, were deep in debt. Unemployment was high. Then on August 4 Britain honoured her guarantee of Belgian neutrality in the face of an attack by the German army. She declared war. With her, willy-nilly, went her Empire. Canada and the world changed for evermore.

Britain called the tune but there was no question about Canada's response. Sir Wilfrid Laurier had said it in 1910: "When Britain is at war, Canada is at war." There was no doubt in the mind of an Ashbury boy or that of his family. Uphold the Empire, fear God and honour the King: a straightforward clarion call to duty for the Canadian of British stock. Anyway, only the gloomiest pessimist believed the war would go on past Christmas. If you didn't get in quickly, you'd miss it. Ashbury old boys flocked to the colours. No one, of course, had any notion of the carnage that was to devour the young manhood of Europe, Britain, and her dominions and colonies over the next four years.

Colonel Sam Hughes, the messianic Minister of Militia, launched a massive, chaotic recruiting campaign. Militia units in towns and cities across Canada leapt to arms. In Ottawa the Governor General's Foot Guards' recruiting office overflowed. Ranks swelled. Adventurous – and out-of-work – young Canadians flocked to join up. In jig time they were aboard trains, heading for Valcartier outside Quebec. A huge tent city sprang up overnight. By September 4 it bulged with 32,000 men and 8000 horses, and even – one week later – eight Ashbury boys with their bicycles!

They were members of the cadet corps, specially selected, drilled and briefed by the redoubtable Sergeant-Major Turner and impeccably uniformed. Down to Valcartier they went, headed by the fleet-footed Roy Maclaren. For two weeks they ran messages and did camp chores from early morning to late at night. Blistering hot by day, freezing by night, "The Lucky Eight," as they proudly signed their report in the *Ashburian*, "... slept on the ground – four in a tent – three blankets apiece and a blessed Balaklava bonnet . . . . Turning out on a black wet midnight to deliver telegrams through three miles of tents – roads deep in mud – well, these were the occasions to wonder why the mischief we had come . . . . No football team worked harder!"

They saw Sam Hughes careering madly around the enormous camp. Watching the whole of "Canada's Answer" on the move, marching past the Duke of Connaught, "gave one an idea of the force and impact of an army corps thrown against the ranks of the enemy." They would soon lose that illusion personally in the trenches, barbed wire and dreadful mire of a new kind of war. At the end of September the boys watched the huge, scarcely trained, meagrely equipped Canadian contingent move out to Quebec to board ocean liners and sail for England. They itched to be with them, of course, but back they went, a proud little contingent, to the dull routine of school until they themselves joined up.

And inside two years every one of them had: William Muirhead, Gunner, wounded at Passchendaele 1917; Geoffrey Birkett, Lieutenant, Royal Canadian

Dragoons, then RAF; Cecil Wood, Lieutenant, Royal Flying Corps, wounded 1917; Allan Code, Lieutenant, Royal Flying Corps, wounded 1918; Roy Maclaren, Lieutenant, gassed 1918; Gordon Ross, Lieutenant, Royal Canadian Artillery; Robert Morris, Lieutenant, wounded at Ypres 1917; Reginald Sladen, Lieutenant, Princess Patricia's, killed at Vimy Ridge.

CHAPTER 4
THE GREAT WAR YEARS

To "The Lucky Eight," coming back to Ashbury after Valcartier was like crawling back into a cocoon. They'd played war in the cadet corps for years, they'd soaked in ideas of Empire, the Mother Country and the natural destiny of Canada to fight for Britain. But now they'd seen it happen: the vast mustering, the incredible, stirring spectacle of an army of Canadians, scarcely older than themselves, actually marching off to war.

Back at Ashbury Roy Maclaren was 1st Lieutenant of the cadet corps under CO Des MacMahon. That seemed pretty tame now, though Sergeant-Major Turner made things as tough as he could. Like his predecessor, he was the very model of the Imperial Army NCO and a master of the dressing-down in blistering barracks-room language. That, in his tradition, was all part of the process of turning his "young gentlemen" into potential officers. G.P. took no issue with that, except for the language. Fred Oliver watched aghast as he actually dressed down the Sergeant-Major himself, punctuating each word he was NOT to use with a jab of his cane. There was no doubt who was in charge at Ashbury College.

But for schoolmastering and the Church, G.P. might well have been a military man himself. He steered his most promising boys to RMC or the Naval College. He had a very strong sense of order and was always a firm, fair disciplinarian. Caning was part of it in the manner of the day. The strap on the hand was for lesser offences. The mildest punishment was detention, meted out by masters in "quarters" – 15-minute bites. You worked off the week's total on Saturday morning or you could take the option of having it "whacked off" by the Head at one stroke of the strap for each quarter.

Roy Maclaren had come to Ashbury in 1909, the school's last year on Argyle, and he was followed by his younger brother James N. The Maclarens had been the first settlers in Torbolton Township, and the boys' grandfather James bought out the Buckingham sawmills and timber limits on the Lievre in the 1860s and built his family empire.

Most of the Buckingham Maclaren boys had gone off to Upper Canada College before, but Ashbury was closer and, by that time, had a high reputation. To two young fellows from Buckingham, though, it had a distinctly English flavour. Gowns and English accents among the masters; cricket, which Roy never liked; soccer, which they played after the football season, though they couldn't get any other school to play. Most of the masters were English, including, since Fleury's departure in 1908, the French teachers.

D.E.C. Wood was a notch up in French: he'd been at the University of Paris. And the Housemaster, C.H. Hooper, had been at Queen's and had taught at Highfield School in Hamilton. Hooper was very well liked and totally involved in the school and the boys. He started the Scout Troop and ran the rifle shooting. He was an enthusiast and a good organizer, and both Scouts and shooting were exceptionally popular. Every summer he went off on Algonquin Park canoe trips and often took boys with him. After a wasting illness, tended faithfully by Fred Oliver, he died at the school in December 1915.

N.A. Creeth had his MSc from Manchester, which didn't quite meet G.P.'s strong Oxbridge preference. The Rev. Dr. Voohris was an unusual addition. He'd appeared at the Chapel dedication in 1913. MA (Princeton) and PhD (New York University), he'd come back to teach classics and junior English. He stayed until after the war.

"Professor" W.H. Hewitt, with his broad Lancashire accent, acted as trainer for the football team and also coached track and field. He was a muscular young man, posed like Charles Atlas for his *Ashburian* photo, bare-chested with pumped-up biceps. Full-time on staff since 1912, he was bursting with energy and immersed in the life of the school. He was to stay on for 12 years. Miss Edwards, who had come in 1911, taught music, German and junior English until she left to start her own small preparatory school in 1924.

Roy Maclaren captained the football team in his last two years. They had won the St. Alban's Cup for the three-way, home-and-home championship in 1913, but lost it to LCC in the fall of 1914. Poor St. Alban's was in a slump and was slaughtered by LCC 126–2 and by Ashbury 106–6. On the ice Maclaren was a fast and bruising defenceman and, if the record book's to be believed, quite astounding on the track.

It ran in the family. Young James was the school's top tennis player. The second year the courts were laid out, he won the junior doubles and the senior singles. By the winter of 1915 he was playing left wing on the first hockey team. The professionals, since 1911, had dropped to six players but the school league still put the seventh man, the rover, on the ice.

There were two sides to life for Ashbury boys during these years – the daily routine and the war. They chafed at the first and itched to be in the second. The excitement and glamour hadn't dimmed and there wasn't one who didn't wish, or at least appear to wish, to be in the fighting. If they wanted an example among the old boys, there was Lieutenant Henry Bate. He had gone to Valcartier with the first contingent but was turned back because he'd had an earlier attack of appendicitis. He rushed back to Ottawa, had his uncomplaining appendix removed and was set to go with the second contingent.

The boys quickly heard of the adventures of the first old boys in action. Rastus Reid, Donald Lindsay and T.S. Critchley were on board HMS *Berwick* when she captured a German armed merchant cruiser and two transports. Old boys in the Imperial Army, and there were quite a few, were quickly at the front. Lieutenant Jack Eliot was decorated for carrying a wounded comrade to safety under fire and getting wounded himself. Captain Oliver Dickey was mentioned in dispatches. Each, as the *Ashburian* put it, was "a splendid example of true British pluck and grit."

Among the staff, D.E. Cecil Wood had gone back to England in June and had joined up as soon as war broke out. The affable and popular Captain Weston was off to England to join his old regiment. He'd started at Ashbury as Bursar in 1908 and became Secretary of the Board as well. It got harder and harder for G.P. to find adequate staff to fill in.

The first Canadian contingent, which the boys had seen march out of Valcartier, trained in England that winter and the first Division got to France in March 1915. In April they were decimated in the second battle of Ypres when chlorine gas was used for the first time in history by the Germans. The Ross rifle that had proved so accurate on the Rockcliffe ranges was a disaster in its first test in battle. It overheated and jammed, and too many good men died.

Gordon Carling, Ashbury 1894, carried a Ross rifle in that battle. He was a Corporal in Princess Patricia's Light Infantry (PPCLI) and he was knocked out by the gas. But he stayed on the front line as the battalion grimly held on. Telephone lines were gone. Carling ran dispatches. He was hit three times by shrapnel. A bullet went clean through him. The Princess Pats were virtually wiped out: they lost 511, all ranks. Gordon Carling, with a charmed life, was one of the 52 who were left.

At Closing 1915, the arrangements were the same as usual. Oliver had the grounds beautifully mown. The mower was horse-drawn, of course, and he needed no reminder from the Head to scoop up the manure. He'd set out the smudge-pots. Rockcliffe mosquitoes were famous. The seasonal deluge of caterpillars dropping from the trees on ladies' hats caused less mirth than usual. The festive feeling was dampened. The casualty lists had brought the war from the realm of another distant South African adventure. This would be a long and bloody conflict.

Two younger Carlings in the crowd, along with everyone there – indeed, all Canada – knew about Ypres and the PPCLI. They too would go. And they did: John to the Royal Naval Air Service, to die of illness in London; Lewis to be invalided home from the army. Gordon, who by fall was back in Ottawa on leave, told the *Journal* he wanted to return to France. He did, was promoted to Captain, was wounded and died. Henry Bate caught up with the overseas contingent of the Royal Canadian Dragoons. He was wounded on the Somme, came home, returned to the front and finally was invalided home, permanently unfit. Many of the 1915 graduates joined up straightaway. Roy Maclaren went via RMC to the artillery and was gassed in 1918. His brother Jim went straight in as a gunner in a trench mortar battery.

Philip Woollcombe was already overseas as a sergeant, and he ended as a captain. Edward and George, both slated for the Naval College, were too young to get to sea. But G.P. watched and prayed as two-thirds of "his boys" from his school's beginning, almost as dear to him as his own sons, went off to war. Every one of them had been under his personal care. Each had been touched by his unflinching concept of loyalty, honour and duty. The death or maiming of any one of them was a personal blow. Every old boy overseas got his free copy of the *Ashburian*. G.P also wrote reams of letters to them, and they to him. There was no typist or stenographer at Ashbury, and when Fred Oliver did his early morning cleaning he'd always see stacks of handwritten letters on G.P.'s desk ready to be mailed.

Captain Weston had been replaced as Bursar by Miss Hammell. G.P. called her his "financial fortress," worth her weight in gold. Teaching staff were in short supply and constantly changing as the war took its toll. G.P. had to take whatever he could get in the way of masters and that meant a much heavier load on him to maintain standards. After Hooper's untimely death, he worked for his warrant as a Scoutmaster, took over the Ashbury Troop himself and added Wolf Cubs for the younger boys. Evenings were the time to call Oliver for rounds to spot work to be done. More often than not they'd stop in the Chapel and the two of them would drop to their knees for a few minutes of prayer for the boys at war.

Mrs. Woollcombe was a tower of strength in the school's domestic department, tracking down new staff, supervising the kitchen, watching sanitation. Her pioneer roots showed. She'd refuse a wagon-load of provisions if it had been covered with a horse-blanket. In summer peak times, when the Ottawa Valley overflowed with produce and fruit piled in from Niagara, she bought great quantities and mustered staff and her children for preserving bees. She trusted only her own canning for the boys, no one else's. By summer's end the shelves that Oliver had built in the basement storeroom groaned with dozens of sealed jars full of pickles, jams and preserves for the coming year. A housekeeper was hired later in the war which gave her a little more time for her own two children and three step-children. But Jessie Woollcombe kept on her keen-eyed overseeing role until G.P. retired.

The faithful Oliver took on anything and everything and never needed direction. Drainage in Rockcliffe was poor and melting snow meant floods. To keep the furnace going he slept at night on a bench in the boiler room, set his alarm clock at two-hour intervals and pumped out before the water reached the gratings. He was constantly sparring with Mr. Short, who owned the corner house on Springfield Road, over the state of the fence. It was a high board one, but cricket balls insisted on going over the top and boys found ways of getting through, trampling things a bit and – according to Mr. Short, who was likely quite right – filching produce from his well-tended garden. Short took to collecting cricket balls and returning them via Oliver but only when he'd nailed all loose boards firmly back in place.

Oliver's quietly self-effacing personality hid a quite remarkable talent. He was an accomplished and comical ventriloquist, always in demand to entertain the boys. One such show took place inside a gigantic snow-house the juniors made, supported by a frame Oliver had built for them. They lit it with candles for an evening show and presented him with a fine box of cigars.

The war years saw Ashbury grow as a school. And it matured, as the country matured and hardened, tempered by the terrible loss of its young men. The appalling casualty lists from France included too many Ashbury names – names read out in Chapel, names the boys knew, names connected to faces in team pictures on the walls, names on the silver trophies arrayed and presented each Closing Day. Graduating classes now weren't just stepping out with high hopes to university or college or the world of business. The names called out on those deceptively sunny June Closing afternoons to accept prizes too often appeared themselves on the dreaded lists. Still, the spirit never flagged. The *Ashburian* Editorial in 1917 said, "We hear very frequently that Old Boys have left Canada to do their bit for the Empire and we are looking forward, if the war lasts, to going overseas ourselves."

Life at the school, of course, went on. Games continued, some against new competition. A sally to Renfrew, the very cradle of hockey, home of the famous Millionaires, to play the Collegiate, proved more than the team could handle. They lost 13–1. Outings for lectures, concerts and variety shows at the Russell Theatre continued. Moving pictures weren't entirely new, but in November 1915 all the boarders went to see that milestone epic "The Birth of a Nation."

That was the year the Rockcliffe Preparatory School for boys and girls started in an old farmhouse over on Buena Vista Avenue. The Headmistress was Mrs. H.

Philpott whose husband taught at Ashbury. Her little school was patronized mainly by Rockcliffe families and in a few years, with their initiative and support, it developed into Elmwood School for Girls. The driving force was Mrs. Harry Southam who was the daughter of Thomas Ahearn, strongly backed by Mrs. Edward Fauquier and Mrs. Norman Wilson – Cairine Wilson, who in 1930 became Canada's first female Senator.

The two schools and their Boards, Ottawa being the kind of town it was, were linked from the start. G.P. welcomed Elmwood, especially as it took little boys and many of them could be coaxed along to Ashbury. Also the advent of suitable young ladies nearby to stimulate the social graces via dances and even theatricals was clearly an advantage. Ashbury boarders, of course, greeted the new school with joy unbounded. They were linked by a wooden walkway, built in earlier years so one could navigate dry-shod from Mariposa to Buena Vista en route to the streetcar stop at the Rockcliffe end-of-the-line loop. Buena Vista had a good surface and in fact was the first and only road in Rockcliffe to have a sidewalk. Boys being boys and girls girls, the traffic built up between the two schools, both decorous and illicit. Soon it was hard to imagine one without the other.

The wartime editions of the *Ashburian* were rather thin. They carried the customary play-by-play accounts of games, and school notes. The joke pages and "schoolboy howlers," which had been regular, lengthy and, by today's tastes, pretty feeble, carried on. Everything else was sparser, perhaps because in 1917 all the editorial work and writing was taken over by the boys. With no master as Editor to prise contributions from the reluctant, there were far fewer literary offerings. There were news items, however. The new Governor General, the Duke of Devonshire, took an interest in the school. He and his family often came to Sunday Chapel, and his son Lord Charles Cavendish entered the school in 1917.

Hamlet S. Philpott, a replacement master, an Oxonian who taught (what else?) classics and English and whose wife was Elmwood's first Headmistress, sparked the formation of the Ashbury College Debating Society in the fall of 1915. Debating wasn't new. The first debate on record had been in 1911; the subject: compulsory military service.

Wartime conscription was a contentious and deeply divisive political issue and didn't go through Parliament until after the great Canadian triumph at Vimy Ridge on Easter Monday 1917. Four divisions – 40,000 men – stormed the Ridge. Over three thousand were killed and 7000 wounded – 25 percent casualties. George Brown won the Military Cross that day, only to be killed six months later. Henri Taschereau was wounded there; Forbes Stuart, MC, was wounded for the third time. Tennis champion Melbourne O'Halloran, who'd been wounded a year before, won the MC.

At sea, while U-boats sank 5000 merchant ships, navy casualties were light. Rastus Reid survived the sinking of his destroyer in the Mediterranean. Charlie Beard commanded his own destroyer. Edward Woollcombe and Ted Orde were cadets at the Naval College in the catastrophic Halifax explosion. Orde lost an eye. Val Godfrey fought at Jutland, then in submarines. Finally, as Cyril Inderwick described it for the *Ashburian*, came the surrender of the mighty German High Seas Fleet at Scapa Flow.

Before that last act though, at 2:00 a.m. on November 11, 1918, sirens and factory whistles woke the school. The Armistice! No one went back to sleep. It was a day of delirious celebration. Motor lorries were rounded up, and the whole school headed

into the city armed with drums, bugles, tin pans, milk cans – anything that would add
to their own uproarious shouts, cheers, school yells. In the centre of the city they
plunged into the surging, wildly cheering throng. That day, not to be forgotten by
anyone old enough to walk, was marked in *Ashburian* verse:

> *Forward the School Brigade,*
> *Was there a boy dismayed,*
> *Not tho' the crowd knew*
> *Ashbury had thundered.*
> *Theirs but to make reply*
> *Ours but to yell and cry:*
> *Straight into Bank and Sparks*
> *Rode our One Hundred.*

A whole generation on both sides of the war to end all wars had paid a monstrous price.
Of a population of only 8 million, Canada lost 60,000 of its vigorous young people;
the same number were maimed for life. Ashbury's sons had been in the forefront. By
June 1918, 453 boys had passed through Ashbury college. Sixty-two percent of them
– 282 old boys, plus nine masters – had gone to war. Two hundred and two were
commissioned. Thirty-nine were decorated. Among them were Percy Biggar, twice
winner of the Governor General's Medal, who won the Belgian Croix de Guerre;
Edouard de Bellefeuille Panet (who had graduated in 1899), who became a Brigadier-
General, was mentioned in dispatches and won the DSO, CMG and Croix de
Chevalier, Légion d'honneur (France); Sergeant-Major Turner, promoted to Captain,
who won the Military Cross; and Willis O'Connor, who won the DSO.

But 39 old boys and three masters were killed, 80 were wounded or invalided out.
It was a terrible toll. By 1918 over a quarter of all the boys who had ever been at
Ashbury College, the oldest around 40, the youngest 16, had been killed, crippled or
invalided in war.

William Brooke, captured at Ypres, died in prison; Alan Beddoe, wounded at
Ypres, was a prisoner for three years; Hugh Billings was killed while serving in the
Royal Flying Corps and his brother Charlie was wounded; Everett Dyson Currier,
Cyril's brother, who had fought in the South African War, was killed on the Somme;
Hugh Hughson was wounded in the same battle, and Jack was invalided home; Des
MacMahon was wounded at Cambrai; Nicholas Sparks was wounded.

John Russell Woods, the Chairman's son, had gone overseas with the Governor
General's Foot Guards. Promoted in the field, twice mentioned in dispatches, he was
the first Canadian to be commissioned in the Brigade of Guards – in Sergeant-Major
Carwardine's Coldstreams in fact – and he left a fine record of leadership and bravery.
He was killed on the Somme.

G.P.'s memories also included the Gilmour boys from the school's first decade.
Four of them fought in the war. Allan U. and John F. had both seen service in South
Africa. Allan was wounded at Ypres and killed a year later. John was wounded on
the Somme. Sutherland and H.L. got through untouched.

Some were partly lucky. Nixie Newcombe was hit by shrapnel in the trenches
at Messines in 1916. It cut the carotid artery. Another soldier managed to control the

bleeding long enough to get him to the doctor, one Captain Colin Webb Johnson, a brilliant man, it happened, who later became surgeon to the Queen. Nixie recovered at length in Middlesex Hospital, London, though he was dogged all through his life by a disability, and a scar that was more than simply physical.

There were many, many more and every one of them was known personally to the Head. At the service of Thanksgiving in the Ashbury Chapel, the Roll of Honour was read out, as it would be every November 11 – Armistice Day, later called Remembrance Day – throughout Ashbury's life. No one there could have felt the losses of those four dreadful years more profoundly than G.P. Woollcombe himself.

In spite of the great surge of vitality and success that had taken Ashbury through to the war years, serious questions had been posed around the Board table about the future of the school. War or no war, vibrant institution though it was, there were basic problems to be sorted out. The Argyle property stood vacant. In the wake of its ambitious building, Ashbury owed too much on debentures and preferred stock and it simply couldn't service the debt. Taxes in Rockcliffe were slight at the time, but under the Ontario Assessment Act of 1910 it was subject to municipal taxation as a share capital corporation.

In January 1915 W.H. Rowley died. He had been President, Chairman of the Board and a tireless Ashbury supporter for 24 years. Lt. Col. James Woods had a big pair of shoes to fill. He was the natural choice, though: he had been Vice-President since 1906; he was an energetic, successful businessman, whose company plants in Ottawa and Hull were booming because of the war; and his son, John Russell Woods, fated to be killed in two years' time, had had five happy years in the school on Argyle.

The possibility of reshaping Ashbury as a public foundation had been raised originally by J.B. Fraser in 1910. He was a supporter and shareholder of St. Andrew's College, Toronto, a share capital corporation like Ashbury. Like Ashbury it had financed a major building programme with privately placed debentures and shares, and had got in over its head. St. Andrew's benefactor and principal shareholder was Lord Strathcona and he had taken the lead by turning in all his shares and making a large donation so the company could be converted to a foundation with a clean slate.

Sharing Strathcona's Scottish origin meant sharing a regard for education that approached reverence. Fraser now took a leaf out of his friend's book. Backed by his business partner and brother, he offered to pay off Ashbury's debt to their own company and to turn in their personal securities on condition that no more debt was loaded onto the property without the agreement of three-quarters of the share- and bondholders, according to their interest.

That gave the lead. But to establish Fraser's proposed foundation, over 50 more holders of shares, bonds and debentures, mostly the long-term supporters of the school, would have to turn in their investments. Shareholders' and lenders' money, invested over the years with the prospect of reasonable return, stood against the survival of Ashbury College as a proven, valuable institution. G.P. set about the delicate and difficult task of canvassing them all.

Those handwritten letters Oliver had seen stacked on G.P.'s desk in the morning weren't only cheering letters to his boys at the front and condolences to bereft families.

Many of them asked shareholders to say goodbye to money he himself had encouraged them to subscribe. In some cases they were people of quite limited means. It was a painful process. For a man like Woollcombe, it was unthinkable to let anyone down. He had always swept everything ahead of him with unbounded and infectious confidence. The Board had backed him, of course, but Ashbury had always been his show. Notably, and typically, it was G.P. and not Orde the lawyer or another top company officer who took on the unhappy task.

He gave up his personal holding in common shares. Their face value was no more than $3800 but they were fully a third of those outstanding. With them went any prospects of dividends. But far more important, his share in the equity built up so painstakingly since 1891 was gone. One-third ownership in valuable land and a fine building, the prospect of eventual reward, comfortable retirement on the proceeds of selling out to a worthy successor – all that was gone. Utterly dedicated to his avocation as he was, he had been blind to the hard basic facts of the business world. The day of the schoolmaster-entrepreneur was past. From now on G.P. Woollcombe would virtually be an employee of the Board of Directors.

A few debenture holders demurred; in some cases it was unhappily more than they could afford to lose. But by 1918 most outstanding securities were in. Face value: $70,000 in bonds and preferred, $10,000 in common shares. For their part, the Frasers surrendered their $20,000, mostly in bonds and preferred shares, a full quarter of the outstanding total. On top of that, they donated $32,000 to retire the Ashbury debt to their own company. Others contributed another $7500 in cash.

Thanks to the leadership and philanthropy of the lumber-merchant Frasers, Ashbury College Company Ltd. was all but free and clear. There was still a mortgage on the Argyle property, now rented out to the government at $2000 a year for a House of Commons restaurant, and there were still a few unconverted debentures outstanding. But the company wound up on April 30, 1918, and a charter for a new company without share capital was granted on July 18.

The stated objects of Ashbury College Incorporated were to take over the assets and obligations of the old company and "to carry on at or near the City of Ottawa a boarding and day school and college for the education of boys, girls or both." The 58 people who had surrendered their shares, waived a debt in the old company or made donations at the time of the restructuring were named Founders and rewarded with one vote for every $100 contributed. Thus, for example, out of 1134 votes, the Frasers had 515, James Woods 65, the Duke of Devonshire 5. George Woollcombe had a mere 38.

Woollcombe's ability aside, it was lumbering – lumbering drive and lumbering money – that built Ashbury College, just as it had built Ottawa itself. Rowley and his friends had supported George Woollcombe from the start and had stayed behind him through some very hard times. Accompanying G.P.'s sad sense of personal failure was the certainty that he had never failed them or his school or his boys.

The original backers of 1891, the Founders of 1918, and the supporters and parents through those first 27 formative years included politicians like Sir Charles Tupper and A.G. Blair; nation-builders of the stature of Sir Sandford Fleming; Ottawa entrepreneurs Tom Ahearn and Warren Soper; manufacturers Woods and Blackburn; businessmen like Plunket Taylor, the Carlings, the Heneys and the Sherwoods;

publisher P.D. Ross of the *Journal* and the *Citizen*'s Harry and Wilson Southam; and merchants like R.J. Devlin. Outstandingly though, they included the names of the great Ottawa Valley lumbering families: Aylen, Booth, Bronson, Bryson, Caldwell, Currier, Davidson, Eddy, Edwards, Egan, Fraser, Gilmour, Hughson, Maclaren, McLachlin, Perley, Wright.

The first generations, which had done so well in the hurly-burly lumbering business weren't, by and large, well educated or cultivated men themselves. But they wanted a first-class education for their children and everything that education could bring: solid values, manners and deportment, and that priceless ingredient for business, politics or, indeed, practically any pursuit in Canada – friends and connections. The old boy network. They were men who recognized value when they saw it, and they were prepared to pay. They had no qualms in giving up shares. George Woollcombe had certainly not lost stature in their eyes. He had moulded a fine school for them and for Ottawa, and they were still behind him.

Ashbury College was well structured now, well supported and well led. It was attracting boarders not only from Ottawa Valley towns but from Montreal, Quebec and the Maritimes. The demand for places was strong. In fact, in the last summer of the war, the Headmaster had moved out of his east wing residence and into a rented house, 2 Cloverdale Road, to make room for more boarders. His reputation and the fast-widening constituency of his school were reflected in the Board of Directors elected by the Founders in 1918.

Lt. Col. James Woods was President and Chairman of the Board. G.P. Woollcombe was Secretary-Treasurer. Other members were J.B. Fraser, F.A. Heney and John Orde, all from Ottawa; John Burstall of Quebec; F.L. Wanklyn, Harold Hampson and A.E. Holt of Montreal; and F.B. McCurdy, MP, of Halifax. Each was a person of substance and the parent of an Ashbury boy present or past. Woods, Woollcombe, Fraser, Orde, Burstall and Wanklyn formed the first Executive Committee.

Now the war was over and the League of Nations, first proposed by US President Woodrow Wilson at the Paris Peace Conference, was born. The Western world set about rebuilding, determined that no such catastrophic war, such slaughter of a whole generation, would ever happen again. The seeds of failure and renewed war lay in the disastrous reparations demanded of Germany and in the United States' refusal to join the League. But at Ashbury College hopes, as everywhere, were high. The school was soon on the crest of the post-war boom.

George Penrose Woollcombe, the Founding Headmaster, 1891-1933. Intellect and purpose speak from this portrait of 1908. He was ordained as an Anglican priest in 1903.

1891-1894
Victoria Chambers, corner of
Wellington and O'Connor Streets
"Mr. Woollcombe's School"

1894-1900
186 Wellington Street
"Ashbury House School"

1900-1910
70 Argyle Avenue
"Ashbury College"

1910-1991
Mariposa Avenue, Rockcliffe Park "Ashbury College"

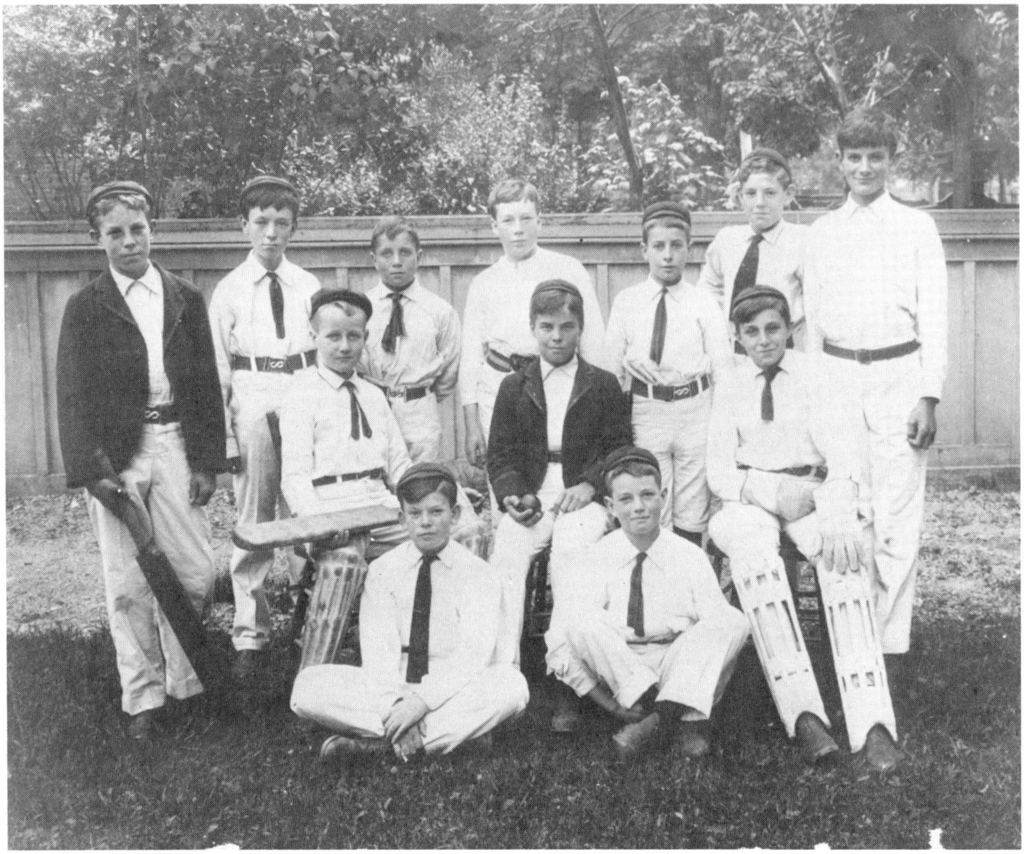

Junior Cricket XI   1904-1905

Standing (from left): Colville Sinclair, Edmond F. Newcombe, Tubby Bate, Geoffrey Burbidge, Leigh Bishop, B.Barnes, Palmer Wright
Seated: Drummond Burn, Donald Ellard, Richard Spain
Front: W.H. Trenholme, Charles Fleming

G.P. Woollcombe was a keen cricketer himself and made sport and physical fitness a part of Ashbury life from its beginnings. "Nixie" Newcombe (standing, second from left) became the longest-standing and most deeply dedicated member of the Board of Governors

Ashbury College 1904-1905

Back Row:(from left) ?, O.C. Dawson, ?, Harry Wright, Donald A. Blair, Charles Keeling, Eric Irwin, Kenneth MacPherson, W. Witcher, Alex Anderson

4th Row: Arthur Sparks, W.H. Trenholme, Edmond F. Newcombe, Philip Woollcombe, Reginald Orde, B.Barnes, Donald Ellard, Geoffrey Burbidge, Colville Sinclair, Gordon Spencer, Drummond Burn, Charles Fleming

3rd Row: John Ward Hughson, Murray Greene, Thomas Carling, ?, Alex Fraser, Richard Spain, Rolland Ellard, Gibson (?), ?, Sam Matthews, Charles Butterworth, Palmer Wright, Tubby Bate

2nd Row: James Bryson, Charles Emery,Esq., Monsieur J. Fleury, J.R. Montizambert, Esq., George Penrose Woollcombe, Esq., ?, Charles E. Read, Ewen McLachlin

Two standing behind Montizambert and Woollcombe: ?, Leigh Bishop

Front Row : John Aylen, Gordon Perley, ?, Trennick Bate, Hugh Hughson, Kenneth Slater, John Roberts Allan, ?, St. Barbe Sladen, John Woods

Ashbury Footballers 1908

Ashbury played St. John's in Montreal (later Lower Canada College) and Bishop's College School, Lennoxville. Before moving to Rockliffe in 1910, home games were often played at Lansdowne Park.

Cadet Corps 1909

The Ashbury College Cadet Corps was founded in 1905 and flourished under the strong hand of Sergeant -Major Carwardine, late of the Coldstream Guards, from 1907 to 1912. All boys from Form III were "expected to join." Behind is the Victoria Memorial Museum (now the Canadian Museum of Nature) in the final stages of construction.

Ashbury College, Rockcliffe 1912

Across Mariposa Avenue, the new Chapel, with assembly hall and "Siberia" underneath, was joined to the main building by a single storey passageway. Fred Oliver's stone fence lined the gravel road.

The 6th Form Boarders   1916

Back Row (from left): J. Malcolm, J.B. Carling, A.E.D. Tremain, G.D.G. Barwis, W.D. Benson
2nd Row: C.H. Goldstein, G.A. Bate, A.B.H. Wiggins,Esq., L.W. Jackson, E.K. Davidson
Front Row : J.H. Gibbs, J.N. MacLaren, T.S. Crocket

All fought in World War I. J. Carling died, Malcolm, Benson and Bate were wounded, and Malcolm won the Military Cross.

Physical Training 1917

"Professor" Hewitt conducts a class behind the school. On the left is the annex originally built as the Headmaster's house. On the right is the original gym. The Memorial Wing was added to it in 1924.

Gymnastics Team 1917

"Professor" W.H. Hewitt(centre top), Physical Training Instructor 1912-1924, sets off his gym team's figure on the parallel bars with a long-arm balance.

Expedition in Algonquin Park, January 1914
left to right: Desmond MacMahon, Maurice Burns, Masters C.H. Hooper, A.B. Wiggins and D.E.C. Wood, Cecil Wood

Ashbury College Scout Troop 1916
Front Row (from left): H. Tamplet. E.W.T. Gill, G.P. Woollcombe, G.P. Sladen, L.H. Burpee
Back Row: F.W. Ritchie, F.G. Adams, W.G. Evans, F.D. Bliss, H.R. Hampson, E.T.C. Orde, J. Burstall

Scouting had a great world-wide surge of growth early in the century and Ashbury had one of the first troops in Ottawa. Frank Bliss was the son of an early leader of Canadian scouting. Frank took over as Scoutmaster. In the seventies, he hosted Ashbury teams playing in the Toronto area. G.P.'s dog's name was Rex.

The Cadets Corps   1918

War had ground on in France for four years. Over thirty ex-members of the Ashbury Corps had been killed already and scores wounded. Senior boys like Cadet Captain W.G. Evans (left) and Cadet Lieutenants Charles Hamilton and Jim Armstrong (on the right, behind Sergeant Mockridge) were ready to enlist as soon as they graduated.

Ashbury College Hockey Team   1912

Back Row(from left): A.Roy Maclaren, R.W. White, D.E.C. Wood, Esq., W.M. Irvin, W.G. Gibb

Front Row : H.M. Hughson, L.E. Bowie, D.F. Verner, Capt., G.A. Strubbe, J.W. Hennessy

Inset: W.H. Wickware

The Captain, David Verner, was a fine school athlete. He was also remarkable in sleight-of-hand. As Dai Vernon, he became a famed professional magician. All these boys served unscathed through World War II.

The Assembly Hall   1916
(now called Rhodes Hall)

G.P. stands on the right in front of the radiator, hands gripping the collar of his gown.
The electric lighting was lauded as using the latest indirect technique. There are about 80 boys in the picture. Full enrolment was over 100.

Ashbury College   1915

8th Row(from left): L. Burpee, W. Moore, ?, L. Jackson, Earl Scott, Ken Bryson, Peter Bate, Jim Armstrong, Frank Bliss, Bert Tremaine, H. Bogart, W. Benson, ?, Ted Orde, S. Woods
7th Row: ?, ?, L. Hart, ?, K. Davidson; 6th Row: Leo Palmer, C. Barwis, Gault, Edward Prince,?;
5th Row: Monty Taschereau, ?, Maclaren, ?, J. Burstall, Charles Thoburn; 4th Row: Wynward Evans, ?, James Bell, David Wanklyn; 3rd Row: ?, Colin Molson, Don Jones, Arthur Evans, Paul Drummond, ?, Bay Smith, Henry Blakeney, ?, Adams, ?; 2nd Row: Willie Angus, ?, E.W.T. Gill, H. Hampson, Ed Woollcombe, Colin McLaughlin, ?, E. Burstall, Frank Ritchie, Gilbert Sladen, Harry Tamplet;
Front Row : ?, Larriat Smith, Fowler, Hammy deBury, Brian Meridith, George Guthrie, Billy Graham, Fonnar, F.T. Gill, Guy Rhodes, Gilbert Fauquier

Jack McMahon took this photo of the popcorn wagon on Mariposa in 1919.

Ashbury College   1928

This was the year the Rowley classrooms were added between the Chapel and the main building. Other than asphalt on Mariposa and the disappearance of horse-drawn deliveries very little changed until the addition of the first phase of Argyle in 1953.

The Prefects 1922-23

Back Row (from left): C.L. Yuile, F.C. Holt, A.M. Irvine
Front Row : F.G. Heney, K.H. Tremain, E.M. Pacaud

Ken Tremain, Captain of the School was captain of football, hockey
and cricket. Marsh Irvine was Captain of the School in 1923-24 and
Captain of Football.

The Staff 1924

Back Row(from left): K.C. (Casey) Cassells, J.R. Pattisson, E.C.N. Edwards, Henry King
Front Row : Edwin Ker, Harry Wright, Rev.G.P. Woollcombe, W.H. Brodie, Rev. H. Chester-Master

All were Englishmen with degrees mostly from Oxford or Cambridge. Harry Wright was the core of the teaching staff and became Headmaster in 1933.

Tennis 1925

left to right: John Arnold, who was runner up in school singles in 1925 and champion in 1926; Ned Pacaud, winner in 1925 and also best cricket bat; Harry Wright, science and mathematics teacher and later Headmaster and a fine bowler; Ned Rhodes PHOTO: COURTESY JOHN ARNOLD

Fred Oliver and friend often entertained the boys. Apart from this special talent, Fred was the backbone of plant and grounds care and maintenance from 1911 to 1952.

Boxing Champions 1928

Back Row (from left): Edwin Ker, Esq., John Rowley, Edward Elwood, Sergeant - Major F.W. Stone
2nd Row: Ken MacKenzie, Joe Irvin, Adam Fauquier
Front Row : Roger Rowley, Jim Symington

Joe Irvin, heavyweight champion, also captained football, hockey, cricket and soccer and won the Connaught Cup for gymnastics – the most outstanding sports record in Ashbury history – and he wore a mustache! All these boys served in World War II. John Rowley and Jim Symington were killed in action. John had won the DSO; his brother Roger won it twice. Sergeant-Major Stone was physical training and cadet corps instructor 1924-1938.

Chapter 5
The Wake of War

The war wasn't yet over for several thousand Canadian soldiers, some old Ashburians included. An Allied expeditionary force was occupied against the Red Army in northern Russia until the spring. However, there were few Canadian casualties in the war against the Bolsheviks, and during that winter Ashbury took the name as its own in the form of Bolshevik hockey.

Teams were small then, perhaps carrying a couple of spares. So there was always a sizeable group too old for the intermediate team and not good enough to make the first. A scrub league satisfied the requirement that everybody get out and play. Its members dubbed themselves the Bolsheviks. Playing on the outdoor rink with dubious ice conditions, through uncertain weather and with cast-off equipment, now took on a special mystique.

The Bolsheviks would play in any conditions, with or without skates, with highly flexible rules, various substitutes for pucks, outrageous clothing and endless *joie de vivre*. One great thing about Bolshevik hockey was that very few of the masters, being English, knew the proper rules or could skate, much less handle the puck. So, unruly revolutionary boys versus inept masters translated into memorable Bolshevik hockey events. All this was commemorated in cryptic reports in the *Ashburian*, something of a send-up on the laborious period-by-period accounts of every first and intermediate game in every season that filled its pages.

The terrible worldwide influenza epidemic shut down the school for some weeks, but Christmas 1918 was still a time to celebrate the end of the war. At Ashbury the annual dance was the biggest ever, preceded as usual by much application of various pomades and potions to keep the hair in its appointed place. Then came an invitation addressed to all the seniors from the Duke of Devonshire to a ball at Government House in honour of his daughter, Lady Rachel Cavendish.

It was, as one might expect, an absolutely splendid affair. The *Ashburian* Editor, Bill Hutchinson, reported on it himself, taking a small leaf perhaps from the *Citizen*'s social column: "... all the young ladies looked extremely sweet: their dainty dresses and the blue uniforms of the RMC cadets made a very pretty picture." A little wistful, one detects? A year in age and an RMC uniform could turn even a properly pomaded Ashbury senior into a wallflower.

From 1919 there was a full school, an operating surplus, a healthy increase in the Headmaster's salary, even a resolution by the Board to investigate a staff pension scheme for senior masters. Such an idea was rather advanced for the times. A man (women hardly counted as independent beings, though they did get the vote federally in 1918) was expected to set things up for his own retirement unless his children were going to care for him. Railway companies had pensions. But other than the post office, civil servants', war widows' and veterans' disability pensions, the nation's first venture in the field was the Old Age Pension Act of 1927. The federal government split the cost with the provinces of a maximum $20 a month pension at age 70, subject, in the manner of the day, to a means test.

Ashbury's Board didn't in fact act on the matter until Senator A.C. Hardy (an Ashbury parent and later grandparent) made a $1000 gift to start a fund in 1926. He specified that it should be the start of a permanent endowment fund, with the interest only to be used. The fund was increased by $1000 from healthy revenue for a couple of years, but no permanent policy emerged.

In 1919, the year of the Board's initial resolution on the pension scheme, a place was made for an old boys' representative on the Board. Nixie Newcombe, the Association President, was acclaimed to the position and began his 27 years service. At the same meeting, the Headmaster floated the idea of a memorial to fallen old boys.

That same year, Guy and Peter Simonds came all the way from Victoria, where their father had retired as a colonel. Guy was slated for the army and Ashbury's RMC entry record was most impressive. Peter, a good deal younger, tagged along. He'd been raised by mother and sister while his father had been at war, and Ashbury was a pretty frightening place for a small boy with its strict discipline and all-male authoritarian atmosphere.

Boarding school wasn't everybody's game, and Peter was desperately homesick. He missed his pet spaniel, which he used to sneak into his bed at home. He had some unhappy experiences sleep-walking, perhaps looking fruitlessly for his little friend. There was the overwhelming feeling that his parents had condemned him to prison, though the quarters, food and comforts were really very good.

Discipline and its related benefit – being raised as a gentleman by Dr. Woollcome – were the main attractions for parents. G.P. was very stern, very fair, unflappable, always completely poised and with a very distinct presence. He was a martinet, but a kindly one. While he was the one who administered the cane and the strap – and quite often at that – he was still a father-figure, especially to the younger boys. An innate gentleness came through to them. Corporal punishment, which he meted out as a duty, was to him a just and basic part of the system he so fully embraced.

D.E. Cecil Wood was back at Ashbury from the war. He was a dignified, rather unbending officer-type. But unlike most of the masters, who hammered out their lessons by rote in the manner of the day, Wood enlightened his Shakespeare classes by encouraging questions. Peter Simonds was puzzled by the word "whore" in one passage and Wood sidestepped a bit and told him "a whore is a loose woman." Young Peter was quite satisfied, picturing a rather uncoordinated female whose clothes hung loosely about her. His friend Kingsley Cousens had an awkward teenage sister who fitted just that description. Delighted with his new word, Peter found an opportunity to remark knowingly that Cousens' sister was "just an old whore." Cousens was a little more worldly than Simonds. Friendship swept aside, he came instantly to his sister's defence. A rousing bareknuckled, bloody-nosed fight ensued behind the school. A neighbour rushed in and broke it up, and the dishevelled pair were summoned into G.P.'s office in turn. Cousens, a man of honour to the last, refused to repeat Simonds' insult and was caned. Simonds, for reasons best known to G.P., got off with a lecture.

After their battle royal the two, being boys in a system where the shared threat was from the hierarchy that ruled from aloft, remained fast friends. Whether it was related to further investigations isn't clear, but they did sneak off to the burlesque theatre down by the railway station, as was the custom to see the can-can dancers. In those days a boy's muddled knowledge of sexual matters came mainly from half-informed peers. G.P. did dispense some advice to older boys, but old boy memory retains only his dire warning to "beware the girl with the sore on her lip."

Running into seniors at the burlesque, like older brother Guy Simmonds and his friend Jack McMahon, was no problem for the youngsters. They were all up to the same thing, plus smoking cigarettes, which wasn't allowed at school. The school food was pretty good by comparison to that at Bishops, TCS and Lakefield, as travelling teams reported, but it was inevitably dull. The favoured Saturday fare at Bowles Lunch was a chopped steak sandwich and blueberry pie.

Pocket money then was 50 cents a week for seniors. The small boys had to make do with 25 cents, and only prudent saving could finance a burlesque or movie outing, with a David Harum sundae or ice cream soda at Weldon Graham's on Sparks Street and enough left over for car fare back to school.

For the seniors, with their relative freedom and perhaps some extra money from home, there were plenty of sporting events. Ottawa was one of the great hockey towns of Canada and they could go to the NHL games. The Silver Seven had taken the Stanley Cup in 1903, 1904 and 1905. The Ottawa Senators had been the first professional team to win it in 1909. Ashbury boys cheered them to victory again in 1920, 1921, 1923 and 1927. Eddie Gerard, one of hockey's greats, coached Ashbury in those years. He played for the Ottawa team that won the World's Champion Hockey Series in 1920. No one minded freezing in unheated Dey's Arena. Ashbury had ice time there for the first team on Wednesday afternoons and for important games. When the Auditorium opened in 1923 at the corner of O'Connor and Argyle, it was pure luxury by comparison.

There was football, too, at Lansdowne Park. Ottawa won its first Grey Cup in 1925. Jack McMahon, a fine Ashbury football player, racked up a great record at RMC and was back in Ottawa in 1926 playing for Winnipeg in the Grey Cup. Ottawa won.

Peter Simonds' homesickness was allayed a good deal by the stocky, robust, little gym instructor, Mr. Hewitt. He was a superb gymnast and teacher and a warm-hearted, thoroughly human fellow who was a father to all the boys in the lower forms. He it was who encouraged the youngsters to dream up great schemes and work away at them. The annual giant snow-house project called for grand plans and organization; indeed, it had a complete club with committee and membership oath. It ended with a sumptuous evening feed for invited guests in the completed house, attractively lit inside with lanterns. A roaring fire outside roasted hot dogs, which the boys each saved a nickel a week to buy. Some thoughtful neighbouring mothers supplied ice cream and doughnuts. Health-conscious Mrs. Woollcombe donated fruit.

One year Hewitt also inspired the junior boys to build a most ingenious series of "panoramas" which they staged for the whole school, with songs and accompaniment by the school orchestra. The show followed a winter term of raiding the carpenter's shop and Oliver's cubbyhole for tools and bits and pieces, and of much sawing and hammering. Finally the curtain unveiled depictions of 11 cities from Halifax to Victoria, including Niagara Falls. Seniors had been enlisted to eulogize each one. There was a mysteriously working mill with real splashing water. The finale was the Battle of the Somme with gunfire, smoke and flashes, the rattle of machine guns and the cries of the wounded. Hewitt understood well that boys are happiest when they're busy or, conversely, that the devil makes work for idle hands.

"Fritzy" Fitzgerald's idle hands got a bit carried away when he purloined one of Oliver's hatchets and began to chop down a nicely shaped elm behind the main wing. He was stopped by a master. The tree survived a near-fatal scar and grew into the stately giant that succumbed at last to Dutch Elm disease in the seventies. A boy of some initiative, Fritzy wired his locker door to an electrical outlet as a substitute for a padlock.

To promote debating, G.P. took a direct hand as President of the Debating Society. In 1920-21 the motions included: "The city of Halifax provides more advantages as a place of residence than the city of Ottawa" (lost by a margin of 16); "the present strength of the British navy should not be reduced" (a squeaker decided by the Speaker's vote); "if the United States and Japan went to war, Great Britain would fight with Japan" (won by two votes); "Ireland is a wronged country" (rejected by a large majority); "the ex-Kaiser of Germany should be brought to trial before a court of the Allies" (won by two votes).

The final motion – and by all accounts the most hotly debated – was that "Prohibition has been beneficial to Canada." Perhaps seeking to divert the mood of the House, the Headmaster intervened with comments on the historical increase in life expectancy since liquor consumption had been reduced. In spite of that, the spirited arguments led by none other than R.R. Labatt and seconded by the soldierly Guy Simonds swung a crushing defeat of the motion.

The 1920-21 school year was the most successful ever. There were 74 boarders and 34 day boys. More boarders had to be turned away. Of 10 in the graduating class, Alex Campbell won first place in Arts in the McGill matriculation, William Sharples second place in Science. Guy Simonds took the nation's second-place entry to RMC on his first step towards becoming Canada's most outstanding field commander of World War II. Sidney Lane was third on the RMC list and Jack McMahon seventh. Lorn Maclaren passed second into the Royal Naval College of Canada – his was the last year of entry. Andy Brewin, whose parents were missionaries in the Orient, won first place in the open scholarship exams for Radley School in England. He came back to Canada and eventually sat in Parliament for the NDP.

The Duke of Devonshire spoke at Closing, before being replaced by Baron Byng of Vimy. He praised "the splendid spirit of the school which like its prototypes, Eton, Harrow, Winchester, Marlborough, Rugby and the other famous English schools, has always stood for playing the game, and for loyalty to Empire. Unity, democratic ideals and cooperation form the keystone to everything that has made your college famous."

This was music to the Headmaster's ears. Certainly he had modelled Ashbury as a miniature version of those famous English public schools. The academic accent was on classics. Sports were dominant, as they were in all schools like it in Canada and nearly all in England and the United States. Performance in sports had a lot to do with pecking order, privilege and the selection of prefects. Masters were expected to be sportsmen, and a record on university playing fields was a strong recommendation.

The only boy among the 10 school-leavers of 1921 who didn't matriculate was Edward Burstall, and he was a super-athlete. He'd been on the first football team for two years, hockey for three (captain in 1921) and cricket for four years (captain for the last three). His father had financed a cricket tour that spring to play TCS, Upper Canada College and Appleby. Dire forecasts of academic failure among the graduating class due to such distractions were given the lie by the splendid matriculation results – except for young Burstall's. His father no doubt had second thoughts about his own generosity. Having missed university, Edward Burstall joined the RCMP and died in a fire a few years later in northern Saskatchewan.

It had been a fine cricket season, though. The school beat Bishop's for the first time in five years. On top of two wins and a loss on the tour, they beat the RCMP, the Ottawa Cricket Club and the Parents. For the Parents, Messrs. Southam and Bogert scored 51 between them, while the rest of their side got 9. The enthusiastic Burstall Sr. got a duck's egg himself but had the satisfaction of finally bowling out his son, who'd topped the boys' scoring with 43. That night the Parents, as was now the annual custom, treated the team to the Cricket Dinner at the Country Club on the Aylmer Road. The Club had been started in 1908 and you could get there by car or very speedily by the streetcar that ended up in Aylmer.

Swimming was a popular pastime for all Ottawa and the boys had various favourite spots. Britannia Beach, a fast streetcar ride right through without transfer from Rockcliffe, was pristine. The handiest Ottawa river swimming for Ashbury was at the New Edinburgh Canoe Club and it certainly showed physical evidence of city sewers debouching not so far upstream. No one seemed to make the connection with the standard ailment known as "summer ear" that the school doctor and his colleagues treated regularly.

But for the boys, Mackay Lake was the obvious place for the first swimming of the season. Only one or two houses overlooked it, but using it meant sneaking out of school with a towel concealed under the jacket. There was talk of quicksand. For some years swimming there was banned by the Head and that made it not only more fun but a mandatory rite of spring.

By this time, G.P. was in his fifties and didn't take part in sports. But he was always lean, wiry and fit. He was a great walker and, winter and summer, unless the weather was particularly foul, he eschewed the streetcar and strode downtown, cane swinging briskly, to do such business as he had.

It often included lunch at the Rideau Club, opposite the centre gate of the Parliament Buildings. It was a convivial place – though G.P. would stick to his single glass of sherry – filled daily with MPs and senior civil servants, as well as the city's business and professional leaders. Cabinet members gathered at the large round table in the dining room that was always theirs for lunch.

Ashbury Board members and fathers were, almost by definition, members of the Club. (In over a hundred years of joint history, 40 percent of the Club's presidents have been Ashbury old boys, governors or parents.) A glance at the visitors' register on the hall porter's desk at the front of the fine curved staircase told G.P. which of them had a guest that day, and from where. That would lead to an introduction to one of the steady stream of well-placed gentlemen from across the country who came to knock on the government's door.

The Rideau Club was a fine place to keep in touch, keep oneself (and one's school) in view, to massage current parents and to hunt for new ones. G.P. made great strides. Numbers of applications from elsewhere in Canada increased. An important connection was Selwyn House, the leading preparatory school for young Anglo-Montrealers. G.P. cultivated it well, starting regular sports fixtures between the schools. Competing with Bishop's, he netted a steady stream of graduates for his boarder beds.

The school was flourishing and the Board was happy to record annual operating surpluses running to $10,000 in 1922 – when they decided to build the Headmaster a house – and again in 1923. Woollcombe's salary had reached $4800 plus housing by 1920 and the school was paying his Rockcliffe rent. He was also voted a $500 bonus each year, plus an "extraordinary" bonus of $500 in 1925 and 1926 because of the outstanding success of the school.

But plans for a major memorial addition moved slowly. In 1920 the *Ashburian* had raised a cry of frustration. A.W. Darnell, the staff member who was business manager and treasurer, quoted other schools' magazines. War memorial expansion projects were going on apace elsewhere. One school was raising $1.25 million for new equipment, staff salaries and pensions; $100,000 had been subscribed the first day. Another was spending $150,000 for a new building; $50,000 had been pledged by two supporters right away. A third school had already built a new boarding house and was planning another. A fourth was building a preparatory school. The demand for places was never greater. What was Ashbury doing?

Darnell's article, which tacitly criticized the Board, sounds brave for a master but it certainly had G.P.'s backing. It didn't stir much action, though. When the campaign eventually started, there was no instant pony-up as there had been at those other schools. Governors made modest contributions and left the fund-raising to G.P. By 1923 he had raised only $20,000 from 65 donors. Confident that there'd be more to follow, the Board decided to go ahead. G.P. wrote reams of letters and printed repeated pleas in the *Ashburian*. Still, the response from old boys and parents was disappointingly weak.

With his own stern, unwavering vision, G.P. saw donation to the school as an old boy's duty. His was the hard sell. Still trying to drum up money to clear the debt after the wing was finally opened, he published the names of the 24 contributing old boys in the *Ashburian* with the amounts each had given (half gave $10, the most was $250, total $805). His accompanying exhortation: "Surely this does not represent the number of old boys who wish to help! May I take this opportunity of again asking all old boys who have not yet sent in a donation to do so at once, even if it is only $10."

G.P. had been on the trail of funds for the new building in 1910 and the Chapel in 1912, and then had had the painful business of bringing in all the shares and debentures until 1919. A lecture from the old Headmaster now was hardly calculated to raise a warm response. It seemed to old boys that Ashbury was always after money. Their cash contribution to various campaigns was a disappointment to successive Boards and Headmasters for over 50 years.

The original idea for a memorial addition was a new wing with a gymnasium and swimming pool, more bedrooms above and new lavatories, a shooting gallery and manual training room below. The gym was scaled down to a modest size (though it had to serve until 1985, when it was turned into the library). The pool was eliminated. In the existing school, the dining room would be enlarged, the old gym converted to classrooms with living space above and a new central heating plant for the whole school fitted in the basement. Plans for the new Headmaster's house were already in hand from the earlier decision, and the contracts were let together. Old boy Allan Keefer, working with J.A. Ewart, again donated his architectural and supervising services.

During the financial agonizing J.B. Fraser stepped quietly forward once again. In 1917 his key offer to turn in his shares had transformed Ashbury's prospects. He had stipulated then that three-quarters of the founding shares must be voted in favour of any new mortgage on the school's property. He held by far the most votes in the newly incorporated Ashbury and by a long shot he had the most in way of security to lose.

It must have been a great disappointment to Fraser and Woollcombe that no one else among all these substantial men they knew so well was prepared to fill the benefactor's shoes. Still, Fraser waived his old condition in favour of any arrangement to benefit the school that Gilbert Fauquier, who was now handling finances, approved.

When the bills were paid – $18,000 for the Headmaster's house and $66,000 for the Memorial Wing – the shortfall from donations and transfers from the operating account was covered by a $30,000 mortgage loan from Sun Life at 6 1/2 percent. Observing Ashbury's strong financial record over recent years, the Company voluntarily waived any personal guarantees by the Governors.

The Memorial Wing was formally opened on Closing Day, June 11, 1924, by the new Governor General, Lord Byng. It was a splendid addition to the school, built of the same brick and joined to the main building by a short enclosed passageway. It had a substantial outside entrance of its own, surmounted by a square tower giving the impression of battlements above.

The gym was big in comparison to the old one and it was well heated. That was good news for all those who'd suffered the "Goosepimple Parade" – boys with the first PT class of the day had changed in the icy locker room amid a liberal quantity of snow knocked off day boys' boots and clothing; then they'd rushed to the bitterly cold gym where Mr. Hewitt had restored their circulation. Now there was comparative warmth and fine new equipment that over 70 parents had kicked in to buy.

On the same floor there was a science laboratory and classroom. This made for a considerable advance in the curriculum and opened up all the delights of bunsen burners, chemical stinks and mild explosions under the gimlet eye of science master Harry Wright. Above, there were rooms for 10 boys and four masters, all miraculously fitted with basins and running hot and cold water. At the end of the upper corridor was a fire escape, a ready-made sally-port for exploring the Saturday night allures of Rockcliffe (with Elmwood nearby) and the steamier temptations of Ottawa and Hull just a streetcar ride away.

The school was now an institution, firmly established in bricks and mortar and in reputation. The Rev. George Woollcombe, Headmaster of 33 years' standing, was an institution himself, not just in Ottawa but throughout Canada, renowned as a widely respected educator. That was his accolade when McGill University awarded him an honorary LLD in 1926. All was now in place for a fine new phase in Ashbury's history.

CHAPTER 6
THE ROARING TWENTIES

With the Memorial Wing in place, everything in the fall term of 1924 was looking up. In charge of the fine new gym was Sergeant-Major F.W. Stone. Rock-solid as his name, he was an old Imperial with years in the Hampshire Regiment soldiering around the Empire and latterly on the Physical Training staff at Aldershot in England. He took over the physical training and gymnastic instruction at Ashbury, and he replaced the militia NCOs who had trained the cadet corps on a part-time basis. He ran the cadets with a firm and efficient hand and instructed rifle shooting.

Replacing W.H. Hewitt was no easy task. In his 12 years at Ashbury the "Professor" had thoroughly endeared himself to all with his warm-hearted involvement, especially with the junior boys. He continued to live out at the far end of the streetcar line in Britannia; though occupied with other affairs, he kept up his connection with Ashbury. Right into the 1930s he was business manager, treasurer and advertising salesman for the *Ashburian*.

Sergeant-Major Stone's army-conditioned demeanour may have been a bit forbidding at first but under it there was a heart of gold. Here was a thoroughly admirable man, first-rate at his job and very quickly a mainstay of the school. He and Oliver and, indeed, Hewitt brought to Canada and Ashbury that solid set of values – constancy, sense of duty, reliability, steady application of a well-trained hand and self-effacing pride in a job well done – which came with the best from Britain. They were true gentlemen, though in their native land the word would scarcely have been applied to one of their station in life.

Stone had fought in the Gallipoli debacle, had been badly wounded fighting in Mesopotamia and he had a fund of stories. He taught the boys boxing, properly emphasizing "the manly art of self defence." Boxing had begun in the old gym in Hewitt's last year. He'd got in touch with some expert judges from the YMCA and had set up the first competition at short notice. The resourceful Oliver had rigged up a ring with four fence-posts, cast-off rope, a scrounged canvas and a good deal of wire.

Under Sergeant-Major Stone boxing and the annual tournament became a feature of Ashbury life. The boys hammered merrily at each other in the ring, wore their shiners like medals and cheered their house-mates on. Mothers fretted over facial damage. Fathers heartily approved. Benefactors put up trophies for every imaginable combination of weight and class. Stone himself was a formidable boxer and Gregor Guthrie and friends were awed to see him lay out one of the masters, Edwin Ker.

Ker was an eccentric – such were not unknown at Ashbury, nor were they undesirable as such – who liked to teach himself new sports. Guthrie and Co. watched him during their cadet parades as he pounded, or sought to pound, a tennis ball against the wall between swift glances at a book lying open beside him on the grass. His book-taught boxing was no match for the Sergeant-Major's, but he was extraordinarily keen.

When the tournament approached, he organized a training programme with a special diet, early morning runs and practice bouts before breakfast.

He was a small dour Scot, a first-rate English teacher and a fine cross-country runner. Strange are the things that stick in people's minds, but Alistair Graham and Ross McMaster swore he changed his socks five times a day, washed them himself and dried them on the radiators. Graham and Bill Eakin, among many, suffered Ker's favoured punishment of copying out endless columns of the dictionary which had to be correct to the last comma. Bill Eakin found you could dicker with Ker and work off so many columns by going with him on his early morning run. He'd lead Bill and the rest at a good clip around Mackay Lake and circle behind Elmwood, where the girls would hang out the windows in their nightgowns to jeer them by.

To McMaster, Campbell Merrett, Pat Bogert and others who'd come from Selwyn House, and Bill Eakin who'd spent some years in a French school in Montreal, the French as taught by W.H.H.C. "Steve" Brodie was less than impressive. Not since M. Fleury had there been a native French-speaking teacher at Ashbury. To Gregor Guthrie, who was shaky in French, Brodie was stern and demanding and Guthrie dreaded sitting at his French table at lunch. But Brodie was affable out of the classroom and a somewhat romantic figure. He limped from a war wound collected in Mesopotamia, and he was one of the leading actors with the Ottawa Little Theatre.

Eldon Grier, who was the best junior rifle shot in the school and who went on to a career as a painter and art teacher, remembered the arts at Ashbury as conspicuously absent. The year after he left, though (1930), Steve Brodie had a good deal to do with reviving drama. The Ashbury College Literary and Dramatic Society was formed that year and brought it back full tilt with *Julius Caesar*. Ambitious indeed, it called for 35 parts. Brodie played Brutus. No doubt through his connections, Ottawa's leading theatrical light, Leslie Chance, directed the final rehearsals and the production was staged in the Little Theatre. It drew a full house, including the Governor General and Lady Willingdon, won raves in the *Citizen* and cleared $250 for the library fund. Then it went on tour to Montreal and got more plaudits from the *Star*. Justifiably flushed with success, the Society held its "first annual" dinner at the Chateau that spring.

Brodie's nickname "Steve" was bestowed by the boys. They took it, most improbably, from one Steve Brodie who sought fame – fatally, as it turned out – by leaping, with a good deal of fanfare, from the Brooklyn Bridge. Ashbury's Brodie married G.P.'s elder daughter Maithol. Their firstborn, Robert Woollcombe Brodie, was baptized by his grandfather in the Chapel in September 1928. Brodie stayed at Ashbury from 1922 until he fell foul of a new administration in the mid-thirties.

G.P. didn't always get the best on his forays to England and there was a steady turnover of staff. Robin Pattison, for instance, was a horseman, a super rugger player, sprinter and cricketer; but he had a violent temper and turned purple when crossed in class, the veins on his forehead apparently about to burst. He was another war casualty. G.P. fired him in 1930 after repeated warnings about constantly favouring certain boys.

Classroom order was maintained by a shifting crew of characters using hair-pulling, whacks with rulers and well-aimed blackboard erasers. Rev. Chester-Master, a handsome, blustery man who'd won an MC and wore his medal ribbons on his clerical suit, was the champion at side-burn tweeking: he plucked a clump of hair from

John Edward's head, roots, scalp and all. He took his foibles back to England where he became Headmaster of the well-established Bishop's Stortford School which had educated Cecil Rhodes.

Casey Cassels – a volatile, peppery little fellow with sandy hair – was a hair-twister too, but he also had his own distinctive way of sinking thumb and finger painfully into the culprit's thigh. He had the much-desired athletic credentials, with his Cambridge "blue" in cricket and soccer, and his cap for playing field hockey for Britain. He wore mufflers and a seedy white blazer with Cambridge colours. Over it, as was the custom in class, he wore a gown in an advanced state of greasy decay.

Cassels was keen on rowing, played a good game of tennis, acted with the Ottawa Drama League, had a certain raffish charm and a reputation as a "cut-up" with the girls. But he'd seen better times and, in his latter days at least (he lasted from 1922 to 1928), he frequently brought crashing hangovers and the reek of last night's alcohol to the classroom. Then he would ease himself into his chair and tilt it back – until the famous morning when he fell asleep and Roger Rowley and Co. tied a string to it and yanked.

One particularly unpleasant fellow came in 1925 – Rev. H. Newton "Speedy" Meyers. He was, for a time, the Housemaster. A favourite Ashbury sport was "curling" in the corridor, using the fibreboard valet boxes intended for sending out laundry and dry-cleaning. Peter Roberts got six on the bare backside from Speedy for that heinous crime. The man showed a sadistic zest for caning. Charlie Gale challenged him once with "I think you enjoy this" and he backed down. But he delivered six cuts to Roger Rowley and when Rowley stood up gave him six more and drew blood.

Roger was something of a lightning rod for beatings. He was often in G.P.'s office before Chapel and at recess, then in the prefects' study at 3:00 p.m. for a strapping for some disaster in his fagging duties like using black polish on a prefect's brown shoes – and all on the same day! But that session with Speedy Meyers was too much. He'd been boarding that year and he packed, got a taxi and went home for the rest of the term. Meyers was gone by 1930.

Normally, Roger and his older brother John were day boys. They lived in Sandy Hill and every morning they piled into a handsome old Red Line Taxi – black bottom, red stripe, gray top – along with Barry and Justin O'Brien, Gregor and John Guthrie, Blair Gilmour and John Basset. The only problem was that they lacked the perennial excuse of tardy boys that the streetcar was late.

Henry King was a decent sort, a good Latin and history teacher and a husky rugger-playing type. He earned the boys' admiration by learning to play hockey – and pretty well for an Englishman. He was the acknowledged eraser champion and could unerringly pick off a boy in the back row.

E. Colin Edwards was ex-Royal Navy, a solid teacher and disciplinarian and a good athlete. He stayed only from 1923 to 1926 and went off to join the boom in Montreal. He returned later, though, having been hit by the Depression, and he contributed a great deal to the school. He was a good pianist and played the organ in Chapel. For a bet one Sunday at Evensong he played his own hymnified arrangement of "Yes, We Have No Bananas." The only person who didn't notice was G.P. Off again at the same time and for the same reason as Brodie, Edwards went back to England and became a housemaster at Eton. Roger Rowley had a cheerful chance reunion with him at Paddington Station during the London Blitz.

Harry Wright acted for the Head when he was away. Wright had arrived the year after the war with degrees from Capetown and Sheffield universities to teach mathematics and science, and he did so very well indeed. Ashbury had always been strong on classics, but boys with a real interest in science were better off in their final years elsewhere. One such boy was Tuzo Wilson. His father was a civil servant, an engineer with the Scots' firm belief in education. The family lived on Rideau Terrace and Tuzo – he was known as Jock – was one of the small boys who went to Mrs. Philpott's Elmwood, then on to Ashbury. He'd been tutored at home before Elmwood and found school easy, so he was always ahead for his age and always the smallest in his class. He went on to Lisgar Collegiate in 1925 for his senior matriculation, and then to the University of Toronto. Lisgar teachers, he'd found, were far better trained than the well-educated, erudite Oxbridge men who predominated at Ashbury. So started an internationally renowned scientific and academic career. His work on the tectonic plate theory and his appointments as first Principal of Erindale College and first Director-General of the Ontario Science Centre are among the best known of his outstanding achievements.

But with the new lab in the Memorial Wing Wright was able to expand the Ashbury programme. He was a first-rate teacher and had a rigorous intellectual approach, urging his students always to ask "why." Campbell Merrett had real respect for him and years later, when he was a well-established architect in Montreal, he designed the memorial plaque in the Chapel preserving the style of the twenties, the time he had learned so much from Harry Wright.

Wright was a dour, expressionless character whose closest approach to humour was educated sarcasm. Smiles rarely softened his thin-lipped mouth, and laughter was next to unknown. When Peter Roberts asked his permission to go to see a French theatre company perform, Wright's eyes got even smaller; he labelled it "a disgusting cabaret act" and turned the request down flat. Harry Wright was the one who kept the school and its assorted characters in day-to-day order, but he simply did not believe in fun.

Looming over all this, commanding unreserved respect, was Rev. G.P. Woollcombe himself. He taught classics, scripture and history (English, not Canadian). But mainly he impressed moral values on the boys and the meaning of duty and responsibility. His "Well, my boy . . .," with piercing eyes gazing through wire-rimmed bifocals over steepled, tapping fingers, held one transfixed. His right forefinger jabbed the chest to make a point – usually reinforced by "read, mark, learn and inwardly digest" or an apt Latin phrase or a favourite from the Bible like "and with one accord they all began to make excuses." But he was still, under it all, essentially kind, human and approachable. A true man of God. At least two nights a week he did evening rounds of the dormitories; he knew everyone and talked to all.

Predictably, he was dead set against boys smoking. But it was now very much accepted in society and he had a good deal of pressure (from some mothers particularly, no doubt egged on by their sons) to allow it. He discussed with Oliver his embarrassment over going to a parent's house and being offered the cigarette box by the smirking boy in question, who would then light up nonchalantly himself. Smoking remained forbidden at the school, but of course boys found times and places to indulge. Oliver never became any kind of ally in suppressing it, or in enforcing any other routine rules. His policy of "hear no evil, see no evil, speak no evil" was based on the fact that he genuinely loved the boys. He even abetted certain crimes, like leaving the rifle range unlocked when word got to him that a particular late night feed was on.

The punishment for smoking was invariably a caning from the Head. As many besides Roger Rowley had occasion to note, it was always begun with "This hurts me more than it hurts you," and ended with "Go, my boy, and sin no more." There was nothing hypocritical about G.P. He really meant it. Caning or the strap was to him – contrary to the dark urges of a Speedy Meyers – a necessary part of the system.

G.P.'s only respite was his annual trip to England to fill out his constantly changing staff. He offered low salaries for Canada, though attractive to Englishmen, with bed and board thrown in. So they were mostly single men and a lot took a stint at Ashbury as their ticket to opportunity (or, in some cases, escape!) in Canada. For some, who were well qualified but proved unsuited for teaching, he could usually find a job in the civil service. Some, as we've seen, would be misfits anywhere. It took a strong hand at the helm, and the backing of a sound first lieutenant like Wright, to keep the ship on course.

There's no doubt that by the late 1920s G.P. Woollcombe had had an extraordinarily hard-working life. He had, of course, achieved a great deal. The school, which had started out to serve the special needs of Ottawa's upper crust, had become one of the elite boarding schools of central Canada. It was completely Woollcombe's school, essentially a one-man show. But, aged 60 now, with close to 40 years in command and some health problems, he could hardly give his school the energy and drive of earlier times.

In 1928 G.P. proposed that the Board provide him with a retirement allowance. A campaign to raise a pension fund was discussed, to be focused on Montreal because it might have more success in the booming financial centre of Canada than in Ottawa. But nothing was done. The experienced Board of very substantial businessmen in fact directed no accumulation for any purpose at all – nothing for depreciation, building replacement or expansion, scholarships or bursaries. Ashbury's business was very soundly attended day by day and year by year, but the future was blithely ignored.

G.P. couldn't ignore his. In early 1929, over 60 and with retirement looming, he put a proposal to the Board and was promised a retirement allowance not less than $3000, and $1000 per year for Mrs. Woollcombe should she survive him.

Ashbury had, of course, a high level of energy of its own, more perhaps on the playing field than in the classroom. All through this time there were plenty of coaches on staff for soccer and cricket, but with so few Canadian masters the hockey and football coaches came from the professional Ottawa teams and most were outstanding. Lisgar and Glebe Collegiates were always tough nuts in hockey, but they were often cracked. Overall, the school teams did pretty well on the regular St. Albans – LCC – Bishop's circuit, with cricket against Ridley, TCS and St. Andrew's. J.S. "Pop" Irvin was the finest athlete of the time. In fact he was acclaimed the outstanding schoolboy athlete in Ottawa in 1928, his last year before he went on to RMC.

The peak year for hockey was 1929: played 28; won 16; lost 8; drawn 4; goals for, 110; goals against, 51. The coach was the Ottawa Senators' star right-winger,

Frank Finnigan. The team had already played 11 games when Upper Canada College came to Ottawa to play during the Christmas holidays. Charlie Stanfield – one of five Nova Scotia Stanfields at Ashbury between 1922 and 1934 – cut short a week of his holidays and came back from Truro to play. Upper Canada scored first, right-winger Peter Smellie evened it up at four minutes in the third period. Then defenceman Stanfield broke away from his own blueline and scored the winner unassisted. The stuff of schoolboy dreams!

That was also the first year an Ashbury hockey team played in Toronto. They beat the highly touted University of Toronto School, but dropped the return game against UCC. The *Ashburian*'s report ascribed a certain listlessness on the team to the tough game the day before, but it was far more likely to have been late attendance at the Casino Theatre where, as was well known through the schoolboy network, strip-tease dancers performed such as Ottawa had never seen. At the sensational season's end, Lewis Bates topped the scoring, Gordon Southam came second, Peter Smellie third.

House matches in all sports had got on a regular footing in 1924. A Games Committee was formed that year, made up of the Headmaster, the Games master, five boys elected from the sixth and upper fifth forms and all those who'd won school colours. Their major decision was to divide the school into Reds, Whites and Greens for games in all seasons. This didn't engender much enthusiasm, so in the fall term of 1927, they changed to home-town "houses": Ottawa House, Montreal House and Dominion House for all the rest. Henceforth no quarter was given. The first House Captains were respectively Pop Irvin, J.T. Lafleur and Ken Mackenzie. By year's end 1927-28, Dominion House was the winner. In 1930 Board member Norman Wilson donated the House Challenge Shield. In 1935, with numbers down, the Houses were reduced to A and B, and renamed the following year Connaught and Woollcombe.

1924 had been a great year for new sporting endeavours. The new gym was used for badminton, which was growing as fast as tennis had when the school moved to Rockcliffe. Fifteen boys signed up for rowing. Casey Cassels was in charge and the Ottawa Rowing Club lent boats and facilities. Two years later, the Ashbury four raced against Glebe and Lisgar over half a mile and came second to Glebe.

That year was the first for competitive skiing. Four boys entered the junior cross-country race at the Ottawa Ski Club and were hopelessly outclassed. But in 1927 Garland and Mackenzie came second and third in the Ottawa junior ski-jumping championship on the Rockcliffe jump. The following year, they went off to Montreal to jump in the Quebec Seniors. Skiing became a regular House competition event. From opening day around the seasons the school was a busy place.

But while Ashbury was building a life of its own, indeed doing a little bit of roaring of its own in the "roaring twenties," changes were taking place in the makeup of Ottawa: changes in its society and leadership, changes in the industry that had charged it so dynamically in the first place. The hugely successful lumber barons of late nineteenth-century Ottawa had had their day. They were, by and large, a pretty tough cut of self-made man. Many of that first generation, like Booth, Bronson and Hughson, were Yankees. They had piled up enormous wealth in a single generation, but they weren't generally on the Governor General's guest lists.

These men were certainly determined to give their children the right education to get them up the tree. That included – be they boys or girls – acquiring the social and cultural graces and the best connections. But cultural interests weren't their own long suit. Nor, generally, was philanthropy. Lumbering names are commemorated in street names bestowed by Ottawa and Hull city councillors, but it took America's Andrew Carnegie to fund Ottawa's public library at the corner of Metcalfe and Laurier in 1906. There are exceptions, notably the Perley Hospital, but other than the industry the lumber barons built they left few monuments to themselves in the way of lasting charitable foundations, concert halls, endowed institutions, public parks.

Change in the industry was gradual and overlapping. J.R. Booth watched his last huge raft of square-cut timber glide slowly down the Ottawa River in 1904. It was 96 years since Philomen Wright had floated the first one to Quebec. Now sawn lumber and matches, which in their own time had supplanted squared timber, had been overtaken by pulp, paper and hydro power. In fact, 1902 marked the lumber mills' peak. Nineteen of them throughout the Valley produced 613 million board feet and J.R. Booth, W.C. Edwards and the McLachlins of Arnprior were the biggest. By and large, the great industries of the Ottawa River watershed moved gradually into the hands of big corporations and became directed from the financial centres of the continent, not from Ottawa.

Again there were exceptions – like the Maclarens, whose personal direction of their Buckingham-based industry lasted into the 1980s. And there were surviving local enterprises. The Edwards, Wright and Davidson names and family direction, for example, stayed on in lumber retailing and building supplies for varying lengths of time. Woods Manufacturing thrived in family hands until it was taken over years later in the seventies. But durable Canadian dynasties, like the Molsons of Montreal, the Prices of Quebec, the Eatons of Toronto, which continued to flourish on the businesses they'd founded, didn't grow in Ottawa soil.

Apocryphal this may be, but J.R. Booth, getting out of a taxi in front of the Chateau Laurier one day, gave the driver, as was his custom, a nickel tip. The man muttered sourly, "Young John always gives me fifty cents." Mr. Booth growled back, "But I'm not a rich man's son." Following in giants' shadows, ensuing generations didn't lack, but neither did they build.

At Ashbury, new men, younger men, were taking places on the Board. Harry Southam and his brother Wilson were Founders, and Harry joined the Board in 1922. They published the *Ottawa Citizen*. Their father William Southam, owner of the *Hamilton Spectator* from 1877, had bought the long-established Ottawa paper in 1896. The competing *Ottawa Journal* had been bought by P.D. Ross in 1899 and he too was an Ashbury Founder. The first Southam Ashbury boy, William Cargill, had come in 1910 when the school moved to Rockcliffe. In the 1920s there were Gordon, D. Cargill, J.D., Robert and Hamilton, then the post-war generation – Chris, Peter and Ross in the 1950s and Rick and Wilson in the 1960s.

The first old boy Board member was E.F. Nixie Newcombe. After the war he'd worked for a time in Montreal, was called to the bar in Toronto, then joined in a law partnership in Ottawa. The Newcombe name was very well known in legal circles. Nixie's father had topped a distinguished career as Deputy Minister of Justice with appointment as a Justice of the Supreme Court. Nixie was a loner and he soon moved to a one-man practice. His mainstay was representing out-of-town lawyer clients filing their cases to appear before the Supreme Court.

When that wise old original, now Mr. Justice John Orde, stood down, Newcombe took over as Ashbury's legal adviser. Except in the early days of his partnership when there was careful accounting of time and disbursements on his modest bills, he made no charge for his endless services. G.P. still chivvied him like a school-boy though. Twitting him about slow action on a mortgage he wrote, "You will remember among the 'ills' of life quoted by Hamlet is 'The Law's delay.'"

Newcombe served actively, faithfully, at times almost singlehandedly, from 1921 until his death – virtually in harness – in 1949. His correspondence for Ashbury was a model of clarity. His decisions weren't always right but, as we shall see, he practically carried the place on his back for years. At more than one critical juncture he literally saved the school from total demise. His son Peter was at the school from 1932 to 1941, served on the Board, did yeoman service at another critical time and was elected Chairman in Ashbury's hundredth year.

Gilbert Fauquier Sr., a Founder, became a member of the Board of Directors in 1922 and gradually became more influential, moving up to head the Executive Committee by 1931. He was Chairman in 1933 and 1934 and stepped down in 1938. The Fauquier brothers, Gilbert and Edward, were major figures in constuction. They built railroads and part of the Halifax dockside. Gilbert headed the Ottawa Improvement Commission. His oldest boy Gilbert started at Ashbury in 1915 and ended as head prefect in 1925. John was head prefect in 1927. Adam and David followed. Their cousin Edward finished in 1935.

Response from old boys to the Memorial Fund in the early twenties had been, as we've seen, lukewarm. After the enthusiastic pre-war start of an Association, the *Ashburian* carried a solid and informative Old Boys' Supplement. It petered out after the war and only in 1926 did the main body of the magazine include much in the way of old boys' notes. They got fatter as time went on, but the Association itself had withered on the vine.

It wasn't until 1930 that the Association was revived with the "first annual" reunion and dinner under President Arthur Evans, Secretary John Bogert and Treasurer Haden Wallis. Memories were short. The "first annual" had actually been held at the Royal Ottawa Golf Club in 1914. This one was held at the Mount Royal Hotel in Montreal. Sixty attended, of whom all but five lived there. Besides the current McGill crowd, a lot of the Ottawans had ended up working where the action was, in the financial centre of the country. Of the three officers and the eight committee members – John and Gilbert Fauquier, Leo Palmer, Ryland Daniels, Keith Davidson, Philip Scott, John Molson and Philip Woollcombe – only Keith Davidson lived in Ottawa, still in lumbering.

Montreal continued as the centre of the Association and the annual dinners were held there. G.P. attended of course. In 1932 Jim Armstrong got a Toronto branch going with committee members Ted Orde, E.P. Taylor, Lawrence Jackson and C.A. Thorburn. Shirley Woods and Gordon Southam were on the central committee representing Ottawa, but there was no Ottawa "branch" of the Montreal-based Association.

The old Ottawa community of supporters had been less than open-handed too.

There was an ambivalence about Ashbury that dogged it for many years – right through in fact until the eighties. It had changed in 1910 from the Ottawa day school with a few boarders to the Rockcliffe boarding school with a minority of day boys. From then on G.P. spent a great deal of energy looking outside Ottawa for his students. Only about a third, who came rather automatically from the wealthy old families or who were sons of transient parliamentarians or civil servants, were Ottawa day boys. With G.P.'s active promotion, the Montrealers, by 1926, formed at least another third, the rest of Canada accounting for the scattered balance.

Fifteen of the 63 Founders of 1920 were Montrealers. Among them, Sir Andrew Macphail was most influential. He had been Professor of both History and Medicine at McGill since 1907, was one of Canada's most distinguished academics and a prolific author. He'd clearly been impressed with Woollcombe. He'd seen G.P.'s boys coming on to McGill, sent his son to Ashbury and was a very significant power for the school in Montreal. P. Cowans, Dr. D. Mackenzie and Ross McMaster, all Montreal parents, joined the Board in 1926.

There's no doubt that living in a boarding school has always generated the highest levels of loyalty. But few Ottawans, the obvious ones to look to for support, were – for equally obvious reasons – among them. The advantage of having the nation's capital just down the road was a regular promotional point. But as the city expanded in the twenties, and Rockcliffe became more populated, Ashbury had less of the attraction of the isolated country boarding school. The bucolic quiet of small-town Lennoxville, Port Hope, St. Catharines or Aurora had more appeal – to some parents, if not to boys – than did Rockcliffe with its fast transport to the fleshpots of Ottawa's Byward market and the far-famed raunchiness of "Little Chicago," as Hull was known right across North America in the twenties. These were good times though and enrolment was strong. The boom was on, prosperity everywhere; the stock market kept climbing, soaring in fact; all was right with the world, and Ashbury's place in it was firmly established and well secured.

Then in 1928, J.B. Fraser, a shareholder of record since 1900, stood down from the Board. As well as providing wise advice and tireless work for all those years, he was, without question, Ashbury's greatest benefactor. The day he announced his resignation, in fact, Mrs. W.H. Rowley donated $4000 in memory of her late husband, who had died in 1915. This was on top of her memorial gift of a pipe organ for the Chapel in 1924. Mr. Rowley's abiding interest in George Woollcombe's school had had a great deal to do with its success. His lifelong interests showed in his active membership in the Anglican Synod and chairing of the Synod's committee on religious education in schools. Now the Rowley classrooms met the needs of steady growth. Symbolically they joined the Chapel to the school. That durable linkage remained a fundamental element in the life of Ashbury College, a singularly fitting memorial to one captain of industry's life's work, in education and in his church.

But benevolence was limited even in these high times. That year G.P. announced a campaign for funds to build an infirmary. The target was $25,000, but by spring 1929 only $10,000 had come in. Again the fund-raising approach was rather heavy handed. G.P.'s urging verged on scolding. He exhorted old boys to "follow the example" of other important schools and "wealthy persons" who had sons at the school to show their interest.

Ashbury College, though, was at its peak. The old Argyle property, badly dilapidated by now, was finally sold in June 1929 for a knockdown price of $7500. Ever widening his net, G.P. spent July in Winnipeg confidently drumming in new blood. But events were conspiring against him. Ottawa that summer had a serious outbreak of infantile paralysis, as poliomyelitis was called then. In the fall there were vacancies at the school for the first time in years.

Then on Black Friday in October 1929, the bottom dropped out of the New York stock market. Montreal and Toronto followed suit. The gigantic paper gains of the hysterical boom days disappeared. Fortunes were blown away overnight. By fall 1930 there were fewer boys at Ashbury. The decline had started. Montreal, the financial capital of Canada and the biggest supplier of Ashbury boarders, was very hard hit. No one could predict the consequences then, but the Great Depression which followed the crash changed the world, changed Canada and changed the prosperous and productive course of Ashbury College for many years to come.

CHAPTER 7

THE END OF AN ERA

The Annual General Meeting of June 1931 acclaimed G.P. Woollcombe President of Ashbury College and Chairman of the Board of Governors – and still Headmaster. This quite unprecedented move was announced to the school at Closing in the presence of the Governor General. It appeared to be the ultimate honour for the man who had built the school and led it for 40 years.

The fact is that a search for a nationally distinguished figure as President – Woollcombe had mentioned Sir Robert Borden or Sir George Perley – had drawn a blank. Gilbert Fauquier, who was certainly prominent in his own right, became President of the Executive Committee of the Board, with Harry Southam and Nixie Newcombe as members. Miss Emma Hammell, the faithful school secretary and G.P.'s "financial fortress," became Secretary-Treasurer of the Board, the post that G.P. had filled since first incorporation in 1900.

It was the first time anyone ever suggested G.P. might need some assistance. He was 64. He showed no signs of stepping down but, having raised the subject of his own retirement a couple of years before, it was clearly time the Governors made some plans. Harry Wright, science and mathematics master since 1919 and long-time deputizer for G.P., was officially appointed Assistant Headmaster.

The year 1930 had marked a downturn. Enrolment sagged. Many businessmen, professional people and investors had lost heavily, hit by the economic slump. The expense of private school was something a hard-pressed family could do without. G.P. tapped a new market by starting a regular junior school in the fall of 1931 and he appointed his son-in-law Steve Brodie as its Head. This was well received and drew some more boys from Ottawa, but it couldn't turn the tide.

By 1933 numbers had dropped below 100. Only 55 were boarders and some 20 empty beds made bad news for the balance sheet. The comfortable debt-reducing margins were gone with the student numbers. Deficits followed one upon the next. Staff salaries were cut by 5 percent. A bigger deficit the following year meant another 5 percent cut. The school had to borrow operating funds from the Bank of Montreal.

It was a sad and baffling time for G.P. He had spent his whole working life building up Ashbury College. Always it had moved steadily ahead. He was 65 now. His great contribution should surely have earned him the satisfaction of leaving his school in good shape. But external events had overtaken his declining vitality. In the spring of 1933, after a long illness, he felt he should be relieved. Harry Wright was appointed Headmaster and assumed the traditional position of Secretary-Treasurer of the Board. G.P., who stayed on the Board, thereupon proposed further reductions in Headmaster's, staff's and domestic employees' pay. He continued as Counsel to the Board, but within a year he and Mrs. Woollcombe went off to live in England. He was fulfilling his retirement dream – back to his family roots to become an English country parson.

The advent of a younger man was no doubt expected to revive Ashbury's fortunes, but Harry Wright's time as Headmaster of Ashbury College was unsuccessful, unhappy and short. He was a fine mathematics and science teacher and well respected in the school. He lacked administrative experience and ability, but principally he was short on the personality, presence, social ease and stature, and the leadership qualities that a successful Headmaster must have. He had taught for 14 years in G.P. Woollcombe's shadow and never came out in the sun. The Board knew Wright well and it was their business to select the new Head. But G.P. obviously was the major influence in choosing his own successor, and in this most important choice of all, a lifetime of sound judgement let him and his own Ashbury College down. Harry Wright simply wasn't the man for the job.

It was certainly no easy time. Staff cutbacks followed dropping enrolment. Only top matriculation results would attract new students. Two masters, B.K.T. Howis and Kenneth Castle, were dropped in the summer of 1935 due to mediocre results in languages and history. Their successor – one for two – was Arthur Donovan Brain, who was an open Classical Scholar at Exeter College, Oxford, and had a BA from Toronto. We will hear a good deal more of Mr. Brain.

Late 1935 was a crucial time. Nixie Newcombe had become Chairman in 1934, but during this period the Governors wrestled with school problems, meeting mostly at the Ritz-Carlton Hotel in Montreal. That was where the influence lay. The majority of Ashbury boarders had come from Montreal and, Depression or no, it was still the financial centre of Canada. Ross McMaster, a Founder, was President of the Steel Company of Canada headquartered there and he took a strong hand. He spent a great deal of time on Ashbury's affairs, giving sound, informed advice to the harried Chairman. His son, D. Ross, was on the Board now as President of the Old Boys Association.

Newcombe had worked extraordinarily hard for Ashbury for close to 20 years. As a lawyer his advice was included without question. Accounts for his services were rare and minimal. He had a good legal mind, and was a demon for work. With Woollcombe gone and Wright not coping, an enormous amount had, by default, to be taken up by the Board. And by default there it fell on Newcombe.

He was not a strong leader, never the boardroom equivalent of the powerful Ottawa and Montreal men on the Board, men like Woods, Southam, Fauquier, Wilson, McMaster. He got things done himself – but he wasn't the man to harness the team. There was help and advice from the others, but there was no structure, no committees charged with responsibilities, none of the organized approach to myriad problems that such men insisted upon in their own businesses. For 40 years under Woollcombe's strong hand such a structure had never been seen as necessary. No doubt he would have resented it. At a time like this, when everyone was beset with his own business problems, who wanted to be chairman? So Nixie Newcombe, the factotum, carried the load.

The outstanding mortgage with Sun Life had been reduced by now to under $10,000 and, when Newcombe sought to increase it to $20,000 for some working capital, the company declined unless the Governors were prepared to give personal guarantees. Sun Life was quite happy that the value of Ashbury's property was ten times the amount, but a glance at the statements showed the business steadily running down. There were only 71 boys now. Day boys stayed about level but there were only 30 boarders, and each year saw more red ink on the balance sheet with no provision for depreciation. Revenue had fallen from $71,000 to $40,000 over the previous four years.

McMaster, a Sun Life director, interceded with Treasurer E.A. Macnutt – they were on a "Dear Mac," "Dear Ross" basis. The keen-eyed, ear-to-the-ground mortgage man noted that Bishop's, under new Head Crawford Grier, was full. TCS, with a new man, Philip Ketchum, at the helm, and Lower Canada, Ashbury's other competitors in the Montreal market, had turned the corner and their enrolment was rising. Selwyn House graduates were almost all going to Bishop's without the usual share to Ashbury. Also, Macnutt was getting poor reports on Wright's capability. He wasn't getting out there, pulling in new boys. Sun Life would insist on personal guarantees for any extension of the loan. The long-term, well-earned reputation of Ashbury College was not just at stake; it had all but disappeared.

By the fall of 1935 Wright was more than prepared to be relieved as Headmaster and go back to teaching. Newcombe took that message to a down-in-the-mouth Board meeting in Montreal to try and divine how the school's fortunes could be restored. Macnutt had underscored Woollcombe's retirement allowance as a heavy item in a very thin operation. Woollcombe had pressed for a funded pension as early as 1928 but had accepted the Board's assurances of an annual income as a guarantee. His son, Edward, was asked to restructure some insurance in favour of the Woollcombe offspring to partly redress the balance, and the retirement allowance was cut in half to a miserly $1500.

A new Headmaster was essential. And a first-rate one. And fast. Confidence among prospective parents had to be rebuilt to turn things around by the fall of 1936. Colin Edwards was the only potential candidate on Ashbury's staff, but he was felt to have too little experience. A few enquiries were made for a Canadian candidate. The Chairman took on the task himself, but there was no serious systematic search, no letters to Canadian Headmasters.

Without doubt there was a strong leaning towards Englishmen in Ashbury circles. There was G.P. himself, and over the years he had mostly drawn his staff from England, preferring Oxford or Cambridge graduates with a classical education. Virtually all had gone to English public schools so they automatically knew the form.

Ottawa's outlook hadn't changed much from the turn of the century. The accent, manners and erudition – superficial or otherwise – that were the Englishman's trademark still held the social set in thrall. A polished English aide-de-camp at Government House was a prize for an Ottawa debutante. Add a title and he was the jackpot. English veneer counted more than Canadian roots. Woollcombe, though Canada was unquestionably his country and in every way his wife's, had the indelible English stamp. An Englishman, an Oxbridge man, it was accepted with blind confidence, would do well as Ashbury's new Head.

And there were, of course, few Canadian equivalents of the English public school, very few Canadians who'd been at private boarding schools, fewer still who look on schoolmastering as a fulfilling career. Still, the thirties saw broadly educated and experienced Canadian-born Headmasters appointed at Bishop's, TCS and St.

Andrew's, to name a few. Most were solidly, and some brilliantly, successful in spite of Depression problems. Whatever the Ashbury Governors' individual views, they agreed that they couldn't afford another blunder like the last. Then they left this all-crucial task in the lone hands of Nixie Newcombe.

Major Frederick Ney of the National Council of Education office in Toronto was asked in late January 1936 to do a search via his connections in England. Among others his enquiries reached J.F. Roxburgh, the famed founding Headmaster of Stowe School, who had stirred the stagnant waters of the British public schools in the twenties. He had no one he could recommend but wrote back: "The Headship of Ashbury looks most attractive. (I suppose you would think me too old for it at 47!)." Ney must have painted a most optimistic picture of a near-moribund institution. Had Roxburgh been serious, though, it would indeed have been a coup for Ashbury and would most likely have signalled a dramatic turnaround.

In early April 1936 a search committee of one, Nixie Newcombe, arrived in London. Using his Club, the Traveller's, he interviewed some of Ney's candidates. He also met Nicholas Archdale, Headmaster of Chartham Towers, a preparatory school in Camberley. Ney had introduced them. His National Council of Education arranged yearly visits, cricket tours and exchanges between Canadian and English schools. Chartham Towers was involved and Ney's son was there. Newcombe, interested in a change of scene for his junior Ashburian son Peter, sent him over that spring for a term with Archdale. Peter was back at Ashbury to start the 1936 fall term; Michael Ney came later in 1939. With no more ado Archdale was Newcombe's choice. He came out for a visit, was accepted by the Board and returned to Ottawa in August as the new Headmaster.

In the meantime, to keep the school's nose above water the Governors passed the hat. Starting with themselves they raised a little short of $10,000. They chased up every prospect, even to the point of pressing Senator Hardy (without success) to release his $1000 from the stagnant pension fund. Times were tough indeed. When the Old Boys Association was asked by Newcombe to chip in with a fund-raising campaign, their committee, chaired by young Ross McMaster, dug in its heels. Gilbert Fauquier junior wrote to McMaster senior that it would only undermine their current efforts to bolster the Association and to very little effect.

Thanking the Governors for putting up their own money, Fauquier wrote: "One of the great complaints of most boys since leaving school has been that when they returned to the School, or been asked to join the Association, it has always been a question of putting up money and for that reason many of them have fought shy of having very much to do with the school." George Woollcombe's relentless fund-raising was coming home to roost. Gilbert Fauquier's frank statement would be heard again. And again.

But on the surface all seemed serene and "Perfect summer weather smiled on the lovely grounds of Ashbury College on Saturday afternoon to welcome the annual sports and end-of-term exercises . . ." wrote the *Ottawa Citizen* that June. Full 60 column inches included Who's Who on the platform and Wright's complete Head-master's report, right down to the details of Lee Snelling's fine 7 for 84 cricket bowling average and old boy Robert L. Stanfield's North British Centennial Bursary and Overseas Essay Prize in Arts. "Only one occurrence served to cast a shadow on the happiness of the day – the formal announcement of the resignation as Headmaster of H.F. Wright."

In spite of all that was brewing in the Boardroom, life at the school, except for sliding numbers, didn't change. To the small boys coming to Ashbury in the late twenties and early thirties, it could be a pretty fearsome place. Three years at Elmwood, as with Hamilton Southam, Bill Hadley or the Rowleys, wasn't much preparation for the hurly-burly life. One of the less attractive tribal rites dictated that in each lower form someone – invariably the least popular – was elected "Queen of the May." At its worst, each unfortunate "Queen" had to push a shoepolish tin around the corridors with his nose, submit to having his face blackened and be paraded blindfolded past Elmwood. This was apparently condoned by the staff as part of the character-building process.

It was of course mandatory for youngsters to learn to play "peg." It took place at recess in the quadrangle behind the Housemaster's house, which at the time was gravel rather than grass. Rules kept shifting, but basically if you were "up" you'd stand in a three-foot circle with a stick and flail at a fat three-inch "peg" tossed in by your opponent. If you missed and it landed in the circle, you'd then hit it smartly on one of its tapered ends, thus flipping it up so you could smack it afar. Not infrequently the peg hit a window. The patient Oliver quietly repaired them, "no names, no pack drill."

Oliver called the game "tip cat," which casts the suspicion that he might have been the one who introduced Ashbury boys to the minor bane of his own busy life. Another theory says it might have been invented by F.E.B. "Wiggy" Whitfield who came in 1927. He was an Englishman who'd been in the Royal Flying Corps in the war. He taught various subjects and was a great games man – football, hockey, track and field, cricket. "Peg" certainly taught you to keep your eye on the ball. Wiggy was well liked. He lived nearby and even in dead of winter he never wore an overcoat, just strode briskly along with a muffler and a large pair of fur gauntlets, his trousers always four inches above his shoes.

Ashbury in retrospect strikes many different chords. To Charlie Gale, as he grew between 1926 and 1934 from short pants and the standard winter breeches into long trousers and climbed the school ladder, the intense, disciplinary approach to living and learning was rigid and rule-bound in the extreme. His was an Ottawa family but for a good deal of the time he boarded. The teaching was patchy – Wright, he found outstanding; Whitfield very good, and friendly in class and at sports. There was the inept Cassels; and the gangling B.K.T. Howis teaching Latin with a crib-book open in front of him; Speedy Meyers he despised.

It helped one to get ahead, it seemed to Gale, if parents helped the school. Backward students were moved up with the rest at the end of the year, pass or fail. The small classes could handle that, and the provincial matric exams were the final arbiter. With the Depression on, every place counted.

Gale wasn't much of an athlete, though he liked being able to play on the lesser teams, enjoyed the physical workouts in gym and, as manager of the first hockey team, worked well with Wiggy Whitfield. Overall, it was skill in sports that marked out the heroes and the chosen leaders and, it seemed to him, appointments of certain prefects were tainted with influence. Though he passed for McGill, he and his family were persuaded he should go back for a final year for his Ontario senior matric. Thus

Charlie got to be a prefect himself!

Roll calls. Lines and quarters and gatings and canings. Day boys were outsiders in a way because they were largely out of the line of fire. Adversity is great glue and there was real camaraderie among boarders: skiing in Rockcliffe Park where there was a tea room and you could sneak a smoke; occasional forays to Hull; crossing the river by the ferry to the taverns – anything to beat the system; all part of the game.

With all of this Gale learned about life – how to stand up for himself and others and get on using his own resources. In sum, whether it was calculated or not, it was all a pretty good preparation for a cold hard world. He wouldn't have missed it, remembered it with wry affection and brought back a strong independent, analytical mind in later years to support the school as an old boy and Chairman of the Board through some very difficult times.

To a free spirit like Peter Roberts beating the system was a great game. Considerable genius was applied to tormenting the masters who couldn't handle boys – and boys' antennae would detect that in an instant. Getting older, the opposite sex became, of course, the big preoccupation. Some older boys, it was whispered, managed liasons with the younger maids who waited on table. The Head, of course, had applicants for those positions very carefully screened and in G.P.'s time he insisted that they should not be Roman Catholics. The reason can only be surmised.

Attaining the sixth form, Roberts moved to one of the choice rooms over the gym. There at the end of the passage was the fire escape, Jacob's ladder, leading downwards to imagined Heaven. Every Sunday afternoon there was a tea-dance in the Jasper Room at the Chateau Laurier, garishly adorned with western murals and fake totem poles. The tea-dance was a reasonably legitimate and affordable outing and marvellously different from the dancing classes at Elmwood. Peter and three friends managed to meet four delightful girls there and charm them into a rendezvous.

The following Saturday night, with the window carefully greased in advance, came the stealthy descent of the fire escape, the swing out, the breathless five-foot drop at the bottom and the run to a darkened car waiting in Lindenlea. Much conspiratorial giggling and cuddling en route to Chez Henri in Hull. Upstairs was a private room available for such racy purposes. Beer and a bottle of sherry! Nirvana (for 1935)! Well after midnight, the goodnight kisses, the euphoric ascent of the fire escape to lie abed and dream of the next time.

Peter, who had the required gift of the gab, as evidenced by great success later on in radio broadcasting in the States, made sure there was a next time, and a next. To be caught and soaked – beaten, gated, anything – would have been worth every minute. But to get away with it . . .!! And they did, many times. Was the Housemaster really asleep? Was the fire escape viewed indulgently as a safety valve for seniors? A safer alternative perhaps than raiding the maids' quarters? Who will ever know?

Bob Stanfield had come to Ashbury in 1929 from Truro for his last three years of school, following two cousins and a brother. He was headed eventually for Dalhousie and the family felt it was a good thing for Nova Scotian boys to get a broader perspective on the world. Contact with an aging G.P. Woollcombe was impressive but limited. Teaching was uneven. The generally bleak condition of the school was disappointing at first, 'til he saw other schools on games trips.

Sports were the great thing. Stanfield played first team hockey and cricket, and he and Tom Beauclerk won the tennis doubles. He revelled in the gym. Sergeant-Major Stone, that thoroughly kind and human person, gave him endless help and encouragement. Patient, constant practice and R.L. Stanfield won the Connaught Cup for gymnastics. He was a prefect and wrote for the *Ashburian*. Good experience, good friends, good memories, but altogether – in retrospect – too much stress at the school on conformity. But that was of course the thrust of the institutions of the day.

The *Ashburian*'s 1932 capsule of Stanfield's hockey: "Sound defenceman with an excellent knowledge of the game. Although handicapped by lack of weight and speed, he used his head well. A most unselfish player." Those words could almost have been written about his distinguished political career.

Unlike music, art didn't have much of a place at Ashbury. The occasional talent, like Alan Beddoe's or, in the thirties, Bob Hyndman's, found an outlet caricaturing in the *Ashburian*. Talent makes its own way. Beddoe became Canada's leading authority on heraldry. Hyndman, no academic wizard as he himself acknowledged, went on to study art in Toronto. He took time out to be a fighter pilot in the war, painted as a war artist, then became a noted landscape artist and portraitist. He painted the portraits of Headmasters Woollcombe, Perry, Joyce and Macoun that hang in the school.

When he was young, Hamilton Southam attended school patchily, going south in the winter with his family and a tutor. He was the last of that generation of brothers (Bill, John and Cargill) and cousins (Gordon and Bob) to leave Ashbury. He actively hated team games but enjoyed the gym – liked the feeling of keeping fit – and it stuck. He ducked boxing, but the wise Sergeant-Major set up a bout between him and Bill Hadley. The two were close friends, ahead for their age and a lot smaller than their classmates. Stone, whose favourite expression, "I've got eyes in the back o' me head I have," applied to human relations just as much as it did to stamping out trouble, knew the two had had a falling out. A good flail at each other in the ring and all was restored.

Southam didn't get much from Brodie's French, taught virtually as a dead language. It was some years later that he made himself fluent. But G.P. filled him with a deep respect for the classics. On top of enhancing understanding of his own and other languages, Latin was one of those arcane accomplishments that served him well when he became Chancellor of Dalhousie University. The Chancellor there is obliged by tradition to address the Convocation in Latin. Southam was quite capable of writing his own speeches and delivering them with well-turned elegance.

Like Latin, the thousands of lines of poetry one was obliged to learn by heart stayed in his mind, as they do with most people of that generation, as a permanent source of delight. So did the Anglican liturgy learned in Chapel (he'd been raised a Christian Scientist) and the rich words of the King James version. He was lucky enough to be at Ashbury when Steve Brodie was leading the great Shakespeare revival. According to old boy Ted Devlin, Ottawa's respected drama critic, young Southam played Gratiano in *The Merchant of Venice* "lightly with exactly the right touch of flippancy." The great passages of *The Merchant*, *As You Like It* and *Macbeth* which he declaimed at Ashbury stayed lifetime favourites. All good stuff for the future first Director-General of Canada's National Arts Centre.

To Avery Stairs, Ashbury was a place to board and to work up his math and science to get into RMC, and it worked. Wright was fine in math, though he was annoyed at Stairs' pronunciation of "centimetre" in the French mode and the way he crossed his sevens à la Europe. Conformity. "Lud" Johnson was first-rate in physics and chemistry and coached Stairs in running. Stairs had been at school in Switzerland for two years. At Ashbury, the lack of association with girls and not being allowed to drop into Ottawa's non-existent cafes for a glass of wine seemed pretty immature.

In many ways it was. But Ashbury in the thirties certainly had a life of its own.

CHAPTER 8
NICHOLAS ARCHDALE

Nicholas Archdale arrived in Ottawa in August 1936 with his wife Sheila, two small girls, a cook, a housemaid and a dog, and moved easily into Rockcliffe society. For a car Newcombe had recommended he buy a new Dodge at $900. His salary was $4000, with Ashbury House rent-free. Assistant live-in masters got $1800. Fees were now $750 per year for senior boarders, $210 for day boys.

Archdale was a charming man, slight, compact, with thinning hair. He was a first-class athlete with his Oxford "blue" in football – soccer to Canadians; he had played for the University in water polo, field hockey and lacrosse and for his College in cricket and tennis. The most noticeable picture on his office wall was one of himself in football rig shaking hands with King George V. He was an immediate success in the boys' eyes because of his skills on the playing field. Here was a Head who was out there with them. When handling a football his feet, to the awe of the soccer players, were like another pair of hands. Soccer had a good deal more stress, and success, through Archdale's time as Head.

To give him a clear deck the Board had already cut staff, put the rest on term-to-term employment status and dropped the position of Headmaster of the Junior School. B.K.T. Howis and K.B. Castle, who had been replaced by A.D. Brain the previous September, at last got a term's severance pay. The Board's first directive to the new Head was simply to increase efficiency and reduce overheads as soon as possible.

Archdale's first real look at Ashbury College jolted him out of any illusion that he or the school were in for an easy or prosperous time. In a report to the Board that November he painted a dismal picture of a leaderless, atrophied institution. The staff, he reported, was disorganized and disinterested; boys were disgruntled with no vestige of loyalty or affection for the school. Discipline, in his view, scarcely existed, while the boys delighted in breaking the multitude of petty rules. Teaching was by rote and memory with no provision for the gifted or the slow. Laziness was condoned.

In his message to the school via the *Ashburian* he pointedly wrote, "There must be discipline but it should be self-discipline, with authority more in the role of a reminder than in that of a dictator." The photograph printed with it was in stark contrast to his predecessors'. Harry Wright's pale eyes had looked right at you, rivetted you. So had G.P.'s dark ones. They were men of determination, men in charge. Archdale's photo showed a young, handsome aesthete, gazing off-stage right with an air of poetic wistfulness. Certainly not the determined man of action.

In his report to the Governors he may have gone overboard a bit. Painting the situation so bleakly at the start would make a new broom look even better in the end. But what more unhappy, negative things could be said about any school? He had indeed inherited a mess. What had happened to the golden age of G.P. Woollcombe?

Archdale didn't think that age was in fact so golden. To him it was outmoded.

Also, the long line of predominantly English schoolmasters meant that Ashbury was bound to be a small copy of the English public school. Wright had gone off to Bishop's. Of the seven on staff when the new Head arrived, only Humphrey Porritt was Canadian.

Whether Archdale was trying to make things more Canadian or just didn't take to them, the solid old hands Wiggy Whitfield, Steve Brodie and Sergeant-Major Stone were soon out. Whitfield was summarily cut off at Easter and he brought a suit for compensation. None of the three got any kind of pension. There was no true replacement for that pillar of the school, the Sergeant-Major. Brodie fell on his feet: he became arbiter of English in the developing Canadian Broadcasting Corporation, the one who set and supervised the standards of syntax and diction for announcers. Without seeking to impose his English accent, he provided the hallmark that distinguishes CBC public affairs announcing to this day.

Archdale's report had marked all the others as "possible": Arthur Brain especially promising, Porritt a good schoolmaster if kept in check, Colin Edwards a good influence, and Lud Johnson a capable scientist, good with the boys. In his second year, though, Archdale fell out with Edwards, well regarded at Ashbury from 1923 to 1926 and again since 1933. Edwards was Housemaster and Senior Master but Archdale said his structured, Woollcombe-style discipline was outmoded. Back in England Edwards became a Housemaster at Eton.

Mrs Archdale, who was of formidable presence and dictatorial bent, had meanwhile plunged into the school's domestic affairs and tangled with the nurse, housekeeper and sewing room staff. For years, since giving up detailed supervision during the war, Mrs Woollcombe had been "Honorary Housekeeper," advising on domestic arrangements. All had gone smoothly. Mrs Archdale had no doubt controlled such matters at Chartham Towers but at Ashbury she put noses badly out of joint and the Board had to intervene and insist that the Headmaster himself be responsible. Charming the Archdales may have been socially, but neither of them knew much about getting the best from those who worked for them.

Reputations can topple almost overnight, and they take a very long time to rebuild. It was one thing for Archdale to diagnose the problem, another to fix it. The situation called for leadership well above the ordinary and Archdale simply didn't have it. Successful he may have been at running his prep school for young boys in a set-piece situation in England, but he was up against especially difficult times and in a country he had never experienced. Worst of all, he was a lazy, self-indulgent man. And weak.

Archdale gave Brain top marks among his staff ("efficient, modern, adaptable, full of ideas, inclined to sarcasm . . .") and he was quite happy to let him take over the day-to-day administration. Rather than spending that freed-up time promoting the school and finding new students, Archdale succumbed to personal interests, sports and social activities. The Rockcliffe Tennis Club saw a good deal more of him than did the school office. The Archdales were quickly taken into Rockcliffe's cozy social circuit, restricted as it was by hard times. Nick soon collected a reputation as a ladies' man. In neither capability nor inclination did N.M. Archdale meet the very considerable challenge of the time.

There were changes to the Board. Sons of the very early Ashbury supporters were joining now – J.D. Fraser, Fred Bronson, John Rowley and Shirley Woods among them. They had their inherited Founders' votes and their interest in the school as old boys. Some had sons at the school. The weight on the Board was now shifting back towards Ottawa, though the Old Boys' Association stayed centred in Montreal. Newcombe stepped down as Chairman in 1938 and after a pause Shirley Woods took over. It was still Nixie, though, who carried the real load.

The best will in the world couldn't get Ashbury back on an even financial footing until it started growing in numbers and reputation. The top criterion for a new Head had been the ability to meet and impress the public and parents. Archdale's affability wasn't enough. Systematic hard work was needed. Competing schools had recovered and were growing. Ashbury, in low regard, was going lower.

To those who straddled the three regimes, the changes weren't perceptible or immediate. Bill Grant came to Ashbury at the age of nine and found himself slightly taller than G.P. The current name for Harry Wright was "Acid." His son Geoffrey, two years ahead of Grant, was "Acid-drop." Wright, most surprisingly, was a good Chapel organist and an excellent teacher of piano and choir. Even with that his ordered approach prevailed. Having tried vainly to get a consistently tuneful voice from Bill Grant, he included him in an important choir performance because he wanted the pews filled precisely. His dire warning: Mime the words lustily, Grant, but on pain of death utter not one single sound. His voice fully changed, Grant went on to major in everything. By the time he left he was the only four-colour man – football, soccer, hockey, cricket – of his day and he was Captain of the School and won the Governor General's Medal to top it off.

Don Maclaren enjoyed singing more than Grant. He and Ian Barclay made up in volume what they lacked in finesse and they figured in rousing renditions of Gilbert and Sullivan, backing Lud Johnson who was renowned for his rendering of "When Constabulary Duty's to Be Done (to be done) . . . ."

Fagging for prefects was fraught with traps, many of which produced a fanning. Maclaren's roommate, Andreas Heuser, made a habit of filling the wash-basin – they were fitted in some rooms now – when he was called to the prefects' study. He'd race back after his beating and cool his backside gratefully in the cold water. Maclaren and Barclay, along with Bob Stedman, L.J. McCallum and Peter Viets, were prefects with Grant and finally on the delivering end themselves.

As day boys spanning 1932 to 1943, Bert Lawrence and younger brother Barney were somewhat out of the line of fire, though their lives still centred around the school. For Bert, who was Governor General's Medallist in 1940, his eight years instilled in him English ethics, Roman discipline and Greek thought. Presumably it all helped him through law practice and the rough and tumble of local politics to cabinet office in Queen's Park. Barney, the athlete, topped just about every sport and was Captain of the School in 1943. Post-war, squash became his main event. Skill and the energy of a charging rhino won him many titles and he played for Canada against the U.S.A. in the Lapham Cup series every year from 1950 to 1991.

Things really hadn't changed. That generation didn't take as dark a view of the school's heavy-handed discipline as Archdale professed. It was part of the game. But it's not surprising that after G.P.'s 42-year regime some changes were due. Beginning in Wright's time, though numbers were sliding, fresh ideas had blown through the corridors.

The *Ashburian* reflected a significant change. In 1935 it was given an expanded format and zippier design and style. Over the next four years it grew from the average 50 pages to over 80. There was far more input from the boys. In fact, it was almost entirely their work now and had a good deal more vitality. The editorial staff grew from one master in charge and a couple of assistant boys (and Hewitt as business manager) to the Editor-in-Chief, Mr. Humphrey Porritt, and a dozen boys in both senior and junior schools. Interestingly there'd been a similar re-vitalizing of the *Ashburian* in 1917, but with a change of the man in charge it had slipped back.

The new *Ashburian* missed Bob Hyndman's outstanding caricatures that headed various sections – hockey, football, cadets, editorial, old boys, etc. The regular numbing reports of games continued, including pages of detailed cricket scores. But now all the reporting, even to drama criticism, was done by the boys rather than being wheedled from the staff.

Porritt obviously had to persuade Wright, the scientist, of the benefits of the expensive change. He knew his man. In his first editorial – the only piece written by a master – he said: "Writing, says Bacon, maketh an exact man, and if the *Ashburian* can only have the satisfaction of making boys appreciate the value and necessity of exactitude in the world to-day it will have surely justified its existence."

There was far more about the boys themselves: thumbnail sketches and photos of the prefects, pictures taken by the boys of informal groups, accounts of their own activities, ski trips, the cadet corps in field manoeuvres with the Governor General's Foot Guards, and attractive angles of the school itself. The formal photos now included suavely posed groups of prefects and the *Ashburian* staff. The dress for these was uniformly a double-breasted dark blue suit with school tie, and white handkerchief folded neatly in the breast pocket.

Avery Dunning wrote an intriguing account of a trip to the 1936 Olympics in Berlin with a group organized by Major Ney and his National Council of Education. The Canadian boys, with their counterparts from other countries, were herded into an army camp with armed soldiers about and the feeling that if you didn't turn out on time there'd be a bayonet under your nose. Accommodation and food were at the concentration-camp level. The boys were marched around to various gigantic spectacles to hear Hitler and Goering harangue the crowds. A chilling experience.

Besides feature articles there was a wide selection of literary efforts, poems and stories that showed a remarkably high standard. Small boys' work figured in their own junior section. The *Ashburian* really got people writing.

Humphrey Porritt, the man behind the change, had started in the Junior School with Brodie and was an absolutely first-rate teacher of English. He could capture a boy's imagination and open up new horizons to the least interested. Those with capability flourished in their reading habits, their understanding and appreciation of literature, and in their own writing. Shakespeare came alive. Porritt took a hand in dramatics and leavened the solemn, massive productions of whole Shakespearian plays by presenting key excerpts and one-act plays by other writers. Performing the Bard's plays had a practical function, though. Each year Toronto selected one for study. It was bound to figure in the matric exam and certain passages had, of course, to be learned by heart.

Porritt also leavened the classics by introducing American authors, even the modern ones like Faulkner and Hemingway. He kept his students up on bright new writers arriving on the pages of *The New Yorker* and *Esquire*. Copies of *Esquire* were in great demand too by those of less literary bent because they carried the monthly "Petty Girl" – curvaceous, transparently clothed, the popular pin-up of the day. Debating, which had lapsed for years, took on a new lease under his guidance, and there were debating trips to Bishop's.

With a Bishop's MA, Porritt was one of the few Canadians on the staff, though he had distinctly English mannerisms. He was a bachelor and lived in a room over the gym. One of his legs was badly crippled. He wore a boot with a four-inch sole and clumped about with a pronounced limp. He couldn't take the usual part in games but he certainly compensated. He was a mentally active, cultivated and entertaining man, though something of a snob. In common with many other Ashbury masters over the years, he was a busy Ottawa Drama Leaguer. He dressed with an indefinable touch of elegance and was seen from time to time heading off for a social affair in white tie, tails, opera cape and topper. He cut quite a dash and was, it was rumoured, pursuing the older sister of an Ashbury boy. Then he was said to be in love with the beautiful daughter of a prominent and extremely rich Montreal family.

Sadly, though, Humphrey Porritt took to booze. The stilted Ashbury life? His little hutch of a room over the gym? His unfortunate physical handicap? Rejection by his beloved? A sense of guilt when war came and he couldn't join up? He had more than enough talent and gave a great deal of himself to many. But he lost his grip and the school condoned him for far too long. Don Maclaren played Hamlet in the churchyard and duel scenes in December 1938, his last year. A couple of years later, Porritt invited him to a performance of *Hamlet* in Montreal. Debonair as of old and outstanding company for such an evening, he was in fast-declining straits.

"G.P.," and after him, "Acid." When Archdale arrived bearing the initials N.M.A. could boys dub him anything but "Enema"? Archdale inherited the good, the bad and the eccentric as his staff, but he considered Arthur Donovan Brain the best in every way. Brain had been in Canada long enough to acquire a BA from the University of Toronto and get some teaching experience. He was reminiscent of the portraits of Henry VIII: four-square, solid as a rock, with a big head and strong jaw and a look in his eye that bespoke supreme confidence in his own infallibility and dire consequences to anyone who questioned it. There was a lot of the Elizabethan in Arthur Brain.

He'd plunge right into the scrimmage at football practices wearing rugger gear, not football pads. Tackling him on the soccer field was like tangling with a Mack truck. He loved cricket, though he talked a far more remarkable game than he played. No generation of Ashbury boys got by without hearing him declare that if his middle finger had been a quarter of an inch longer he'd have been the finest medium-paced bowler in England. No generation lacks its tale of the time that "A.D.B." or "Donovan" or "Buggy" was bowled first ball or was knocked for three sixes in a single over.

The school couldn't afford to pay outside coaches or even referees for interschool games. A.D.B. always wanted to be in charge of whatever was going on and he loved to coach and referee. He'd have done both in the same game if it had been allowed.

If his knowledge of rules and technique was thin, his confidence never wavered. There's no doubt at all that his refereeing and umpiring decisions were blatantly weighted towards Ashbury College. He was, in point of fact, a cheat.

He also fancied himself as a boxer. He was invariably a judge in competitions and he liked to spar with the boys to teach them a thing or two. Lee Snelling, who was no slouch with the gloves, caught him a beauty and laid him out – which put Lee's stock way up with everyone but A.D.B.

In the classroom Brain was rigorous and demanding and ruled with a rod of iron. Yet he inspired any who had a thirst for knowledge. He had a remarkable grasp of classics and an extraordinary command of Latin and Greek. Sometimes he turned his hand to teaching French, though he couldn't speak the language at all. To boys with good minds or academic potential he could be the finest influence in their whole school and university career. To the average boys – especially the lower end of the scale – he could be a bully, even a monster. He had a mind like a prehistoric computer and he never forgot anything. On the flats his footfalls were unmistakable; a whiff of his pipe tobacco and you took cover. Whatever side of A.D.B you were on, you always knew he was around.

He had a flair for detailed administration and an unlimited capacity for work. Taking over the details from Archdale suited him completely. In 1938 he moved into the Housemaster's quarters in the Annex. The Brains' first house guests, the Right Reverend Lord Bishop of Niagara and Mrs. L.W. Broughall, were Mrs. Brain's parents. The Brains became part and parcel of the school. Barbara was particularly outgoing, warm and friendly.

When, rarely, Brain left the school to go downtown, he wore a bowler hat planted squarely on his massive head. He delighted in the titles and positions of Housemaster and Senior Master which gave him (under the nominal direction of Archdale) total control over the school, except for the money and perhaps the domestic staff. If he wasn't in charge of something those responsible bent to his will or he soon took over. With the weak N.M.A. taking little more than a ceremonial part, A.D.B. ran the place. His ideas of discipline didn't coincide with his Head's. Not for him Archdale's idea of authority in the role of "reminder": A.D.B. was, and always would be, the dictator.

The Old Boys' Notes in the *Ashburian* in 1938 reflected the war clouds that were scudding over Europe. At RMC that year Michael MacBrien was Battalion Sergeant-Major, and Bill Hadley took the Bronze Medal and the Artillery Prize. Bill MacBrien was promoted to Flight Lieutenant in the RCAF. Eric Ernshaw, accepted for the RCN, had gone to England for training; Norman Beard was already there. John and Roger Rowley were both Lieutenants in Ottawa's Cameron Highlanders.

On the lighter side, Lou Bates had landed the part of captain of a hockey team in an English movie called "I See Ice" with the Lancashire comedian George Formby. And that summer Charles Burrows, still at the school, won the Dominion Boys' Singles Tennis Championship.

The same year Archdale ran a competition for a school motto. The winning entry, Probitas, Virtus, Comitas – freely translated Honour, Courage, Grace – had no name attached. One can't help suspecting a plot involving Arthur Brain.

The teaching staff by now totalled seven including the Head, down from 11 in 1933. But it was now much more Canadian: E.B. Mercer, Dalhousie; W.A.G.

McLeish, McMaster; H. Porritt, Bishop's. Brain had his Toronto degree, though he was English to the last. J.W. Johnson had a Toronto science degree as well as one from Oxford. His nickname "Lud" came from his Midlands-English pronunciation of "lad." He was physically powerful, a direct, no-nonsense man without the cultural niceties and with a clear contempt for what he considered Oxbridge snobbery. He was a thoroughly inspiring science teacher and a fine tennis player. Barney Lawrence started his racquets career being coached by Lud Johnson at 6:00 a.m. at the Rockcliffe Tennis Club. Only A.A.V. "Swamp" Waterfield and Archdale were pure Oxonians. There's no record of Board directives to Archdale. With jobs so hard to find, he'd hardly have had trouble filling the slots. He'd hired some very good men and it seems he was indeed trying to build a Canadian school.

Whatever. The 1939 McGill matriculation results were poor. There were fewer than 70 boys and less than half were boarders. There was the serious problem of debt. Closing Day, though, is always an occasion for expressions of high hope and confidence. Praise tends to be lavished, deserved or no. Fine words and all, Ashbury College was undoubtedly at its lowest ebb.

Just about every Ashbury room had a radio now, or at least a crystal set with earphones, and they brought in Hitler's raving speeches punctuated by the "Sieg Heils" of vast cheering crowds and the ominous sound of marching feet. In the eleventh hour, the summer of 1939, Ottawa gave a tremendous welcome to His Majesty King George VI and his wonderfully warm and responsive Queen, Elizabeth. Ashbury turned out en masse on Parliament Hill for a great parade in their Majesties' honour and acted as ushers. The Royal Tour across Canada, more than any other factor, stiffened the country's allegiance to Britain. When Germany invaded Poland and disregarded Prime Minister Neville Chamberlain's ultimatum to withdraw, Britain, on September 3, declared war. On September 10 Canada followed suit.

As in the previous conflict, Ashbury was represented right at the start, this time by its Founder. Canon Woollcombe, aged 72, was returning to Canada in the passenger liner *Athenia* when, on September 4, she was torpedoed by a German U-boat off northern Ireland. G.P., true to his intrepid self, calmly collected his overcoat and lifejacket from his cabin and got into his assigned lifeboat. It pulled safely away as the ship went down. He took his turn at the oars and led his fellow survivors in prayer as they awaited rescue on the empty sea. They were picked up eventually by the *City of Flint*. G.P. tended the injured, conducted services and was a tower of spiritual strength among the survivors. Back in Ottawa he got on with his church work as though nothing had happened.

There was no question of the country's response. And Ashbury's old boys responded – many for the second time – just as selflessly as they had 25 years before. But this time there was none of the naive excitement of 1914. Memories of war were too fresh. Bert Lawrence's poem was published in the *Ottawa Citizen* in June 1940, the month he graduated to RMC en route to the army and a Military Cross in Normandy:

"On the Death of Youth in Battle"

In no little daughter's laughing eyes
Is his smile reborn.
Ne'er a son to carry on his name;
Youth for whom we mourn.

Yet children hath he more than any man,
The nation's little ones, safely at play,
Are his.

Their heritage he bought with his dear life,
They too shall fight the wrongs he did defy,
His sacrifice hath cut a pattern for their lives;
He lives: he cannot die.

Junior School Group

Back Row (from left): J.M. Brown, W.A. Grant, A.J. Perley-Robertson, A.S. Purdy
4th Row: G. Perley-Robertson, J.C. Viets, D.A. Cassils, R.B. Stannard, J.H. Colvil
3rd Row: G. Bryson, E. Spafford, A.B.R. Lawrence, A. Heuser, R.B. Hobbs, D. Maclaren,
2nd Row: T.M. Galt, S. Hopper, V.J. Wilgress, R.B. Bailey, E.P. Newcombe, E.D. Wilgress, G.K. Wright
Front Row : E.L. Macdonald, L.S. Magor, W.H.C. Brodie, Esq., H.M. Porritt, Esq., H.D. Snelling, H.J. Ronalds

"Steve" Brodie was the first Head of the Junior School. Humphrey Porritt was in his first year.

***Julius Caesar* - 1930**

Back Row (from left): D. Gillies, C. Eliot, J. Magor, R. Leathem, W.H. Brodie, H. Hammond, M. Menzies, G. Perodeau, G. Witcher, F. Macorquodale, J. Rowley, D. Mathias, R. Wodehouse, W. Robertson, G. Wodehouse, M. Grant, F. Sherwood, G. Abel, P. Smellie, H. Fensom, A. McCarthy, B. Ritchie
Front Row : (seated on floor) S. Macdonnell, R. Stanfield, J. Calder

The Ashbury College Dramatic Society presented *Julius Caesar* at the Ottawa Little Theatre on the Ides of March 1930. Steve Brodie, the producer, played Brutus and nabbed the shiniest armour as befitted the "noblest Roman of them all."

The Mock Parliament   1937

Staged by the Debating Society, directed by Humphrey Porritt. Highlights, as reported by Gerald "Flap" Green were: the impossible budget introduced by Finance Minister David Ghent; the speech by the Leader of the CCF party which conveyed nothing at all and the bibulous Member for Carp (Lee Snelling) insisting he heard tom-toms and demanding a statement from the Ministry of Justice on unrest in the Indian reservations.

First Hockey Team 1931-32

Back Row (from left): Fauquier, F.E.B. Whitfield, Esq., G. MacCarthy, F.A. Heubach, E. Allen
2nd Row: J. McGuckin, R. Stanfield, L.R. Thomas (Capt.), J. Allen
Front Row: G. Stanfield, J. Symington, T.W. Beauclerk, J.S. Galt, R. Coristine

This was the year the Old Boys Association presented the trophy for annual competition with Bishop's and LCC.
Ashbury won! The team played 17 games, won 11, lost 5, drew 1. Goals for:46; goals against: 30.

Soccer Team   1942

Back Row (from left): H.F. Bulpit, H.P. Harben, R. Bourget, S. Pegram, A. Hurtley, N.M. Archdale, Esq.
2nd Row: E. Grove, P. Richardson, R.G.R. Lawrence, Capt., I.F.C. Cole, R. Heaven
Front Row : C.P. Prance, P. Grove

Headmaster N.M. Archdale was a soccer "blue" from Oxford and a fine athlete and coach. He gave the game
a boost. So, during the war years, did the Abinger Hill boys. Barney Lawrence became Canada's ranking senior
squash player.

Canada's outstanding field soldier of World War II

Major General Guy Simonds (1920 - 21) receives the Distinguished Service Order from Lieutenant General Bernard Montgomery in 1943 for his leadership in command of the Canadian Forces in the invasion of Sicily. General Simonds went on to command the 2nd Canadian Corps and accepted the surrender of the German armies in Northwest Europe in 1945.

Some 1947 and 1948 graduates with Arthur Brain – who else in that stance with his pipe 'afume ?

Back Row (from left): John Nesbitt, Graham "Kid" Knight, Arthur Brain, John "Newt" McBride, Robert "Puggy" Patterson

Front Row : Frank Rose, Alan " Pass" Holmes, John "Tubby" Pettigrew, Tim Kenny, Christopher Hampson, Arthur MacRae, Tony Price

PHOTO: COURTESY JOHN NESBITT

Cadet Inspection, Spring 1946

Rear Admiral Percy Nelles, Chief of the Naval Staff, inspects the junior stretcher-bearers. Bert Lawrence, Cadet Corps C.O., sports faultlessly rolled WW II puttees. He went to RMC then the army and won the M.C. in Normandy. The school was at its smallest in over 30 years. N.M. Archdale brings up the rear.

Abinger Hill Group 1940

Friends rallied to help when over 50 boys from Abinger Hill School were suddenly evacuated from England in July 1940 to spend the war years at Ashbury. Mrs. Agnes Etherington (in white hat) welcomed this group at her summer home near Chaffey's Locks. The man in the rear is Richard Sykes. On his left is the Matron, Miss Lee. For these boys, life in Canada was an exciting adventure but very far from home.

The Ski Team 1946-47

Back Row (from left): C.L. Ogden Glass, Esq., W.R. Wright, Esq.
2nd Row: S. Price, G. Knight, D. Gardner
Front Row : G. Ross, P. Lighthall, T. Price, C. Hampson, A. Holmes

The Prices led Ashbury strongly into competitive skiing after the war with plenty of encouragement from Oggie Glass.

"Hay Fever" – The Ashbury - Elmwood Players   1949

Standing (from left): Judy Nesbitt, Chris Hart, Betsy Alexandor, Don Hall, Sallie McCarter, Peter Hargreaves
Seated : Judy McCulloch, Robin MacNeil, Jackie Nothnagel

Duke Belcher was the producer. Robin MacNeil, the lead, went on via the Ottawa Little Theatre and radio to television, three books and eminence in public affairs analysis in the MacNeil-Lehrer News Hour.

PHOTO: THE OTTAWA CITIZEN

First Hockey Team 1946-47

Back Row (from left): John Nesbitt, David Fair, Doug Poaps, Robert Paterson, Jim Fleck, John Pettigrew, Tim Kenny
Front Row : Don Watson, Doug Heney, Walter Scott, Jay Dover, Doug Hall, Jim McBride, Moe Zilberg

Ashbury re-entered the Ottawa Senior Interscholastic League after many years with a great deal of enthusiasm but little success.

The 60th Anniversary Weekend   1951

left to right: Joe Irvin, Roger Rowley, Bert Lawrence, Bob Southam, Headmaster Ron Perry, Ned Rhodes

All these old boys were Governors, all but Rowley chaired the Board, all sent sons to the school. Ron Perry was responsible for planting some 1500 trees on the Ashbury grounds.

Closing, June 7, 1951

On the left in the front row is Canon G.P. Woollcombe in his last appearance at the school he founded 60 years before. He had assisted at the Leaving Service that morning. Next to him, Hon. George Drew, M.P., Viscountess Alexander, Viscount Alexander, who presented the Governor General's Medal to John Fraser, and behind Headmaster Ron Perry, Vice-Chairman Ned Rhodes.

Cadet Corps Inspection 1959

Arrival of the inspection officer, Vice Admiral Harry DeWolf, was heralded by a fly-past of jet fighters. The bugle band was in its second year, the Guard of Honour dressed in bearskins and red tunics, courtesy of the Governor General's Foot Guards. The Junior Corps Drill Squad performed; the Midget March Past included all of height three feet and under.

Ray Anderson (1954 -1991) Athletic Director, physical training instructor and officer in charge of Cadets had his busiest time of year around Inspection Day. The P.T. and gym display that always followed inspection was, like the corps, a full school turn-out.

Boxing Champions 1950-51

Back Row (from left): G.S. Wharton, G.E. Turnbull, L. Cardinal, R.E.L. Gill, J. Luyken
2nd Row: J. Hamill, G.C. Carne, R.G. Ross
Front Row : A.B. Maclaren, E.T. Mulkins, T.D. Hornell

From 1924 to 1960 the boxing tournament was a popular annual event. There were long-standing trophies for every event.   PHOTO: CAPITAL PRESS SERVICE

CHAPTER 9
ABINGER HILL

In the spring of 1940 Hitler's Panzers ripped through the Low Countries and France. The remnants of Britain's army were plucked from the beaches of Dunkirk. Britain was alone and under siege. Parents who could find friends or had contacts in North America were encouraged to send their children away. The ubiquitous Major Ney, in England at the time, plunged in for Ashbury, quite unbidden. An English prep school that he and Archdale knew, Abinger Hill, headed by James Harrison, was interested in being evacuated en masse. Most of the parents had agreed on the condition their children were kept together under Harrison's care. And Ashbury, Ney knew, had space galore.

There was a fast exchange of cables in the last two weeks of June:

Archdale
Ashbury College

HAVE SUGGESTED ABINGER TEMPORARILY AMALGAMATE ASHBURY
HAVE PUT PROPOSAL HARRISON PARENTS NOW BEING CONSULTED
HERE IS GREAT OPPORTUNITY HELP THIS CRITICAL TIME

Ney

Ney
London

DELIGHTED HAVE ABINGER JOIN US IF FUNDS AVAILABLE TO COVER BARE EXPENSES

Archdale

Harrison
Abinger

DELIGHTED TO HEAR YOUR COMING PRESUME NEY HAS ARRANGED FUNDS WE HAVE NONE

Archdale

Archdale
Ashbury College

FIFTY SAILING VERY SHORTLY EAGER ANTICIPATION BE-
LIEVE FINANCE ALL RIGHT

Harrison

———————————

Heaven-sent! A chance to help Britain through this terrible time *and* 50 new boarders in the bargain. A great opportunity for Archdale and Ashbury in *their* critical time.

Parents of British boarding school children, mainly people of some means of course, leaped at chances of an organized evacuation. Any child who could be moved out to safety would have a far better chance to live in freedom and be one less mouth to feed in Britain. On top of that, Abinger Hill School was in the front-line south of England and had been taken over by the Army. The Canadian government had opened the doors in this fast-moving emergency and set up a scheme to put unsupported children in the care of the Children's Aid Society.

Archdale's "yes" to Abinger in such circumstances was a natural human move. The Board met on June 17 to discuss the implications. It was their first meeting in a year, a rather casual treatment of Ashbury's pressing problems. Now there were war guests actually on the way with no answer as to who would pay Archdale's undefined "bare expenses." Long-time Governor and financial guarantor Harry Southam took a hard look at Ashbury's finances. Watt Creighton, the genial and sympathetic manager of the Bank of Montreal, gave him the picture. It was pretty bleak.

The $20,000 credit at the bank, endorsed by eight Governors and friends, was overstretched and the school was sliding further into debt. By September it wouldn't be able to carry on another day unless guarantors for more credit could be found. That, deemed Southam, was a good deal less than likely. And now here was Abinger Hill, about to land on the doorstep, with no apparent way of getting funds from beleaguered Britain.

Harry and Wilson Southam, Norman Wilson and Dr. T.H. Leggett were joint guarantors of the outstanding $60,000 mortgage, now with North American Life. As well, Mrs. Harry Southam and Senator Cairine Wilson had endorsed half the bank credit between them. Southam put the hard case: unless Abinger money came through, plus enough Canadian new boys in the fall to run a year without an even bigger deficit, Ashbury must liquidate. The school would close. The endorsers of mortgage and bank credit, on the line for $80,000 between them, would have to take over the debts and the property. Subdivided for houses, the available 10 acres would bring $6000-$7000 an acre. That was in normal times, which these were not. Eventually they would get some of their money back, but Ashbury would be no more.

Meantime, Abinger Hill, divided between Canadian Pacific's *Duchess of Rich-mond* and *Montrose*, ran the U-boat gauntlet. There were 55 small boys altogether, aged eight to 12, and some 18 of their little sisters who had been sent to Abinger earlier in the war to get them away from the dangers of London bombing. In a matter of a few brief days each of these youngsters' lives had been set on end. Snatched from apparently secure surroundings, herded aboard the awesome grey-painted steam-ships, and taken across a menacing ocean towards an undefined future in a land of which they knew nothing with their families far behind, they were alternately agog with excitement, miserably seasick and overwhelmed with longing for home. It was very much on the cards that they would never see those families or those homes again. In fact the very next evacuee ship was torpedoed with tragic loss and no more groups like theirs were sent.

The first lot were under the care of the Headmaster, G. James K. Harrison. To the bafflement of customs officers, ship's crew and the reception party at the Montreal dockside, all the children called him "Mrs Hippo." ("Mrs Hippo" was an English comic strip character who ran a school for a mischievous lot of small animals.) With them came assistant master Richard A. Sykes and the matron, Miss Lee. The rearguard was tended by Mrs. Harrison and two parents, Mrs Acworth and Mrs Webb.

They arrived in Ottawa in early June with $2000 cash and no arrangements at all for getting any more money from Britain. The Harrison family itself was intact – James and his wife, young son Jonathan (called "Baby Hippo") and his sister Julie, and their very large mottled Great Dane, Georgina. Peter and Thomas Crump's sister came too but, unlike the Harrisons, their parents were in England and very far away.

Ashbury parents and friends rallied around. An anonymous well-wisher sent several boys off to Camp Kagawong, including Baby Hippo. His sister and several other girls were taken by the Viets family to Blue Sea Lake. Maclarens, Perley-Robertsons, Newcombes and many other Ashbury families took others off to their various cottages and homes. Mrs Etherington, whose ward Douglas Moulton was at Ashbury, took a good 20 of them to her summer place, Fettercairn Island, near Chaffey's Locks on Indian Lake. It remained, as so many did, an open house for the duration.

Safe and sound through that deceptively lovely summer, the evacuees heard news on the radio of Hitler massing his landing craft in the French ports, stepping up the U-boat war and air attacks, lining up the lamb and its beaten, depleted army for the slaughter. Britain stood alone with the Commonwealth, steeled for invasion, massive bombing of her cities, death, destruction, starvation. Their own families were right there.

But nearer at hand Ashbury was broke and literally on the very edge of closing down. Without doubt that's what the numbers said, and there were those outstanding notes. But old soldier Nixie Newcombe manned the barricade. It was a patriotic duty, he wrote to his fellow Board members. There was a war on and this was something Ashbury could do for Britain in its time of mortal danger. They must stand by these children, invited or not; otherwise they'd be scattered as charges of Children's Aid. Harrison had given their parents a commitment that they wouldn't be separated. If they could all just hang on, there must be some way of getting money from the U.K.

Ashbury was by no means the only Canadian school that opened its arms, inadvertently or not, to English school children. The matter was raised in two Houses of Commons – Ottawa and Westminster. Under pressure from Canada, the British Treasury allowed parents to pay school fees into sterling accounts in England. They could be invested in the U.K. but couldn't be sent out of the country; they could, theoretically, be used as collateral for borrowing in Canada and released at the end of the war. But as the great air battle raged in the clear English autumn skies, prospects for a victory were dim.

The Ashbury Board set out to raise emergency funds and somehow muddle through, for a year at least. Willy-nilly the school opened in September. The war had brought in more Canadian boys too. Across Canada there were fathers in the services, families moving about. Ottawa was growing fast, with swelling government. At Closing in June there'd been 63 boys on the rolls. In September there were 191, Abinger included, and about 100 were boarders. The place was transformed. The press coverage of Abinger Hill was the best promotion Ashbury had had in years.

Harrison was made Headmaster of the Junior School, of which his boys made up the lion's share. He kept his own school's name and spirit alive. The *Ashburian* had a special section for the *Abinger Times*. There was no doubt about their identity: English voices and accents, and small-boy expressions and clothes – shorts, of course, but they soon got used to breeches for the winter until they grew into long trousers. To Ashbury boys, age for age, they were alarmingly advanced in their schooling.

A campaign began in January under Board member General Charles Maclaren and Nixie Newcombe. They asked people to put up $500 towards a boy's boarding fees, or take a boy into their home and pay $150 day fees, or subscribe to a $20,000 Trust Fund to help in their support. Contributions would be paid back from the English funds if and when the war was won. That veteran fund-raiser G.P. Woollcombe provided a list of prospects.

Montreal campaign committee member Judge Gregor Barclay, whose son Ian had graduated in 1939, was asked to canvass, among others, the Bronfman family. There was no reason to suppose they'd be other than sympathetic towards helping British children, but there'd never been a Bronfman at Ashbury College. As well, Judge Barclay was the wrong man to ask. During the previous war, following a stint in the trenches with the P.P.C.L.I., he had been with the Judge Advocate of the Canadian army involved in prosecuting Sam Bronfman for bootlegging to the troops! Added to that, the Barclay family "adopted" Abingerite Glin Bennet. When they had him for the holidays they found he was so homesick boarding that they moved him to their Montreal home and sent him to Selwyn House as a day boy. There he was a classmate of Edgar Bronfman's. Canada was a small country.

In any event most of the money was raised in Ottawa since Montreal as a centre of Ashbury interest had all but disappeared. By the end of 1941 the sterling account in London was receiving the equivalent of $500 per child per year from the Abinger Hill Council. Archdale had quoted that figure at the outset without anyone's agreement, though it was less than the Ashbury fee of $650. Abinger was actually collecting over $700 and withholding the balance. The school had been requisitioned by the army, but its supporters were determined to keep Abinger alive for a post-war restart by Harrison, keeping up the interest on their debentures, storing furniture, paying insurance, lawyers and accountants.

In the meantime, Mrs. Harrison and the two other ladies had set up the Abinger girls, including her daughter, in a makeshift school in Hotel des Pins in Montebello, which they rented from a friendly owner. They attracted some local children too, but by the middle of winter living conditions became unacceptable. The Ottawa Board of Trade stepped in, contracted with the Ottawa Ladies' College to take all the girls as boarders, paid the fees ($400 per year, plus $10 per month for incidentals) and set up a "blocked" account like Ashbury's in London to collect from parents. This worked quite well until the Ladies' College was closed in 1942 and their school building was taken over by the army. Most of the girls moved on for a while to a school in St. Sauveur des Monts, then to King's Hall, Compton. Glin Bennet's and the Crumps' sisters were sponsored at Elmwood for a time.

There were pangs of loneliness of course. The Bennets, for example, didn't see their mother for three years or their father, an army doctor, for five. Some had sad experiences, but for most of the English children the new country held untold wonders. Summer cottage lake life was a great adventure. Friendly sources turned up skates and skis and outdoor clothing. Hacking away on the hockey rink and getting better by the season, skiing in Rockcliffe Park with the dizzy plunge down the landing of the ski-jump to run out on the river ice below, sleigh ride parties, tobogganing – all were new delights. In soccer and cricket they were streets ahead.

As time went on the Abinger Hill boys integrated more and more into Ashbury and added a tremendous amount to the life of the school. By their last year their Lewin Chapman was Captain of the School and valedictorian after Barney Lawrence. James Harrison had developed a most interesting clientele for his school. Michael Arlen's father (of the same name) was a well-known novelist, as was Daniel Farson's father Negley. Andrew Murdoch's father was a leading concert pianist. He, sadly, died while Andrew was in Canada. Simon and Sebastian Rathbone were nephews of actor Basil Rathbone, famed for playing Sherlock Holmes. David Drumlanrig was the heir to the title Marquess of Queensberry. Peter and Martin Macintosh came from the toffee-making family. James, Charles and Frank McNabb, sons of The McNabb, head of their clan, formed a Scottish entente with the Buckingham Maclarens that was to last many years. And Hugh Noyes' father, Alfred Noyes, was already known to the legions of Ashbury boys who'd never forget the opening lines of his poem *The Highwayman*:

> *The wind was a torrent of darkness among the gusty trees,*
> *The moon was a ghostly galleon tossed upon cloudy seas . . . .*

Dan Farson and Michael Arlen both followed their fathers as writers. From their first Ashbury days they were on the magazine staff. Michael J. Arlen, among his extensive writings, became a regular contributor to the *New Yorker*. Each published a book in the early seventies that reflected their time at Ashbury. They changed the names of staff members, but it would be hard to equate "Keyhole Kay" in Farson's *Out of Step* with anyone other than the squint-eyed H.B. "Keyhole" MacKay, and his "Bolder" could be no one else but Humphrey Porritt.

> *. . . Mr Bolder was the most civilised master in the school and an alcoholic. One rebellious evening, all the masters found reason to be absent – except Mr Bolder who was past caring and was given the crucifying assignment of evening prayers. Much cruelty was done to the masters in the name of religion.*
> *Evening prayers were so confused that Mr Bolder made no attempt*

at keeping order. Boys walked and talked; Mr Huggins marched out muttering madly and some boy took his place and played jazz, badly, on the organ. There were outbursts of clapping; the Bible had vanished from the lectern, so after standing behind it patiently for a while, Mr Bolder walked down the aisle again and out of the chapel. It wasn't a walk so much as a roll, not because he was drunk but due to a limp from a club foot. One of the prefects stepped behind Mr Bolder and placed his hands on his shoulders, and another boy did the same to the prefect, and so on, until a line of several hundred boys rolled their serpentine way to Mr Bolder's room where he sank into a chair, shattered in every way, while boys stole the bottles from his cupboard and helped themselves to anything they fancied.

He left soon after this and someone heard that he had taken a 'cure'. Several months later I was waiting in the lobby of the big hotel in Ottawa when I saw him walk in quietly and go to a reading room where he turned over the pages of a magazine. He was hardly recognisable, immaculately shabby, sober to the point of transparency: a ghost of a man. He looked up suddenly, saw me, and limped out.

Sykes' was the only name Arlen, in his book *Exiles*, didn't change. This fine schoolmaster, who clearly understood boys so well, soon left to join the army in England, ended up in the tank corps and was badly wounded.

Some other English boys, outside the Abinger crowd, turned up. Michael d'Aeth, for example, had set off in the blacked-out train from London for Liverpool, alone with his little sister, clutching his precious new fly-rod. They saw a ship in their convoy torpedoed and go down like a stone, heard the terrifying sounds of night explosions. They joined their mother in Bermuda, then moved to Jamaica. Michael came to Ashbury foster-parented by Captain and Mrs. Roger Bidwell, whose son Tony was at Ashbury. Michael's naval officer father had been a shipmate of Captain Bidwell's early in the war and was killed in action at sea.

For Ashbury, it was a hand-to-mouth existence. Negotiation to get sterling released dragged on. The red tape unwound slowly in London but assurances that all would be well didn't pay Ashbury's bills. In April 1942 Newcombe wrote to the Immigration Branch in Ottawa saying that Ashbury had exhausted all its resources and couldn't pay its monthly trade accounts. There was $40,000 sitting in Ashbury's account in London; unless it was released, the school would close at the end of April and the Abinger boys would become a government charge. In two weeks a cabled advance of $24,500 arrived. It was an emergency transfusion. The British Treasury had ruled that $600 per year per child could be sent to Canada.

Dealing at such a distance was difficult and fraught with misunderstandings. Abinger's Council was determined to keep its school alive. Many English parents, now in the services on sharply reduced incomes, had trouble with fees. Ashbury understood all this but was caring for their boys at a loss and was on the verge of going under.

Shirley Woods, with his own business to run in difficult times, couldn't give the attention and leadership as Chairman that all this demanded. In December 1941, the same month the Japanese attacked Pearl Harbour and brought the United States into the war, he had resigned. Again, Newcombe became the not-so-willing horse and took over the Chair once more, as well as the host of problems he was handling already. From his own law office, which had to be run too, he carried the whole load of endless correspondence, the complex, often frustrating, dealing on finances with Abinger's Council and with Harrison. He was also the trustee, with General Maclaren, for the trust accounts and the real working hand on the small Executive Committee that now carried on the business of the school in the face of Archdale's shortcomings.

After a long wrangle, Abinger agreed to raise the originally understood fee of $500 to $600 a year. Ashbury absorbed interest on the long-overdue English accounts and some $4000 in extras, which parents would normally pay. It carried six Abinger boys whose parents could pay only token fees. It provided room and board in holiday periods, books in the early terms and sports trips, all at no charge.

As well, Ashbury was constantly begging help for the Abinger contingent. And Ottawa was generous. The members of the Dentists' Association, for example, contributed their services free of charge. Heney's Fuel waived interest payments on long-overdue accounts. Many people took boys on outings and for the holidays, and gave them clothes and sports equipment. When accounts were finally settled in late 1944, contributors to the initial $20,000 Abinger fund were offered repayment. Over half of it was waived.

The Abinger numbers slowly dropped. Six, by parents' choice, went to Putney School in Vermont which had a high reputation for special education problems. Some, ready for English public school, went home in 1943. All had gone by the summer of 1944. Fortunately, before then Canadian enrolment had solidly increased. The fall term of 1944 began without Abinger but with 123 boys.

The accounts were at last settled. Letters of thanks and good wishes were exchanged by the Ashbury Board and the Abinger Council. Over four difficult years many Canadian-English friendships had been formed. Letters flowed between families. While the Maclarens and Kennys in Buckingham looked after Charles, James and Frank McNabb during holidays, for example, Don Maclaren, in the army, was most hospitably received by the senior McNabbs in Scotland.

Abinger did in fact live on in a different property in Surrey under the name Ashfold School, headed by James Harrison. Richard Sykes came back to teach. Jonathan Harrison went on to Oxford. In his final year he stroked the University eight. In the classic annual race on the Thames that year between the two universities, the Cambridge boat was stroked by an Abinger-Ashbury schoolmate, Michael Marshall.

Ashbury nearly ruined itself harbouring the Abinger boys. But, paradoxically, if it hadn't been for Abinger arriving just when it did, there's little doubt that Ashbury wouldn't be here today and Rockcliffe would have 10 more acres of houses. The survival was due far more to a sense of patriotic duty and obligation to see Britain through than any loyalty to Ashbury College itself. The English boys brought to Ashbury a real sense of the scope and meaning of the war. As well, Harrison and Sykes brought a badly needed shot in the arm to a nigh-moribund school. On the other side of the coin, Ashbury saved Abinger. Without it Harrison's school would have broken up and been very hard put to have survived the war. This chance encounter, then, wrought a happy outcome for both schools from those years of tragedy and strife.

But Abinger Hill School left no memorial at Ashbury College, planted no tree, affixed no plaque in the Chapel. Certainly, with the shakiness of Archdale's regime and the continued presence and strength of James Harrison, there wasn't much to divert the boys' loyalty. Abinger, not Ashbury, was their school and their sense of loneliness so far from their families was bound to have coloured their feelings.

And neither, indeed, did Ashbury bestow any memento on Abinger, or its successor Ashfold, to mark their mutual life-saving. The only reminder was that Abingerites were all kept on the list of Ashbury old boys and continued to get those periodic appeals for funds. It is sad to reflect that nothing was left except fading memories to commemorate this tale of two schools in Canada during World War II.

Chapter 10

The War Years

The war years 1939-1945 showed that Ashbury old boys had the same built-in sense of service to King and country as had their fathers. Over 500 joined up for active service. Canadians on the "home front" – when the imminence of catastrophe really struck home with Dunkirk in the summer of 1940 – reacted with energy and spirit.

The country as a whole geared up to a tremendous effort, not just in producing armed forces but in mounting a gigantic industrial thrust. The war in fact ended the Depression. There were virtually no unemployed. Women joined the forces, releasing men for the front line. They took industrial jobs they had never dreamed of doing before.

People made do. There were shortages, but Ottawa stayed pretty comfortable compared to the places around the embattled world where so many Ashburians found themselves in the thick of it. Generally, though, the spirit was to get on with it. "There's a war on" was a good enough reason for accepting just about any inconven ience or upheaval. People rose to the occasion. The wheels of the country were turning again. But the years 1939-1945 marked a rough time in Ashbury's history.

The school was, as we have seen in the Abinger Hill story, hanging on the ropes by the end of the school year 1940. Archdale was the author of a good deal of misfortune. He was a lax administrator. His letters more often than not started with an apology for failing to take action sooner. It was Archdale who in December 1940 had quoted a fee of $500 per child per year to the Abinger Hill Council.

Finding staff – teaching and domestic – became a problem for all schools, of course. This hit Ashbury harder than it should have because Nicholas Archdale was a poor manager. He was unable to get on with those under him who seemingly didn't conform to his ideas. From the abrupt, ill-handled dismissal of Wiggy Whitfield in 1937, most people leaving Ashbury College did so in a cloud of acrimony. Rather than correction by a mature leader, it was too often confrontation. He was quarrelsome and abrasive too on picayune business matters. Newcombe, as a lawyer and as Chairman, was frequently up to his ears in sorting such things out.

In 1941 Archdale pressed Shirley Woods (they corresponded on a first-name basis; Newcombe and Archdale did not) for an increase in his $4000 salary. The cost of living was certainly soaring. His most repeated concern was that he had no margin for doing the entertaining he should. The amount was niggardly, but there wasn't enough money in the coffers – or conviction by this time – to increase it. He never did get more.

No doubt Mrs. Archdale contributed to the problem. She certainly had sailed into the domestic area with guns blazing when they first arrived. She was a far stronger character than her husband. Their marriage, sadly, failed during this time and – cause, effect, or both – Archdale's attentions were too often elsewhere than the Headmaster's office.

Alcoholism, like it or not, could affect an institution of learning just as it could any other kind. Ashbury around this time had a bit more than its share. Humphrey Porritt, the engaging, witty and at times inspired teacher of English, turned increasingly and obviously to drink. By 1941 it was standard practice, when Porritt was duty master, for the Captain of Boarders, Geoff Hughson, to check his room above the gym around 5:30 p.m. to see if he was up to taking charge in the dining hall and at evening chapel. More often than not he wasn't – as observed by Dan Farson and the whole school, except Archdale who was rarely there – and the senior boy did the job. At least it was good training in taking charge – as Geoff found when he joined the navy.

Porritt was finally dismissed in 1941. He took with him a nice letter of recommendation from the Headmaster not, of course, mentioning the real reason he'd been fired. Engaging man that he was, he cadged money around Ottawa, then Montreal, using Ashbury credentials and contacts. The last report on him came from old boy John Sharp's father, O.R. Sharp, at head office, Bank of Montreal. Porritt tried to touch John, just back from the war in North Africa and in hospital, for a loan. Then he found his way west and forged Air Vice-Marshal Croil's signature on cheques he passed at the Bank of Montreal in Vancouver. George and Tom Croil had been at Ashbury with him. He served some time and sank finally from sight.

The war of course meant a lot of staff changes. Brain stayed as anchor-man – fortunately, because without him the organization would probably have fallen apart. The Abinger boys, when they first arrived, thought that calling the Assistant Headmaster "Mr. Brain" was some odd Canadian custom. Harrison, an outstanding schoolmaster who could stand up to him and so had his respect, kept the juniors firmly under his charge. Thus, at the start, they came under A.D.B. only indirectly. Still, to them he was an ogre. It was their piping voices that dubbed him "Ashbury's Damn Bugger," shortened, in course of time, to the familiar "Buggy."

Lud Johnson, off to the army, was replaced in the chemistry lab by Rev. Wilhelm Shultze Tigges, a big hulking fellow with an array of European degrees. Swamp Waterfield, who was well liked, went back to England right at the outset. Before he left he was married in the Ashbury Chapel to Mary Malloch, sister of old boy George Malloch. Geoff Hughson and some of the other senior boys were ushers. Waterfield went into Intelligence, was captured and shot.

W.A.G. "Mucker" McLeish was a big strapping fellow who left his mark before he went off to the RCAF. There was bad blood between him and Joe Thomas, who was just as big and just as strapping, and Joe publicly challenged him to a boxing match. Duly staged, it was a ferocious set-to. McLeish taught physical training and had a good command of ring-craft. He could very likely have laid Joe out, but the match ended in a draw. Honour satisfied.

Strange characters appeared. Some, like Keyhole MacKay, ran a merciless gauntlet. Mr. Meizer was a fugitive from another school for some unknown but widely suspected reason. Tormented by the boys, he broke down in class, weeping "you know about me . . . ." Rev. T.C.B. Boon was a kindly, helpful man and a good teacher. E.D. Harrison (no relation to the Abinger Head) didn't last long. Called "Wings" because of his big ears, he lost what little control he had when a senior class ganged up on him and held his head under the cold tap.

"Captain" R.F. Travers came poshly garbed in the uniform of the Grenadier

Guards, gloves, swagger stick, accent, the lot. He somehow got two rooms instead of the regular one per master, and furnished them richly with his own effects. His sherry supply was filched in a well-executed operation by some Abingerites – the Crumps were in the know – and he loudly and vainly demanded expulsion for the unknown felons. He was universally seen as a fake, if a picturesque one, but he did go off and join some workaday unit of the Canadian army as a second lieutenant. Captain H. Dare, MC, on the other hand, was a genuine soldier from the previous war. He was missing some fingers and had some tales to tell.

David Polk arrived in the sweltering August of 1940. With New England frugality and natural lack of pretension, he lugged his heavy suitcases from the Union Station via the streetcar. He was a fun-loving man of adventurous bent, and when he'd graduated from Dartmouth he taught at Yardly Court, an English prep school. Casting further afield, he applied to Abinger Hill and Ashbury, among others. Ashbury won him and he arrived, remarkably enough, right on the heels of the Abinger influx.

Polk teaching with Harrison and, for a short while, Sykes made three first-class men in the Junior School. Teaching was Polky's lifework but wanderlust and war took him off to sea in 1942. He sailed in the US Merchant Service as ship's purser-cum-"doctor." Back he came to Ashbury in 1947 to dedicate a lifetime as the school's most universally beloved teacher.

Another find was A.B. Belcher. He had graduated from RMC at the end of the previous war but had a chronic heart problem and couldn't get into the forces. He had notable poise, charm and *savoir-faire*, a fine sense of humour and a certain air of faded, tweedy elegance. He was soon dubbed "Duke." He took over Porritt's hey-day role as the man who could make the English language leap to life. Duke came from Bobcaygeon and under his air of impoverished aristocracy lay a real woodsman and a capable guide. In the fall, one could often see his week-end's bag of ducks or partridge hanging outside his window readying for the pot. He had an inclination to the bottle. It didn't match Porritt's, but jovial evenings at the Claude Tavern down on Beechwood brought on jaded mornings, drawn visage and shaky hands. Withal, he had a fine flair for teaching the language and in spite of his eccentricities – in many ways because of them – he was dearly loved by those he taught and those who worked with him. He pitched into dramatics with a real flair and later took over the *Ashburian* too.

As Porritt had lost his grip, so the *Ashburian* had slid. Its quite respectable standard of reporting, prose and poetry had sagged. Right through the war the only artworks in it were poorly executed lino-cuts. Abingerite Peter Crump found no encouragement at Ashbury for his own interest in art, or music for that matter, which had been so well fostered in England.

There was talent on the *Ashburian* staff, though. Dan Farson and Michael Arlen worked on the Junior *Ashburian*, combined with the Abinger Hill magazine, under the Editor, future Prime Minister John N. Turner. Farson sparked a student newspaper called "Panorama." It started off as a daily news-sheet to keep people up on the war, and developed into a weekly with far more refreshing articles and comment than the staid *Ashburian*.

It wasn't easy running anything in wartime. But Archdale's incompetence was clear, at least to Nixie Newcombe who spent so much time of necessity nudging him and taking on a substantial share of running the business end of the school – for example, sorting out financial dealings with Abinger Hill. There was certainly a wartime shortage of good men but, whatever the reason, the Board came only halfway to grips with the problem.

In December 1941, at a Board meeting (not attended by Archdale), Shirley Woods resigned as Chairman. At the same meeting, Newcombe (not there either) was asked to become Chairman, backed with a small Executive Committee to carry on the business affairs of the school. Reluctantly he agreed to be acting Chairman for three months to get financial affairs in order.

The Executive Committee consisted of Newcombe, Harry Southam, Charles H. Maclaren and Norman Wilson, with G.P. Woollcombe as consultant and the Headmaster as Secretary. It met weekly at the school and approved all expenditures. Newcombe became the real working member of the committee, as he had been before he resigned the Chair in 1938. This committee was something of a War Cabinet and the Board as a whole agreed to accept short, telephoned notices of meetings to approve the Executive's actions. It's not clear who, other than Newcombe, attended. Archdale was officially the Secretary but, deliberately or by default, if any minutes were recorded none survive. The committee virtually took away all Archdale's authority over school administration. He'd abdicated day-to-day matters to Brain, so now he was nothing but an expensive figurehead.

Newcombe's patience with Archdale came to an end in an intriguing incident. Masters were in very short supply, and a German-Jewish wartime internee called Rosenberg had applied to teach at Ashbury. Internees were allowed to take jobs and Jewish Germans, though officially "enemy aliens," could hardly be counted as supporters of Adolf Hitler. Rosenberg was well qualified but had already been turned down by Upper Canada College.

A Mrs Osborne had discussed Rosenberg's case with the camp commandant and offered him lodgings outside the camp if he was employed by Ashbury. Archdale turned him down and was assailed in his office by Mrs Osborne for refusing to employ a Jew. Archdale told her the Executive Committee had turned the man down because he was German and parents might object. Then he went on to say in writing that "both in the US and Canada experience has shown that once a private school holds out as taking Jewish boys the tendency is for other people to withdraw their support." Ashbury, he said, had to look to its investment.

Archdale in fact hadn't discussed the matter ahead of time and Newcombe told him in no uncertain terms that he was to do nothing without approval of the committee and must maintain absolute silence on all matters to do with school management and affairs. Hardly a vote of confidence.

Anti-Semitism ran strongly in Canadian society then. Prime Minister Mackenzie King himself had set an ugly example before the war and it continued. In living memory most private clubs, mostly in unwritten rules, had excluded Jews, as had the majority of independent schools. A few Jewish boys attended Ashbury in G.P. Woollcombe's day and there was the odd one in the war years, mainly from foreign missions and Abinger Hill. But overall they were a rarity.

The issue wasn't in the open at Ashbury but it was there. In 1944 Archdale sought approval to accept Chris Nowakowski. His parents were Polish war refugees, and he felt they deserved some financial consideration. The Chairman advised him to check the Nowakowskis weren't Jews: "You and I may not have strong feelings on the subject but a lot of other people do and might be unwilling to send their boys." Archdale had checked already. They weren't.

Well before Chris finished his outstanding Ashbury career in 1955, there was, happily, no such reservation. Ottawa's Jewish community had grown steadily and strongly since 1892 when Jacob Mirsky became Rabbi at the city's first synagogue on Murray Street. (The largest donations towards its building, incidentally, came from J.R. Booth and Senator W.C. Edwards.) Rabbi Mirsky's great-grandsons, Stephan, Peter, Michael and Phillip, came to Ashbury in the late fifties.

With Archdale as Secretary-Treasurer of the Board as well as of the Executive, no full Board minutes are on record for 1942 or 1944. At the one recorded meeting in 1943 the main item was to turn over the vestige of the staff pension fund, started in 1926 by Senator Hardy, to the general revenue. A disenchanted Judge Gregor Barclay wrote in 1945 that he and other Montreal Governors had had no report of a meeting since 1939 and no word whatsoever from Ashbury since the fund drive ending in 1941. He resigned.

In 1942 the Ottawa Ladies' College, founded in 1869, closed when its buildings were taken over for the Canadian Women's Army Corps. Noting this, Harry Southam proposed a searching look at the question of private schools after the war. If there was, as he suspected, no clear future for them, perhaps now was the time to sell to the government.

Newcombe believed there was a future if properly qualified Canadians could be found. In the short term, he felt strongly that Ashbury was obliged to see the war through. Government support in getting funds out of England, Abinger Hill's need for a home and the many Ashbury boarders who had no homes to go to as their parents were away in the war – all this made it a duty to keep the place going.

Not all agreed. Shirley Woods got a real estate agent to open talks with the Defence Department. Captain Duncan MacTavish, a prominent Ottawa lawyer in the wartime navy's legal office, spoke to his father-in-law Harry Southam, who seemed to favour investigating a sale. The Superintendent of the Women's Royal Canadian Naval Service inspected the school and pronounced it would be ideal as a training school for Wrens. Newcombe got wind of it and he, Maclaren and Norman Wilson dug in. Ashbury was not in the market. It would only go if expropriated and that didn't happen. Another near-run thing.

Shirley Woods was an old boy, son of the second long-term Ashbury Chairman and a Chairman himself. He'd sent three boys to school and they were pretty active characters. John had, among other capers, managed to wire a thunder-flash to the ignition of Arthur Brain's car. It produced a thoroughly satisfying whistle and explosion, clouds of smoke, and fury in the heart of A.D.B.. In 1943 John's Ashbury career ended with a fracas that arose after he'd jabbed some tormentor in the rear end with the point of a compass. He was shot off briskly to TCS, thus laying the base for some kind of future record as the only Ashbury Chairman (the third of the Woods' line at that) to have been expelled from the school. Brother Guthrie went to TCS with him and, the following year, Shirley. Their father apparently wasn't all that enchanted with his old school.

By June 1943, with enrolment at 153, a teaching staff of 10 and funds coming through the Abinger Hill account, debt was under control and the financial prospects good. Soon the endorsers for bank credit were off the hook. But Newcombe had lost all confidence in Archdale and told his fellow committee members they couldn't work together and he, Newcombe, intended to resign.

The school, he said, wasn't doing its job. Feedback from parents was discouraging, as were results. Archdale wasn't interested in the boys or the old boys, only in a social set which had nothing to do with the school. He kept Newcombe in the dark on school operation, went his own way and balked at the Board's directions. There was a very high staff turn-over. New men couldn't get on with Archdale and nearly always left after some kind of dispute to go elsewhere and do well. Newcombe counted it somewhat bizarre that little Elizabeth Archdale was dressed in boys' clothes and attending Ashbury classes. The Chairman ("Acting" for three months only a full 18 months before) and Headmaster simply couldn't work together.

The answer from Harry Southam was: "Frankly, if you cannot be persuaded, notwithstanding the difficult, trying and well-nigh unbearable conditions under which you are serving the school so admirably, generously and patiently, to continue to lead the Board of Governors it is my view that we shall have to close the school." Norman Wilson said he wouldn't continue on the Board without Newcombe as Chairman. There was some difference in perception, however. Newcombe said to Gregor Barclay in 1945 that Harry Southam was the "real permanent head of the Board." His own task as acting Chairman had been just to stabilize the finances. Newcombe had his inconsistencies, but his talents and his time and his extraordinary loyalty to the school were used, perhaps unthinkingly but quite unmercifully, by the others. Nixie would always do it.

But no one would come to grips with the root problem – the Headmaster. Newcombe stayed. Incredibly Archdale, whom Newcombe had brought to Ashbury in 1936, did too. And the school, through all its travails, somehow managed to survive. In 1944 Newcombe could report the bank debt cleared and endorsers released. The mortgage with North American Life was up-to-date. Those who had supported Abinger Hill were reimbursed or wrote their expenses off as donations. On top of that, the 1944 Ontario matriculation results were startling.

Charles Eliot, still a student – and a brilliant one, headed for a distinguished academic career – worked out a detailed comparison of matric honours at eight schools for Arthur Brain. Eliot's precise calculations showed Ashbury on top, then TCS and Elmwood, and some way behind the five leading Ottawa high schools. There was a strong element of Abinger boys writing that year of course, but some things were going right.

Games against traditional rivals were curtailed quite a lot because of wartime travel restrictions, but more local matches made up for it. First teams in soccer and cricket won more games than they lost. In 1943-44 both had clean sweeps. The English boys certainly had a good deal to do with that, but so did Archdale's interest. Soccer, in fact, had had winning seasons right from 1937, when he had given it a boost. On the other side of the coin, hockey tapered off in numbers of games and in success. Football teams, in each war year, steadily lost more than they won.

Archdale had pretty well abdicated other than for show. He couldn't move on the business or administrative level without the Executive approving. Arthur Brain, who met him every morning in his office to go through the business of the day, was the backbone of the place and firmly in charge of the school's operation.

Abinger had gone by that summer of 1944, and the fall term opened with 127 boys. The Archdales' divorce was proceeding. Whether it was the social impropriety of such an event or simply exhaustion of ill-placed indulgence isn't clear, but in September it was mutually agreed that Archdale would leave in the spring. He and the Board said nice things about each other. Civility at all costs. Arthur Brain took over in all but name for the balance of the school year. As Newcombe held things together at the business level, so Brain – strong-willed and demanding as he was – kept the operating end going. He wasn't infallible of course and discipline and teaching standards, except for a few standouts, had pretty well crumbled away. The strong contingent of English boys had kept the standard up in spite of the teaching.

Tony Price's classmates, who weren't the best of students, were scared stiff of the mathematics exam on which they might or might not be recommended for their junior matriculation. Rising to the challenge, Price conned Brain out of his key chain and the paper was duly purloined. Then Michael Shenstone was called in from the Upper Sixth. Shenstone, who was about to win the Governor General's Medal, was the absolute whizz in everything and it was no trick for him to work the paper through. He pointed out, though, that if everyone in that lot did well the jig would be up. So he dashed off a dozen individually graded papers. He slotted Peter Richardson for 60 percent; Scott Price and Dim Sablin were slated for the low 50s. And someone, Shenstone insisted, had to fail. Grossly unfair it seems to the one who'd beaten Buggy Brain, but Tony Price was elected. He was coming back next year and he'd have another shot. Schoolboy honour takes some strange turns.

Arthur Brain, quite understandably, looked upon himself as Archdale's heir. He had worked tirelessly, endlessly and with total loyalty. He had taken over by default and strong personality just about everything Archdale should have been doing. But he wasn't the man for the job and Nixie Newcombe had to tell him. His value as a teacher was appreciated and he was most effective, even indispensable, as a second-in-command. But he was far too abrupt, too abrasive, with parents particularly. He simply had the wrong personality for a Headmaster. So Brain was passed over and that was the turning point of his life.

Over all these years, beyond the day-by-day routine of school affairs, loomed the war. Abinger Hill had brought it right to hand. Then the names of old boys filtered in with word of their exploits, decorations, deaths. Names of the fallen were read out in Chapel again after little more than 20 years. Each Closing Day another graduating class left and most, eager to go, joined up.

The first to die was Flying Officer William Tudhope who'd won the DFC on an earlier operation. Next was Flying Officer Frederick Lambart. Both were with the RAF. In the fall of 1940 Commander Charlie Beard commanded HMCS *Prince Robert* in the capture of a German cargo ship. In the spring his son, Midshipman Norman Beard, an old boy, was killed when HMS *Hood* was blown sky-high by the German battleship *Bismarck*.

In the spring of 1941 the list of those killed included Flying Officer Michael MacBrien, Second Lieutenant A.W. MacDonald, Pilot Officer J.E. Wood, Pilot Officer Lionel Emens, Flying Officer Angus Alexander and Air Gunner Ian MacDonald. By war's end over 500 had gone off to fight. Thirty-two were killed. Lt. Col. John Rowley, commanding the Cameron Highlanders, was mentioned in dispatches. The award of a DSO came through after he'd been killed in a later action. Captain Jim Symington was killed on the very last day of the fighting in Europe.

Major-General Guy Simonds, Ashbury, RMC, every inch the professional soldier, commanded the 1st Canadian Division in Sicily and won the DSO. He was promoted Lieutenant-General and went on to command the 2nd Canadian Corps in Northwest Europe, then the whole First Canadian Army through the crucial battles along the Scheldt. He was Canada's outstanding field commander of the war and capped a brilliant career as Chief of the General Staff from 1951 to 1955.

During Simonds' drive north from Normandy, Lt. Col. Roger Rowley commanded the battalion spearheading the assault on Boulogne. It was massively fortified. He and the tank commander, Major Bill Joyce of the Fort Garry Horse, could see that a lethal nest of anti-tank guns stood in the way. That night Lieutenant Peter Smellie of the Cameron Highlanders, who'd been at Ashbury with Rowley, let his platoon over open ground right beneath the guns. At first light he blasted them out with grenades. Rowley's infantry and Joyce's tanks charged through. Boulogne fell. All three were decorated, mainly for that action. Rowley and Joyce won the DSO, Smellie the MC. They were to meet again when W.A. Joyce became Headmaster of Ashbury College in 1966.

Meantime, John Fauquier had been flying with the Pathfinders and the Dambusters. He'd been a bush-pilot, jumped in quickly when the war started and rose to be Air Commodore and the most decorated flyer in the RCAF. Rear Admiral H.E. Rastus Reid commanded the naval forces based in Newfoundland, then became Vice-Chief of Naval Staff. Out at sea, Fred Sherwood, the first Naval Reserve officer to command a Royal Navy submarine, was attacking Japanese shipping. Bob Hyndman flew fighters, then worked for a time as a war artist. Another fine Ashbury artist recording the war was Eric Riordan.

Old Ashburians responded as instantly and as bravely as the earlier generation had. But unlike the earlier war when G.P. Woollcombe had hand-written reams of letters to his boys, they didn't hear much from their old school.

Nicholas Archdale bowed out in June 1945 and the usual pleasantries were dutifully exchanged at the Closing. In his farewell speech Archdale made the point that Canadian schools shouldn't try to be imitations of English ones but should be their own distinctive selves. Perhaps that was the kind of thinking that had attracted Newcombe back in 1936. They were wise words, but the man who said them hadn't had the fibre for the job. And it had taken nine years for the Board to turf him out.

Dr. Grove, head of the Chilean diplomatic mission in Ottawa, had found Archdale a job as headmaster of the MacKay School for English-speaking boys in Valparaiso. Three Grove boys, Eduardo, Jorge and Patricio, were at Ashbury. It's unlikely that Dr. Grove got much thanks from the MacKay School. Archdale was at a low ebb there, very much alone, his children back in England with his ex-wife. He didn't last. He made his way back to Canada and a series of teaching jobs in smaller communities.

He shied away from Ottawa, avoiding those he had known in better days. Arthur Brain kept him up on school affairs with occasional mailings. He was teaching in Chilliwack Senior High School in December 1955 when he died of a heart attack at a meeting of the local Little Theatre, aged 53. He had made a good place for himself in the community, restored his grip on himself and never, as had Porritt, presumed on his old Ashbury connections.

It would have been far better for both Nicholas Archdale and Ashbury College had they never met. The plaque placed by the Board to his memory in the Chapel marks a melancholy time in the life of a Headmaster and his school.

CHAPTER **11**

C.L. OGDEN GLASS

Nicholas Archdale wrote his resignation letter to the Chairman on September 1, 1944. It was formally accepted by the Board in January, 1945. Again, a one-man selection committee of Nixie Newcombe handled the matter, but he had already made very clear that this time there was no looking to England. The Board's preference was specifically for men educated in Canadian private schools and universities and who had been in one of the services during the war.

The word got around other schools via the Headmasters' Association and drew responses from well-qualified men at Bishop's, Upper Canada, Lower Canada, St. Andrew's and King's. Lieutenant Ogden Glass, RCNVR, serving at sea in the frigate HMCS *Thetford Mines* as First Lieutenant., heard about the possible opening in late fall 1944. Ashbury old boy Lieutenant-Commander John Roberts Allan, RCNVR, happened to be the Commanding Officer of *Thetford Mines* and got the word from Barclay Robinson, President of the Ashbury Old Boys Association, who was with the navy in Halifax. Allan and Robinson plus Jim Oppe, another old boy wartime naval officer who knew Glass well and admired his qualities, all pushed his case.

Oggie Glass was a Montrealer, a graduate of BCS and Bishop's University, a Rhodes Scholar with an MA from Oxford, and he had taught for two years at BCS. He was an outstanding scholar and first-rate athlete and debater. As a naval officer he made a strong mark as an instructor and at sea. As applications were arriving on Newcombe's desk in Ottawa, *Thetford Mines*, with two other Canadian ships, was sinking a German U-boat near England, and John Roberts Allan was winning the Distinguished Service Cross.

Glass didn't mention the action in his formal application for the Headmastership of Ashbury College, written just four days later. Of all the principal applicants he was the youngest at 32, with the shortest experience as a schoolmaster. But he was by a long shot the most appealing and the most promising. There was still a war to fight against Japan, but the forces were being reduced and only those who volunteered to stay on were being sent to the Pacific. A letter from the Chairman to Douglas Abbott, Minister for Naval Services, and his release was quickly approved. He was aboard a returning troopship on Victory in Europe Day, May 8, 1945, and in Ottawa as the fourth incumbent and first Canadian Headmaster of Ashbury College at the end of the month.

Archdale had left not a word for his successor. When Glass arrived at the school with Newcombe, Arthur Brain, who was in charge, said he'd get prefect Ted Pilgrim to show him around while he, Brain, had a talk with the Chairman! If he thought he could put the new boy Headmaster in his place and stay in charge as he had with Archdale, he was mistaken.

Glass had the traditional independent school approach – structured and disciplined, with a hierarchy of prefects – and in the Canadian setting. He was a first-rate role model, the image of his record – independent school, athlete, Rhodes Scholar, wartime officer – and young with personality and presence. And his wife Janet was charming, capable and most attractive. They were both immediately accepted by the boys. His nickname instantly was "Clog" – it pays to have a set of initials that make an inoffensive acronym.

Glass believed strongly in the merits of the private boarding school education, the fact that a boy was exposed to the school's influence around the clock. His first priority was high academic standards and that meant building a strong teaching staff. He believed in compulsory games though one needn't excel. He believed in Christianity. If the library was the mind of the school, the Chapel was its soul. He wanted the school to have a Canadian identity. Next, he believed it important to know all the boys personally and earn their trust. He wanted a strong disciplinary system based on firmness and that trust. He believed in corporal punishment, sparingly applied. He found it was out of control and used indiscriminately, especially by Arthur Brain.

Despite Newcombe's straight talk, there's no doubt Brain felt that he should have been Headmaster himself. He had become erratic and irascible, often in the extreme, and he and Glass were bound to meet head on. One morning in the dining hall he bellowed that when he said grace everyone bowed their heads – even the Catholics. This outraged the boys' sense of fair play and John Smith, Captain of the School, complained to the Head.

Small things built up. Every morning before breakfast, rain or shine, the whole school mustered at the front door to run out the driveway, along Mariposa, and back in, completing the circle. This little exercise to get the blood stirring had been going on as long as anyone could remember and was supervised by the duty prefect. On one particular morning Brain appeared and loudly and publicly berated Smith and a fellow prefect for not running themselves. Smith went to Glass to say that he and all the prefects were walking out to protest Brain's contemptuous treatment.

They did walk out, and they were duly disciplined. As this capped a whole series of complaints and problems, Glass felt Brain must leave. Newcombe agreed, but Brain had nowhere to go. There was no pension plan and nothing in the coffers to offer a reasonable settlement for 10 years of extraordinary service. The decision was to keep him on probation with his authority to wield the cane withdrawn.

The new Head's first impressions had been bleak. The plant had run down to a dangerous degree, in part because of the war, and so badly he was ashamed to show parents around. The staff he found shabby, though Duke Belcher, shabbiness personified, was very good at his job. Glass believed in a strongly structured school and a traditional one – gowns on the staff, for example, threadbare though they might be. He had the naval sense of good order as well as his experience at Bishop's behind him, and he took a firm hold where it was badly needed.

He felt he had to run a tight ship and he did. But the financial situation was still very shaky. Essential building repair had to be financed by a $6000 overdraft. The $60,000 mortgage had just been renewed with the two Southams and Norman Wilson as guarantors (Dr. Leggett had resigned from the Board) and interest had to be paid. Glass's first budget in January 1946 projected a loss of $4500.

The struggle to keep Ashbury College afloat, get it shipshape and on a new and steady course took its toll. The new Headmaster missed his first Closing because he was in hospital with a serious attack of stomach ulcers. They no doubt had started at sea. Glass had been seasick from his first experience in a little corvette, and as First Lieutenant of *Thetford Mines* he carried heavy responsibility; altogether it was an effective recipe for ulcers. Fortunately, as he was a veteran the two months' hospital bills were paid. The school had no provision for sick leave with pay nor, in those pre-medicare days, any funds for hospital bills.

In that first year Glass had worked with the eight other Ontario members of the Canadian Headmasters Association on a brief to the province's Royal Commission on Education. All the schools – Appleby, Hillfield, Lakefield, Pickering, Ridley, St. Andrew's, Trinity and Upper Canada – were Protestant and for boys only; all, except Hillfield, took boarders. They pointed out first that they had all started because various groups, at one time or another, wanted more for their children than the public system provided.

With slight variations each wanted religious instruction and regular worship, physical training and participation in games, elementary military training through cadet corps, additional studies like music, art and shopwork, study of "foreign languages" (presumably including French) starting before high school, public speaking, debating and dramatics, small classes (the average ratio of masters to boys was 1:12.4) and the close individual contacts between boys and staff made possible when they lived in their own community. They expected their teaching staff to have wide experience as well as learning, and their Headmasters weren't restricted in selecting them. All the schools stressed development of spiritual dimensions, character and leadership. Their objectives had survived the years.

Independence had given them the flexibility to experiment and they had introduced and developed in Canada a number of innovations like outdoor education, counselling, intelligence testing, arts and crafts, music and drama. The case was made for the value of independence and for the role of the independent schools in the overall educational system.

Government interference wasn't much of a concern at the time. The Commission had been set up by Tory Premier George Drew, whose son Edward came to Ashbury in 1952 when Mr Drew became the federal Conservative leader. Neither was there any help. But the brief was something of a reaffirmation of values and faith, a statement of purpose for the independent school in a new age. Glass ran it in the *Ashburian in toto* as salutary reading for those who questioned the school's relevance and as a pitch for mustering badly needed support.

The need for money to improve the plant was very clear. War, which had had such a profound effect on yet another generation of Canadians, gave the drive once more. Thirty-two old boys and masters had given their lives out of over 500 who had served. The proportion was thankfully half the dreadful rate of the earlier war and reflected Canada's overall experience. But Ashbury could once again be very proud of its sons' contribution to their country.

Barclay Robinson, President of the Montreal Old Boys Association, was on the Executive Committee of the Board from 1946. He spurred an Old Boys Association Memorial Campaign. Quite apart from the campaign, the Symington family of Montreal had already made a handsome gift to the school, having the dining hall extended and panelled in memory of Captain James Symington, who had been killed on May 6, 1945, the last day of the fighting in Europe. National Revenue gave a ruling that for the first time made donations to the school income tax-deductible.

But there was something missing. G.P. Woollcombe had written stacks of letters to "his boys" during World War I. He'd seen that they all got the *Ashburian* free, and he'd had a tasteful booklet printed afterwards honouring their war service. Archdale had written no letters. Old boys at war had heard little from their old school except rumours that it was in poor shape. Afterwards, unlike most other schools, no "old boys at war" publication was produced. Most, who were catching up with university or finding jobs, had little money to spare. The campaign never got off the ground.

Glass did a remarkable job turning the school around. By May 1948 he could report full enrolment (174 boys, 101 of them boarders) and improvements in teaching staff, discipline and academic success. Results had steadily improved. From 1941 to 1945, only 50 percent of the senior matriculation papers written were passed in spite of the good showing in 1944. In 1947 the pass rate was up to 80 percent.

With fees raised to $850 for senior boarders, Glass projected a surplus. The Board's vote of confidence was a salary increase to $5000. While he was increasingly happy with the tone of the school and what was being achieved, boarding and sports facilities were still badly wanting and the state of the plant was downright poor – the worst, in fact, he had ever seen in a private school.

In June 1948 Charles Gale, President of the Ottawa Old Boys Association, announced the first general campaign in Ashbury's history. It aimed to raise $150,000 – $100,000 for a Memorial Wing and $50,000 for an endowment fund. Architects' sketches printed in the *Citizen* showed a splendid new wing with a curved facade behind the Chapel, facing Glenwood. It was to house 50 more boarders and six classrooms.

The next year Gale, wartime navy veteran and now a chartered accountant, became the auditor and began regular systematic examinations of the school's financial state. He noted there was no provision in the budget for regular repair and depreciation, let alone new building. There never had been. There was no reserve. All the money for the new wing would have to be donated or borrowed.

Glass wasn't quite on the same track. He saw that day boys' fees weren't carrying their share of the load, and he believed firmly in the merits of the country boarding school à la BCS versus the city day school like LCC. With some 70 day boys to 100 boarders, Ashbury was neither fish nor fowl. The Rockcliffe location provided the temptations of Hull, its fleshpots reported in lurid detail by imaginative day boys on Monday mornings. Rockcliffe land had leaped in value. The answer, he felt quite strongly, was to sell the property and move.

In 1949 he found an ideal piece of land some 30 miles down the Ottawa River. His idea was to concentrate on boarders and bus the day boys out. Newcombe, still Chairman, was sceptical. He fussed over lack of water mains. Really he remembered the reaction of Ottawans when Ashbury was nearly turned into an all-boarding school in 1914. The possible move and the opposing idea of two new staff houses were considered by the Board, but the financial situation got worse rather than better.

Glass had, though, done a very sound job strengthening the staff. Early on he'd demoted Brain from Senior Master and Housemaster, in charge of everything, to

Assistant Headmaster, which made him answerable to the Head. Of the old hands he'd made Belcher the Senior School Housemaster and thus the one most directly involved with the boys. In his delightful memoir *Wordstruck*, Robin MacNeil gives a vivid picture of Belcher as he appeared to them:

> *In slighting the men who taught us English, I do some injustice to one man, A.B. Belcher, whose very diffidence had charisma. He appeared each morning, haggard and drawn (we guessed from drink), a strand of uncombable hair falling over his watery eyes, shaky long fingers stained with nicotine, like the lip under his thin mustache, his old tweed jacket buttoned an inch too tight. He seemed always on the borderline of not having been able to get there at all that morning. His handsome but ravaged face wore many sorrows, yet, through all the seediness, he conveyed refinement, even hauteur. For that reason he was nicknamed the "Duke."*
>
> *I felt some complicity with him and embarrassed for him on his ghastlier mornings, when his voice rasped and his fingers twitched. I assumed that some private agony had blighted his life and he was soldiering on with dignity, like a character in a Terence Rattigan play. I had reason to be tolerant: for three years he gave me progressively better parts in the school play, which he always directed. Then I saw the evening side of Belcher – freshly shaved, hair combed, a silk handkerchief in his breast pocket, handsome in a well-used way, and stimulated to be in female company. The plays were produced jointly with our sister school, Elmwood, a few blocks away, and rehearsals were conducted there. The presence of an Elmwood mistress and the older girls, who were in fact young women, brought out much charm and gallantry. I felt conscious of a rival for female interest.*
>
> *In the mornings he was again a grumpy, laconic man, looking at us from deep eye pockets; his cigarette reluctantly snuffed out in the last second before class began. Yet, almost perversely, he communicated discrimination and sensibility. You understood what he admired and that, if he did, it must be admirable. Between the sarcasms and the ironies, occasional smiles, the rare warm reading of a line or two, an aesthetic sense leaked through. If you are looking for enthusiasm, you'll find it. Hungry for encouragement, you will squeeze it out of a stone.*

Robin MacNeil (his actual first name was Robert) went on via stage and radio to become American television's most respected commentator on public affairs. Duke Belcher's unique projection of English, his stage directing in Noel Coward's "Hay Fever" and all the annual plays, and his own particular individualism and character were among the things of value that MacNeil took away from Ashbury College in those late-forties days. A great deal of Duke Belcher's unique, eccentric self went off into the future with every boy he taught.

Miss Irene Woodburn, an outstanding musician and music teacher, came in 1945. Mrs Elsie Hunter, who had taught so well in the Junior School since 1939, stayed on. And good men were back from the war. The Junior School Housemaster from 1946 was Lt. Col. E.G. Brine, a very capable ex-British army engineer. David Polk rejoined in 1947 to stay. In the Senior School, J. Allan Powell had come with Glass. He was an old boy from Ottawa, a Toronto and Cambridge graduate, a wartime Fleet Air Arm pilot, an erudite English teacher and a totally dedicated cricketer. And he was known as "Curly" because of his bald head.

Money was short. Salaries were low in a racing economy. As one solution, Glass brought graduates back each fall as assistants to fill some gaps before they went on to university. Ted Pilgrim, who later became Headmaster of Ridley, and John Hooper filled that role for bed and board and token pay. A long-termer who came in Glass's first year and who was a stalwart until 1966 was Leonard Sibley. Major Hugh Woods came in 1946 to take physical training and cadets. He was replaced by Captain G.W. Higgs for a while and came back in 1950. Gymnastics didn't reach its former glory, but these men did first-rate work with the cadet corps. In 1946 and 1947 it won the Col. L.P. Sherwood Cup for the best in the Ottawa district. The corps on parade included 40 juniors smartly turned out in blazers, school caps and white shorts. The inspecting officer in 1946 was an old boy – Vice-Admiral H.E. Rastus Reid, Chief of the Naval Staff.

Donald Macdonald, who'd come to Ashbury in 1941 as a day boy, left in 1948 having spent a fair bit of time in the ranks of the cadet corps. It was his only exposure to military affairs in fact until he became Minister of National Defence in 1970. To scotch one bit of Ashbury folklore, Macdonald's nickname "Thumper" – after Walt Disney's cheerful and likable rabbit with the huge feet – got pinned on him later by his fraternity brothers at the University of Toronto.

Glass put a lot of emphasis on sports and coached first team football himself. The teams got progressively stronger. In his last year, the fall of 1949, Bob Darby was Captain and the team took the Ashbury Old Boys' Cup with two wins against Bishop's. In the season they won five, drew two and lost one.

The school hadn't competed in skiing since 1938. Tony Price, a first-rate skier, worked hard to get it going again as a recognized sport. With encouragement from the Head, he got 60 boys signed up for the winter of 1947. The team had limited success and did better the next year, captained by Scott Price. They had some backing in the meet against LCC and Bishop's from Tony Price, who by then was Captain of the Bishop's University ski team. Then in 1949 Gillies Ross (Captain), Scott Price, Larry Wood, Evan Gill and Bob Bryce took the three-way meet in slalom, downhill and cross-country from Bishop's and LCC. The next year the same team, less Ross, did it again. Skiing at Ashbury was back on the map. Hockey was to take a little longer. In 1947 the school re-entered the Ottawa Senior Interscholastic League away over its head and began working from the bottom up.

There was time in spring for half a dozen cricket matches and the team made respectable showings. The best bowler in 1949 was Robin MacNeil. The pinnacle of his cricket career wasn't in taking most of the wickets against Bishop's, which he regularly did. It happened, as he recounts in *Wordstruck*, in the annual match against the staff. Arthur Brain was the first man in.

> *Our captain was a thin, funny French Nicaraguan named Henrique Dreyfus. As I walked back to begin my runup to bowl the first ball, Dreyfus*

> *whispered, "A dollar if you bowl him out first ball!" I laughed and turned.*
> *Brain was a very competent batsman and we all expected him to be in there*
> *for hours, knocking up a respectable thirty or forty runs before lunch. Brain*
> *expected it too.*
>
> *He despatched my first few balls smartly, earning three runs. I gave*
> *the next ball no particular thought. The invisible hand guided it to a perfect*
> *length, exactly between his two outside stumps, with a slight spin that made*
> *it break inwards. He put his front leg out in the proper fashion, made the*
> *conventional blocking stroke, and hit the ball smartly – straight into my*
> *hands. The umpire shouted "Out" and he was out – 'caught and bowled',*
> *in the cricket expression: both by me. He was totally astonished. So was*
> *I. He straightened up, muttered "Extraordinarily good ball," and walked*
> *off the field – the very long walk back – humiliated. My teammates confined*
> *their jubilation behind the traditional polite clapping, and Dreyfus said,*
> *"Oh, tough luck, sir." But the air was electric with joy. The bastard who*
> *terrorized us all was vanquished.*
>
> *I had a blissful moment and then, in the long wait for another batsman,*
> *felt some regret for the man whose moment of glory had been snuffed out.*
> *Suddenly I knew him: not the monster I believed, but a competent man, not*
> *more, hiding his inadequacies by making himself haughty and feared. Life*
> *has never dealt me as pure a moment since. I took six more wickets in that*
> *match. Is there life after high school? I must have doubted it that day.*

Most memories tend to distort with time. But MacNeil's account stands up precisely to the record in the *Ashburian*. The magazine had doubled in size in three years and part of that was accounted for by including, as of old, the detailed cricket score-sheets. To enjoy the game was to love it with a passion.

"Snake" Dreyfus was team captain and leading batsman that year. He had come from Guatemala in 1944 speaking French and Spanish and practically no English, and he had become Captain of the School. In his valedictory in 1949 he remembered the warmth and friendship that had greeted a frightened young stranger in this strange northern land when he'd first arrived.

In 1950 G.P. Woollcombe appealed again for an increase in his pension. He was turned down – again – because the school couldn't afford it. Back in 1929 the Board had recorded that he would get $3000 as an annual pension, with Mrs. Woollcombe to receive $1000 if he predeceased her. Payment began when G.P. retired in 1933 but it was halved to $1500 in 1935. During his years in England he had a small church living, and after he came back to Canada via his adventures with U-boats and the sea in 1939, he was a Sunday assistant at All Saints Church near his home in Sandy Hill.

He raised the question of a modest increase by letter to the Chairman a number of times. Each time the answer was the same: the school couldn't afford it. In 1946 G.P. had said he "would be exceedingly grateful" for an increase of $500 a year, and he added: "as I am now entering my 80th year the school will not be burdened with me very much longer." Later that year he wrote that he had had to hire a practical nurse to take care of his invalid wife. Still no increase. Then his doctor told him, aged 80, that he should take things more easily and leave his church work. Another appeal for an increment whenever he finally stopped at All Saints brought an undertaking. In January 1947, when declining health finally forced him to end his part-time work in the church, his Ashbury pension went up to $2000 a year.

In his final appeal – his 1950 request for a modest increase – he said that the remaining years that "Ashbury will suffer in my behalf will be necessarily very few." His request was realized a full year later. Bare months after that, on July 2, 1951, G.P. Woollcombe died. His memorial is the large stained-glass window in the centre of the north side of the Chapel. Its dedication says:

> To the Glory of God and in loving memory of
> Canon G.P. Woollcombe M.A., L.L.D., 1867-1951.
> Founder and Headmaster of Ashbury College 1891-1933.
> Honour, Courage, Grace

Those three words, the English rendering of Ashbury's motto, summed up a lifetime of human service, most profoundly dedicated to "his boys." The three main panels illustrate his lifelong work as Teacher, Counsellor and Preacher. After a determined campaign by Headmaster Ronald Perry, the window was finally installed and dedicated in 1961. That the school's founder, driving force and guiding spirit for 42 years had been let down on an undertaking by the Board, then literally had to beg for years for a sum that could have been covered by a tiny increase in fees and further that it took 10 years to establish a memorial casts a dark shadow on Ashbury's story.

Nixie Newcombe hadn't lived to see it. He had died instantly in March 1949 when his car hit a streetcar on Sussex Drive. He had worked on the Old Boys Association from its earliest days. From 1919 he served 30 years on the Board. He was Chairman from 1934 to 1938, then again from 1941 until his death. For his last 15 years, whether in the Chair or out, he was the lone core of the working Board. He contributed untold hours and endless professional application entirely on his own account.

Newcombe's decisions and actions weren't always right. An all-important duty of an independent school Board is to choose the Headmaster. In 1936 a flimsy process left it effectively to Newcombe to pick the new man. His choice of Archdale proved disastrous and he suffered him too long. After he had convinced himself of the man's incompetence, he was somehow unable to muster the support to dismiss him.

But Newcombe was the one who doggedly kept things going, who dug in twice against proposals to pack the school up during the war. Ogden Glass's name got in the ring through the haphazard fortunes of war, but it was Newcombe who pulled the threads together and Glass was an outstanding choice.

Others on the Board attended meetings, though by no means faithfully. Others provided money in most unpromising circumstances. They often came up with a helping hand or the clout needed to turn a situation. But only Newcombe was the willing horse. In the Woollcombe days, virtually everything was done by the Headmaster. But when the going got rough, with the Woollcombe leadership gone, with Ashbury College an embarrassment and a burden, those who had the real power let the workaholic – and sometimes erratic – Nixie Newcombe do it all.

When Newcombe died, Harry Southam, who had been Vice-Chairman, became acting Chairman briefly until Duncan MacTavish was elected. MacTavish was a prominent and highly regarded Ottawa lawyer, neither an old boy nor previously a member of the Board. He was a wise, experienced individual and he was, as we noted at the time when Ashbury nearly became a training school for navy Wrens, Harry Southam's son-in-law.

Duncan MacTavish gave Oggie Glass unstinting time and the kind of support and sage advice that a good Headmaster, who had his own administration under control, needed from time to time from his Chairman. But their relationship was short. In early 1950, Crawford Grier, long the Headmaster of Bishop's College School, suddenly stepped down. Bishop's first and most obvious choice was Oggie Glass, the old boy ex-master who had brought new life to Ashbury College. Grier in fact had recommended Glass most highly to Ashbury in 1945.

Quite naturally Glass was strongly drawn. Bishop's, the school and the university, were what he called the "heartland of my youth." It would have been a self-inflicted wound to turn the offer down. The prospects at Ashbury were bleak. Enrolment had slipped to 152. The bank overdraft had crept up to $17,000. In a year and a half the Memorial and Endowment Fund had raised only $40,000. Members of the Board agreed to campaign themselves for another $50,000. Clearly, though, it would be some time before Glass could expect any improvement in the general dilapidation – the very reason that Ashbury wasn't competing successfully.

The Canadian economy, transformed by the war, was moving strongly. Montreal and Toronto old money had grown and supported schools like Bishop's, Ridley and TCS. But Ashbury was still in tough times. Montreal House and Dominion House, the symbols of the twenties and of the enduring loyalty of boarding boys, were no more. The base that G.P. Woollcombe had built so strongly had been badly shaken by the crash of 1929. The Wright and Archdale years had eroded it almost completely. Glass, a Montrealer himself, had done his best to rebuild it. He had set up a Selwyn House bursary to reopen that source. He had also begun to exploit the school's multi-national potential and its unique location in the capital. He went on the campaign trail himself, but dynamic, personable and thoroughly competent though he was, he found Ashbury a very hard sell.

The Ottawa lumber baron fortunes that had built and sustained George Woollcombe's school had long since dispersed, and the industries those giants had founded were now in the hands of strangers in head offices in other cities. Government, with its ever-expanding bureaucracy, was now Ottawa's biggest industry. But most of its senior members came from elsewhere in Canada. Since the days of Sir Sandford Fleming, the civil service had never been a fertile field for fund-raising by such as Ashbury College. And Ottawa was building new institutions.

In the huge post-war demand for university places, little Carleton College burst into a full-blown university and that seemed a far more relevant place for Ottawa philanthropists to leave their mark. Among other substantial donations, when it moved to its fine site between the Rideau River and the Canal in 1959, over a quarter of the land, 37 acres, had been donated by Harry Southam, Norman Wilson and Cameron Edwards.

Ashbury needed another Headmaster of sterling qualities and the Board struck a selection committee. Glass was quite taken aback when Arthur Brain asked him for a recommendation. He declined. Further, he advised his successor, Ronald Perry, to get rid of him. It says something for the place that Brain holds in the annals of Ashbury College that this is the only piece of turnover advice that both these Headmasters can recall to this day.

CHAPTER **12**

RONALD PERRY

In appointing Ronald Perry as the new Headmaster in 1950, the Board was making a distinct departure from the traditional thrust and direction of Ashbury College. Born in 1902, Perry's early years were on the traditional track. His father was an Anglican clergyman. He spent six years at Bishop Ridley College while his father had a parish in St. Catharines, a year at school in England, then finished his matriculation at St. Catharines and Hamilton Collegiates. He took his BA at Toronto, then an MA at Columbia University's Teachers' College. Columbia was the well-spring of the John Dewey "child-centred" progressive education movement in North America.

As a teenager he'd met Taylor Statten, who was an outstanding Canadian pioneer in boys' work, through the YMCA and scouting. Statten was a charismatic outdoorsman and the founder of Camps Ahmek for boys and Wapomeo for girls on Canoe Lake in Algonquin Park. Perry summered there regularly as a camp counsellor, became an expert at canoe-tripping and wrote two first-rate little books, "The Canoe and You" and "Canoe Trip Camping."

In 1926 Joe McCulley, long-time friend and fellow Ahmek camper, was selected as Headmaster of Pickering College. Pickering, closed for some years, had been founded by Quakers in 1842. It had now been reopened by the Society of Friends. With Quaker philosophy and McCulley's direction it became the beachhead of progressive education in Ontario. Taylor Statten became the Director of Character Education, virtually the guidance counsellor, the first in any school in Canada.

Progressive education was poles apart from the mainstream and particularly from the mainstream of independent schools. Boys who played games against Pickering reported, agog, that the boys there smoked in their rooms or wherever they wanted, and called the masters by their first names. The Headmaster, to everyone, was "Joe"!

Ron Perry was not altogether in line with the Pickering outlook or with McCulley's declared pacifism. When war broke out he joined the RCAF. Close to 40, he became an administrative officer, spent six months in Britain as chief administrator of 6th Bomber Group RCAF, then came back to Canada to run a summer camp programme for air force dependants.

Post-war, he worked in university administration in Toronto and still summered at Camp Ahmek. In fact it was the Ahmek connection that brought about his appointment. Ned Rhodes and Joe Irvin, among quite a few Ashbury-connected people, sent their sons to Ahmek. Dr. King Rowan-Legg, whose boys later went to Ashbury, was camp doctor. He it was who phoned Ron Perry to say the headship of Ashbury was open.

In April 1950, faced with Glass's late announcement, the Board appointed a search committee of Chairman Duncan MacTavish and old boy Board members Ned Rhodes, Sr., Roger Rowley, Bill Eakin and Charles Gale. There was no lengthy deliberation, no meeting of the whole committee, no statement of objectives, no consultation, in fact no search. Rowley, a career soldier, was away; Eakin lived in Montreal. Neither was consulted. Gale, told by MacTavish they had just the right man, joined him and Rhodes, plus Irvin and Rowan-Legg – neither of whom was on the Board – to interview Perry.

There was no alternative candidate, no discussion of educational philosophy or methods, no exchange of ideas on how either the Board or the new Headmaster saw the school being run. If the Board was expecting it to continue in its structured, hierarchical, traditional way, it didn't make that clear to the candidate. If Perry expected to change the school on progressive lines, he didn't lay this on the table and get a mandate. But his background in progressive education was perfectly clear. Unless key members of the Board were uninformed on matters educational, they were making a conscious move to put Ashbury on the progressive education track, a basic change from its traditional philosophy, without reference to the Board at large.

Ronald Perry was a friendly, easy, very kind and very considerate man. He engendered strong mutual loyalties. When Dr. Harry Whitley retired within the year, King Rowan-Legg became the school physician and stayed until he retired from practice in 1982. Joe Irvin, who had been Ashbury's all-time great athlete before going to RMC in 1928, joined the Board in 1954, became Chairman in 1957-58 and in 1961 was appointed Director of Administration working for the Headmaster.

Perry was also a builder. The third Headmaster to register his misgivings at the inadequate facilities, he set about improvements as effectively as he could. Short of money, he could at least beautify. Most of the trees that screen and grace the campus and give it such special charm today were planted at his direction. Many a delinquent worked off detentions in this way in the early morning; in a little over 10 years, 1500 trees were planted.

He could see the school plant had to expand and enrolment had to increase. It was an uphill struggle. The Old Boys Association post-war campaign had raised only around $30,000 and most had been drained away on essential refurbishing and patching up. Ned Rhodes gave the money to renovate the assembly room under the Chapel, including new lighting. This attack on shabbiness was so notable that the room was immediately called Rhodes Hall. Tax-deductibility of donations reared as a problem under the existing charter. Ned instigated a look at it and proposed a new charter at the Annual General Meeting in October 1952. The Board was heavy on numbers, light in interest; six attended. The Executive was armed with 77 proxies, though, and the new charter passed.

A new Building and Improvement Fund started in 1953 and plans were drawn up for the Argyle wing, more or less as it is now and far less grand than the earlier plan for the Glenwood side. At that, money was so short that only the first stage, a single storey, one-quarter of the final building, opened in 1954. It was dedicated to the memory of old boys killed in the war. Captain George Woollcombe, the Founder's son, unveiled the plaque. Pre-war, he had become a chartered accountant. He served at sea and ashore during the war, then stayed in the permanent navy, the career his father had had in mind for him back in 1920.

The cost of Argyle stage one was $30,000. By 1955 there was only $25,000 in the Building and Improvement Fund, so a mortgage for $100,000 was raised to pay off the old mortgage, settle building costs and cut the overdraft. A second storey was added in 1958 for some $40,000. The architecture was in the utilitarian, no-frills, rectangular style of the fifties like the school buildings springing up all over the fast-growing country. The flat roof, horizontal lines and broad window openings made no concession to the original style, though the brick itself and the laying of the courses followed the old.

Half-way there and the slow-moving campaign wasn't covering the costs. Perry pushed up enrolment and crammed boys in, including a lot of junior boarders, trying to pay for building out of revenue. This crowding in living conditions and classrooms was counter to the policy of the Board and therein lay the seeds of disagreement.

In 1962, the physics laboratory was added, largely with a gift from Cargill Southam. Two years later, a very interesting plan was developed by old boy Campbell Merrett, a prominent Montreal architect. It would extend Argyle westward and run a partly cloistered wing north from there to an extension of the annex, thus enclosing a quadrangle. It was to include a proper-sized gymnasium, classrooms and more living quarters, and the price tag was $600,000.

That was too rich for Ashbury's blood; the renewed campaign raised only one-third. So sails were trimmed. During 1966, 12 years after it was begun, Argyle was extended to the west, doubling its size and adding four classrooms and the Southam library. There the expansion stopped. But Ron Perry wasn't there to see the ribbon cut. He had left Ashbury after Closing that year.

His absorption with the outdoors had gone on. In his first year, with Ned Rhodes' support, he found a cabin in the Gatineau to be used mainly for skiing weekends. It was close to Camp Fortune – as the *Ashburian* said, "only a forty-minute hike." The ski team was in good shape for cross-country racing.

On his own account Perry bought a property in the Haliburton Highlands and started Camp Kawabi in 1954. His 30 summers with Taylor Statten gave him the experience. Most of the boys and girls came from Ottawa, a good number from Ashbury. He ran the off-season business from the school and left Arthur Brain in charge in the summer. Some of the Board felt it was a conflict for the Head. His view was that the summer was his own.

His Kawabi business manager was Bill Slattery, a 1952 Ashbury graduate whom Perry had taken on the school staff as a tutor and crafts instructor. Bill was nothing if not plausible, and durable. He left the Kawabi books in a mess and dipped into the Ashbury tuck shop accounts. When he left, he falsified a university degree which he never had, forged a recommendation from Ashbury and actually landed a job as assistant headmaster of a respectable boys' school in the States. He even found a handy summer job there for David Polk who, like most of the staff on slim Ashbury salaries, needed it to make ends meet. Plausible indeed. He died in the USA.

Perry was an industrious image-builder and he made sure the school kept its unbroken line of visits from Governors General. Field Marshall, The Right Honour-able Earl Alexander of Tunis, the famous wartime general, had his sons, Shane, then Brian, at the school between 1946 and 1952. Expansion and reorganization called for adding a house to the long-standing Woollcombe and Connaught. Perry got his approval to call it "Alexander House" and also to name him the school's first "Visitor." It was an office with no defined duties and his name stood above the Board of

Governors' list until long after he had left Canada in Perry's last year as Head.

At Perry's instigation the Mothers' Guild was begun with Maryon Rhodes as first president. It grew over the years as the Ladies' Guild, then the Ashbury Guild, into an exceptionally effective supporting arm of the school.

The cadet corps was polished up and annual inspections, always by a distinguished senior officer, were turned into social occasions. Ceremonial red jackets and bearskins borrowed from the Governor General's Foot Guards set off the honour guard.

Perry organized such events very well and he was an easy and affable host who thought of all the details. He developed cordial relations with the press and got good coverage. He wasn't academically inclined. He took no classes himself, feeling the Head had more than enough other things to do. He delegated the school operation pretty well *in toto* to Arthur Brain, who was now named Assistant Headmaster and Director of Studies. Compromise, not confrontation, was Perry's way. On discipline he believed in reason and counsel, not punishment, and certainly not corporal punishment.

He had bridled at Oggie Glass's advice to get rid of Arthur Brain and chose to bide his time and see for himself. Brain – brilliant, a bully, and deeply disappointed for the second time in his 15 Ashbury years that he himself was not Headmaster – could brook no methods other than his own. His way was terror. In fact the first thing he showed the new Head was a bundle of canes. But Perry never came out flat and banned beatings. Nor did he take the responsibility himself. Brain knew that any boy who ended up on the Headmaster's mat would get a talking to, which in his mind was no answer. Rules must be enforced. So he simply kept on using the cane. So, following him, did the Housemasters and others. To know it was going on, one had but to read Eric Detchon's ditty in the 1959 *Ashburian*. He titled it "Inevitable":

> *"Sir" came stealthily down the aisle:*
> *I didn't know he knew.*
> *I threw my book across the room;*
> *He caned me black and blue!*

Caught cribbing? No matter. The end result was the ever-ready cane.

Perry's aversion to beating wasn't only because it substituted pain for reason. He was disturbed about the sexual gratification connected with caning in some people's makeup, though he had no reason to believe any of his staff were thus inclined.

His presence had first been felt by the boys in the school-shattering change of banning beatings by the prefects. How, wondered Allan McCulloch, who was Captain of the School in 1951-52, could they possibly keep order? To their surprise they found they could. But substitute physical torments emerged, like making the culprit kneel on his own hands on the floor of the prefects' common room. Standing "nose to the wall" in a corridor with hands behind the back and having the ear tweaked did for lesser offences. Hierarchical bullying didn't disappear. And corporal punishment was an issue that simmered, unhealthy and unresolved.

Ronald Perry didn't have a strong, direct impact on the boys at large, but in the meantime school life, as always, went on. The 60th anniversary, 1951-52, was celebrated with an outline of the school's history in the annual issue of the *Ashburian* published at the end of the school year. Old boys presented the school with the portrait of G.P. Woollcombe by Robert Hyndman. In the Chapel the new stained-glass window over the altar was dedicated to the old boys and staff who had died in World War II. It was unveiled by the Founder's son, Captain Woollcombe. At the same service the honour roll plaques for both wars were unveiled by old boys Roger Rowley and Bill Eakin.

Canadians were at war again and had been since 1950, in Korea this time, under the flag of the United Nations. There had been no great call to arms as in the two earlier wars. Canada sent three destroyers right at the start, followed by a newly recruited brigade. The air force provided air transport.

The cadet corps paraded specially for inspection by Brigadier Pat Bogert in the spring of 1952. He was an old boy and a professional soldier with a fine record in World War II, and he was off to Korea to command the brigade. He eventually retired as a Major-General, CBE, DSO, CD. Cadets were much in vogue, and very strong at Ashbury. Crew cuts predominated among boys anyhow, and Captain G.W. Higgs, who was in charge, and Cadet Major Andy Pritchard had no trouble with hair hanging over the collar.

The regular inspection day brought Lieutenant-General Guy Simonds, CB, CBE, DSO, CD, Chief of the General Staff, back to his old school as reviewing officer. There were 36 parades that year, including one memorable mock battle in the woods near the New Edinburgh Canoe Club, complete with blank ammunition and thunderflashes. About the same time Lieutenant John Woods, the thunderflash ace who'd booby-trapped Arthur Brain's car in the last war, was doing some real fighting in Korea. The corps lined the procession route for Princess Elizabeth and Prince Philip on their royal tour. Later in 1952 the Princess became the Queen when her father, King George VI, died. Lord and Lady Alexander came to the memorial service in the Ashbury Chapel.

The Chaplain was Rev. W.J. Lord. Coincidentally, the master who took the Roman Catholics off to mass on Sundays was R.G. Bob Devine – a tough disciplinarian, belying the name. The Director of Studies was Arthur Brain. A small boy coming to Ashbury for the first time had reason to be bemused!

There were some solid long-term staff members in addition to A.D. Brain. Leonard Sibley, the Senior Master, could kindle interest in chemistry among the least scientifically inclined; Duke Belcher, Upper School Housemaster, not only managed his house charges well in his laconic way, but continued to inspire boys in English and drama; Curly Powell, with an acute mind and caustic wit, taught mathematics in the senior grades. He suffered neither the fools nor the less than able; in spring he had a great deal of time for cricket.

David Polk had come back again in 1947. He taught history and geography to Grades 11-13 and in 1953 took charge of the junior school. That was his place. Exactly. Generations found that with David Polk learning was fun, that classes could be a delight, that poetry could gladden the heart and open horizons to the mind. His love of the sea had been reinforced by his years afloat.

Who will ever forget – "I must down to the seas again, to the lonely sea and the sky..." or *Cardigan Bays'* "Clean, green, windy billows," or the magic of *Cargoes.*

And all of it was learned by legions of boys for David Polk, by heart, to be treasured in the mind for life. Polky's love of life, sense of fun and gentle wit never left him nor will he ever cease to touch those thousands whom he taught.

All manner of club activities came and went – International Relations, Science, Cercle français, Music, Photography – and Polky took on the Geography Club. Enthusiasms vary. After a short time it failed to attract any members among the boys and it was appropriated by the staff. Notice from Polk of "a meeting of the Geography Club," passed along with a wink to fellow members of the masters' common room – who had little enough money for any kind of fun – was the signal for a genial gathering down the hill at the Claude Tavern.

Among the short-term members of the Geography Club was Tony Price. After Ashbury he'd taken his BA at Bishop's, then taught for two years at BCS, including a year under Oggie Glass. He came back as Housemaster of the junior school for a couple of years, before deciding that the total dedication to the special world of schoolmastering that he saw in such as David Polk wasn't in his makeup. He wisely went off to study law.

He'd been paid $1750 a year at Bishop's and got the princely sum of $2000 at Ashbury plus board, of course, and a tiny bedroom in the Memorial Wing. Tom Lawson, who soon went on to a lifetime career at TCS, was in the same boat. All the staff taught pretty well every period; on slack days they might have one spare. They stood duty master every third day, including weekends. And of course they all coached teams, which often meant weekends travelling. Lawson coached first football. Price coached third football and the ski team.

Tony Price had been a great competitor at school himself and he coached the skiers of 1952 to a clean sweep. John Gill was Captain, with Ned Rhodes, Gerry Ross, Chris Nowakowski, David Scott and the fast-improving Chris Gill, Henry Eschauzier and Billy Baer. For the big meet versus LCC and Bishop's, they had plenty of backing from old boys Evan Gill, Harry Price and Dick "Tusker" Wright, a respected ex-master, who had taught for three years with Glass and had coached skiing in 1947. The 1952 team brought Ashbury the Cochand Cup for the team championship of the three schools.

Those were the days of the laced leather boot, immovable toe-irons and the "long-thong," which bound the boot irrevocably and lethally to the ski for slalom and downhill racing without benefit of safety release. Racing was a chancy affair and the spiral fracture an occupational hazard. Scott and Rhodes had legs in plaster for part of the season but emerged for the big events. David Polk was master in charge of skiing before and after Price, without any skiing ability or coaching skill but with his own invariably good-natured organizing powers.

The Christmas party, December 1951, featured Tom Lawson's quartet, Mrs. Row's Memorial Wing choir (the juniors lived over the gym now), and a radio show by prefects advertising "Uncle Sibley's Fluoride Flea Powder." Fred Oliver performed his comical, topical, always up-to-date ventriloquist act with his friend "Henry." Over 40 years of entertaining Ashbury boys and it had never palled. As far as the school was concerned, Fred and Henry outclassed Edgar Bergen and Charlie McCarthy, who'd been one of radio's most popular acts for years.

This was the year, 1951, when Ottawa's first television station, CBOT, went on the air. The days of radio acts and of self-entertainment, as in the annual Christmas party, were numbered. But perhaps some competition would do no harm. One visiting speaker that year, as the *Ashburian* reported without comment, was a Mr Humphrey, "for the 9th consecutive year with his slides of British Columbia."

That Christmas party was, too, Fred Oliver's swan song. He left in June after 41 years at Ashbury. He had taken on every imaginable task in his time – engineer, boilerman, iceman, groundsman, carpenter, plumber, electrician. In earlier days, when the boys were required to keep their windows open on the coldest winter nights, Fred would go around and close them at 5:00 a.m. before he stoked up the furnace and got some heat running through the rads. When he brought the boys' trunks down from the attic for packing at the end of term, he could always find a key on his bunch to substitute for the one that was lost. If some treasure had been left behind, he could always be counted upon to tuck it safely away.

He was physically strong, even at 70. As well as his hand-piled stone wall, he had made the intermediate playing field himself, with its fine, level, well-drained turf, from the area that had filled each spring with 12 feet of water. He'd fitted his horses with leather overshoes to reduce damage to the turf while mowing. Then he'd moved easily to the first tractor and kept it and its successors going, often miraculously.

And he was equally strong in character. To any who needed a hand or a word, from a new Headmaster to an old hand to the newest new boy, he was a guide, philosopher and friend. You could absolutely depend on Fred Oliver and on his kindness, wisdom and humour. It was the same with his wife. Mrs. Oliver for years had turned out first-rate fare as head cook, and then run the sewing room. She, like her husband, was always ready to lend a hand at anything, to rise to a crisis at the drop of a hat.

Long hours, low pay and hard work: what Mrs Woollcombe offered Fred Oliver in 1911 held to the last. "Overtime" wasn't in the Ashbury lexicon, and he and his wife put in endless hours without more pay. Neither ever expected it or grudged one minute of their lives. Such people are rare. They and Ashbury College just happened to suit each other as perfectly as it is possible to do. Even more remarkable was that another man made of the same stuff came along straightaway. His name was Ted Marshall, and the next 22 years of Ashbury people remember him as fondly as the earlier 41 recall Fred Oliver.

Another of those one-of-a-kind fits was Duke Belcher. It's hard to imagine him employed, or even employable, anywhere else. He kept love of language alive and kicking, and indeed infused it with respectability in a place where jocks ruled pretty well supreme. And, his strength of character somehow shining through his shabbiness, he quietly commanded the respect of all.

Belcher had taken over direction of the *Ashburian* in 1947. His name wasn't noted in that issue, but his hand is clear from the first words of the Editorial to the photographs and layout and the number and quality of the contributions.

And in the first issue after Ron Perry arrived who else would have editorially greeted the new Headmaster with "winter's sullen tale is told, and spring, the troubadour, has slipped almost imperceptibly into his coloured coat and strings his jocund lute"? Poetry lived. For years Belcher orchestrated the annual poetry reading contest. Seniors, intermediates and juniors read a set piece, a sight piece and a selection of their own. He brought in established poets and distinguished academics to adjudicate.

It was Duke who made dramatics interesting and fun. No small part of the attraction, of course, was the Ashbury-Elmwood Players combination which he engineered. And the Ottawa Little Theatre where they performed rekindled his bohemian spark, stirred memories of Broadway days and intrigued his young players. The stage, with Duke as interlocutor, had captured the likes of Robin MacNeil. On this 60th anniversary of acting at Ashbury, another Players' alumnus, Gordon Fischel, gave a trophy for the best contribution to Ashbury dramatics. Self-effacingly, Fischel called it the David Garrick Cup for Dramatic Arts.

But Belcher never picked any of the seventeeth-century or earlier pieces that the great Garrick played. He avoided Shakespeare – it was too close to schoolwork. He mostly chose light comedy. John Fraser won the Garrick Cup the first two years for his parts in typical Belcher selections, *Eliza Comes to Stay* and *Nothing But the Truth*. Sometimes it was Noel Coward, sometimes a bit of G.B. Shaw. He reached high in 1954 with *The Playboy of the Western World*.

In public speaking, choice of subject reflected the day's concerns. The same John Fraser, who was also a Governor General's medalist, won the senior title, talking on "Civil Defence." Dull as ditch-water it sounds, but "The Bomb" loomed then as a constant terror and there was a deadly fascination in notions of clinging to life in fall-out shelters, then creeping out to repopulate the world. More fancifully, Gordon Gale was the winning junior, speaking on "Flying Saucers."

Science with Sibley was moving up in importance. There was a lot of emphasis on it with the extraordinary blossoming of science and technology stimulated by Canada's role in NATO and North American defence. The year's Science Notes included a full five pages on university, laboratory and industrial tours by the boys. The new Head was putting science forward as the centre of Ashbury's scholastic thrust. Major improvements in facilities were needed if that were to come about.

CHAPTER 13

THE IMAGE OF ASHBURY

The school was competing not just with other independent schools for boarders but with a highly developed and very effective public system, and Ottawa's was no exception. The post-war baby boom put a huge bulge through the system, starting in the fifties. Through the 1960s the elementary school population increased by 40 percent, the high schools by a massive 120 percent.

Great sums were being spent on building new schools and updating the old, on new labs and equipment, expansion and upgrading of everything from libraries and sports facilities to instructional methods and teachers' qualifications. In the fifties more than half the high-school teachers had honours degrees; all had a year of teachers' college.

Unions were building their power, and teachers were seeing more equitable reward for their exacting and important work. Between 1947 and 1955 the purchasing power of high-school teachers' salaries increased by 24 percent, for elementary teachers 35 percent. Teachers' college enrolment quadrupled in the 1950s but there was a serious teacher shortage in the high schools that wasn't over until the late 1960s.

The gap between independent school teachers' salaries and benefits and those in the public system continued growing. By the nature of the job, the independent school teacher put in far more hours and was paid less for the privilege. Ashbury had some first-rate people, but bringing in the right ones to build and maintain a good all-round staff was an endless problem. The public system was leaving Ashbury, with its minimum budgets, further and further behind.

The school could point to small classes, personal attention, no girls – a plus point in many people's view – and sports for all. But it had no claim to educational breadth or scholastic excellence, to modern equipment or advanced facilities. The Dewey concepts of child-centred education, the progressive theory in which Ron Perry had been reared, had been set back by the war. The approach in the public system was generally traditional – textbooks by the page, memorizing, lots of homework and tests, Shakespeare plays, quadratic equations, all to be mastered for success in the departmental examinations.

Public high school, independent school – everyone wrote the same exams. The results were there each year to see, and Ashbury couldn't point to notable results. Neither could it claim a more disciplined approach to education. That only became possible after the Hall-Dennis Report wrought sweeping changes in the public system in the late sixties.

So, unless being a boarder was important for some reason, what was the relevance of Ashbury College? The ability to handle special learning or social difficulties? (It was tending towards a repository for some families' problems but without specialists to cope.) Closer communication with teachers? (Smaller classes, certainly, and the strong involvement outside the classroom.) Better-educated teachers? (No longer; many were less well educated, few had formal teacher training.)

What generation hasn't thought the schools are crumbling and their children going to hell in a handcart? But the high-school student culture of the 1950s was hardly threatening. In standard fashion for boys: V-neck sweaters and a white T-shirt with draped trousers, hair in a brush cut or ducktail; for girls: sweaters and skirts, white bobby socks and penny loafers. Just as much a uniform as Ashbury blazers and ties and Elmwood tunics.

"Going steady" was in. Elvis Presley, very much alive, well and gyrating, raised adult eyebrows. Dire pronouncements said rock-and-roll was inciting the younger generation to unbridled sex. And TV, up to an average of 15 hours a week for high-school students, would be their ruination. But the high-schoolers' aim was joining the good life, and really this was a pretty conservative, unadventurous lot. So what was the difference?

The 1958 *Ashburian* carried an article titled "Private School vs Public School." It was unsigned and thus emanated from aloft. The greatest difference, it said, was the control over the boys' time. The private school boy was fully occupied; however, with everything organized, he turned out less self-reliant. The private school with compulsory sports meant even the least talented had a go and got plenty of exercise. In both systems "members of the student body look after most of the discipline outside of class." (Appointed prefects on one hand, elected student council on the other.)

Finally, this: "In a sense, the most noticeable difference between the two methods of education is the polish that a private school imparts to an individual. It is the consideration of this refinement that no state school can ever give, and it is this refinement which, when parents are debating whether to send a boy to state or private school, often causes them to decide in favour of the private."

Polish. If that was the *raison d'être* for an Ashbury College, it would take some selling. Ashbury College badly needed an image of its own. After a couple of years as Head, Ron Perry had gone full out for building up sports. He had the backing and help of Ned Rhodes, Board Chairman from 1951 to 1954. In the fall of 1953, C.B. "Tiny" Hermann, late great lineman of the Ottawa Rough Riders, came in to coach football. The previous year the team had lost seven out of eight, including humiliation by Bishop's at 33-0. In Tiny's first year his team won the Bishop's Old Boys Trophy (Ashbury, Bishop's, Lower Canada College). Then in 1954 he coached the most successful football team in Ashbury history.

The record: undefeated in eight games against the traditional LCC and Bishop's, plus Lisgar, Carleton Place and Arnprior high schools; 150 points for, 34 against. The Bishop's Trophy came home again. Chris Nowakowski was Captain. For the first time ever, the *Ashburian* recorded football scoring statistics. The high scorers: Ned Rhodes, Joe Irvin, Chris Nowakowski, Mike Widdrington and Billy Baer. The football dinner drew a full dozen Board members. Ned Rhodes, the quarterback, won the Lee Snelling Trophy for most valuable player.

Nothing succeeds like success. The effect, right through the school, was electric. And it wasn't a flash in the pan. There was depth. Old boy Barry O'Brien, who was President of the Ottawa Rough Riders, coached the seconds, and there were two strong junior teams to feed the top. Next year the firsts, captained by Joe Irvin, won every game again; in 1956, with Bruce Hillary as captain, they lost only one. The Founder's heart would have stirred to see it. His grandson, Stephen Woollcombe, was a strong guard on that team, Captain of the School and heavyweight boxing champion, plus winner of the English and Latin sixth-form prizes, the Nelson Shield and the Southam Cup.

Tiny Hermann's monumental bulk on the sidelines and his bellow rattling the upper windows in the school were part of the fall scene now. Blasting, demonstrating, encouraging, and sharing his professional knowledge of the game were all part of his magic. Ashbury was the power in its league. In 1957 the Bishop's Trophy stayed where it was for the fifth consecutive year. Mervin Sutherland, a beefy 220-pound guard, captained the team as well as the school. Next year Ashbury kept the Bishop's Trophy again, but the season was a little off the peak with a record of 4-3-1. Joe Irvin was assistant coach that year before going to McGill. He played football and hockey for the university and, when he graduated, he played football for the Riders.

The 1958 team was first-rate. It was fast but light, and it was injury-prone. The era of big, heavy Ashbury teams with strings of victories was waning. Tiny Hermann ended his Ashbury time at the close of the 1962 season. He, and the strong crop of young athletes he'd had to work with, had given the whole school a tremendous lift.

The strength of the material showed right through. These were fine hockey years too. Lude Check, an ex-Ottawa Senator, coached the team in 1955 to the best season in years. Joe Irvin, the captain, led the season's scoring. Jim Wedd was a standout in the nets. Against Norwood he stopped 55 of 57 shots for a 5-2 win. They beat TCS for the first time in many years.

In 1962, with Bruce Hillary coaching (he was back from university and on the teaching staff), Ashbury finished first in the newly formed Ottawa High School Hockey League. In a 12-game season (6-5-1) Bob Berry was high man by a long shot. He scored 36 goals, 57 points – and 42 minutes in the penalty box: altogether a sure thing for a career in the NHL. As vice-captain of football the previous fall, he'd scored an Ashbury season's record of 51 points. He went on to Michigan State for football, to Vermont and then to Sir George Williams in Montreal for hockey; he played on the national team and then went to the NHL.

Skiing took off again in 1954 with Bruce Heggtveit, a former Canadian cross-country champion, as coach. Bruce and his brother Eugene had been the powers at Glebe who had edged Ashbury out of the high school championship in 1938. In 1957, captained by Ross Southam and coached by Frank Macintyre, the senior team won the Dalton Wood Trophy for the Ottawa and District Championship. John Rowan-Legg led the downhill and cross-country. They took the trophy again the following year, and the next too, with Chris Nowakowski back as coach.

From 1954 there was a surge of activity in just about every sport. Rowing was revived by Peter Falstrup-Fischer, who had joined the staff for a couple of years. He was a fine athlete and got squash going, using the Minto Club courts. He started Saturday morning riding too. Badminton had a boost, and a full-scale swimming meet was held at the Chateau Laurier. Basketball had been revived two years back by A.H. Snelgrove, a cadaverous Newfoundlander with the ideal beanpole build himself but not much know-how and over 70. Still, the game was gaining popularity. Boxing and gymnastics too were getting a lot more attention. This upsurge of all-round interest was certainly spearheaded by the football victories. But the fact that it was consolidated and sustained had a great deal to do with the arrival on the Ashbury scene of Ray Anderson.

Three years back the Head had started searching for an instructor for cadets and physical training. Over in England Lt. Col. Roger Rowley interviewed some likely candidates recommended by the British army. On the short list of two were T.L. Weatherall and R.J. Anderson. Both had recently left the army as NCOs thoroughly trained in physical education. Weatherall, the senior of the two, got the job and replaced Captain Higgs in the fall of 1953.

If Ashbury thought it was getting another Sergeant-Major Stone – and it hadn't had the likes of Stone since he'd left in 1938 – it was mistaken. Certainly Terry Weatherall was well qualified. He was a fine gymnast. He knew how to train young soldiers and he had all the skills and knowledge the British Army Physical Training College could give him. That, in the 1950s, was way ahead of the old-line Imperial soldier. But Sergeant-Major Stone, whom those of Rowley's age at Ashbury remembered so well, was a human being who understood young people. Weatherall was a very tough individual indeed and a bit too much for Ashbury College.

He always started his morning PT classes with everyone on their knees, facing the proper direction and bowing to a deity of his own particular choice. His was a no-questions-asked, rod-of-iron, my-way-or-nothing approach that by year's end had everyone on the staff shaking in their shoes. He had to go. For fear of mayhem, perhaps, he wasn't given his marching orders until after Closing. He went back to his own milieu, got a commission in the Canadian army in physical training and successfully coached a number of national teams in boxing and track and field. To each his own.

It was late June 1954 when Leonard Sibley cabled R.J. Anderson to come and fill the breach. Anderson had served in the regular British army in Korea on warfare training and as a specialist in remedial health. He was settling into civvie life, but in stagnant England he felt he was waiting for someone to die to get ahead. He and his fiancée Eve agreed he'd go out to Canada for a year and try it, and young Mr. Anderson arrived at Ashbury, full of energy and ambition, to take up a career in a bright new world.

It might have been the start of a Dickens novel. He'd be excused some misgivings at the down-at-heel buildings, gloomy basement with the boys' butt-room reeking of nicotine even in mid-summer, at the dark subterranean passage, laced with pipes and wires concealing unknown creatures and threatening the top of his head, leading him at last to the small, sad excuse for a gymnasium.

Up under the eaves in the annex he found a little hutch of a room for himself and a bathroom which he shared with the occupants of three others. They were the Chaplain, Rev. E.G. Kettleborough – "Kettles," squat and round as his name suggests, quiet and sincere and a bit too gentle for the hurly-burly of Ashbury – and Duke Belcher and Leonard Sibley. Clearly, in the matter of Ashbury people, Dickens was at work here too.

"Sib's" room was the clubroom. Once the term started, it overflowed every evening after study with 15 or 20 senior boys. They simply drifted in, sprawled everywhere, consumed peanut butter and jam sandwiches, chocolate cookies, cheese and crackers, and drank coffee. Sib always presided in his easy, smiling genial way, his record player a background for the chatter. When the hoi polloi had gone to bed, the prefects stayed on for the 11:00 p.m. news. After they left the live-in staff would drift in for a friendly glass of rye and water and some good conversation.

Regularly once a week, on Saturdays, Sib headed down the hill to Beechwood, ran his laundry through the laundromat and came back laden with the supplies for the next week's nightly feeds and, from time to time, a bottle of rye. He'd stroll off again later and treat himself to a steak dinner at the Eastview Hotel. Once a year in summer he'd pay a short visit to his family at Brome in the Eastern Townships. But Ashbury was his real home.

He had a BSc from McGill and he was a fine science teacher. His lab and classroom periods were an incitement to learning, a stirring of the imagination. There was a constant bustle about him and always a smile. From first thing in the morning he was on the move, charging everywhere at once, his gown streaming behind.

He played the organ in Chapel every morning except Fridays. That day "Sharpy" Snelgrove (he never missed a caper in class) took over and Sib led the weekly sing-song. With the whole school there, he didn't go for quality. He strode up and down the aisle, gown flying, arms flailing, urging, "Open your mouths. Sing up! LOUDER!"

At any time he was there with wise advice if a boy had a problem with his work or personal life – even agony over a girlfriend. He was constantly at work. In 1950 the new Head had made him Senior Master in an attempt to diffuse the omnipotence of Arthur Brain and he took over a lot of the interminable detail. Lists and rosters for everything – Chapel Reading, Duty Prefect, Duty Master, Closing programme and prize list, the programmes for every event, travel for the holidays – all were Sib's. It's impossible to imagine him anywhere but Ashbury and equally hard to imagine Ashbury in those years without him. In humanity and scholarship it would have been diminished. For 21 years it was his life.

Like Sibley, Duke Belcher, Arthur Brain and David Polk were part and parcel of that era – and Ray Anderson joined them – but they all had outside interests. Belcher, on his slim salary, lived an easy-going bachelor life. He had his room with its view back over the playing fields, his books and his theatre. He wrote poetry. He loved crafting his Editorial for the *Ashburian*, weaving in all manner of classical allusions with ever-fresh, imaginative, if highly coloured, turns of phrase. He had his weekends with rod and gun. He would go to Bobcaygeon in the holidays and do some guiding. He'd go to Toronto where, for a time, he had a wife; at some point they separated. Echoing his earlier days on bohemian Broadway, he had a lady friend – or two – who lived conveniently near the school. Mornings, he'd still pinch out his cigarette, tuck it in his cuff and shuffle, drawn and ragged, into the classroom in his maroon bedroom slippers. His heart murmurs – both physical and emotional – never left him. At times just able to cope with the day, he'd still stir magic in the minds of those least inclined to the beauties of the English language.

David Polk, always humorous, fun-loving and articulate, was a good friend and a fine duck-hunting companion. David and his wife Eleanor were raising their family of three Ashbury-bound boys, Michael, David and Nicholas, in a little house on neighbouring Union Street they were managing to buy with slim salary pickings.

Arthur Brain, his wife Barbara and their children had moved out of the annex to a house of their own before Ray Anderson arrived. Brain had an unceasingly active range of interests. Bowler-hatted, he'd make his weekly expedition to the central branch of the Ottawa Public Library on Metcalfe Street. He'd take out three books: one was to expand his knowledge of an area of his special expertise; the second concerned a subject of which he knew nothing (and which, as time went on, according to him, got close to unobtainable); the third was purely for pleasure, a novel, even a thriller.

Over the years he'd developed quite a reputation amongst classical scholars. In earlier *Ashburians* and elsewhere, he was referred to as "Sometime Open Classical Scholar of Exeter College, Oxford." He hadn't taken a degree at Oxford, but the title had a far grander ring than his prosaic BA, Toronto.

Those who'd heard him boasting about his bowling in cricket – and who hadn't? – might have been sceptical about his claims to expertise in other fields. But at any rate he was invited, in the winter of 1956, to spend five months as the acting Head of Classics at Haverford University. Haverford, near Philadelphia, had a high standing in liberal arts, particularly in classics. He got a leave of absence from Ashbury and off he went.

He was very warmly received. His encyclopaedic mind had full play in first-class intellectual surroundings. He revelled in it. This was the place where he could spend the rest of his academic life. And there was a permanent opening for him too. A comfortable salary; a delightful, civilized university precinct; all the prestige and intellectual stimulation a scholar could ask; none of that endless, dead-end grind as perpetual second-in-command of a small boys' school. Surely this was beyond his and Barbara's dreams. Surely too it would have solved Ron Perry's dilemma – how to offload Brain without actually seeming to do so. The two were poles apart, yet Perry hadn't grasped the nettle.

But Ashbury, Brain felt, needed him. Twice frustrated in his ambition to be Head, he'd slaved away to keep the place together. He'd thrown body and soul into trying to keep it running the way he felt it should, first under the incompetent Archdale, then under Glass's firm control, now with Perry's friendly hands-off style. Utterly incompatible as he and Perry were on their basic approach to educating boys, he'd convinced himself long since that Ashbury would go down the drain without him. There were times indeed when he'd held the place together, and there was perverse satisfaction in feeling indispensable to people who'd handed him such deep disappointments in his chosen life.

The tragic fact of the matter was not so much that Ashbury needed Arthur Brain. Arthur Brain needed Ashbury College. There alone he had power. And back he came. Sibley, Belcher and others over many years found happiness and a unique place for their often eccentric personalities – personalities that would have been hard pressed to find another haven. They – and David Polk too, who was unique though not answering to "eccentric" – found true contentment in their own particular way in their long years at the school. Arthur Brain's last years, though, were shadowed with disappointed dreams.

In some "The Bug" engendered real affection. Graham Jackson had been Captain of the School in both 1953 and 1954. He returned in 1958 to teach but, unlike Bill Slattery (who'd been his roommate), he'd got a real BA, from Bishop's. He suffered through Brain's interminable staff meetings. They thrashed out each boy's progress in detail, starting after supper and ending often at 3:00 a.m.. A.D.B.'s instructions to the staff on how they should handle each of their students were succinct and not a little characteristic. Jackson, with an innate instinct for history, had the wit to jot them down on the last page of his mark book. There are 28 unique "Bugisms" in all. For the student of Arthur Brain, Ashbury College and pedagogical history, it's an archival gem. A mere selection:

Bear down! Wallop! Give him the boots! Young toad! I'll cane him before afternoon school! The Brute, eh? (it was one of his nicknames). Flog him! Torture! Split him up three ways!! Clout him! Thrash him every morning! Young swab! Rip his buttons off and drum him out the front gate!!

Most ominous of all was "Send him to me!" The raging of the totally one-sided "interview" next day could be heard through A.D.B.'s office door right down the corridor. The culprit, roundly thrashed, would rocket out the door. Brain would stroll out after him, amiably chatting to whomever happened to stand quaking in his path.

On the other side of his character, though, which some like Graham Jackson saw, were kindness, generosity and, of course, a wide-ranging mind, remarkable memory and scholarly capability and style. Ashbury's letter of recommendation when Jackson went to teach elsewhere was written and signed by A.D.B. (not by the Head) and was a masterpiece of memory and thoughtful, constructive comment.

To those with average minds (and, more particularly, below-average) Brain was a bully and a terror. He knew no carrot, only the stick. But he gave a great deal of care and provided unbounded stimulus to those with the most promising intellects. Old Ashburians who went on to scholarly achievement, like Gillies Ross, Tony Bidwell, Don Macdonald, Rodney Moore, C.W. Eliot, and Georges Verhaegen, Ashbury's third two-time Governor General's medalist, all look back to A.D.B. for their mental conditioning and their inspiration to learn.

On the physical conditioning side, Ray Anderson quickly and surely became the key man. He and Eve were married back in England in the summer of 1955 and out they came to a new life. He ran cadets and took the whole school from Grade 1 to 13 in physical training. He took over as soccer coach from Ian Spencer, an outspoken Australian who bequeathed him, along with the team, the un-English habit of shouting from the sidelines. Spencer, who was also an outstanding bridge player, went off to head the Halifax Grammar School. Anderson, a fine soccer player, did a great deal for the Ashbury game.

Right at the outset he had a nose-to-nose with Arthur Brain. The whole athletic programme had been coordinated for many years by the Sports Council. It was made up of the prefects, who were in charge of the various sports. A.D.B. (who else?) was secretary. He invited the new Director of Physical Training to sit in. Then, when Anderson made some suggestions, the bully in Brain tried putting the upstart new boy firmly in his place.

It didn't work. R.J.A. had run sports programmes for 1200 troops, he'd had lives in his care. He knew his business and he knew people, and he wasn't one to push around. He made that quickly clear to A.D.B. who just as quickly backed down. It was simply a matter of drawing the line. From that moment Brain treated him with due respect and Anderson took firm, sensible and thoroughly capable control over the whole programme of physical education and sports.

He took over basketball coaching from Sharpy Snelgrove. The gym was far too small so they practised at the YMCA and used the Rockcliffe Public School gym for home games. In 1957 the team was undefeated. Anderson had arrived at the start of Tiny Hermann's regime and found that, with Tiny getting everything he asked for, then Lude Check doing the same for hockey, other activities were getting short shrift. He worked hard to even things up and eventually turned the annual football dinner into the sports dinner. In the early sixties the time of the outside professional coaches died out.

Gymnastics, tennis, boxing, soccer, track and field – everything he coached himself benefitted from the Anderson touch. Besides those, he coordinated all sports activities most capably. There were changes, of course. Every sport needed competent staff coaching. When Falstrup-Fischer left, for instance, rowing and riding died out.

Boxing had been going steadily since 1923. The Head had never liked it; he felt it was a crude sport for young people and they could too easily get damaged. But it was long established and popular, so he didn't make a change. Anderson, as with all his predecessors, taught thoroughly and stressed the traditional "manly art of self-defence." Opponents were carefully matched and fitted with gloves of the right weight to minimize injury. The annual tournament was a major event, hard and cleanly fought and high on house rivalry.

Inevitably there were minor injuries and, just as back in 1923, some parental misgivings. Dr. Rowan-Legg was against boxing too and the Head eventually put an end to it in 1959. For the record, in the last Ashbury heavyweight championship bout, John Gamble won the decision over Ross Southam; Woollcombe House won with 50 points over Connaught and Alexander with 47 each. The great array of silver boxing trophies was laid to rest. But there was a revival. David Polk, with his years of experience with small boys, restored boxing to the junior school in 1961.

In the Perry years Ashbury first teams had some spectacular seasons. They had a good share of the independent school honours and overall they did well against high schools with their big populations. The main reason was that everyone played at all ages and all levels. The school didn't shine academically. Cultural interests were fostered to some extent, especially through Irene Woodburn's fine music programme in the junior school and the interest in the Ashbury-Elmwood Players. The tiny gym and other sports facilities were scarcely adequate. But with the support and encouragement of the Head, the overall involvement of the staff and the outstanding capability and ceaseless energy of Ray Anderson, the school had a first-rate all-round sports programme for everyone. That, in Ron Perry's time, as he had set out to make it, was certainly the prominent attribute of Ashbury College.

CHAPTER **14**

HIERARCHICAL DIFFICULTIES

Day-to-day school life, matters that concern the students, seldom seem affected by that remote body "the Board." Ashbury's Board in G.P. Woollcombe's time kept corporate affairs in order and looked to supplying money for capital projects. The school was, without question, entirely in the hands of the Head. From 1933 on, with Wright and Archdale, the Board had to take an increasing hand in actual administration. The power lay with the few who had financial control either by guaranteeing loans or being potential major donors. There was for a time in the Archdale regime an executive committee that virtually took over the Headmaster's main responsibilities. Otherwise, execution of business, insofar as it concerned the Board, was left to Nixie Newcombe as an executive committee of one.

With Glass running a competent administration, the Board had little input except in matters of finance, casting about for funds and advising and supporting the Head on request. After Newcombe's death a proper Executive Committee of the Board took shape. It started as a small group, rising to around 12, that took on the chore of doing the whole Board's work more or less as a matter of duty. Most were old boys, younger men, established now in professions and business, mostly in Ottawa, with sons of their own at, or likely to go to, the school. What they'd learned at Ashbury in traditional pre-war times had served them well when war came. Almost without exception they were wartime officers and that had reinforced their school-taught respect for structure, order and discipline. They expected that kind of schooling for their sons.

Otherwise they kept a good distance from anything to do with educational philosophy or method or administration – that was the Headmaster's business, and the familiar old departmental matriculation was the yardstick. They occupied themselves mainly with trying to find money to get the school back in the running. Most, if put to it, favoured corporal punishment but under defined control. As it turned out, with Perry as Head and Brain in charge of students, they got the former without the latter.

Chairmen from 1950 to 1958 were successively Duncan MacTavish, Ned Rhodes, Sr., Bob Southam and Joe Irvin, Sr. All were Perry supporters from the start; it was the group that had put him in. In the fall of 1958 Charles Gale took the Chair. Since early Woollcombe days the Headmaster had been Secretary of the Board, but there had been growing disquiet among some of the Executive and a feeling that Perry's minutes were prone to interpret things his way, that he ignored or deflected their direction when it suited.

They disagreed on enrolment. The Executive wanted to limit the school to what they felt the accommodation, facilities and desirable class size could properly handle. Perry wanted to build enrolment and he did, by cramming boys into marginal quarters particularly in the junior school. By 1960 numbers had risen to 288 and it was a very tight squeeze. There was a teaching staff of 18, plus Miss Woodburn, the outstanding music teacher, and two unqualified men. Bill Slattery was still assistant junior

Housemaster; Michael Sherwood was tutoring and coaching hockey for bed and board while studying at Carleton. The qualified regular staff made a less than favourable student-teacher ratio of 16:1.

To be viable Ashbury certainly had to get bigger. But it was stuck with too little space and no money. Boarders were what paid and Perry took pretty well every boy he could find. Some he took for the human reason that he could help them; that was right and proper and always seen as part of the school's role. But numbers of questionable apples must be kept in judicious proportion to the whole barrel, and there was too little in the way of bursary and scholarship funding for selective strengthening. Too many had been problems at home or in other schools. The behaviour they brought with them incited the kind of instant, strong-armed response that was the stock-in-trade of the Arthur Brains. Weekends were thin on organized activities for boarders. The lure of the night spots of Hull was still there and Ottawa was much more open. It didn't take much ingenuity to get around the roll-calls and bed-checks. Affluent times meant day boys had access to cars. There were plenty of willing accomplices in the traditional sneakout down the fire escape.

Some faithful old boys pulled their sons out, disenchanted. Negative aspects are quickly magnified. Reputations are made – and unmade much more swiftly – by word of mouth. Ashbury became spoken of too often as "the zoo," a school of last resort, a place where parents with money enough could dump their problems. Exaggerated, but with a disturbing core of truth.

With the split between the Headmaster's outlook on discipline and his staff's execution, it suffered from the worst malaise – inconsistency. Incidents involving punishment too often became Board matters. Perry believed the Board's business was to stick to fund-raising and to let the Headmaster run the school as in the straightforward G.P. Woollcombe days. Perry wasn't a Woollcombe. A lot of the questioning was well founded.

Some, though, was petty and disruptive interference. One influential member was angered that his son hadn't been made Captain of the School. Unfortunately, to satisfy such expressed or sometimes perceived parental aspirations, Perry temporized. He opened up the positions of Captain of Day Boys and Captain of Boarders, and sometimes Co-Captains of the School at the top, to 16 senior prefects in all. It was a pretty hefty doling out of privilege and authority with very little responsibility and it debased the coinage.

The fact is the Board was not very successful at fund-raising and the Head was not really in charge of the school. He spoke with real personal conviction to parents, Board and public about bringing out the best in a boy through reason and understanding. But those humanitarian concepts of developing character in boys certainly didn't pervade his school.

By 1960, under Chairman Gale, the Executive was riding much closer herd on Perry. Old boy Bill Hadley, who was a lawyer, took over his duties as Secretary of the Board. Gale, a chartered accountant, insisted on the Headmaster's accountability to the Board. There was no question of misappropriation – except in Slattery's dealings over the tuck shop – but budgets were closely scrutinized now and expenditures examined for consistency with Board policy, enrolment among them.

In January 1961, in the Headmaster's absence, the Executive established a subcommittee on standards and enrolment. Bob Southam (who wasn't there either) opposed it strongly at the next meeting. Lines were being drawn within the Board. Mutual confidence was crumbling. Incidents, differences and personality clashes between Perry and the working core of the Executive came to a head at the end of the year. They decided he should go.

Gale, who liked precise answers to direct questions, went to Perry's office in January 1961 with Bert Lawrence and told him they wanted to replace him that summer. Perry dug in and fought back. He had a lot of staunch friends and he pulled out every stop to muster support. The staff was divided, with most older hands like Brain, Sibley and Snelgrove firmly loyal to their Head. Curly Powell's tenure had ended abruptly in 1958. Normally, changes were made in March, but Powell got his notice after Closing. He was an old Ottawa friend of the Board members. Rightly or wrongly, Perry believed he'd been talking against him.

But Perry wasn't going to leave without a fight. Apart from his conviction that he was building a good school and that the Board was out of line trespassing on his preserve, where would he go? He was approaching 60. The landmark Old Age Security Act of 1951 had provided the first universal pension without a means test – $40 a month at age 70. Senator Hardy's forward thinking on a private Ashbury plan in the twenties had never taken root. In spite of the annual discomfitting reminders of G.P. Woollcombe's circumstances, the Board did nothing about staff pensions until Perry himself pushed it. One of his earliest proposals to the Board, in 1950, was for a participatory pension plan. By 1954 his persistence got a modest one in place. But benefits were still pretty meagre.

Chairman Gale called a meeting of the full Board. It was held in mid-February 1961 in the less-than-salubrious basement of the Eastview Hotel. Heavy campaigning brought the biggest turnout ever: it flushed out many of the 30-odd Governors who hadn't been to a meeting in years and polarized it from the start. George Woollcombe, on the Board though not the Executive, had urged Gale and Perry privately to work things out. He spoke at the start of the meeting, supported neither side and repeated his plea.

Charles Gale presented the Executive's recommendation. Ron Perry hit back. He had had a substantial raise in 1958, with the plaudits of the Board on record. Matriculation results that year were above the average of Ottawa high schools. Ashbury's standards, he said, were at least equal to those of local schools. As to philosophy, he believed "in the right and desirability of every boy to live without fear or terror in an environment where there is understanding, encouragement and trust."

Then, for those concerned about lack of discipline, he reported that the Director of Studies, Senior Master and Housemasters had his authority to use the cane (or strap in the junior school) and that corporal punishment was used an average of twice a week. On the one hand, his belief; on the other, the way things actually were.

The house was divided. Perry had consulted Duncan MacTavish on his legal position and armed him with his resignation letter. MacTavish, who was still on the Board, moved that any decision be postponed for a year and that McGill's Director of Education, Professor D.C. Munroe, be asked to report and advise on the relationship between Headmaster and Board.

The majority went for MacTavish's compromise and he kept Perry's letter in his pocket. It was a non-decision. Professor Munroe produced a report in the spring, and joined the Board for a couple of years. He made useful proposals for restructuring the Board into a smaller, more actively involved and better informed body. But the basic matters – whole-hearted confidence between Headmaster and Board, confidence of the whole Board in its Executive Committee, and unanimity of purpose in the 12-man Executive – went unresolved.

Bill Hadley resigned, but there was no wholesale change. Perry stayed as Headmaster, though no longer on the Board. He counted it a victory, but Ashbury supporters were cut right down the middle. Most were men who ran into each other professionally and socially, in their offices, at their clubs, on the golf course, at cocktail parties. Ottawa was a small town, Ashbury was a tight circle and this was a hot subject. In the staff common room an atmosphere of wariness at the very least prevailed. The boys couldn't help but know their Headmaster and the Board were at odds and who was on who's side. It all did a great deal of no good to Ashbury.

And it simmered. Trust had gone. Executive Committees, smaller now and composed mainly of men who had gone through the controversy, still lacked unqualified confidence in the Head. Closely involved and successively Chairmen over the next five years were Bert Lawrence, Geoff Hughson, Dick Ross and Don Maclaren. None of them was happy with the Head and an uneasy situation prevailed.

Perry was genuinely liked and strongly supported by many people, but his message, the one in which he fervently believed, didn't get through. Academically the school wasn't strong. That was not his forte. There were good teachers – Sibley in science, Belcher, Brain in his own way – but the staff was very uneven. Sports were the biggest thing – Perry had made them so – and life pretty well revolved around them. The prefects, the school leadership, came from the athletes' ranks. If you were bright in class too, that was okay; but the studious, the intellectually superior, if they lacked prowess on the playing field, hardly rated until Closing Day. And now, with the glory days of first team triumphs on the wane, Ashbury's spirits sagged.

And then there was another blow. In April 1963, after 20 Ashbury years, Duke Belcher's warm and gallant heart gave out and he died in harness. So ended his steadying influence as a Housemaster, his quality as a gentleman, tattered though he might be, and his inspired teaching of English. Gone too was the influence of a cultivated, civilized mind. All these were elements that Ashbury College could ill afford to lose.

His old students and friends dedicated a window to him in the Chapel. It includes a beehive, the Royal Military College crest, a dove carrying a quill pen, a trillium for his beloved Ontario woods and a smiling theatrical mask. Beneath are repeated the last two lines of one of his poems:

> *And God runs quiet fingers*
> *Through the tired hair of the world.*

Another loss that year was Elsie Hunter, retired from teaching juniors, mostly in a tiny subterranean classroom. She had been a well-loved pillar of the place since 1939. David Polk had the junior school humming smoothly in an even-handed, happy and up-beat way. He and the Head stayed rather at arm's length and the junior school remained his own preserve. Little boys passed happily through the firm but gentle hands of Mrs Dalton, then Elsie Hunter and the male staff like Ian Spencer whom Polk took on. It was quite a leap for them moving to the bottom rung of the senior ladder in the territory of overbearing prefects and the dreaded Buggy Brain.

There was a real dividing line. In Michael Sherwood's early days as a junior school tutor, he ticked off a senior school boy for some obvious dress infraction. He was promptly summoned to the prefects' study to be told to keep his hands off. The senior school was a rough-and-tumble place, still ruled by the iron hand as exemplified and passed down the line by Arthur Brain. It was a place where you endured the slings and arrows 'til the day when you reached the prefectorial heights and could mete them out yourself.

No promotional campaign could have matched the attention the school got in February 1964. There'd been an outbreak of thefts from armouries in Quebec and the army called in weapons and ammunition from various units that might be targets. Ashbury's cadet corps was on the list and Ray Anderson was told a party would come at 9:45 p.m. to pick up all their arms. It didn't arrive until very late and the spectacle of army vehicles rumbling through Rockcliffe and fully armed soldiery stomping about the school in the small hours caused quite a stir and attracted a keen young reporter.

In no time it was on TV. The army assaulting an innocent school in the middle of the night was just too good for the political cartoonists and the Opposition to ignore. For two days questions were fired across the floor of the House of Commons. Newspapers across the land called Ashbury "the Eton of Canada" with its "now world famous Cadet Corps." The story strung out for six weeks. It hit *Maclean's* and *Time* with a picture of the corps on parade. Enquiries poured into the office from all over Canada at a quite unprecedented rate.

It wasn't this incident that attracted Emperor Haile Selassie of Ethiopia to Ashbury, but it could have had something to do with his gift of a magnificent leopard skin for the bass drummer in the band. The Emperor's grandson, Prince Michael Makonnen, and two great-grandsons, John and Michael Mengesha, were at Ashbury between 1963 and 1966. The introduction came via Robert Thompson, MP, leader of the Social Credit Party, who had met The Lion of Judah, as he was titled, on peace-seeking missions to Africa.

From the 1961 showdown, relations between the Head and the Board were uneasy at best. In 1966 Perry and Chairman Dick Ross disagreed over some matter of handling the last stage of building Argyle. Ross and Don Maclaren, who was with him in Perry's office, believed he had overstepped his authority. Perry offered his resignation. Ross accepted it on the spot and this time the Board concurred.

Ronald Perry left Ashbury College that summer aged 64 after 16 years as Head. He bore with him his conviction that he was the victim of ill-will, of a vendetta by personal enemies. He maintained his view of the Board as dabblers in education – the field of his expertise, not theirs. They should, he firmly believed, have stuck to raising funds and left the school entirely to him. He took a year's salary with him and his pension of $155 per month from the modest plan he had pushed through the Board himself.

Indefatigable still, he started his own school, Rosseau Lake, on a fine lakeside property in Muskoka given by Lady Eaton. He endured extraordinary difficulties there, including eight fires, through the distempered times of student unrest and the rising drug culture. He finally retired at age 72 to live in Port Colborne with his wife, Mary.

Ron Perry retained an abiding affection for Ashbury and most of its people; many will return that affection 'til they die. He had done everything in his power to build the school. He had tilled tirelessly for money in a stony field. And he did indeed build where others could well have given up.

The Southams, who were his mentors, had led the donations. The library, a large room on the top floor at the west end of Argyle, was dedicated to the memory of Harry and Wilson Southam. This marked a long Ashbury connection starting with Wilson's son William H.C. as a student in 1910. The two senior Southams were among the Founders of 1920. Harry was on the Board from 1922 until 1953, and was Chairman and Vice-Chairman. Certainly he was its single most influential member. In his last 20 years, if not in the Chair, he was the *éminence grise.*

Harry's sons went to Ashbury; Bob graduated in 1930, overlapped his father on the Board from 1948, was Chairman from 1954 to 1956 and finally a Life Governor; Gordon was on the Board from 1949 to 1964. Bob's son Ross was at the school in the 50s and Rick in the 60s. Wilson's sons William, John David, Cargill and Hamilton graduated between 1914 and 1934. Cargill's son Wilson graduated in 1964. Hamilton's sons Peter and Christopher in 1958. Following the pattern of a Southam on the Board Rick joined it in 1977. Southam influence had made Ron Perry Headmaster. Through all his travails he retained their unwavering support.

The last stage of Argyle opened after Perry left. But it was really his. So were the three staff houses built on the grounds in 1965 and 1966 – architecturally undistinguished, but serving a very useful function. The fine trees that give such character and colour to the campus season-round are very much a Perry contribution. He boosted the student body by well over 50 percent. He put Ashbury on the athletic map. And he is remembered by a great many as a compassionate, kind and considerate man.

With Ronald Perry's departure in June 1966, fully half of the regular teaching staff of 24 left too, either by choice or by decision of the new regime. At Closing Rick Southam (Captain of the School), Bruce Deacon, Arthur Ault and John Cotton said the school's goodbyes with words and gifts to Messrs. Perry, Brain, Sibley and Snelgrove. Between them these four totalled 80 years of Ashbury service. Arthur Brain decided it was time to go after 31 years; Leonard Sibley left by choice because of his intense loyalty to his Head. Snelgrove, at 74, was overdue for retirement.

Under the polite veneer of the sun-filled Closing afternoon – prizes galore, tea in the marquee, graceful women with hats and summer dresses, light airs by the Governor General's Foot Guards band – feelings ran very deep. And there was a last kick at the controversy. When the 1966 issue of the *Ashburian* reached its readers in the fall, the three pages that carried the expected tribute to the departing Head had been excised.

In a remaining archival copy it survives, unsigned, written perhaps by Arthur Brain. Quite properly the writer lauded Perry for his building, his humanity and compassion. But, he wrote, he had met his moment as had "Thomas à Becket, with a display of fortitude that has illuminated history, although his Constitutions of Claredon were no more significant to his purpose than were Mr. Perry's hierarchical difficulties to his . . . ." Thus casting the Board as Henry II, whose ragings over à Becket as "this turbulent priest" incited his minions to hack the martyr to pieces on the altar steps, he went on to scourge them further: "The school cannot be properly directed from outside," he wrote, and finished with the hope that "the future policy of those who offer direction from 'outside' will be one of understanding, sound judgement and an appreciation of the infinite number of problems that arise in the daily life of the School."

Censoring the press? Concealing criticism? School magazines served, in the words of the song, to accentuate the positive, eliminate the negative. But the Board, after all was said and done, was in charge. Using the *Ashburian* to tell them to keep their nose out of the school's affairs was not only inappropriate, it was dead wrong. And thus, unhappily, Ron Perry didn't get what credit he was due in public print.

So ended an uneven, turbulent time, a time when Ashbury College grew but was certainly not at its best. For a majority of boys, though, there were happy times in plenty. There's always a challenge in beating the system, always fun in it, more especially when it's heavy-handed; and there's great comradeship in adversity. Sports were more important than studies and for most they were more fun. There were some first-rate people on the staff and the boys would usually find help and encouragement if they sought it out.

The anonymous eulogist might better have invoked the analogy of Hamlet, not for the venom-tip't sword, but for the tragedy of the man – and this applied to the Board as well – who couldn't make up his mind.

The Staff 1954-55

Back Row (from left): W.E. Slattery, D.L. Polk, Jr. Housemaster; R.G. Devine, J.K. Jobling, A.H.N. Snelgrove, L.I.H. Spencer, P.F. Falstrup-Fischer, R.J. Anderson, Rev. E.G. Kettleborough
Front Row : A.B. Belcher, Sr. Housemaster; Miss I. Woodburn, A.D. Brain, Asst. Headmaster; R.H. Perry, Headmaster; L.H. Sibley, Sr. Master; J.A. Powell, Mrs. F.E. Hunter, Mrs. H.F. Dalton
Absent: J.M.P. Rees

Music for Juniors

Irene Woodburn Wright taught every boy who went through the junior school between 1945 and 1967. Besides the recorder and singing she had a gift for imparting appreciation and understanding of music.

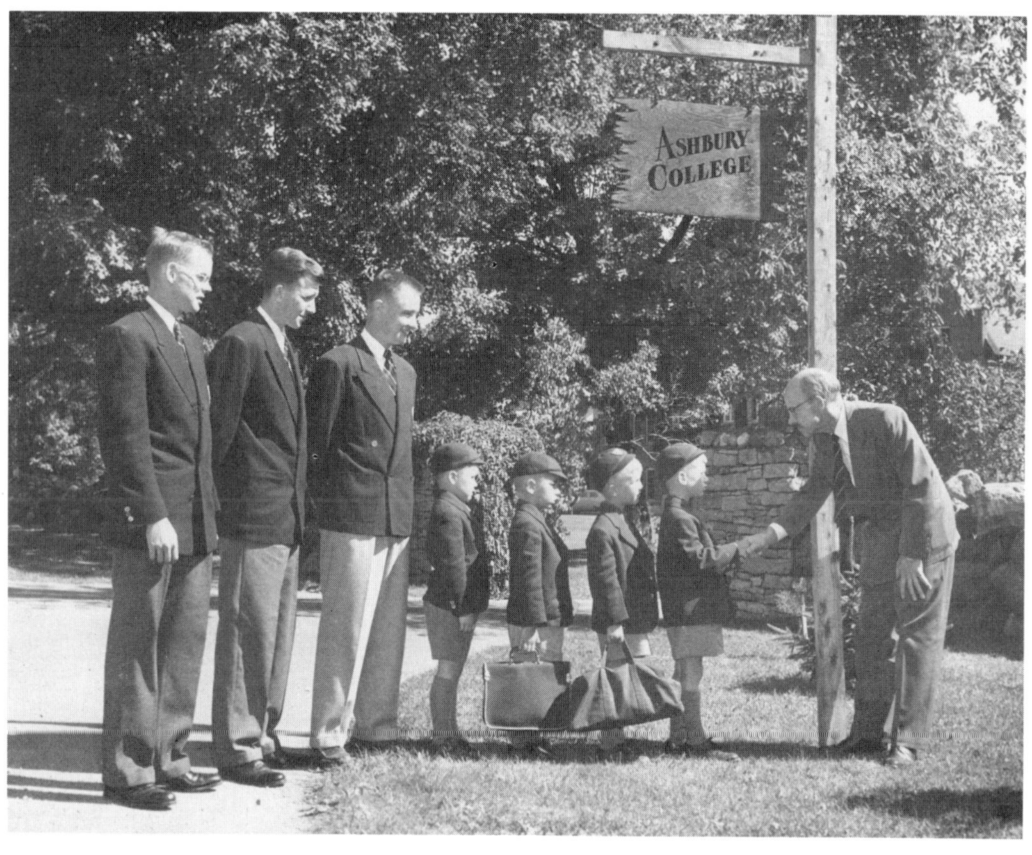

First Day of School - 1954

Ronald Perry (Headmaster 1950 - 1966) raised enrolment to record numbers, saw the first half of Argyle built and everything in place for its completion. The junior school started boys at Grade 1 throughout his time.

Football Dinner 1955

Left to right: Gregor Grant, Tiny Hermann, Joe Irvin Jr., (who also captained hockey) Mac Killaly, Richard York, Vic Rivers

Tiny Hermann, ex-Ottawa Rough Rider great, inspired Ashbury's football team to a record of 25 wins and 4 losses over the four years from 1953 to 1956. They won the BCS Old Boys Trophy three times captained by Chris Nowakowski, Joe Irvin Jr. and Bruce Hillary.

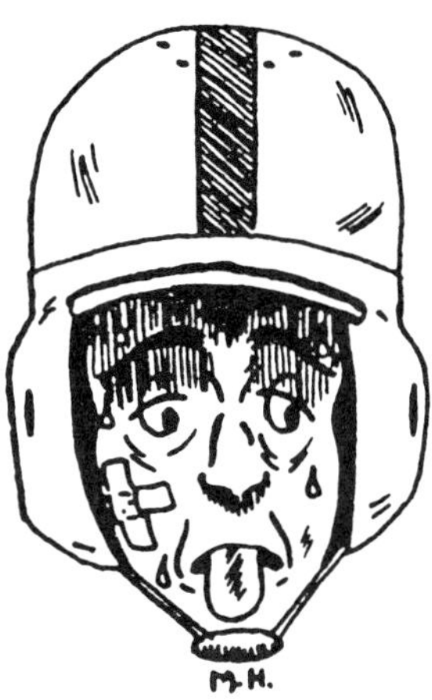

Old Boys sons   1958

from bottom of stairs (left to right): Peter Elwood, Michael Hadley; Roger Rowley, James McPhail; Brian Merrett; Christopher Coristine, David Minnes; John Gamble, Sam Gamble Jr., Ronald Perry, Headmaster

First Football Team 1954-55

Back Row (from left): A. Wurtele, P.A. Riddell, E.J. Drew, B.K. Hillary, H. Kahle, T.M. Devine, L. Ochoa, D.I.T. Gamble
3rd Row: C.P. Hermann, Esq., D. Graham, A.W. Lackey, D.M.T. Widdrington, R.C. Pennington, J.M. Grant, R.E.B. Kemp, R.H. Perry, Esq.
2nd Row: J.B. Wedd, A.B. Wells, J.S. Irvin,(Vice-Capt.), C. Nowakowski, (Capt.), E.N. Rhodes, L.M. Killaly, F.W. Baer
Front Row : R.B. Grogan, M.I. Lawson, C.L. Gill, P.G. Beavers, S.A. Azubel, J.G. Marshall

Winners of the BCS Old Boys Trophy and undefeated in eight games.

The Choir

The Chapel, the choir and candlelit Christmas services are part of every alumnus' memories of the school.

The Chapel was built on simple classic lines in 1912 for a school of 100 boys. It has been used daily and on Sundays in term-time ever since. The Chaplain has always been Anglican in the Founder's tradition, but students of all religions pray or meditate together – with today's school of 500 in three "sittings."

Junior Track and Field - 1959-60

Back Row (from left): A.S.F. Wright, G.R.V. Benskin, P.R. Ryde, M.H.E. Sherwood, Esq., T.F. Hurdman, D.A.P. Gamble, C.J. Roche
2nd Row: H.K. Reed, C.H.C. Grant, M.S. Polk, Co-Captain; M. Feller, Co-Captain; T.G. Bell, B.J. Cooper, D.C. Polk
Front Row : J.V. Hearne, G.C.G. Bowie, R.J. Millar, M.L. Peterson, D.H. Nettleton, I.S. Cosh, P.M. Anketell-Jones

A junior school gym display at the parents' reception in 1968. Richard Larocque was the high-diver.

Most distinguished Canadians. The Right Honourable General Georges Vanier DSO, MC, CB, Governor General of Canada and Madame Vanier were welcomed by Ronald Perry to the inspection of the Cadet Corps in May, 1965. General Vanier was the 12th consecutive Governor General to visit the school.

Leonard H. Sibley, 1945 - 1966

As well as teaching science and chores like the annual prize line-up, Sib's room in the annex was open every evening to senior boys after study for snacks, music and conversation. He was a mainstay of the school.

First Soccer Team 1966-67
Ottawa High School Champions

Back Row (from left): A.D. MacDougall, P.A. Church, M.J. Lang, R.H. Hall-Brooks, W.D. Smith, A. Egan, Esq., (Assist. Coach)
2nd Row: R.J. Anderson, Esq., (Coach) I.D. MacKenzie, P.G. Loftus, W.J. Stevenson, P.Dyson, J.M. Mulaner, D.C. Polk, W.A. Joyce, Esq., Headmaster
Front Row : G. Woolsey, R.J. Millar, O.L. Lawson, (Capt.), J.H. Smellie (V.Capt), R.H. Armitage

Dining in Symington Hall 1967-68

For economy the boys waited on table themselves in Symington Hall from the late sixties, but service had always been family style and continues so today.

On Parliament Hill   1973

Old boy MPs Andy Brewin, Robert Stanfield, John Turner and Donald MacDonald with Ian Rhodes and Nigel Macleod, Captain of the School.   PHOTO: JOHN EVANS

Fathers and Sons   1977

Back Row (from left): Fred Maclaren, Donald Flam, Ned Rhodes, Mark Viets, Digby Viets, Brock Mordy, Michael Nesbitt, Blair Mordy, Joell Gallaman, Sam Gamble
Front Row : Fergus Maclaren, Stephen Flam, Jamie Woods, John Woods, John Nesbitt, Michael Gallaman, Mitchell Rosenberg and Dennis Gamble

Fifteen sons of old boys attended Ashbury in 1976-77. Nine fathers came to Closing Day.

PHOTO: JOHN EVANS

The Staff 1971-72

Back Row (from left): V.J. Burczak, P.H. Josselyn, H.J. Robertson, B. Wallin, G.J. McGuire, F.T. Jones, J.L. Beedell, B.B. Bellamy, D.L. Polk

2nd Row: P.J. Flynn, G.W. Babbitt, G. Armstrong, T.C. Tottenham, J.H. Humphreys, W.W. Byford, J.A. Glover, E.E. Green, R.J. Anderson

Front Row: Mrs. G.W. Babbitt, H. Penton, C.J. Inns, Housemaster of Woollcombe House; J.J. Marland, Assistant Headmaster; W.A. Joyce, Headmaster; M.H.E. Sherwood, Master-in-charge of the Junior School; G.W. Thomson, Housemaster of Connaught House; K.D. Niles, Mrs. J.T. Linn

Three Characters 1973

Three Ashbury characters (from left): Arthur Brain (1935-66), Ted Marshall (1954-76) and Alan "Curly" Powell (old boy 1929-34, staff 1946-58) meet at the old boys' dinner in 1973. The speaker was Ontario "super-minister," Bert Lawrence, the Provincial Secretary of Resource Development.

Cyril Currier (1894-1898) broke ground for the additions of 1973 operating a backhoe. Cyril was Ashbury's oldest old boy, always fit and active, through until he died in his 101st year in 1985. On the right of the photo is Ned Rhodes, Jr., Chairman of the Board. PHOTO: CANADIAN PRESS

CHAPTER 15
WILLIAM JOYCE

In the summer of 1966 William Anderson Joyce became Ashbury's sixth Headmaster. His coming was heralded by tremors through the school. Any new Head is bound to bring change and he'll always be greeted warily, perhaps even with suspicion, until he's shown his stuff. But W.A. Joyce faced more than that. The differences had gone on for a long time unresolved, the lines had been drawn and loyalties among the old-guard staff and many of the older boys so strongly forged that there was real reluctance to accepting him. Besides, that remote body the Board had dictated a shaking-up of their school and had chosen an iron-fisted soldier to do the job.

Things military were regarded with suspicion, even contempt, at this time, particularly among the young. The Vietnam War had been grinding on since 1962 and the deep trauma it had wrought in the USA had spread, not only to Canada but to Europe as well. At Ashbury talk of dreaded things to come at Colonel Joyce's hands had spread through the ranks. The prefects already chosen for the coming year got together during the summer. There were 10 (as against 16 the year before): Kennedy Lawson was to be Captain of the School; Bill Stevenson, Captain of Woollcombe; Jim Smellie, Captain of Connaught; Michael Evans, Peter MacPhail, David Polk, Christopher Stone, Bill Hogarth, Jack Steenbakkers and Michael Wennberg.

Those who were in Ottawa huddled at the Smellies' house, second-guessing the changes to come, deploring the high-handedness of the Board. Along with the previous Head, half the teaching staff had already been swept out by this martinet whom they hadn't even seen. Even though Buggy Brain had become more and more erratic, the affectionate memories eclipsed the outrageous. Sib would be sorely missed, as in his way would Sharpy Snelgrove.

Jim Smellie had come to Ashbury reluctantly in 1962 and survived – among other things – threats of beating by a certain classmate, possessed of more brawn than brain, if he didn't help him cheat in a math exam. (Jim didn't, and was agile enough to escape retribution.) Now he and the rest had risen through the rough-and-tumble to the prefectorial heights at last. In common with prefects of any era, they didn't want change impinging on their bailiwick and there was no doubt change was coming. There was strong talk of leaving the school en bloc.

Jim's mother, Fran Smellie, was President of the Mothers' Guild and one of the first people the new Head met when he arrived. She had come to size him up; she had never met him, though her husband Peter had – in battle in 1944. She brought back her impressions to the boys and told them they'd be well advised to go back in the fall. That, as surely as Peter's grenade attack at Boulogne, cleared the way. But, as in 1944, there was still some heavy fighting to come.

W.A. Joyce (W.A.J. quickly became "Wadje" at Ashbury, following the acronym tradition) was raised in Winnipeg and went off to Appleby College in Oakville from 1930 to 1934. He then spent four years at the Royal Military College, Kingston.

There were very few openings in the permanent army then. He joined the reserve –
Winnipeg's Fort Garry Horse – and spent another year at the University of Manitoba
finishing his degree in Civil Engineering. When war broke out he was on a survey
gang for the Canadian Pacific Railway – the only job in those hard times a fresh-minted
engineer could get.

He joined up as soon as war started; he and Peggy Snyder of Waterloo were
married before he went overseas in 1941 and distinguished himself in battle. After the
war he worked for the National Research Council, then the mortgage department of
an insurance company, and in 1950 an old friend, Rusty Bell, who was Headmaster
of Appleby, asked him if he'd like to join his staff. Appleby had some 300 boys then,
mostly boarders. Joyce was Director of Maintenance first, then taught math and
physics. After four years he became a housemaster.

In 1964 he felt it was time for a move. He got a position at Tunbridge School in
England for a year under Michael McCrum, who later became Headmaster of Eton and
then Master of Corpus Christi College, Cambridge. McCrum recommended him to
Uppingham, another solidly established public school. In late 1965, on a trip to
Canada, Joyce heard that Ashbury was looking for a new Head and he applied. Later
he flew back for an interview and got the job.

The selection committee consisted of Board Chairman Dick Ross, Vice-Chairman Don Maclaren and Commander C. Herbert Little. Commander Little had taught
at Upper Canada College in the thirties and he was an accomplished linguist. He had
joined the navy at the start of the war and was now serving in Naval Headquarters with
Commodore Dick Ross and Captain George Woollcombe. He'd been invited to join
the Board as an educational adviser. By now the members of the Board had defined
their objectives for the school. They wanted to see an orderly administration, sound
academic standards and firmly structured organization with even-handed discipline.

At 50 Joyce was a little older than they might have preferred. But his education,
his solid record in traditional schools, his business experience and a distinguished war
record told in his favour. His own background was engineering, math and science, but
he considered English – communicating in one's own language – to be the most
important element in education. He believed strongly in the boarding school. He was
their kind of man with their kind of background, and he got the job.

It was obvious to him that he was taking on a real challenge. The plant left a great
deal to be desired and the Board members hadn't hidden their concerns about staff.
Arthur Brain and Little, it happened, knew each other well from playing cricket
together for years. Brain was given his option and he decided it was time to go. It was
clear to all that there would be more changes and the masters' common room seethed
with rumours that the new broom was going to sweep the lot of them summarily out
the door. In fact, apart from the old hands, the staff had been disturbingly unstable for
some time. Since 1961, there'd been an average of nine changes a year out of a full-
time teaching staff of about 23.

Other than his first quick look when he was interviewed the Headmaster-
designate couldn't spend any time at Ashbury until summer term ended at Uppingham
in August. It had been arranged that Commander Little, corresponding with him,
would select new staff. However, with the state of alarm among the existing staff,
Joyce flew back and interviewed each one.

To Leonard Sibley he said his position was open if he wanted to stay. Sib elected to leave. He must have felt very deeply about Perry and about Brain's decision, because Ashbury had been virtually his home since 1945. It was the last year, too, for A.H. Snelgrove, H.W. Atwood, I.D. Copeland, A.J. Hancock and R.J. Munson. In the junior school Miss W.G. Black, Nancy Jacobsen, P.M. Gillean and Rev. N.C. Peyton left.

W.A.J. appointed J.J. "Jake" Marland as his Assistant Headmaster, replacing Brain and taking on Sibley's duties as Director of Studies too. Marland was a steady, level-headed man, a North-Country Englishman who had spent 17 of his early years, including wartime, at sea as an officer in the merchant marine. He was badly wounded, put in an office ashore, married and then took up teaching. He and his wife, Rosalind, decided to emigrate in 1957 and he taught in Temiskaming. During his first year there he heard about Ashbury from an old boy, made a phone call and came aboard.

Jake Marland was a man with quiet integrity and a completely different style from either of the two men he replaced. Rosalind was a sparkling, warm-hearted dynamo, famous among the many they entertained for her delectable meat pies. Their son Paul graduated from Ashbury in 1960 and became a teacher himself. The Marlands were the first to live in the first staff house built on Mariposa.

Ray Anderson, stalwart since 1954, stayed on. Over in the junior school, rock-solid David Polk stayed. Actually he didn't want to stay in charge; he wanted just to teach and he'd already proposed that Michael Sherwood should come back as his assistant for a year and then take over the reins. Sherwood had started coaching junior school hockey and doing a bit of teaching in 1958 while finishing his degree at Carleton. The following year he'd come on staff, living in at the going rate of $2000 a year. During the divisive events of 1961 when Ron Perry stayed, he decided to go. He was in business for a while but was back teaching at Selwyn House when Herbert Little called him for an interview.

Dr. Kitty Spencer, an experienced expert in remedial reading, stayed on. She'd come to Ashbury first in 1958, and had left for Japan for four years to stay with her oldest son while her second son Michael took his degree in Tokyo. Michael had been Co-Captain of the School at Ashbury with Peter Noel-Bentley in 1961, and he came back in 1965 at the same time as his mother to teach in the senior school for three years. After 1968 Dr. Spencer taught part-time. Michael went into the foreign service and travelled the globe. His son Bob became Captain of the School in 1985 and his daughter Lisa graduated from Ashbury in 1987.

Herbert Dalton came back to teach mathematics. His wife Muriel had joined the staff in 1954. She was a charming, gentle lady who taught all the boys in Grades 1, 2 and 3, jammed together in a dingy basement classroom with scarcely a break other than their daily session with Ray Anderson to work off some steam in the gym. Herbert joined her in her second year to teach mathematics in the senior school and they both stayed until 1964. When he came back this time he taught for another year, then became the Bursar. He died suddenly, of a heart attack, in 1968. Muriel Dalton came back in 1971 as the weekend nurse and continued to do do for another 13 years.

Back in England Joyce hired W.W. Byford to teach chemistry and a new Chaplain and experienced English teacher, Rev. Ian Watson. Watson became Woollcombe's housemaster and, with Arthur Brain gone, he did his best to keep cricket from dying out. Oddly, the team was dominated by a group of keen South Americans at this time and the matches rang with the equivalents of "well bowled, sir" in Spanish.

In the meantime Commander Little put in a busy summer interviewing close to 60 people for the vacant slots. Altogether he made a very valuable contribution to the school at a difficult time simply on the basis of friendship and an interest in independent education. He stayed on the Board for another year.

Betty Babbitt was among the new arrivals in the junior school. Three years later her husband Bill, a retired naval aviator, joined the staff. They provided warm, solid strength there until 1982. Pierre Fortier became the first native-speaking French teacher at Ashbury since J.M. Fleury. Other new arrivals were J.B. Fudakowski, J.G. Shovanek and J. Vincent. Eleven new people out of a teaching staff of 24. The fall term of 1966 opened with a very different school.

Preconceptions aside, W.A. Joyce was a schoolmaster, not a soldier. He'd left the army behind him 20 years before, as had hundreds of thousands of Canada's citizen soldiers. His time at RMC and his wartime service had certainly consolidated his sense of order and discipline and developed his direct approach to whatever was at hand. He was a man who knew how to delegate, and he expected results. There was no doubt about where he stood, or who was in charge. He brought to Ashbury College what it needed at this time in its history – one strong hand firmly at the helm.

Decisions came thick and fast. The first crisis that summer was in the kitchen where the chef of 19 years fell out with under-cook Mark Tatichek. Mark was a post-war new Canadian from Poland who'd started in Ashbury's kitchen in 1958. He'd been summer cook at Camp Kawabi as well and he was a man of talent – and lively temperament. Mrs Tatichek was the school nurse and their son Peter was going through the school. W.A.J. settled the matter briskly and without bloodshed. Mark stayed as cook-manager in the kitchen for another 18 years.

The change in personality and approach in the Headmaster was like a cold bath. Very soon after school assembled in the fall, he found himself unhappy with the tone of the student body. Finances dictated that beds had to be filled, but quality came first. That meant tough decisions. Enrolment had dropped sharply. In the peak year, 1958, it had been up to 293. By 1965 it had slumped to 236. Joyce started with around 240. It was well below capacity but he swiftly put his finger on specific problems and dismissed 20 boys in his first year. The cold bath refreshed.

The tension was there, right from Opening Day. But school affairs go on. By the second week in November the first soccer team, with Ray Anderson's inspired coaching, had knocked off Lisgar, Ridgemont and Woodroffe in the Ottawa high school league. The final was against Ottawa Tech, very strong, undefeated in two years and four-time winners of the City Championship. The game was at Carleton University and the Head turned the whole school out to cheer.

Goals by John Mulaner and Philip Church and great goalkeeping by Russell Armitage pulled the game out of the hat for the first City of Ottawa soccer championship in Ashbury's history. As well, it was a just reward for the years Ray Anderson had spent coaching, getting the school into the Ottawa High School Athletic Association, and taking a leading role in developing soccer in all the Ottawa schools. At the annual sports dinner Anderson had a placard slung around his neck saying: I AM A

LIAR. It was penance for his early season prognostication that there was "no way" the soccer team could win the championship! If there was ever a morale-booster sent from heaven, that single soccer game was it.

Another boost for the school that year was the long-planned extension to Argyle. Ground was broken in September and the new classrooms were in use by spring. Bob Southam officially opened the Southam Library at the west end of the upper floor on Closing Day as a memorial to Wilson and Harry Southam. It was warmly panelled and comfortably furnished. The furniture – easy and upright chairs, tables and shelving – was built to last. It's still in use in the new library.

W.A.J. was a boarding school man and he set out to boost activities for the boys outside the classroom and the playing field. Close to a dozen club activities started, with varying success. Officially there was no Geography Club, though David Polk still chaired periodic meetings.

The new Head developed a larger place for music in the school. With his encouragement Irene Woodburn (now Irene Wright) organized some Sunday evening concerts, mainly with young musicians from the Ottawa area. Unfortunately this was her last year. She had joined the staff in 1943 to teach the juniors music appreciation, and she'd never looked back. Her aim was to encourage the boys to enjoy fine music and form their own tastes, to discover the principles of rhythm, the relationship of harmony and melody and the sounds of the instruments, and to learn something of musical history. She built an award-winning percussion band and introduced the recorder before it became so widely used in schools.

She got every director of the junior school behind her, in particular David Polk. Music wasn't just a frill and it wasn't for sissies; it was part of the life of the junior school, it was fun and the boys loved it. Indeed, in David Polk's view, understanding and loving music was one of a boy's most important lifetime acquisitions even though he did nothing but listen after he left school. Piano and instrumental lessons were available to all students as extras, of course, though facilities were pretty limited. Mrs Woodburn Wright's programme had never extended to the senior school.

The junior choir was always popular and very good. Godfrey Hewitt had been part-time organist and choir master at the school since 1961. In Ottawa music and church circles he was another James Edgar Birch and he was certainly among Canada's top ten in his field. He produced memorable special Chapel services and brought the choir along remarkably.

Since the school's beginnings there'd nearly always been some kind of popular music group making some kind of music – quality commensurate with talent at the time. The rise of the guitar with the 1950s revolution in popular music, then the development (diabolical, as most parents would say) of electronics made it a good deal easier to put something together that passed. But generally, in the senior school, there wasn't much to foster interest in classical or modern music.

That was to change. In the fall of 1967 Geoffrey W. Thomson joined the staff from England as Director of Music and Housemaster of New House, which was added as a boarder house to Connaught and Woollcombe. Music now got a toehold in the senior school in the shape of one period a week for Grades 9, 10 and 11. Rev. Watson had revived the performing arts with an Ashbury-Elmwood production of Gilbert and Sullivan's *Trial by Jury* the year before. But then he'd left. Thomson picked up the threads and produced a rousing rendition of *HMS Pinafore*.

The new Head was keen on the cadet corps, as might well be expected. The image of Colonel Joyce, the military man, was certainly reinforced that first spring when he wore his dark blue dress uniform at the annual inspection, medals agleam. The shades of the past must have been too much to resist. The inspecting officer was Major-General Roger Rowley and the Commanding Officer of the Corps was Cadet Major Jim Smellie.

In W.A.J.'s second year there were only 226 boys enrolled. Building the student body in both strength and numbers would take time and patience. Weeding out was the first stage, but Joyce was by no means the ogre of initial repute. He was convinced that an independent school could and should help young people who had problems that understanding, personal supervision and firm guidance could help. The trick was to keep their numbers in hand. But finances couldn't be discounted and not every selection was ideal. He had his disappointments but strength slowly and steadily improved.

The staff, decimated as it had been, had to be rebuilt. Salaries and benefits, as they had been for years, were below the public level. The expected involvement outside the classroom – the sports and extracurricular activities, evening duties – being a constant example to the boys, the consuming involvement in school life to the inevitable limitations of one's own – all these were not to everyone's taste. Squeaking by financially while living among compatible people was no longer enough. Teachers, through their unions, were gaining more control over conditions of employment and in effect over curriculum – and, with the great changes that were going on, losing it over their students. People with the character, temperament and dedication for the independent school, with first-rate teaching ability to boot, didn't grow on trees.

In 1968, though, with a turnover of 11 again, W.A.J. made some very sound selections. Seven of them – Tim Tottenham, James Glover, Ken Niles, Hugh Robertson, Hugh Penton, John Beedell and Jim Humphreys – became long-termers and the latter five are solid-core Ashbury today. Staff turnover continued to be quite high but such people provided the anchor. By their character, personality and personal example, as well as their dedicated skill, they made enduring contributions to the lives of hundreds of students over more than 20 years.

Another long-term member, Rev. E.E. "Jeep" Green, took over as Chaplain in 1969. Peter Josselyn came to teach English that year, and the next brought Bruce Wallin and George McGuire. Each one of these Ashbury people is different, each very much an individual. They hold one vital characteristic in common and that is all-out dedication to the interests of their students.

One thing hadn't changed and that was the office. Joe Irvin Sr. continued as Director of Administration. In his time at Ashbury from 1918 to 1928 he'd been the finest athlete the school had every produced, and his son Joe followed in those footsteps in the fifties. Joe Sr. joined the Board in 1954 as Vice-Chairman, became Chairman 1956-1957, then resigned to join the salaried staff; he held the post until he died of a sudden heart attack in 1968.

The ladies who had run the office so faithfully, cheerfully and well stayed on. Olive Thurston had been the Headmaster's secretary since 1964. She was efficient, outgoing and entertaining and put up with no nonsense. As parent of Peter (1960-

1966) and stalwart Mothers' Guild member she was always there to lend a hand –
decorating the gym for dances, rigging out the choir boys on Sundays, selling tickets
for old boys' events.

Ethel Pryde, who emigrated from Scotland with her husband and three-year-old
Derek, had been bookkeeper, then Bursar, since 1957. Derek spent 12 years at
Ashbury. Ethel's lifelong friend June Gensey emigrated too and joined her as
secretary in 1960. They found the new Head's manner formal, almost stern, certainly
in comparison with Ron Perry's affable informality. They retained their affection for
the old Headmaster as they developed respect and regard for the new, and they didn't
miss a beat.

The three were the sum total of the office staff (there are 10 today). They worked
on with remarkable and wholehearted dedication, Olive Thurston until 1982; Ethel
and June are there still with 65 years service between them, their Scottish brogues
warmly intact. Far more than just efficent service, they have always projected that
feeling of friendship and family that comes with Ashbury's character. There's
something to be said for an institution that attracts and holds the kind of people who
care less about the pay than about enjoying what they're doing, working hard at it,
making a contribution that's appreciated and getting true satisfaction from a job well
done.

Fred Oliver was a notable example in another field, and so was Ted Marshall who
followed him in 1954. No title came with the job – or rather the whole grab-bag of jobs
– that Ted assumed. He was groundsman, keeper of the tuck shop, custodian of sports
gear and all manner of essentials, bartender par excellence at social gatherings, fixture
at every old boys' event, always in the know, doer of anything that needed doing – and
he loved doing it all. He had the memory of an elephant. He could recall at a glance
every single boy who had gone through the school while he was there. The title
"Steward," which came in course of time, didn't stem from his activities at social
events; it was much closer to its fourteenth-century roots as "a high administrative
officer."

Cricket was Ted's life. When it was time to muster an old boys' team, he got on
the phone and who, from the newest graduate to the highest in the land, could say "no"?
A call from Ted Marshall to a cabinet minister's office went straight, without question,
to the man himself.

Ted had left Ashbury in 1966 for Ridley and, when W.A.J. found that a myriad
detailed jobs weren't being managed well, he heard the laments about Ted's absence.
Some detective work revealed that he hadn't fitted in at Ridley and had gone back to
his native England where he had a job at Ontario House. It just so happened that the
Agent General for Ontario was Jim Armstrong, the Ashbury old boy who had taken
a hand years before in organizing the Old Boys' Association in Toronto. Ted Marshall
was a gem at his job in London but Jim didn't stand in the way. Back came Ted in 1968
and for the next eight years he was a mainstay of Ashbury College, one of those true
gentlemen who gives to life and everyone he encounters far more than he ever takes.
When he left to retire out west in 1976, he planted a maple tree in front of the school.
Just two years later he died of cancer. His ashes came back to be buried among its roots
in the place where his heart had been for so many years.

Canada's centennial, 1967, was marked at Ashbury by two school-shaking changes. First, the venerable game of cricket, introduced at Ashbury by G.P. Woollcombe in 1900, ceased to be the prime sporting rite of spring. Many mourned, though few among the current boys. In latter years enthusiasm had tapered off and it was a far cry now from the days when Arthur Brain was out at the nets at 6:30 a.m., perched on his shooting stick, pipe in mouth, casting his pearls of cricket wisdom before the young swine flailing away with bat and ball.

To the vast majority of Canadians cricket was a baffling anachronism, kept strangely alive in pseudo-British upper-crust enclaves. Later tides of Commonwealth immigration boosted the game but in most parts of the country the independent schools had probably done more than anything else to keep it alive at all.

By now the Ottawa league had shrunk. At the school fewer staff members had the game in their sporting repertoires. To get a school match meant travelling to Lakefield, TCS or Bishop's. The spring season was very short, what with waiting for the pitches to be dry enough and buckling down to exams, and local clubs had barely got their seasons underway. Tennis, track and field and a spring start at soccer replaced cricket.

To Ted Marshall, who'd been born with bat in hand and the game in his blood, this was akin to losing an arm. Wanted or not, he faithfully tended the pitch and for years got old boys' and parents' teams together for friendly matches.

Secondly, the dawn of Canada's second century was marked at Ashbury by the advent of girls. Grade 13 Elmwood students began coming over for mathematics. French was next. More courses were shared; the traffic moved both ways and grew each year. It was a good move for both schools. It offered more credit options with specialized teaching; Jane Kennedy, for example, came in 1973 to teach business studies, an appointment that wouldn't have been possible for either school alone. It broadened opportunities and perspectives; it brought fresh air to cloistered lives.

"Operation Elmwood," from surveillance and scouting, through reconnaissance in force to trophy-taking raids, had occupied Ashbury minds and energies since older girls started going there in the twenties. Having girls around the corridors and classrooms day-to-day took the edge off such clandestine activities to some extent, but they certainly didn't disappear. When "streaking" came in vogue in the mid-seventies Mike Beedell capped them all with a masterfully executed operation. It was timed to the second just before noon. Clad in basketball shoes with a paper bag over his head, he burst in the Elmwood rear door, scattered a gymful of girls like a fox in a barnyard full of chickens, raced through the dining hall to the alarm of the first lunch sitting, bowed politely past the office, sped out the front door and leapt into a waiting car for a clean getaway.

W.A. Joyce was the fourth Headmaster to deplore the rundown state of the plant. In 1968 the property on Springfield Road called Dunkerton House was bought by an anonymous benefactor and leased to the school pending eventual transfer for use variously as dormitory and staff quarters. That certainly helped, but in spite of the modest addition to Argyle, the state of everything from the front entrance to classroom spaces, labs, dormitories and the undersized gym worked directly against the need to raise enrolment. Desperately needed was a set of buildings in which the school could take pride, and that called for substantial work and a lot of money.

But the strife of the early sixties and the upheaval of 1966 had so divided the Ashbury family that a lot of potential financial support had been lost, perhaps for good. Communications had been sporadic. The Old Boys Association was low on drive. An Association newsletter went out intermittently, but other contacts by the school were limited to seemingly incessant appeals for funds. Going right back to the early thirties no campaign had reached its target, and each failed effort to raise money had defeated the next.

Raising the quality of staff and the student body was essential and this was progressing. As regards fund-raising, the new Head could see that a systematic start had to be made on the root problem of cultivating the constituency. David Polk was appointed secretary of the Old Boys Association in 1967. There could have been no better choice. David, already a 24-year institution, was genuinely loved by all.

Next, Major-General Dan Spry became executive treasurer of the Ashbury College Development Fund. He was an outstanding wartime soldier, President of the World Boy Scouts for several years, parent of Toby, and a Board member from 1963. Dan Spry went off to other schools and associations to learn the game and set about gearing up a fund-raising operation. Following the American lead, the major Canadian independent schools had had some version of Polk's and Spry's functions – called "Director of Development" or something similar – for some time. Generally the schools needed about $50,000 a year other than fees for their general operations and that didn't include funds for building projects. They had to work systematically and hard to get it.

The Development Fund was to be fuelled by a sustained campaign rather than a crash appeal for immediate needs. The Ashbury College Fund was incorporated in the United States so supporters there could get some tax benefits for donations. After a couple of years David Polk chose to go back to teaching full-time, but between him and Dan Spry a lot of solid work was done on building mailing lists, tracking down the lost legions and developing contacts.

There was a full measure of confidence between the Head and the Board. A clear structure fostered involvement by committees on education, development, school functions, finance and publicity and fund-raising. Costs were escalating sharply and not just from inflation. In 1967 the Head's proposal to pay a premium for five heads of department added $25,000 to the budget – the fees for 10 senior boarders. Such strengthening was essential and there was a lot of catching up due on all staff salaries. The notion of running the dining hall as a cafeteria to save money was firmly rejected though. Sitting family-style, with a staff member at the head of each table, continued as it always had as an influence for civility. Domestic costs were cut by having the boys wait on table.

A major change in the Ontario school system came in 1967 when the provincial exams were dropped. Examinations for university entrance were now set and marked by each school, so in effect each school set its own standard. The following year the Ministry of Education's Inspector reported positive changes at Ashbury in attitude, discipline and philosophy – due, he remarked, to new leadership. Discipline, in the boys' view, was certainly firm, but it was even-handed and fair. Enrolment was creeping up, to 261 by 1969. Not all were the best and the Headmaster knew it. The turnover was continual. So was financial stringency. W.A.J. and Michael Sherwood drove to Montreal from time to time and headquartered in a modest motel for a couple of days to accomplish two missions – tracking down new students and collecting overdue accounts.

Strengthening the student body depended a good deal on the availability of scholarship and bursary money – scholarships to attract the academically gifted and bursaries to entice good all-rounders who'd contribute to the school but whose parents couldn't pay full fees. In 1969 C.E. Pickering endowed a substantial fund, the income to go to bursaries and scholarships.

Mr. Pickering had five grandsons at Ashbury around that time: Peter, Eric and Tim Wilson and Matthew and Robert Pimm, plus two step-grandsons Hugh and Rob Wilson. At about their time in life, aged 13, young Chester Pickering was living by his wits in the hobo jungles of New England. Ashbury then was only three years old. He got into sales and started a business selling an industrial floor cleaning compound. He came to Canada and – rare for this city – built an industrial empire in Ottawa called Dustbane Enterprises. Among other ventures he had a major hand in building the Lord Elgin Hotel in 1941. Chester Pickering had a heartfelt appreciation of what it could mean to give a youngster the kind of educational opportunity he had never had. He lived to see Ashbury go from strength to strength, and died in 1983 at the ripe age of 101. His memorial is the fine stained-glass window on the south side of the Chapel.

The Old Boys Association started a Tiny Hermann Memorial Scholarship Fund. Results, as with the ongoing fund-raising, were frustratingly slow. But such things take a great deal of time. In 1969, an annual giving campaign began. By 1971, including the Pickering Fund the Headmaster had $19,000 available annually for bursaries and scholarships. Fees that year were $3000 for a senior boarder, $1500 for a junior day boy.

During this time the Association of Governing Bodies of Independent Schools in Ontario was looking for government support. In Quebec, for example, independent schools that met Ministry of Education standards were eligible for an annual grant related to the per-student cost of education in the public system. A fair and just arrangement. Bishop's, for instance, suffered no Ministry interference and was able to charge fees significantly lower than a similar Ontario school. In Quebec, though, the Roman Catholic Church historically had controlled education. Then, in the Quiet Revolution in the sixties when government took over, church schools kept their slice of tax money, and the same had to apply to other independent institutions. No such luck in Ontario.

While the Ministry of Education wouldn't budge on money, its policies naturally bore heavily on the independent school. Huge education budgets over 20 years had put Ashbury far behind the average high school in laboratories, equipment and facilities. Then the 1968 "Living and Learning" Hall-Dennis Report on Ontario school programmes sparked sweeping changes in the whole system.

Unlike the usual jargon-packed official report, Hall-Dennis was in layman's language. It was a national best-seller at 60,000 copies and it got wide support. It recognized the impact of the sixties' popular culture and the sexual revolution. The authors rejected the streaming that had been brought in in the early 1960s. They called for a shift from "content" to "experience" – no more memorizing, no more regurgitating facts. Punishment was demoralizing because it negated moral responsibility –

no more lines or detention. A major point was the introduction of a wide range of course options. Fisher Park High School was one of six in the province to experiment with the credit system. They found it needed computer timetabling and student counselling.

By 1972 the new Ontario credit system was in place across the province. With the new freedom of student choice there was a drop in history and second languages, an increase in sciences, creative arts, social sciences and vocational subjects. English and math stayed the same. Teachers got more flexibility in curriculum design and began a continuing trend to develop competitive courses to attract students to their subject.

To Ashbury, all this meant increased and more specialized staff and equipment. That added up to more money and so more pressure to build numbers in the student body. By 1971 enrolment was up to 290. Two portable classrooms squeezed between the kitchen and Glenwood took some of the pressure. But the whole fabric of the place was outdated, tired and badly run-down. The mere look of the place was a poor advertisement. The Headmaster and junior school director had to swallow hard to stop themselves apologizing when showing prospective parents around.

There was no spare money, nothing for maintenance or improvements. So it was band-aid, do-it-yourself time. Science master Bruce Wallin hired students in the summer to renovate and panel the boys' and live-in masters' rooms. John Beedell led the junior school staff in an entirely spare-time volunteer project to build the boys their own common room. They took a remote attic space in the senior wing, made it over, panelled it and linked it ingeniously to the junior wing by building an enclosed bridge. It survives as the TV room today. Next, they all gave up a long weekend to scrape and paint the boys' rooms.

W.A.J. pushed hard for major renovation and expansion. Architects Murray and Murray worked out an expansion plan. (Tim Murray's Thady, Sean and Sarah and Pat's Patrick, Fiona and Brian all went through Ashbury between 1972 and 1988.) Their proposal in 1971 developed the earlier concept of enclosing the quadrangle, sparked interest and got down to serious figures. The following June, though, William Teron, father of Chris and Willie, who was on the Development Committee, presented a different approach.

Bill Teron had started a small house-building business in Ottawa in the early fifties in conjunction with a contemporary furniture store in which his wife was a partner. He quickly moved on to subdivisions and then to whole towns. Kanata was his concept and he was the one who started it in the sixties. He was a highly successful developer and designer who combined vision and imagination with a gift for devising new, human-scale solutions. The Teron plan for Ashbury was a practical and economical approach to expansion. Developed architecturally by the Murrays, it produced, in two major bites, the Ashbury College configuration of today.

The Board was now chaired by Montreal old boy Charles Brown. He was dynamic, blunt and exceptionally energetic. His colleagues responded to his challenge and in June 1972 they took the bull by the horns. The mortgage was increased from $170,000 to $300,000 to get things started. Plans and specifications were drawn up and the Development Fund was reconstituted into a capital drive called Action Ashbury.

The all-volunteer approach hadn't worked and earlier experience with fund-raising consultants had been less than successful. Action Ashbury hired Tony German as executive director. He had taken early retirement from the navy in 1966. In the fall of 1972 he became the school's first full-time Director of Development, responsible for administering old boys' affairs, fund-raising and public relations. The following year the first Old Boys' Directory in Ashbury's history was published. The campaign committees now had an organized operating base to coordinate their work.

The new Head had run straight into discipline problems. The old thorn – day boys off and running free, while the devil made work on the weekends for idle boarders' hands – jabbed harder these days. Inter-school games in the Ottawa area took place during the week now. Saturday afternoon sports were dying out. W.A.J. proposed Saturday morning classes for all. That went down with day students and their families like the proverbial lead balloon.

And these were the days of seething unrest among the young of North America and Europe. The Vietnam War had taken a terrible toll on young Americans. Their country had lost its bearings. Theirs was a generation of disenchantment. Pot and the pill. Campus unrest, student revolt, the drug culture. Basic values everywhere were challenged. Authority, in schools and universities – any kind of authority – was under siege. Long hair and scraggly beards, sandals, the whiff of marijuana. It was a time, more than any other in memory, for rejection, for dropping out.

The tide moved north. Parents quailed at what was happening in Canadian high schools. The clothes. The music. The drugs. Sex. Discipline was breaking down and it was helped on its way by many aspects of the Hall-Dennis Report. The cry of the sixties, supported by the press and political and educational leaders, had been for individual freedom. "Living and Learning" had been the response. Its essentially child-centred philosophy proposed that, right from elementary school, children shouldn't compete with each other but rather find their own level. Whatever their motivation, high-school students were to be offered courses they were able, or willing, to handle.

Education historian Robert M. Stamp wrote in *The Schools of Ontario* in 1982 that Lloyd Dennis, the unorthodox Toronto elementary school principal who was the prime instigator of the Report, had said in 1970 that "The days of established order, propriety and moral admonition are gone." The concept was one of a move from the "Calvinistic to the Rousseauesque approach," away from "diligent, dutiful, industrious, to engendering independence and developing unique intellect and character."

How to achieve that essentially desirable latter aim without a good touch of the old-fashioned diligence, duty and industry? Schools like Ashbury could steer their own course. They were still inspected by the Ministry but they could draw their own lines, maintain their own rules and set their own demands for students. In 1969, for example, religious education was eliminated in the Ontario public system. (It had been required from 1944, Premier George Drew's time.) Independent schools could, of course, do what they wanted. Many parents, concerned about their children's education and future, approved of the structured approach. Just as generally, the students didn't. To the teen-ager rejecting the traditional ideas of an Ashbury College was being with the times.

Lines were drawn on the visible things that made Ashbury "different." Jackets, ties required, and *no jeans allowed*. Anytime. After generations of the crew cut, long hair was in vogue – but not at Ashbury. These were the visible foci of discontent, the symbols of the hold-out against crumbling values – values cherished by older generations and rejected by the new. Collisions were inevitable – between parent and offspring, student and "the system," student and teacher. There was no question where W.A.J. stood. Corporal punishment, the old bugbear, was still on the books, but administered only by the Headmaster, and rarely. But discipline was certainly strict.

The Head was, by background and beliefs, firmly in favour of the cadet corps. The Ashbury corps had started in 1905 in the days when each high school turned out its corps with pride. It had shone over the years, with regular distinction in rifle shooting and annual inspection reports. It was always an all-hands affair – everyone in the senior school was in the corps. But now things military were out. High-school corps had largely disappeared by the 1970s and many other independent schools were dropping theirs. It reflected the temper of the country. Old boy Donald Macdonald was Minister of National Defence, dealing with the cuts in defence budgets and reductions in strength that had been reducing the armed forces since the late sixties.

The great army raid on Ashbury in 1964 had taken away not only the rifles but a lot of instructional equipment, including radios and field kit. In spite of all the publicity, little of it was restored. To Ray Anderson, officer-in-charge of cadets, the corps lost a lot of its point just drilling for one big parade a year. He withdrew, and other staff members with little military background struggled on.

The whole corps, that is, the whole senior school, went to Camp Petawawa in 1971 for a training camp, but it was the swan song. By the next year cadets had become a subject of deliberate ridicule. The Headmaster, with great reluctance, gave up and that, after 67 years, was the end of the Ashbury College Cadet Corps.

CHAPTER **16**

TURNING POINT

In his valedictory speech of 1969 Bill Haughton had said, "Revolution has not yet come to Ashbury College." The tides of youth were certainly running high but they hadn't actually burst the floodgates. To the turbulence of the times the Headmaster's answer was to shore up the gates, keep his school watertight, maintain traditional standards.

It was a continual struggle. School uniform came under fire. Why couldn't the boys wear sweaters and slacks? Why not blue jeans – youth's universal uniform – after school and on weekends? And what about hair? Long was the fashion. Even the Prime Minister's hung to his collar. And he'd worn sandals and an ascot in the House of Commons.

The public schools were giving up the unequal struggle. Dress codes were no more. Along with such symbols long-accepted respect for order and authority was going down the drain. Classroom discipline was crumbling. Teaching was becoming far more difficult. So was learning. Parents wrung their hands and coped with the tide as they saw best. To many, a stand-fast school like Ashbury looked a good port in the storm.

The Ashbury boy's distinctive dress had always drawn, from some quarters, a sniff about snobbery, but more often than not he'd been proud of his smart turnout. Now, his jacket and tie marked him as right out of the mainstream. In an isolated boarding school everyone was in the same boat; with two-thirds day boys, though, differences loomed large.

There's no doubt that the port-in-the-storm got quite a number of boys who weren't coping elsewhere or whose parents couldn't handle them – some who'd had trouble at more than one school, some with serious drug problems that weren't revealed by parents or previous schools, a few who were plain bad eggs. W.A.J.'s urge to extend a helping hand, plus the need to fill places to stay afloat, added problems. Breaches of discipline tended to be answered with rules. The waves might pound at the floodgates, but Ashbury would hold firm.

The prefects had never been elected by their peers to represent their interests up the line as with a school council. They were appointed by the Head as the right arm of the administration, with power and authority to see that rules were observed and good order prevailed. In return they had privileges and prestige. New boys still fagged for prefects, with chores like shining shoes and taking sweaty football gear down to the locker room to dry. The badge of office was the red prefect's jacket.

The system was based on the boarding school idea. Room captains, appointed by housemasters, were responsible for order in their own part of the boarding bailiwick. The Captain of the School – the head prefect – by tradition lived in as a boarder. Indeed it was a condition of office, though in some earlier years there had been a Captain of Day Boys as well.

By and large the system worked. It provided organization for sports and interhouse competition and all manner of activities. It developed in those wearing the mantle an ability to take charge – though it didn't necessarily bestow the real attributes of "leadership." It helped many boys towards self-confidence. Among the lesser fry it bred skills for the ongoing guerrilla warfare between levels and factions, junior boys, prefects, masters and Head that was part and parcel of boarding school life.

The possibility of abuse was always there. It wasn't universal but new boys certainly ran into some bullying and some prefects were pretty arrogant – as one of the persecuted said, "swollen heads with small minds." It took alert guidance and sound psychology by sensible housemasters to see that firmness didn't become bullying, that privilege didn't lead to licence, that prestige didn't breed conceit. It wasn't easy at any time to find the man who was willing to live in cramped quarters with very little privacy or time to himself and who had the right experience and qualities, as well as being a competent teacher.

If Ashbury's floodgates didn't burst, outside influences more than seeped through the cracks. Drugs came in, as surely as they found their way into any school. The *Ashburian* ran poems on the subject. One began "Hey sonny, tired of wine and beer? Buy some hashish, there's nothing to fear." They cautioned rather than incited. In the close quarters of Ashbury with its high staff-to-student ratio and far greater interaction round the clock than in the high school, the influx of drugs was more controllable than elsewhere. It also raised a new aspect of staff responsibility for the well-being of boarders.

Youthful rejection of authority certainly found expression at Ashbury. In 1970-1971 the Grade 12s, a bright and lively bunch with plenty of ability, were discontented and restless. They chafed at the rules, questioned the reasons for them, felt stifled by regulation. By chance Peter Josselyn's English class brought the core group together. He didn't take their side or encourage rebellion but he saw their deep concern. A capable, wise and human schoolmaster with an open mind, Josselyn turned their ferment to the positive purpose of getting them to think things through, sort out their ideas and muster their arguments logically. The following year the prefects were chosen from their ranks.

Bryan Boyd was appointed Captain of the School and moved in to board, though his home was just around the corner. He had been at Ashbury since Grade 7. He was articulate, quick, a natural leader, excellent student, first-class athlete and also a loner of very independent mind. Unusually, of the 22 Grade 13s that year, 20 were boarders, and it was the boarders, of course, who were most affected and most steamed up.

Marc Duguay had been elected by the boys in 1971. That year the Head had opened two positions to popular vote. Marc would have been chosen anyway. He had come from the Gatineau only two years before by dint of strong family dedication, armed with very little English, a real determination to overcome shaky schooling, and an unquenchable spirit.

There was quiet, level-headed Ed Jokinen, Bill Stratton, Dick Bennet, Jim Bekaj, Bob Kenny, Nigel Macleod, Don Morrison, Kostas Rimsa and Bert Couturier, the leading light of the room captains with the liveliness and wit of his native Quebec City. This was an active and able group, and they were determined to change a system which, as they saw it, stifled initiative, produced discord and simply made them servants of a rigid, unlistening regime.

Prefects should, they felt, be the leaders of the students, representing their views and interests to the administration, not the administration's hatchet men. Why, they argued, should they enforce rules – on haircuts, for instance – that they had had no part in developing? Why did decrees descend from on high with the full expectation that the prefects would implement them without discussion or question? Why did they never sit down as a group to talk to the Headmaster on what, to them, were important issues? They genuinely wanted Ashbury to be a better place. The fact that they didn't feel happy they put down to a structured, rule-riven system with a punishment for any infraction.

When W.A.J. picked the school up and shook it into shape in the late sixties he reckoned it would take him five years with a pretty iron hand to sort things out. Now, after that allotted span, he still had some way to go. The student body still had some questionable spots. He had brought many first-rate people to his staff, but too many weren't of that calibre yet. So he kept a tight rein. And he wasn't a man who sought consensus or spent time explaining his decisions. Certainly the system was rigid, authoritarian, ruled by rules rather than a spirit of its own.

The man of the spirit in another sense, the school Chaplain, was Rev. Eugene E. Green. From pre-war days he'd been known as "Jeep" after a strange little animal character called Eugene the Jeep in the Popeye comic strip. It gave its name, too, to the Allied armies' tough little utility vehicle that saw service in every theatre of war.

Since the Woollcombe days when Head and Chaplain were one, there had always been an Anglican clergyman on staff. In earlier times scripture had been on the curriculum, and the Chaplain had taught regular school subjects too – for economy rather than through qualification – with varying success. When Rev. Ian Watson left, enquiries in the Ottawa diocese turned up Jeep Green.

He looked on Ashbury as his parish. The Chapel and its rituals weren't his focus. His function, he felt, was to be there as a friend – someone to take one's troubles to in confidence; someone to give advice if asked; someone outside the school hierarchy who could perhaps sort out personal things in informal ways. He was the Chaplain at Elmwood too, and his wife Joy was secretary there through the 1970s. Son David went to Ashbury, daughter Katherine to Elmwood.

Jeep's dual chaplaincy lasted for some 15 years. It was ready-made for promoting activities between the two schools – coffee houses, dances, outings. The Greens conducted an educational cruise in the Mediterranean each March break and it was an ongoing success. His confirmation classes included students from both schools and parents as well. At Ashbury his scheduled Chaplain's hours were devoted not to religious studies but to personal development – dating, relations with parents, sexuality, drinking, drugs. When Peter Josselyn took his first-rate talents off to become Headmaster of Queen Margaret School on Vancouver Island, Jeep took over public speaking and debating. On the sports scene he had charge of curling and he promoted activities like the live-in weekend when day boys brought in sleeping bags and shared the boarders' lives.

Chapel had always been part of school routine; it started off each day and it had always been compulsory. Jeep, by nature, was against regimentation in any form. He went along with it, but made his own services more free-form and colloquial. He used the Chapel to project his own ideas about human relations. On certain days the boys ran the services themselves.

In the Ashbury scheme of things, as Jeep saw it, the Headmaster was the priest, the pillar of structured orthodoxy. Jeep Green was the prophet, leading his flock, if necessary, on other paths. His message was not just – in the temper of the times – "Do your own thing," though some certainly took it as that; it was "Do what you believe is right." He was an activist and far more liberal than the Head. The two men's outlooks were bound to clash.

The year 1971-1972 was a watershed year. To start, the Headmaster reported to the Board on drugs and alcohol in the senior school with considerable concern. On top of that the prefects, from the beginning of the school year, were pretty much at odds with the administration. They balked at enforcing rules they hadn't had a hand in making. The bugbear of haircuts, for example. What was and wasn't acceptable had finally been put in the hands of a committee of boys with one staff member. When a higher-up took a direct hand and ordered "Get a haircut," it undermined the system.

The Head, in their view, wasn't listening. But the Chaplain was. He was right next to the prefects' common room in a dank little cubby-hole of an office in the gloomy basement with its overhead pipes. They unburdened themselves on the way they felt about the school and the things they'd like to see changed. Jeep Green was ever willing to listen and by nature sympathetic. The boys seized on a passage from a sermon of his on getting your personal act together, that there was a time for "revolution, not evolution."

Things came to a crunch in the winter of 1972 over, of all things, the death of a rock star. Jimmy Hendrix, an immensely popular British star, died of an overdose of drugs. A group of boys talked to the Chaplain and next morning they put on their own memorial service. Prominent in the Chapel were big posters of Hendrix and also Janice Joplin, who'd died of the same brand of self-destruction. Chaplain Green commented on Hendrix's last words, reported as urging others not to mess up their lives with drugs like him. W.A.J. stalked from the Chapel. With a stroke Jeep Green had put himself on the side of the boys versus the establishment. In no time word flashed around that he was fired as of the end of the year.

The boys at large had great regard for him. He listened to them. The prefects felt Ashbury needed him. They also felt responsible: because he'd supported them, it seemed he was about to lose his job. Bryan Boyd didn't put pressure on any of the other prefects but most said they'd resign if Jeep was fired. Boyd told the Head and wrote to Board members. Whatever happened, the Chaplain's contract was renewed.

Things continued at a slow burn. The prefects weren't cooperative or active in their expected role. The Head's door stayed open to Boyd; they worked together on routine matters, but they really stayed at loggerheads on basic issues.

In April 1972 Boyd wrote a 24-page paper which he called "a personal, biased investigation into Ashbury's problems during the past year." He sent it to Board members, the Head and friends. Slanted certainly, it was a very well-written piece – in that way a credit to Peter Josselyn's teaching. His summation of the Ashbury system was: "the more it insists on obedience, the more resistance it creates."

There was one symbolic victory for the boys. A look at the football and soccer team photos taken in the fall of 1971 shows hair cropped fairly short. The first hockey team, photographed in the following spring, sport some coiffures that reach the collar.

The cadet corps was the next target. Jim Bekaj was the cadet officer commanding and a good one. But the platoon commanders, his fellow prefects, blundered deliberately, reduced drill sessions to shambles. Between them they robbed the corps of its positive aspects and make it an object of ridicule. That spring's inspection was the last in the history of a venerable, and for many years valuable, Ashbury institution. Only a few of the independent school cadet corps survived this period. They were notably the ones with some special regimental affiliation, including a striking uniform rather than the drab old khaki.

This turbulent year ended with the most unusual valedictory address in the annals of Ashbury College. Bryan Boyd shook the usual large and genial crowd at Closing by talking not about athletic and other achievements but about conflict and alienation in a "tense, frustrating year . . . . [N]ot one person out there [who] accepts Ashbury's rules and standards without question." Communications he deemed poor, lack of discipline and student apathy symptoms of alienation.

Pretty strong stuff, and it broke all the bounds of traditional propriety. He made a plea for better relationships between staff and students – both ways. Paradoxically, "[W]e can be proud of Ashbury College even though we may hate it." But, he said, it was a tremendous year because things happened, the school progressed, people got involved. Then, with the whole company agog, he presented the Headmaster with a pair of blue jeans.

Feelings ran high. To most solid staff members Boyd, on a power trip, had stabbed his school in the back. The *Citizen* quoted the valedictory. W.A.J. responded with a letter. Through all of it, though, the driving force on both sides was the good of Ashbury College. While they railed at the restrictions, Boyd and his colleagues loved the school. They wanted to make it – in their eyes – better, and they put themselves out on a limb and risked their own final years to try and do so.

And Bill Joyce, with a very much longer view, showed extraordinary restraint. In fact, he had throughout. He even wore the blue jeans out to dinner that night. His big disappointment was over the valedictory and he quietly told Bryan so. Before Closing he had said Bryan could deliver it on the condition it followed the usual form. Bryan's understanding, given he was allowed on his feet, was that he could speak his mind. With all this going on he'd still won the Governor General's Medal. Ashbury gave Bryan Boyd a pretty good education and three years later W.A.J. welcomed him onto the Ashbury staff as a math tutor as he worked towards his MD. Then, when he set up family practice in Ottawa, he applied for the position Dr. Rowan-Legg had left after 33 years. In 1985 Dr. Bryan Boyd was appointed physician to his old school.

In retrospect he wouldn't give that valedictory again. He had had quite enough of conflict at Ashbury and took no part in university politics. But Marc Duguay did. In the student uprising at York he led the takeover of the Dean's office; such a move had once been discussed at Ashbury. When the class of '72 gathered for its 10-year reunion, Bryan was a doctor, Marc was a rising Montreal lawyer much involved in politics, Ed Jokinen an experienced Air Canada pilot, Nigel Macleod a lawyer and Bert Couturier running a successful hotel business in Quebec. All looked back on their time at Ashbury as a great and positive experience in their lives.

Nigel Macleod was the next school Captain. As a junior prefect through the troubles he had agreed with his seniors on the problems but had stuck to his conviction that they should work through the system, not confront it. The previous year's turmoil had conditioned things for change. He found W.A.J. open to suggestions and easy to work with.

The cadet honour guard, with its red tunics and bearskins (with the hair tucked under), continued for a while as a club activity. Nigel, anti-military though he was, was a member. He also got the Head's agreement to start the Ashbury Representative Council. There were elected class representatives and the aim was to open lines of communication up and down. It had a measure of usefulness, but died in a couple of years .

Things had changed. The troubles of '72 had made their point. No one wanted that tension and turmoil again. Communications had opened up. It was much easier now for the prefects to make their point, attend to their various duties and reflect the feelings of the student body up the line. Also, W.A.J., holding the line on externals like dress and on the basic structured, disciplined approach, preserved the fundamentals. Ashbury WAS different. It had solid, lasting values of its own. As it grew and strengthened in students, staff, administration and plant under his guidance, the basic values on which it was founded were steadily and solidly reaffirmed.

In that same spring of 1972, the Board registered a ringing expression of confidence in the Headmaster. They decided to go ahead with the building plan, put the essential first phase in the works and start a full-scale campaign for total needs at the same time. The building bill was to be $750,000.

On March 14, 1973, Cyril Currier, aged 91, Ashbury's senior old boy, took the controls of a backhoe and broke ground for the new wing. Cyril was a fine and remarkably symbolic choice. He had been at Ashbury from 1894 to 1898 when it was on Wellington Street. Lumbering fortunes waned and Cyril had a modestly successful career in banking. He still meticulously minded the accounts of a number of private estates.

A spade would have done him just as well as a backhoe because he'd always kept himself extraordinarily fit. Cyril had learned about physical fitness from G.P. Woollcombe, starting with those runs from Wellington Street around – and sometimes through – the centre block of the old Parliament Buildings. He'd been active in many sports and he and his wife had been outstanding badminton players.

He'd been a widower for some years. At his summer cottage he split wood and paddled miles by himself. In Ottawa he lived in a little upstairs flat over Laura Secord's at the corner of Bank and Fourth. His daily exercise regimen in the late 1970s included 100 sit-ups and a six-mile walk, likely to the Parliament Buildings and back. If the sidewalks were too icy for safety, he'd climb his stairs 50 times twice a day instead. Add to that a work-out with the chinning bar he'd fitted in the door-frame of his workshop. After he broke a hip in a fall, he took to a bicycle again, revisiting his old days of the penny-farthing.

Cyril's hobby was woodworking. He frugally collected used packing boxes from a fruit merchant. Reusing everything, nails and all, he made neat and sturdy little utility stools, ideal for that extra step-up when working around the house. He gave them away to his countless friends. The author's, still rock-solid as the man who made it, is signed "Cyril Currier April 1977, aged 97." He was a long-time familiar figure at Ashbury events, football games, the Closing. He often walked. Indeed, it was only at the insistence of the Headmaster that he accepted a lift to the groundbreaking.

When Ashbury opened in the fall of 1973, it had been transformed in a way that only those who had lived in, and perversely loved, its air of Dickensian decay could appreciate. Now there was a sense of arrival. Instead of the claustrophobic front access of 1910, you could come up broad steps into the spacious entrance hall, a comfortable sitting area ahead, glassed-in office on the right. Now, to get to Argyle and the gym, you no longer had to descend to the dungeon-like bowels of the basement and grope along a dank passage with a tangle of pipes, low enough overhead to make a tall man stoop. Now you could walk along the wide, well-lit, attractively tiled corridor, the warmly textured brick of the old outside wall on your left, the trim concrete block of five sunny classrooms on your right. You could turn left to the fine new biology labs or climb to the bright new row of 10 double bedrooms above, with a housemaster's apartment and a new infirmary. You could go down wide stairs to senior school and staff common rooms below. Now there was space and light and air, a sense of openness rather than the pinched and huddled feeling of a past gone on too long.

As well, the Symington Dining Hall was extended, with the addition of the southeast corner. Next, there were major renovations to kitchen, electrical systems, fire exits and locker rooms, the main housemaster's residence (west annex) and to all the old dormitory flats.

Cyril Currier with his backhoe and the new wing itself linked deep-rooted Ashbury tradition with a hopeful future. So did the new memorial elements. The front steps were given by Edith Hughson and her son Geoffrey, a former Board Chairman, in memory of Geoff's grandfather, lumberman Ward C. (a Founder), his father John W. (an old boy) and his brother Ward C. who was killed in action on August 26, 1944.

Eric Beardmore (1921-1930), an outstanding school athlete and leader, wartime fighter pilot, businessman and sportsman, had left a bequest to Ashbury in his will. The new entrance hall is his memorial. Set in the hall floor, the fine Ashbury medallion remembers old boy Montague Anderson (1915-1916), an uncle of the Headmaster. The Symington family gave the extension to the dining hall which already marked the life, and death in action on May 6, 1945, of James A. Symington. W.H. Connell of Spencerville, whose grandson Martin was a recent graduate, gave the new biology lab.

All this was proudly on display on "Ashbury Day," October 13, 1973. The band of the Governor General's Foot Guards entertained the big, distinguished crowd and 310 boys, the highest enrolment ever. Ned Rhodes, Jr., the second generation of his family to be Chairman, welcomed their Excellencies, The Right Honourable Roland Michener, Governor General of Canada, and Mrs Michener. Attending them was their press attache, old boy Rodney Moore. Old boy Dr. J. Tuzo Wilson, now world-famed scientist and Principal of Erindale College, gave the address. The Right Reverend W.J. Robinson, Bishop of Ottawa, led the dedication. The Headmaster read out the memorials. The old school hymn rang out: "He who would valiant be . . . ."

The Governor General's words could hardly have summed it all up better: "First-class young men are needed in all the far reaches of this wide land – tough-fibred young men, strong in character, independent in spirit, and disciplined in mind . . . . The heart of a school is in its people rather than its buildings, but the splendid new premises and facilities, and your determination to provide them, are an assurance of the future for both the College and its students."

The Captain of the School, Donald Paterson, showed their Excellencies through the new premises; his father, old boy Donald S., was there to watch. Pride in the new quarters reflected on the real core, the school's spirit. It was a turning point. Enrolment jumped that year by 20 boys, with 107 boarders. The march continued steadily. By 1981 there were 400 all told.

Action Ashbury had set a total target of $3,100,000. First came the $750,000 spent on the completed buildings and renovations. Next, as and when the money was raised, would come a new gymnasium; the old gym would be turned into a proper library and the Southam Library in Argyle converted to classrooms. That would be another $725,000.

Other needs were money to buy Dunkerton House, funds for educational development including strengthened French courses and outdoor education, and a financial foundation of $1.5 million. The aim of the foundation was to boost scholarships and bursaries, raise academic standards and provide for special enrichment projects and plant maintenance. Campaign target: $3.1 million.

Support, for the first time, came from some major foundations. Parents and past parents were systematically approached. In many cases both parents were working specifically so they could keep their sons at Ashbury, still they responded generously.

In 1976 Dunkerton House and also the Jackson property on Springfield Road were purchased. The campaign total rose slowly. By the end of 1977 the fund stood at $640,000. Parent and Board member Robert Campeau, the Ottawa developer, approached the Ontario government for support. The Wintario lottery was bringing in millions to be freely spent on community projects. Perhaps there might be support for a gymnasium. No luck on any count. In 1978 the school loan stood at $325,000. With enrolment around 370 that was manageable. With the growing school population the elusive new gym was ever more essential, but it would have to wait.

Action Ashbury had plugged away for five years. The corporate campaign had had limited success. Major corporations faced far more requests for funds than they could handle. It wasn't easy to convince their shareholders, who had good causes of their own, that a privileged kind of education for a small number, and in Ottawa, was worthy of support. Without an inside advocate it was pretty well a non-starter, and few of them had old Ashburians holding sway in their boardrooms. Family foundations, though, responded encouragingly when they identified an Ashbury objective with their own. The McLaughlin Foundation set up two scholarships for amounts close to a senior boarder's fees in 1976.

But no major groundswell of support built up. There was no strong base of old-fashioned tribal loyalty, although there were exceptions, of course, and very generous ones, based on a vision of the future. Too oft repeated was the complaint that old boys only heard from Ashbury when it wanted their money. That had been said in G.P. Woollcombe's day. The same refrain could be heard to some degree at any alma mater. But there had indeed been some "dark ages" at Ashbury, apart from the one that Donald Paterson named in 1974. When D. Cargill Southam, long-time faithful supporter that he was, died in 1976 and left a substantial bequest, it was a rare windfall. But the 1973 objective of $3,100,000 was nowhere in sight.

The bright light, though, was the strong support from parents, the group that had very heavy financial responsibilities as it was. On top of that, the Ladies Guild, mostly parents and wives of staff members, got really involved in serious fund-raising of their own. The Guild had been started in 1950 at the instigation of Ron Perry. Initially it was the Mothers' Guild, a get-together group that gave welcome help with the Chapel and the choir. It always had an energetic president. The membership increased and got more active as time went on, and it became an informal vehicle for a two-way flow of information and ideas between parents and school. Each Headmaster's wife was Honorary President. Peggy Joyce had brought a new fund of energy, and the organization grew.

In 1976 the Guild raised the money for two new tennis courts and the resurfacing of the old one. The Ashbury Antique Fair was put together for the first time in 1977 by Mrs Bobbie O'Neill. It quickly became a real annual money-spinner. Over the November long weekend the halls, common rooms and gym were filled with antique dealers and their wares. People came in droves. The dealers did a brisk trade, came back year after year and paid a solid rental for their space. The Fair flourishes today as the Guild's big annual fund-raiser, the source of major material gifts to meet the special needs of the school with a public relations bonus in the bargain.

More important than the money, though, was the strong message from parents that the school was doing things right, because fees had to jump. Costs were rising above inflation. A long and bitter strike by Ottawa Board of Education high-school teachers in 1975 brought a lot of good students to Ashbury's door. Some came desperate to salvage their year. Others came later because the strike had starkly illuminated the conflict between the self-interest of the unions and the vital interests of the students.

Ashbury's student-teacher ratio was 11:1 versus some 16:1 overall in the public system. There were great differences in organization, and the best comparison was that the independent high-school teacher dealt in the classroom – and in assessments, marking, evaluation, advising – with about 60 students, the public system teacher with 180. And all the Ashbury staff, quite unlike many of their public system counterparts, spent many hours outside the classroom in sports and other school activities. They also had much closer contact with parents.

Teaching at Ashbury was for dedicated professionals who liked giving that bit extra and found it more personally rewarding than the public system. Unlike the public sector, though, few independent schools had any kind of published salary scale. Headmasters negotiated staff salaries and contracts individually and kept each other posted on that score, and on fees, through their Heads' associations.

But this Ottawa Board settlement with their teachers left Ashbury staff salaries on average 27 percent behind. They were also in the lower third of the independent schools. It was unacceptable to have such a yawing salary gap, so fees had to rise. In 1975 a senior boarder's fees were $4,100; in 1980, they'd gone up to $6800.

Ashbury families were now mainly Ottawa-based professional people. More and more had both parents working, very often solely so they could pay the fees. They expected high standards for their money, their children's potential expanded, their weak sides helped along and their talents challenged. Few could now send their sons to an Ashbury College just for a good sports programme or to shelter them from the public system, for some notion that it was socially the place to go or just to acquire some "polish."

In 1974 enrolment was 344; with all beds filled, only one-third were boarders. W.A.J. believed as strongly as had G.P. Woollcombe in the value of the boarding school for boys. Without the boarders as the hard core around which the school was formed, it certainly wouldn't have been the same. Increasingly, though, boarding was a service – albeit a valuable one – for families in the federal government or industry who were periodically moved overseas and who got financial help to educate their children.

There was an international flavour among the boarders. In Perry's time, it had been strongly South American. Now the growing element was Chinese boys, mainly from Hong Kong, whose parents took the long view that a Canadian education was an investment in their family's future. Ashbury was their passport to a Canadian university and they were excellent, industrious students. Literally all the beds could have been filled with boys like them, but it was important to keep a balanced school. Following the long-term pattern, foreign diplomats often sent their boys. They too added a different flavour. But itinerants rarely had long-term loyalty.

The fact was that Ashbury was Ottawa-based, and when it came to fund-raising Ottawa was unlike any other Canadian city. There were no great captains of industry, few really monied families. Its business was overwhelmingly government. A civil service doesn't breed philanthropy. Many of its members had their roots elsewhere in Canada and looked forward to going back. Any appeal for monetary support for Ashbury College had to be based on demonstrated excellence in education. Now, under an orderly and confident administration, the academic side of Ashbury College was at last developing real strength.

Back at Closing, 1974, Don Paterson had delivered the valedictory. As at that electric occasion of 1972, his words were his unprompted own. He said: "I have witnessed at first hand the dark ages of Ashbury. The days of prefects with absolute power. The days when student initiative and individuality were unheard of. I have lived through the revolution. I have seen the prefects guide the student body towards total rejection of authority and negativity in their attitude. Now, however, we approach the Golden Age of Ashbury. The prefects no longer control the student; instead they hope to guide him . . . . The students must be even more willing to involve themselves in the school than ever before."

Don's hair, as had become the Ashbury-accepted mode, curled neatly to the collar. The changes were not only bricks and mortar. The most golden of ages is never without its difficulties, but without a shadow of doubt Ashbury had turned a very significant corner and had a clear eye to the future.

CHAPTER **17**

TOWARDS EXCELLENCE

The 1970s saw a sharp decline in public confidence in Ontario's educational system, and indeed this was so across the country. The bloom had gone from student power but disenchantment was abroad among parents. The Hall-Dennis idea of the happy school with individualism and freedom of choice hadn't worked. Academic standards had been sacrificed in the name of individual development.

Under the old system of provincial examinations the pass rate had been 80 percent. In the first year without them 92 percent passed. In 1968 11 percent of high-school graduates were Ontario Scholars with an 80 percent average. By 1973 mark inflation by individual schools had boosted their number by over 50 percent. That created a problem for Ashbury. Inflate with the rest so graduates would get the university of their choice? Or stick with a rigorous standard?

The jaded view of public education was underlined by surveys. Half the people in Ontario believed the standard of reading and writing had dropped. Tests in Ontario universities in 1976 showed 46 percent of freshmen needed remedial English. Veteran school teachers and university people saw a steady decline in standards.

In Ontario there were 94,000 teachers in 1970 – twice as many as in 1960. Now, with projections of a declining student population, school boards were economizing. On the teachers' side, tough American trade union tactics rolled north. Teachers walked out of every public school in Ontario in 1973. Thousands marched on Queen's Park protesting a bill to invalidate mass resignations – their alternative to the right to strike. There were mass resignations by Catholic teachers, illegal strikes in Ottawa and Windsor. In 1975 the Collective Negotiations Act gave Ontario teachers the right to strike. That was the year of the Ottawa Board strike and the large salary increases that put such pressure on Ashbury.

While enrolment declined in the public system because of straight demographics, it leaped in private schools. In 1976 there were 52,000 students in fee-paying schools in Ontario. That was a 32 percent increase in five years. Multiplication of cultural streams brought growing, varied demands for particular religious and secular content in education and there was the continuing concern about the slide in public standards. Ashbury benefitted, of course, with a steady rise in applications. From 1970 to 1980 the teaching staff rose from 28 to 37. Boarders, limited by space, stayed close to the maximum at a little over 100. Demand wasn't that strong for boarding places in fact. In the 10 years after 1974, it stayed static throughout the independent schools while the demand for day school places doubled.

W.A.J. found it very hard to turn down a plea for help. If he felt a boy could be guided in the right direction he'd take him. There's no doubt that some brought problems of their own which sorely taxed the patience and good judgement of housemasters and staff. One young fellow, an orphan living with grandparents, had run away, spent some shadowy time on big city streets and piled up a police record.

W.A.J. gave him a chance – and in this particular case it worked wonders. Year by year the student body grew stronger.

The staff stabilized, strengthened, expanded in numbers and professional diversity. They produced more advanced ideas. There was a change in the character of the Board too. Old boys naturally tend to compare things "now" with "then." More often than not they are guardians of tradition and that will always be an important function. But it's parents, who pay the whopping fees for an education, who compare things with the current alternatives. Parents became more involved and more influential. Board committees worked constructively with increasing input from staff. The Curriculum Committee, for example, had regular staff participation. For the first time in the school's history the Board was getting into hard-core matters of educational consequence.

There were certainly clashes of opinion but confidence between Head and Board found a strength it hadn't known for years. W.A.J. was a sound, hard-nosed administrator with a firm hand on economy, and the place was running in an orderly way. He was authoritarian, certainly. Consultation was not his strong suit. He made decisions briskly, on his own, and wasn't much inclined to prepare the way for those decisions or to explain them. Anything in the nature of an innovation he approached with caution, but once convinced – and if he had the right person for the job – he'd delegate very effectively.

From the fifties there had been various tries for a permanent camp in the Gatineau, mainly as a weekend outlet for boarders. John Beedell had joined the junior school staff in 1968 to teach science and he did it outstandingly. He also had a lot of experience in outdoor education. He was a first-class wilderness man with a knowledge and love of the outdoors that rubbed off on others. It ran quite naturally in his sons, Mike, Jeff and David.

Between the three of them they spanned 1968 to 1980 at Ashbury. Mike became one of Canada's foremost outdoor photographers – his book *Magnetic North*, published in 1983, is a gem – and he is a famed and intrepid Arctic traveller. Among his exploits are sailing (and hauling over the ice) a two-handed catamaran from Alaska to Hudson Bay and a dog-sled trip from Baffin Island to Greenland in 1987.

Given his head by W.A.J., John Beedell made outdoor education part and parcel of Ashbury life. He set up a systematic programme centred around Heney Lake, a two-hour drive up the Gatineau, not far from Mont Ste. Marie. The Harris family, outdoorsmen all, had a large property there where they ran an outdoor programme for various school boards. It was an ideal spot, with lake front and some high, rugged, rocky faces.

Beedell was soon taking junior and senior school classes out on a regular basis, fall, winter and spring, teaching rock-climbing, canoeing, orienteering, camping and wilderness survival skills. A portable classroom, surplus after the 1973 expansion, was parked at Heney Lake as headquarters.

Boys who had had no exposure at all to the outdoors, other than the comforts of a summer cottage and a spin on water skis, found they could sleep in a lean-to in mid-winter snow, paddle through drenching rain, pitch camp, light a fire and cook themselves a satisfying meal. They could rappel off a sheer rock face confident that their friends would tend the rope safely. They could spend a night alone in the bush without a light or another human being within sight or sound. In course of time it was possible to take an Ontario credit course in outdoor ed.

Self-reliance, confidence in one's own capability, appreciation and respect for nature and a real understanding of teamwork and consideration for others, plus the opening up of a sense of adventure, were the natural bonuses. And for many they were there for life. Chris Teron, for one, took those skills and inclinations with him to Lester B. Pearson College of the Pacific. He won a place against stiff competition when it first opened in 1974.

Pearson College, as a new member of the chain of United World Colleges, had a very strong outdoor programme. In his two years there Chris met Louisa, his wife-to-be, and Michel Landry. Landry, a bilingual francophone, came on the Ashbury staff in 1983, joined the outdoor education programme and was in charge after John Beedell was very badly injured in a fall from the roof of a cottage he was building. The Heney Lake base had been dropped in favour of weekend trips to areas best suited to different activities like climbing, canoeing and hiking. Chris and Louisa Teron (recently joined by their baby) and brother Bruce regularly helped out with the Ashbury outdoors groups at places like Palmers Rapids and the Dumoine River. Each time they returned something of those skills and – more important – those values they had gleaned in their earlier years.

Typical of John Beedell's courage was the fact that, as soon as he was mobile, he began working his way step-by-step back towards involvement in Ashbury's affairs. In the meantime Michel Landry adapted the programme to changing needs and demands. With the ongoing support of staff members like Peter Ostrom and Christine Dennison, parents and other friends, outdoor education continued as a vital part of Ashbury College life.

The early 1970s brought a surge of interest in marine biology, oceanography and limnology. A keen group of scuba divers headed by Ian Scarth, Chris Friesen, John Moore, Bill Craig, Ian Burke-Robertson and Janet Moore of Elmwood had followed the spectacular work of Dr. Joe MacInnis, the internationally famed expert on underwater physiology. In 1974 they hatched the idea of building their own underwater classroom for biology studies. They dubbed their project "Neptune" and Heney Lake was the natural base. Dr. MacInnis, a Gatineau dweller himself, generously gave his advice and enthusiastic support.

"Neptune" was entirely student initiated and driven. They got hold of an old boiler and converted it, complete with observation window, air valves and entry port. They scoured Ottawa for donated materials from buckets of paint to steel wire rope, from welding to heavy trucking. Biology teacher Fred Bellware, a scuba diver himself, became staff science advisor. The Headmaster agreed that "Neptune" could be an Ashbury programme as long as it raised its own money and safety was assured. Tony German, Director of Development, undertook to get the habitat safely into position and chased funds. The Canadian National Sportsman's Show made a handsome donation.

Douglas Elsey, the expert who engineered Dr. MacInnis's famed Sub-Igloo Habitat under the Arctic ice, came to advise and help. In a driving weekend snowstorm the students manoeuvred six four-ton grinding stones, cast-offs from Eddy's mill, onto the lake ice, cut holes and dropped the stones for the anchoring system, then surveyed their positions by diving under the ice.

That April, 1975, HRH Prince Charles, a qualified diver himself, heard about "Neptune" on a visit to Canada and summoned 11 of the team to Rideau Hall. Ian Scarth briefed him. He was most impressed with their initiative, intrigued by the winter work, and asked to be kept in touch.

That May 24 weekend there was a big turnout of boys, staff and parents at Heney Lake for outdoor education demonstrations and the "Neptune" launching. Chaplain Jeep Green pronounced the blessing, appropriate to a new vessel going down the ways. With the guidance of Mr Elsey, help from RCMP divers and much heaving and hauling, Ashbury's "underwater classroom" was moored in position, filled with air and tried out. Prince Charles cabled "Good luck to all the human guinea pigs."

"Neptune" got full-page coverage. The CBC had followed it with a film crew on the ice and underwater, and produced a half-hour documentary titled "And You Never Have To Stand In The Hall." It was broadcast on a national television network with a special viewing for Prince Charles at Buckingham Palace.

Next came an air compressor, telephone to shore, furniture and electric light. Ian and Chris stocked it with food and down they went for a remarkable underwater stay of 72 hours. That fall Dr. Tuzo Wilson hosted a reception and presentation on "Neptune" with a showing of the CBC film at the Ontario Science Centre in Toronto.

The habitat was used through the school year. The following summer, 1976, biologist Ross Varley who had joined Ashbury's staff in place of Mr. Bellware took on "Neptune" and scuba diving. The new student leaders Keith Macdonald, John Moore and Brian Baxter, were keen to keep the programme rolling, but at Heney Lake they found the habitat had leaked air and slumped to the bottom.

Lifting it for repair would be expensive and Varley saw ongoing safety problems. Students were certainly keen on diving but there was no assured succession of experts. And getting right down to it, there really wasn't much science teaching or practical investigation at Heney Lake that couldn't be done without the "underwater classroom." Except as an interesting device for divers it would really be more of a liability than an asset. Sadly the boys pushed their habitat into deep water and laid it to rest.

A more manageable and productive project under Varley's guidance later on was a long-term study of biological factors in Mackay Lake. The tail in fact had wagged the dog. The students' enthusiasm had really stemmed from their intense interest in diving. Nonetheless it was an exciting project and a remarkable one for high-school students to conceive, much less turn into reality. It showed what could be done when young people really set their minds to it and were given their head. All of them had learned a great deal. Project "Neptune" was a real adventure and the school was better for it.

Early in 1973 the Board looked with favour on a radical proposal that, as a long-term aim, Ashbury become a fully integrated bilingual school. It was an idea in tune with the times. The Royal Commission on Bilingualism and Biculturalism (1963-69) and the Official Languages Act of 1969 had set the course for institutional bilingualism and established a Commissioner of Official Languages. A command of both languages would become more and more of an asset, indeed an essential, for an aspiring public servant. Ottawans, particularly professionals, were far more aware, and indeed understanding, of bilingualism than most Canadians. For their children

French would be an important tool as well as a cultural asset. Also, Ottawa's francophone professional population was growing rapidly. Their children were a market to be tapped. French immersion had been pioneered and developed by another independent school, the Toronto French School. Rockcliffe Park Public School was among the first in Canada's public systems to be involved.

Since the far-off 1890s with Monsieur Joseph-Marie Fleury, French at Ashbury had been almost exclusively the domain of Englishmen. Hamilton Southam's Ashbury French in the thirties was taught to him by Steve Brodie and others as a dead language, like Latin and Greek. Tony Price learned little in the forties and later became fluent on his own living in Quebec. Rodney Moore came from Selwyn House in the fifties and found Ashbury French sadly lacking. Arthur Brain taught French, as he did Latin and Greek, though he didn't really speak it.

Jimmy Glover had come from England in 1968 as Woollcombe housemaster and to teach modern languages. Clifford Inns came from England to take over Woollcombe in 1970. He, and his wife Linda who headed French at Elmwood, had top English-based qualifications and a genuine interest in French culture. In the junior school Jim Humphreys was fluent and David Polk and Alan Thomas spoke good formal French. Jim Bailey, who taught from 1975 to 1978, was the only mother-tongue French speaker on the staff. So French was still being taught mainly by anglophones, with the accent on the academic approach rather than on communication.

The heady idea of the bilingual school conjured, to the majority of the staff, a murky future. It would certainly mean major changes in many of their lives. The mechanics of implementation loomed large. It wasn't easy to find really competent teachers of French as a second language. The School Board of Greater Montreal, for example, couldn't find enough in Quebec and was hiring from Europe. A parents' questionnaire showed less than majority support and there the notion died.

Quite apart from a bilingual school, most parents did want their sons to have a much better level of fluency in French. Programmes in the Ottawa public system by this time were excellent. Parent/Governor Cynthia Baxter chaired the Curriculum Committee in 1977 and got Board approval to hire a new Head of the French Department to overhaul the programme and take advice from Elmwood.

In Linda Inns' department, the strength of Elmwood's French and Spanish teaching was Judith Sabourin. She was the first French-Canadian to teach there, and for the year 1977-78 W.A.J. hired her to head Ashbury's French Department while she still carried her load at Elmwood. She hired Guy Lemele, an immigrant from France whose wife later came on staff, and Québecer Pierre Gosselin. Suddenly French was a live language in the staff common room. David Morris came from St. Michael's University School in Victoria as department head. After two years Guy Lemele took over.

Board member Robert Campeau pushed for increased use of the language throughout the school. The International Baccalaureate (IB) programme was well established by now. A full IB diploma required a second language and at a substantially higher standard of fluency and communciation competence than the regular Ontario credit. In close collaboration with Elmwood enriched French began in 1977 and was soon available in every grade.

From 1978 geography was offered in French. It was Tony Macoun's subject and he was in charge of the IB. Also he had workmanlike French, attained, oddly, in his days as a British Colonial administrator in the South Pacific. Lemele and Macoun began by team-teaching geographie. *Histoire* and *sociologie* followed. Apart from having the right people on staff, the biggest factor was the cooperation with Elmwood. There were enough students between the two schools for four or five levels of French to be offered in every grade without adding staff to either.

By now some parents who were pleased with French immersion in the public system were concerned that their children, about Grade 6, weren't fully competent in English. It was, in fact, too much to expect. There were assurances and examples to show that this would sort itself out in time but for some that wasn't enough. Moving to a non-immersion public school could mean floundering in English or dropping behind, also risking the loss of their headstart in French. Ashbury, to this group, was especially attractive.

Elmwood cooperation boosted Spanish and German, and made far more options available to students at both schools. It all cost nothing more than the annoyance (to the teaching staff) of the inevitable dallying through the park with a quick puff en route. The case for combining the two schools, alarming as it might be to old boys and old girls too, was gaining ground.

The rebellious sixties had brought slim times to independent schools. By the early seventies the low demand for boarding pushed some revered old New England boys' and girls' schools into combining. Albert College in Belleville, the rare Canadian exception among the old independent schools, had been a co-educational boarding school since it was founded. In Hamilton, Hillfield and Strathallan combined as a co-ed day school. In the Eastern Townships it was Bishop's College School and Compton Hall: Bishop's in 1970 was down 15 percent at 170 boys; Compton was down to 80 girls, and on the verge of going under; in 1972 the girls moved to the Bishop's campus and Compton closed. None of these marriages was made in heaven. Virtually all were arranged unions of hard financial necessity. But in each case of conversion the crustiest confessed that their alma mater should have done it years before.

The forces of society were at work. The sexual revolution had let in a lot of light and air. Women's liberation was an inevitable tide. The very basis of the single-sex school for the late twentieth century was in question. On Ashbury's Board John Woods, in 1976, asked Michael Sherwood to get together with some of the staff and write a viewpoint on co-education. Sherwood, who had headed the junior school for 10 years, co-opted Ken Niles and Tony Macoun. He chose well. Niles, at Ashbury since 1968, was of conservative view, instinctively against such change but intellectually prepared to take an objective look at a serious proposition. Macoun, with only two years in the school, had brought fresh ideas with him from teaching in England.

Their conclusion: in the long term co-education was the right thing for Ashbury College and it should be accepted in principle; however, the time wasn't ripe. Staff, student body, educational standards, reputation, public image – all were moving ahead. First things first. When the school was thoroughly consolidated, that would be the time to move.

The Headmaster's view was that co-education could well be right for the future, but not in his time. With retirement five years hence, it was better left to the next generation. In the meantime there was more than enough to do.

The *Ashburian* staff started *The Independent Press* in 1975-76 to give themselves first-hand experience in creative journalism. Ian Higgins was editor of both publications; Drummond Lister, who was in his second year teaching English, was deft and stimulating as staff advisor. The loft of the old coach house was converted to a newsroom, and both publications fairly burst with energy, with new style, layout and editorial approach. The *Ashburian*, compared to earlier times, was open and cheerfully irreverent, though it lost none of its importance as a historical record. Working with Ian were Brian Baxter (news editor), Graeme Clark, Jeff Beedell, Kevin Reeves, Peter Belicki, George McKenna, Ross Brown, John Lund and David Welch.

Ian's editorial in the *Ashburian* showed the changes in the school through the eyes of an articulate, involved student: "Only three years ago, when I first arrived at Ashbury, the school was still 'The Reform School of Greater Ottawa.' Today, however, the hard work which Don Paterson advocated to bring Ashbury out of its 'Dark Ages' has succeeded, and it is great to be at a school which is now a winner. Ideas, opportunities, projects now see the light at Ashbury, led by interested teachers but run by industrious students."

He cited "Neptune," drivers' education, outdoor education, *The Independent Press*: "The point being that with enough student interest, anything can be done at Ashbury. The teachers, including Mr. Joyce, when one proposes a project will say, almost invariably, 'Yes, let's see how we can do it' rather than 'No, here's why it can't be done.'"

The 1976 cross-country ski team had had the best season in years. They won the Dalton Wood and Art Levitt trophies for both senior and junior high-school championships of the National Capital Region. Jeff Beedell, Michael Evans, Richard Sellers and Ian Higgins set the pace. Ken Niles had guided their conditioning back in the fall with his laconic "get moving or I'll kick your arse in." Hugh Penton, cool and steady, was coaching football. George McGuire coached first soccer with his warm Grenadian stress on "trappin' and headin' the ball, mahn." Other teams had had average, hard-played seasons, enjoying their sport. On the individual level Martin Wostenholme won the Canadian 14 and under tennis singles championship and the US indoor doubles, and was runner-up in the US singles in his age group. He was named Ottawa's Amateur Athlete of the year. But it wasn't fleeting euphoria over athletic victories that sparked the high spirits.

There was indeed, as Ian Higgins had said, a lot going on at Ashbury, things that were exciting and important. Besides those he'd already mentioned, three other major initiatives were brewing at once. A new student magazine *Spectrum* was getting off the ground; the International Baccalaureate was being introduced; the Forum for Young Canadians had had its first four sessions that year and Ashbury students and staff had been crucial in its success.

CHAPTER 18
THE FORUM FOR YOUNG CANADIANS

Ashbury's calendars and prospectuses, since the early 1900s, had always made a point of its unique location in Canada's capital, with Parliament, government and the steadily developing cultural institutions. There was never a shortage of distinguished lecturers or speakers for Closings or special events, never a shortage of resources an imaginative teacher could use to enliven a subject.

Ottawa had always been a city of connections, and from the start G.P. Woollcombe's character and competence had seen that his school was well plugged-in. Among parents there were Governors General (Earl Minto, the Duke of Devonshire, Lord Alexander), cabinet ministers (like E.N. Rhodes, Finance Minister in 1932-35, then Senator; father and grandfather of two Board Chairmen), top public servants from Sir Sandford Fleming through the World War II dollar-a-year men and women (like Phyllis Ross, John Turner's mother).

Many old boys had gone on to the senior ranks of the public service: Hamilton Southam, for example, to External Affairs and then to the National Arts Centre as its first Director; Michael Shenstone as an Ambassador. Many had reached the senior ranks of the Armed Forces with General Guy Simonds as the outstanding example.

Sitting in Parliament in the early 1970s, were four old boy MPs. Robert Stanfield was Progressive Conservative leader, 1967-76. John Turner was first elected in 1962 and served in Liberal cabinets from 1965 to 1975. Donald S. Macdonald was first elected the same year as Turner and was a Liberal Cabinet Minister from 1968 to 1977. Andy Brewin was first elected as an NDP member in 1962.

Ottawans were always somewhat blasé about the panoply of power on their doorsteps. At Ashbury, Hugh Robertson was drawing freely and productively on the political and public establishments to enrich his courses in Canadian studies. He'd found that these busy, highly informed people were remarkably generous with their time.

Director of Development Tony German, involved with fund-raising, was developing the case for Ashbury College to put to philanthropists and captains of industry. He had been casting about for ways to underline its relevance as an independent school, its significance in the broad field of education. Its unique aspect was the Ottawa location, and Robertson's initiatives had shown what could be done to capitalize on this.

Young Canadians visited the capital each year in droves for a quick look at their country's central institutions. Most toured the Parliament Buildings, looked down on the often unseemly zoo of Question Period and went away, bemused, with the disturbing notion that somehow this was the way Canada was governed. Could not some of these young people from across the land be brought to Ottawa under Ashbury's aegis to learn about the real workings of Canada's government in a structured and stimulating way? The school had sound educational credentials and independence of choice. It was beholden to none but its own governors, and it had a live-in facility of its own.

On top of the educational value, a programme that would get young people together would make a contribution to understanding and unity. Since the mid-sixties and the Commission on Bilingualism and Bilculturalism, concerns about Canadian unity had spread wide. Here was a chance to make a contribution. The Headmaster immediately gave the go-ahead and enough of a budget to put together a full proposal.

German consulted Birnie Hodgetts, Director of the Canada Studies Foundation, who had taught at TCS when he was a student there. Hodgetts, with his great breadth of experience, encouraged the embryo ideas and suggested a look at "The Presidential Classroom for Young Americans" in Washington.

German went to see it in action, then arranged for one of Hugh Robertson's leading students, Michael Evans, to attend a regular one-week "Classroom" session. Michael's personal student's-eye report to the Board in March 1975 impressed them deeply and clinched German's proposal for what was now termed "The Forum for Young Canadians." There would be four sessions per year of one full week each consisting of 50 boys and 50 girls. They would be housed at Ashbury in the March break and right after Closing in June, and would be bused daily to the Parliament Buildings, Supreme Court, External Affairs, Press building — wherever the programme took them. Everything would be run in English and French.

Ottawa had several first-rate visit programmes that brought students together, like "Educanada" and the Rotary Club's long-standing "Adventure in Citizenship." They were cultural, social and generally informative. The Forum would be specifically educational. The teachers would be the men and women who actually made government work, and who influenced it — the politicians, the public servants, the press, the pressure groups. The Board backed the project to the hilt.

Right away it drew enthusiastic and informed support. Father Roger Guindon, Rector of the University of Ottawa and a knowledgeable and wise educator, called in James Hurley, a political scientist, who was directing the Parliamentary Intern's programme. Hurley had a profound knowledge of the subject and knew the key people. He was a first-rate teacher, fluently bilingual, and had a great rapport with the young. He became Director of Studies, entirely as a volunteer. Though burning questions would certainly come up in such a gathering of students, he focused on the process of government rather than on political issues of the day. He developed the programme content, identified key people and resources, and took a major active part in every course for over 10 years. He became Chairman from 1983 to 1985 and remains a Director to the present day.

An immediate ally was Alistair Fraser, Clerk of the House of Commons. The Speaker of the House, Hon. James Jerome, without hesitation said "yes" to committee rooms with simultaneous interpretation, the use of the Commons Chamber itself and his own participation in sessions on the workings of the House. The Speaker of the Senate, Hon. Renaude Lapointe, added the Senate's and her own personal support. She actually had a change made in the Senate's rules to allow Forum students to sit in the Senators' seats when she conducted sessions in the Chamber. Successors in these key offices are fully behind the Forum to this day.

Everyone at every level said "yes." Party leaders and Whips agreed to ongoing participation. Senator Eugene Forsey, Canada's most respected voice in constitutional matters, agreed to lead off each course. The Forum was to be strictly non-partisan. Parliamentarians of all parties agreed to pitch in whenever asked.

The public service was just as enthusiastic. The policy for getting speakers was to shoot for the top. John Carson, Chairman of the Public Service Commission, and Gordon Robertson, Clerk of the Privy Council, agreed to take part. So did the Chief Electoral Officer, Jean Marc Hamel. Such people added real momentum. Mr. Carson agreed to find young, bilingual, professional public servants to act as "counsellors" for groups of students. The Medical Director, Rear Admiral Richard Roberts, undertook to provide nursing officers for live-in medical support. The Canadian Labour Congress, Canadian Teachers' Federation and the School Trustees Association provided resources, communications and support.

With Ashbury bed and board at minimal cost, the break-even fee worked out at $150 for the full week, plus the travel. Open House Canada, a Secretary of State youth travel programme, came up with enough funds so that from Inuvik, Halifax or Hawkesbury no student would have to pay more than $90 for travel. Money for fees and travel would have to be raised locally. With support from its President, Sam Hughes, the Canadian Chamber of Commerce spread word to its members. So did Rotary, Kiwanis, the Canadian Legion, Club Richelieu and Chevaliers des Colombes. The aim was for service clubs to sponsor students from their local high school; afterwards the students would report back to their sponsors.

To fund and manage the Forum a new body, the Foundation for the Study of the Process of Government in Canada, was incorporated. It held its founding meeting that summer, chaired by Kenneth Lavery who was also on Ashbury's Board. The Foundation's trustees were all active, influential people and they were spread right across Canada. Five of the 18 trustees were also on the Ashbury Board and the Headmaster was a regular member.

As well as Father Guindon, Senator Forsey, Alistair Fraser and Birnie Hodgetts, the heads of the Conference Board of Canada, the Canadian Teachers' Federation and the Science Council of Canada came aboard. Tony German was Executive Director, dividing his time between that and Ashbury duties. The Foundation was funded separately from Ashbury and now had to raise $100,000 to get the Forum rolling for the coming school year. The J.W. McConnell Foundation responded with a major contribution, and seven major corporations very quickly said "yes."

The four party leaders — Prime Minister Trudeau, Robert Stanfield, Ed Broadbent and Raoul Caouette — officially endorsed the Forum. That fall all 2500 high schools and CEGEPs across Canada were invited to nominate students — no more than one per school per session to avoid cliques. In Ashbury's March break 1976, the first two sessions of the Forum for Young Canadians were held, back-to-back. Fifty boys and 50 girls aged 16 to 17 came from across Canada to each of them. There were two more sessions after the school closed in June.

The first Saturday of the first Forum was typical March weather — freezing rain right across eastern Canada. Buses and trains were held up, flights were running hours late. Jim Humphreys of the Ashbury staff, backed by volunteer parents, handled the transport problem with cheerful aplomb. The 100 young people straggled in, full of enthusiasm, sporting their Forum badges, fast friends already with those they had just met en route.

Michael Evans, with his French well polished, handled registrations. One of the last to come in from the storm, near 2:00 a.m., approached the desk with a broad smile and mysterious tongue. Michael responded with a careful welcome in French. More smiles and volubility but no communication until Michael spotted the name on the young man's badge: "Reg Walters, Boat Harbour, Newfoundland." With its own affectionate Newfie joke in hand, the Forum for Young Canadians was in business. Reg was a real contributor to the first session.

All the support that had been promised came through. Senator Forsey shared a whole Sunday evening with Jim Hurley, illuminating the Canadian constitution in an incomparable way. He continued this for every session over the next 10 years. MPs who were ordained clergy — Tommy Douglas, David Macdonald, Alec Patterson — conducted Sunday services in the Chapel. The counsellors from the public service, volunteers all, added immeasurably and incidentally gained a lot themselves. Many of the them volunteered year after year.

From the start the students were demographically in line with provincial and territorial populations, city versus rural and language distribution. Everything was done in English and French assisted by bilingual counsellors and simultaneous interpretation for all the full sessions. The dormitory areas were divided into boys' and girls' sections. Mark Tatichek and his kitchen staff worked right through. From the teaching staff, Jim Humphreys, Jim Bailey, Greer Gardner and Gordon Hyatt worked through the holidays. Humphreys continued with two sessions a year for 10 years. Judith Sabourin of Elmwood was first *mère-poule*. Guy and Therese Lemele and Ross Varley were among others on Ashbury's staff who worked with the Forum for several years. Michael Evans, George Duong and Paul Campbell gave up their holidays to fill the invaluable position of staff assistant. Other Ashbury boys followed their lead until there were enough Forum alumni available to take over.

In those Forum sessions Ashbury College fairly hummed. High-school principals had done their part in selecting bright, outgoing students, full of vitality, questioning, eager to exchange ideas, to learn. They were quite prepared, firmly and politely, to take issue with a Cabinet Minister. From Ashbury Jeff Beedell, Nick Brearton, Graeme Clark and Ian Johnston attended the first year sessions. Graeme recalled being a bit ashamed of the less-than-slubrious dormitory flats. The visitors were somewhat bemused by Ashbury's quaintness but it had its own atmosphere of friendliness, and what was really important, as Graeme quickly found out, was living and working — and playing — together. With such inspiringly bright and warmly friendly young people from across the land, the Forum couldn't go wrong.

Presentations, panels, discussion groups, simulations — the programme was non-stop from Saturday's arrival to the elegant final banquet on Friday evening at the National Arts Centre. Then it was a quick change into jeans to dance in Ashbury's common room 'til it was time for the early buses to the airport and emotion-filled partings from new-found friends. Deliberately there was not attempt to inject a "unity" theme. That feeling, and a very powerful one, simply bubbled up. The most repeated comment volunteered at the end of any session was some version of "I came an Albertan (or Cape Bretonner or Québecer); I left a Canadian."

Barry Turner succeeded German as Director of Development in early 1979. He ran the Forum from Ashbury's Development Office until he left in 1980 and later ran successfully for Parliament in the General Election of 1984. He was succeeded by Keith Cattell in Development. But running both jobs was too much, and the Forum office moved in 1981 to its own quarters, with its own Executive Director, Jane Coté.

The Forum still used the school as a residence, but except for interlinking directorships — including the Headmaster's — it separated from Ashbury. Students from the school attended every year, though, and Ashbury put up two annual scholarships to help them. John Connelly became Executive Director in 1983, then Hon. John Reid in 1985. He had been an MP in 1978-79 and Minister of State for Federal-Provincial Relations. He was supported by the most capable Denise McCulloch, who became Assistant Director in 1982. Then, in 1990 Claire Baxter was appointed Executive Director. (She's no relation to Ashbury Governor and Forum Board member Cynthia Baxter, who has contributed in a major way to both.)

Getting students to come in June proved more and more difficult because of summer jobs. So in 1986 the late sessions were shifted to April/May, using university residences and later the Beacon Arms Hotel. Robert Horowitz, whose family business it was, was an old Ashburian and it had long been a rendezvous for old boys. The Venture Inn has been used more recently.

As time went on it became more difficult to get the right numbers of québecois applicants and to get local sponsorships in Québec. The Foundation got a grant from the McConnell Foundation in 1989 to develop an in-school promotion campaign in the province. Though the Meech Lake atmosphere in the spring of 1990 rolled a cold wave over it, it still had marked success. A growing Alumni Association provided the means for spreading the word in schools across the land. Enthusiasm is infectious. In Alberta, Linda Curyisek, who came to the Forum in its first year, started the Forum for Young Albertans. Her guidance and strong support from provincial and municipal governments keep it flourishing as a valuable educational programme.

When the Forum started in 1976 feminism was taking effect. Girls were finding their place in high-school hierarchies. Student councils were influenced less by jocks. There were new role models: women were increasingly visible in influential fields. Girls were, by and large, showing more interest in public affairs than boys. The Forum selection process had been decentralized right from the start to provincial trustee committees. As applications got more numerous and competitive, girls came to outweigh boys by about 6:4.

Numbers rose to 125 per session to help offset escalating costs, and in March breaks Ashbury's junior school classrooms sprouted cots to squeeze them in. Make-shift though it is, Forum alumni have always felt strongly that living in at Ashbury College, their first and friendly home, provides the right atmosphere, the essence of living and working together, which does so much to give their experience its deep and lasting value.

Without discounting the tremendous contribution from all the outstanding, highly placed men and women who give their time and talents to the Forum, it is true to say that the lasting value lies, not so much in their words of wisdom as in what the students learn from each other. It lies in their discovery of each other —English, French, native, new Canadians — and the common factors that join rather than the differences that divide.

On the Forum's tenth anniversary, it was decided to open sessions to teachers and that became a regular feature. From 1989 special provisions were made for students with physical disabilities and economic disadvantage. By Ashbury's Centennial, Forum sessions had been running for 15 years.

The Forum has always received remarkable support. Successive Speakers of the Commons and the Senate, now Hon. John Fraser and Hon. Guy Charbonneau, have become Honorary Chairmen and active participants. Their senior people, like Beverly Koester who succeeded Alistair Fraser, Claude Desrosiers, Robert Marleau, Charles Lussier, Charles Askwith and Gordon Lovelace, have provided outstanding facilities. Senators and Members of Parliament sit down to dinner with students from their areas. Cabinet ministers, labour leaders, deputy ministers, journalists, heads of major corporations and national associations join in serious discussions. Each Prime Minister has met Forum groups a number of times. So have Opposition leaders.

The educational philosophy of the programme hasn't changed. The content stays essentially the same. The whole-hearted support from all political and government quarters continues. The inspiring calibre, energy and spirit of the students never flag. Forum alumni are closely involved now as volunteers in administration and in running the sessions themselves. Some 7000 of them — the early classes now well established in their careers — form a significant network of well-informed active-minded young Canadians across the land.

Starting and nurturing the Forum for Young Canadians is more than a feather in Ashbury's cap and a point of pride. It stands as a contribution to Canada in very difficult times.

CHAPTER 19
A SPIRIT OF PURPOSE

From the mid-seventies W.A.J.'s steady campaign to build both student body and staff was paying off. Now, between them, there was a strongly growing rapport.

A key factor in this was Ken Niles. His beard and his stern façade were already Ashbury institutions. The staff photograph in the *Ashburian* of 1969 records his long jaw (beardless), big ears and open boyish smile. He grew the beard the next summer. He was going to shave it off just before school opened, but his wife Brenda said he should keep it awhile and he frankly found it easier than shaving every day. If the boys thought a retired hippie was among them, they were dead wrong.

Ken Niles had left Cobourg High School looking for adventure and went off to Britain in 1959 and joined the army. After three years soldiering in Europe as an NCO, he was going to re-enlist. But coming home on leave he met Brenda on board the steamship. She was finishing her MA in history. One thing led to another: new horizons, marriage, his BA at Carleton while she taught high school, then the search for a job.

Teaching appealed but the public system demanded teachers' college. Ashbury didn't. Common currency had labelled it as "Borstal for rich kids," "the zoo." But the Head was rebuilding, looking for good people, and K.D. Niles was his man. In the usual testing of a new arrival, the boys quickly recognized a firm and steady hand. He was, from the start, respected. He immersed himself totally in the school, his students and their interests. He taught because he loved it and he became first-rate in his fields of history, then philosophy.

His impact on Ashbury went far beyond the classroom. He was a traditionalist. He liked things to be orderly and clear-cut. He firmly believed that young people could give their best when they lived in a well-ordered atmosphere where everyone understood the ground rules and the system, above all, was fair. He didn't like some of the things he saw at first — fagging, some bullying too. Nor did he agree with the heavy emphasis on sport.

He was gruff and formal, even forbidding, and the junior boy quailed at the thought of running foul of "Kenner" when it came time to brave the terrors of the senior school. Invariably, though, K.D. Niles had at heart the individual long-term interests of each student. In 1972 the senior boys sensed his sympathy. He saw both sides, and the gulf in communications that lay between them. But youthful intemperance and even arrogance, he feared, would push too far too fast and only set things back. His common-sense and compassion had a lot to do with levelling things out, with laying the base for Don Paterson's "golden age."

W.A.J. knew his people. With his talent for delegation he put Niles in charge of the prefects in 1975. Titles changed, but from then on he was the link with the students, the key to the chain of command, the buffer between the colonel and the troops. Soon he was the one really in direct administrative charge of the senior student body.

From his desk his laser gaze commanded the broad new corridor. He occupied A.D. Brain's old command post, the key tactical position at the school's crossroads. He was of equally strong character but a different man. He presided day by day with even-handed firmness, and always with humanity. Clear and confident lines existed between him and the Head. His announcements, and pronouncements, at lunchtime just a few steps away in Symington Hall would pull things up short, or make things move. The new boy's fear soon changed to respect, and by graduation grew to real and lasting affection.

From the earliest years Ashbury had looked to England as a prime source for schoolmasters. In G.P. Woollcombe's era of the classical education, English public school and Oxbridge background seemed ideal. And Englishmen could generally be hired for less.

W.A. Joyce knew the English market and he went to it quite often. The staff common room was a good deal bigger by this time, of course, and it wasn't, as in the old days dominated by Englishmen. The Head didn't want it so. But he could pick good people and without doubt many who came from outside Canada brought fresh ideas, the energy and initiative of the immigrant and wider international views.

Peter Josselyn, for one, had come in 1969 via 10 years teaching at Shawnigan Lake. He became head of English, and theatre was his special interest. He sparked school productions, mostly Gilbert and Sullivan with Elmwood, and he always took a part himself. Theatre-going was another of his interests. The brand new National Arts Centre was bursting with vitality under the direction of Hamilton Southam. In his first year Josselyn got 100 tickets (at $3.50 subscription price) to each of 16 plays at the NAC — and filled every seat. Ashburians became sophisticated theatre-goers. After the boiling over of 1972, Josselyn became the Director of the Senior School, preceding Niles as the one in direct contact with the boys.

Clifford Inns, who had come from England as housemaster in 1970, moved on as Head at Rothesay after five years. Robin Hinnell had taught briefly in Quebec and Alberta before. From 1975 he brought great strength as head of the mathematics department, then was Director of Studies. His wife Sally taught at Ashbury too for a time. They left in 1987 when Robin became Head of the Halifax Grammar School. David "Doc Hop" Hopkins came in 1975 and stayed. Roger Potter came from Stowe School in England in 1977 on exchange with Ashbury's Hugh Penton.

Ray Anderson and Jake Marland bridged the Perry and the Joyce years. Marland retired in 1976; his wife Ros stayed on applying her personality and talents in charge of the domestic scene. Anderson stayed on until 1991. Alan Thomas came as a housemaster in 1974, following Geoffrey Thomson. An outstanding musician and teacher, he built up a fine programme.

The British Isles weren't the only source of non-Canadians. Bruce Wallin, an American, was a great hand at summertime renovations when money was so short. He lived in as a housemaster, took a leave of absence and came back as business manager for a time. George McGuire, who came in 1970, was a fine science teacher, a gentle man with a brilliant mind and a core of steel. He went home to Grenada in 1978 to become his country's Minister of Education. Guy Lemele had come from France and started at Ashbury in 1977. His wife Therese joined the staff two years later. Michael Jansen was a Rhodesian who'd studied and taught in England, moved to Ottawa in

1976 and right away found an opening at Ashbury as a live-in housemaster teaching English. The boarders were spread then between the three houses — Woollcombe, Connaught and Alexander — and grouped under housemasters by grades. Jansen believed that boarder cohesion would boost their spirit and he sparked the change that made Woollcombe the all-boarder house.

Hugh Robertson, a South African, had come in 1968. He injected new ideas and energy into history and social studies, stimulating his students with his own infectious interest in the larger world. He seized on the newly revived interest in Canadian studies that was sparked that year by a study by Birnie Hodgetts, who later gave valuable advice on the Forum for Young Canadians.

As a Canadian Centennial project Hodgetts had been given a year's sabbatical by TCS to determine what students across the country were being taught about Canadian history, geography and civics. The answer, expressed in his report, "What Culture? What Heritage?," was "precious little." As a result of this the Canada Studies Foundation was started with private funds to try and right the situation; Hodgetts was the first Director.

Robertson took note of this, beefed up Ashbury's Canadian studies, got his classes involved in interschool projects and they started a new publication called *Ashbury News*. The idea was to provide a communications vehicle for high-school students across the country in a regular periodical featuring their writing, inviting their views on Canadian issues. Even in its early, simply duplicated format it caught the interest of the recently retired Prime Minister, Lester Pearson. He wrote an eloquent foreword in the third edition, underscoring the pressing need for Canadians to know each other better.

Robertson raised some seed money from Senator Norman Paterson, father of Donald of the thirties and grandfather of Donald, the 1974 Captain of the School. The magazine blossomed into *Spectrum*, the Canadian student magazine, a first-rate publication, nicely produced, featuring outstanding contributions in English and French from students in every corner of Canada. All the editorial work and layout was done by boys at Ashbury, advised by Robertson. The subscription list grew slowly — too slowly, unfortunately, to keep up with the cost of printing and distribution. Appeals to government departments and the Canada Council fell on stony ground. There was no doubt about the need for and the value of the magazine — Lester Pearson had said it well — but the school couldn't go on subsidizing it indefinitely. *Spectrum* died. It left a legacy of indelible experience and also a national void.

Pursuing other lines of interest, Robertson sparked the first interest in rugger at the school. As well, he looked in some depth at the International Baccalaureate, a new examining system at the high-school graduation level which in the early 1970s was in widening use throughout the world. The IB had been started by a group of educators who were also involved in starting the United World Colleges. It was their answer to the fast-growing number of students in the "global village" trying to qualify for university while being schooled outside their own country. From an office in Switzerland, they developed a central international examination system and made it available in a wide range of languages.

Qualified schools anywhere in the world could join for an annual fee. Their students could then write the IB exams, which were set centrally and graded against a truly international scale. The first IB school in Canada was Lester B. Pearson College of the Pacific which was opened in 1974 as a wonderfully fitting memorial to Canada's Prime Minister and Nobel Prize winner.

Hugh Robertson had discussed the IB with his colleagues and had got a representative to come to speak to them. The individual didn't strike much of a spark, but when A.M. Macoun came from Stowe School in England in 1974, Robertson found a ready ear, a kindred soul and a man of quick and determined action.

Stowe was young to be among the great public schools of England. From its founding in 1923, the first Headmaster, the famed J.F. Roxburgh, broke away from the Victorian tradition. He set his school on a liberal course. His thrust was individuality, the development of the unique qualities of each student, rather than uniformity and the corporate good. He cut into the overwhelming dominance of team sports. He greatly widened the cultural horizons of his students. A sharp difference between Roxbugh's liberal ideas and those of Hall-Dennis was his insistence on rigour and mental discipline.

Roxburgh wrote a critical book called *Eleutheros*, which was very widely read, on the state of the English public schools. In 1936, when Chairman Newcombe was seeking a new Headmaster for Ashbury, Roxburgh had half-jokingly suggested he'd go for the job himself had he not been too old at 47. By an extraordinary coincidence, the nom de plume he'd used for his book was "Dr. Archdale." If Nixie Newcombe had got the real thing when he hired Nicholas Archdale, what a different story Ashbury's would have been! However, the Roxburgh tradition rubbed off on Macoun. Even delayed by 40 years, it contributed significantly to the most notable changes in the history of the school.

Tony Macoun was born and raised in Africa, the son of a Colonial Police Officer and the daughter of a Kenyan settler. He went to school in England at Stowe, then to Oxford for a degree in geography. In 1967 he married and went off to the South Pacific where he was a Colonial Administrative Officer for two years. Career prospects were dim, so he took an opening at his old school as Head of Geography, After two or three years in the slow pace of the British system, he decided to emigrate. He applied to various countries, and met Bill Joyce for an interview in London in March 1974. With his wife Anne and three small children, he joined Ashbury and settled into a staff house in time for the fall term.

Macoun, teaching Grade 13 geography, was hit immediately by the low standard required for university entrance compared to the British A-level. He was disturbed by the absence of outside examinations. He abhorred marking by Bell curve rather than capability. On the other hand, he saw great strength in the liberal choice of subjects and areas for study versus the narrow specialization that by this time boxed in all students — even at Stowe — in the British system.

He happened to know a good deal about the IB because he had applied to Pearson College before it opened. Pearson didn't hire a geographer but Macoun, with his questing mind, got interested and spent some time in the IB London office. An IB diploma, he found, was accepted now by most universities around the world. Success in each subject required a real depth of knowledge and understanding. Students had to use individual initiative and the more deeply they pursued each subject, the greater would be their success. Macoun and Robertson hammered out a proposal to the

Headmaster that Ashbury should join.

Then, before they'd heard back, Dr. Alec Peterson paid a call at Ashbury. He was the founding Director General of the IB and an influential founder of the United World Colleges. He'd heard that Ashbury had expressed some interest and paid an informal call on the Head. By chance Macoun spotted him at lunch in the hall. By another chance the two knew each other from Oxford; Dr. Peterson had been Head of Education when undergraduate Macoun had supported his campaign for city councillor. Dr. Peterson talked to staff in the common room over coffee and ended on the note that, if Ashbury applied, there'd be no problem.

Robertson and Macoun invoked the school's declared policy which, by this time, placed academics first. The annual IB fee was $5000 and there was an examination fee too. An expensive slice of staff time would have to be spent on administration. It would be enormously stimulating for the students and the teaching staff, and also far more demanding. Not all the staff were entirely enchanted and a few were strongly set against such change. So it was no light decision.

The IB assessment was very searching. As well as a written, mail-in exam, it included individual research papers, oral exams, practical assessment, taped listening comprehension tests and a school assessment. Work was spread over two years. Candidates could qualify for certificates in individual subjects at subsidiary or higher level without going for the full diploma. An IB diploma would greatly widen a student's choice of universities, including Oxford, Harvard, Hong Kong and the Sorbonne. In many cases it would get entry into second year.

Persistence and persuasion told. Enough boys and their parent were interested in the challenge. Macoun, who volunteered as coordinator, got approval to start on a trial basis in the fall of 1975. Ashbury was the 55th IB school in the world and the second in Canada after Pearson College. Macoun, Robertson and Niles, and Nicky Davis of Elmwood, led the way with geography, economics, history and English. French came aboard after the major strengthening of that department in 1977. This was a key matter. The complete IB diploma required a full course in one's own language, plus a second language, and at a high standard for both. Mathematics under Robin Hinnell joined the next year, and science with Ross Varley.

An Ashbury student could now elect the regular Ontario credits and write the IB in one or more subjects, or he could go for the full diploma. IB and Ontario credit students worked in the same classrooms. Pearson hadn't had this problem as it offered the IB only. So at Ashbury there was a lot of pioneering to be done. Curricula had to be matched and the Ministry persuaded that a higher level course counted as an Ontario credit. The majority of students still went for their Ontario qualification but the IB — much more demanding on student and teacher both — now set the academic pace.

The full diploma called for six subjects (including one's own and a second language, an option in the study of Man, mathematics and an experimental science), an "extended essay" (a mini-thesis), participation in athletics or art or community service and "Theory of Knowledge" — essentially philosophy. Ken Niles worked on it with the first candidate, Graeme Clark, one-to-one in spare time. There was no equivalent in the Ontario book so Niles wrote the philosophy course, which was then published by the Ministry of Education as a Grade 13 credit. Then he took a place on the IB's North American Subject Committee.

Graeme Clark, in 1978, was the first Ashburian to earn the full IB diploma. The next year there were nine. At the top was David Welch who scored 42 points out of a possible 45. He went on to Harvard and in 1989 co-authored a highly acclaimed book on the Cuban missile crisis of 1962 titled *On the Brink*. Ross Brown since his youngest days had had an extraordinary facility in mathematics. He got 40 points. These students were in the top bracket in the world. Ashbury results overall were right up with the international best.

The IB was far more than a series of examinations. The whole concept — the more one searched outside the classroom, the more deeply one studied, the better the result — was quite different from either the rigid departmental examination system of old or the lack of systematic assessment of the new. The IB was a real challenge for capable young minds. For the individual it expanded the horizons of learning and revealed the rewards of intellectual achievement. For the school as a whole it raised the sights and built the standards.

Teaching counted, of course, in a major way. Mathematics was Robin Hinnell's field. In 1977, Ross Brown had come first out of 21,000 students in the National Junior Mathematics Contest sponsored by the University of Waterloo. He was unique with a perfect paper, the first in 15 years. But Ashbury's team of five was first in Ottawa-Carleton and tenth in Canada. Of the top 15 teams, five were from independent schools. Such results were no accident.

The whole IB system was still developing in the late seventies. W.A.J. gave Macoun his head and he became a member of the North American Board, later of the IB Council based in Switzerland. In Canada Macoun became "Mr. IB," with a unique understanding of melding the IB with the provincial system. Ashbury's name became widely known in informed educational circles.

First-rate students from the Ottawa area who were interested in high achievement were attracted by the IB. It was immediately appealing to diplomatic families, foreign and Canadian, and to overseas students. There was new strength in boarder applications, especially from internationally mobile families. With this new stimulus the whole student body grew in quality even as the school grew in size, standard and reputation.

W.A. Joyce planned to retire in the spring of 1981 when he reached 65. In the fall of 1979 the Board set up a committee to find a new Headmaster. Thirteen years of W.A.J.'s firm hand had wrought many changes. There was a strong student body and staff. The latter were predominantly energetic, fully committed people who thoroughly liked teaching at Ashbury College. They were the kind who liked close, individual contact with their students in and out of the classroom, and often with the parents. As to academic standard, with the International Baccalaureate firmly in place it was the highest ever.

However well-ordered a school may be, there are always some problems. Beds still had to be filled and W.A.J., as always, wouldn't turn away a boy whom he believed needed and could benefit from the help that Ashbury could give. Inevitably there were some misfits, like the boarder who protected his privacy by wiring his door-knob to the wall socket. More serious was an upsurge of drug use in 1977-78 that called for outside help.

Jane Kennedy had been head of business studies since 1973 and by a useful coincidence her husband was an officer on the RCMP's high-school drug squad. Henry Kennedy literally moved into the school for two days, and interviewed every boarder and a lot of day boys. He put a finger on some 50 boys who had used drugs, if only once, some who admitted to selling and two who were actually financing a nasty little trade and making money from their schoolmates. Users attended extra-hours drug education sessions. Perpetrators were rooted out.

The school plant was still deficient. The gym had been inadequate for 30 years, all the more so as the school got bigger. The same applied to the library. The budget barely kept fees, operating expenses and debt management in balance, and was setting next to nothing aside for capital improvements. So such things as gyms and libraries depended on fund-raising and the long-term record on that score had been frustrating.

But good reputations are built on a predominance of the positive over a long period of time. By now Ashbury's had climbed steadily to a position it hadn't enjoyed since the Woollcombe days. By the time of the decisions that led to W.A. Joyce's appointment as Headmaster, the Board was pulling itself into an effective body. At that time it was made up almost entirely of old boys, as it had been since the war; now parents and past parents predominated. Board members were much more active in school affairs. It wasn't a question of interfering with the Headmaster's day-to-day administration. They were concerned with educational policy, curriculum development and long-range planning, going far beyond the traditional matters of finance and fund-raising. They worked closely on committees with members of the staff.

This was a responsible Board, filling its right and proper functions. John Woods, the third generation of his family to head the Board, was Chairman from 1978 to 1982. He was the one who'd prompted the first look at co-education in 1976. Now, with the school on a really firm footing, the stage was set for a period of dramatic and rapid change. Frederic Martin chaired the search committee for a new Headmaster with another parent, Cynthia Baxter, and two old boys, John Woods and Jim Smellie. The Headmaster acted as secretary, not a member of the committee, and there were no head-hunters involved.

New headmasters meant new styles, new ideas, perhaps new departures. So now was the time for the school to define itself and make its own vision very clear, not just to itself but to anyone who aspired to be its Head. In anticipation the Board had set up a Long-Term Planning Committee. It was chaired by Dr. A.G. Sandy Watson, with another Board member, Duncan Edmonds, and staff members Hugh Robertson, Michael Sherwood and Tony Macoun. Their main report, called "A Spirit of Purpose," was ready in spring 1980 for the search committee to send out to those on their short list before they came for their final interviews in September.

The members of the Planning Committee had set their sights on Ashbury's Centennial in 1991 and gathered input from Board, Headmaster, staff and parents. There was no doubt that the future would bring even more turbulence and change in Canada and the world. Only a high-quality school would survive. A first-rate liberal education was the prime goal. The academic programme would be built around the curriculum and philosophy of the International Baccalaureate, with the Ontario system in parallel. They stressed the essential value of music, art, drama, Canadian studies, computer studies, creative thinking, outdoor education and community service. It was essential to retain boarding in the senior school.

They examined Hugh Robertson's concept of Ashbury as "The School of the Commonwealth." Pursuing this, Macoun visited IB centres in Geneva and London, and the committee talked to Dr. Alec Peterson, who was chairman of United World Colleges and Vice-Chairman of the International Baccalaureate, and to Sandy Rampal, Secretary-General of the Commonwealth Secretariat. The aim of the School of the Commonwealth, as with United World Colleges, was to promote international understanding through education.

The proposal: some 40 students would come to Ashbury on full scholarships from Commonwealth countries for the two IB years in Grades 12 and 13. Ottawa was the ideal place for such an ongoing congress of talented young people. The scheme would further the cause of a global society and add a remarkable dimension to the school. It was a breathtaking vision.

In recent years Macoun had been asking old boys what the gaps were in their preparation for university. The common answer was "computers" — and that was in hand — and "the opposite sex." Back in 1976 Sherwood, Niles and Macoun had recommended co-education "when the time was right." Now, all the committee members were convinced it was part and parcel of a properly rounded education. For a "School of the Commonwealth" it was essential.

An obvious avenue, from Ashbury's point of view at least, was a combined venture with Elmwood. There was a long history of cooperation between the schools. Since Elmwood's earliest days there'd been a good deal of overlap among families, parents and Boards. At the time of the study Duncan Edmonds, for example, was on both Boards. Dr. Hannah Sellers was on Elmwood's, her husband, Dr. Frank Sellers, on Ashbury's. The committee talked to Elmwood's Chairman and Governors. Their response was cautious. By the spring of 1980 nothing on that front had been resolved. Whatever the means, though, the time had come, the committee said, for Ashbury to embark on "full co-education."

They also recommended total commitment to excellent French instruction and creating the milieu to stimulate it. Contacts should be developed in Quebec to encourage student exchanges; French-Canadian culture should become part of Ashbury's programme. Participation in the Forum for Young Canadians should be increased and Ashbury should be more closely related, as it had been when the Forum started. They forecast a big expansion of the junior school including kindergarten to Grade 8, though with very few boarders; ideally it should be moved to a nearby separate campus. But the school should maintain its long-time Rockcliffe location. The major physical need was for a full-sized gymnasium and swimming pool.

"A Spirit of Purpose" presented a challenging vision with well-defined objectives. The Board whole-heartedly endorsed it. The school knew where it was headed. Above all, it called for a Headmaster who was totally committed. Thus, there was a clear meeting of minds when the search committee interviewed those on the short list in September 1980. The new Headmaster, appointed by the Board in October to succeed in the summer of 1981, was Anthony M. Macoun. His stamp was firmly on "A Spirit of Purpose." His record at Ashbury stood very clear. In the staff common room, among the boys, the parents, the whole Ashbury community, the choice drew universal acclaim.

That the right man was found within the ranks was a tribute to the strength that W.A. Joyce had so ably and painstakingly built up. Over 20 impressively supported applications had come in from across Canada and from the United States and Britain. They included several headmasters and assistant heads of leading independent schools. If any other tribute was needed to the changes wrought throughout Bill Joyce's regime and the reputation he had built for his school, this was it. When he himself had been interviewed back in 1966, he had been one of two. The *Ashburian*'s columns on his leaving the school called him "Colonel Joyce." "Colonel" wasn't seen now as a title for a tyrant sent to beat boys into line. It was a mark of respect for deep-rooted values, consistently espoused and firmly applied. W.A. Joyce infused Ashbury College with the spirit of purpose which would carry it forward to new, productive heights.

Chapter 20
Anthony Macoun

In-house appointments of Heads of independent schools are generally viewed with ill favour. The only previous one in Ashbury's history, that of Harry Wright in 1933, was followed by a disastrous slide. But that was a quick anointing. Tony Macoun's was the result of the most thorough, systematic selection exercise the Board had ever run, and it was followed by the most concentrated period of progressive growth in the school's history.

Macoun's philosophy of education grew from his own varied experience. He was convinced that the complex challenges of the future could not be met by a technical fix, by any single-dimensioned approach. Ashbury must educate students for all seasons, have them learn how to learn, to think for themselves. It must bring out talent, not pump in skills. The aim was a first-class liberal education concentrating in substantial depth on basic disciplines.

To achieve this Ashbury capitalized on smaller classes, committed teachers, and a curriculum that was traditional and more demanding than in most schools, with the pace set by the International Baccalaureate. But also, in the best tradition of the independent school, it had a responsibility to develop each student's spiritual and physical well-being, social and moral attitudes, character and values. These qualities could best be developed in a structured environment with a strong sense of community. There must be firm standards of admission, conduct and academic progress. Now, after years of steady consolidation under his predecessor's leadership, the way ahead was clear.

As one of its authors, Macoun's commitment to "A Spirit of Purpose" was complete. He had a clear mandate and, typically, he moved with energy and dispatch. The report, dated May 1980, had unreservedly proposed co-education, "possibly in full partnership and co-operation with Elmwood." Before writing it, the committee had talked to a group of Elmwood Governors. Shared classes had been a boon to both schools, allowing much wider choices and more levels of instruction. But there were timetabling, administrative and day-to-day irritants. Most important, it didn't make Ashbury a fully co-educational school. And that was the aim, for educational reasons, not because of financial pressure.

For the Ashbury committee amalgamation was an exciting and obvious field to explore. Two long-established schools so physically close, so long-connected, with the same basic aims and serving a common clientele, seemed natural candidates. There'd been plenty of successful unions in much less promising situations. But to Elmwood, Ashbury was charging ahead with its own interests, without the courtesy of a Board to Board approach, and it was aiming squarely at their market. From the outset there was no real meeting of minds.

Then in October 1980, with the "Spirit of Purpose" report officially accepted and Macoun appointed Headmaster-designate, the Board set up a co-educational committee. Cynthia Baxter chaired it, with Macoun and Sherwood as members. Their first task: to work through the Elmwood possibilities.

The earlier meeting had launched Elmwood's Board on a self-examination of its own. Its staff was quite firmly against amalgamation. The planning committee sent a questionnaire to its constituency and, while it deliberated, there were several meetings over various Ashbury proposals that reached no agreement. The Elmwood planning committee report, completed in May 1981, favoured continued cooperative classes and perhaps the running of the top three grades with Ashbury on a 50-50 control basis. But they shied well clear of any form of amalgamation.

A joint meeting of the two Boards after Macoun became Headmaster turned no common ground. Elmwood saw a place for a girls-only non-denominational school in Ottawa. Ashbury aimed at one school, favouring co-education in junior grades and at least the top three grades, using the two campuses in the most suitable way. Aims simply weren't compatible. Two years of talk and a good deal of uncomfortable friction had brought no progress. Ashbury's Board decided, in February 1982, to press on. Grades 12 and 13 were opened to day girls who wanted to follow the IB. By the end of March 13 had enrolled for the fall term.

Elmwood's Board called off the cooperative class arrangements. On the positive side — certainly stimulated by this whole episode and the burgeoning competition across the village green — Elmwood went through a major planning and expansion phase and came out a far stronger school. Having entered the IB with Ashbury and shared the $5000 annual fee, Elmwood continued to offer it on a close individual basis.

Even with the recession of the early eighties and declining student population, there were plenty of applicants for both schools. Earlier trends continued. Between the mid-1970s and mid-1980s the boarding population in private schools stayed about the same overall, but numbers of private day students doubled. The year 1982-83 was a landmark too as the first year in which more women than men took degrees at Canadian universities. Ashbury opened that year with 434 students, 13 of them girls. There was no decrease, as some had predicted, in the number of boys. On the contrary. There were considerably more applicants than places. And a whole new market had opened up.

The next fall girls entered Grade 11 too, raising numbers to 28. The nine boarders among them came from Madrid, Los Angeles, Washington, Dar es Salaam, Hong Kong, Montreal, Toronto and Ottawa. The old annex, built in 1910 as the Headmaster's house, became the main girls' residence and they used the accommodation in the staff houses as well. Macoun and many of the long-term staff had reservations about admitting girls in Grades 9 and 10 and for the time being he held things as they were.

Unlike the controversy that raged over mere contemplation of co-education at most other boys' schools, there was hardly a murmur from Ashbury's old boys. Some were bemused at the new collective "alumni" and terms like "Dean of Women." But, if a gauge were needed, alumni annual giving that fall took a jump. For senior staff who'd spent most of their careers teaching in boys-only schools, there were qualms. But turnover was very slight: with over 50 on the teaching staff, between 1981 and 1985 only five on average changed each year. Among the boys, especially at the top, there'd been some pretty strong reservations. They liked their school very much as it was. But in the event they liked it even better. Co-education was taken across the board as a positive and welcome step.

Jane Kennedy was the clear choice for Dean of Women. A wise, level-headed, feet-on-the-ground woman who believed in straight talk, she had things moving with the right spirit from the start. And the calibre of the girls was outstanding. No one visiting the school who had known it of old could help being struck by the new atmosphere that pervaded the traditional male preserve. It was quite transformed. Their impact, even in the first small numbers, was phenomenal. There was less of the boisterous hurly-burly but no loss of vitality. There was a new tone, an essential civility about the place, with an up-beat attitude, a feeling of openness, pride in the school and pride in achievement. The following spring every single graduate went on to higher education.

The driving force for excellence, the IB, was now in Michael Jansen's hands as coordinator and consolidator. Tony Macoun stayed on the important international IB bodies and that kept Ashbury contributing to the programme and thoroughly involved.

From the early 1980s a lot of other Canadian schools followed Ashbury's lead. Pearson College was quite untypical, so a steady stream of visitors from across the country beat on Ashbury's door. Jansen found himself dispensing advice and running workshops from Winnipeg to New York. Some independent schools experimented, but Ashbury and Elmwood were the only ones in central Canada to make the IB a permanent fixture.

One of the less eye-catching sections of "A Spirit of Purpose" concerned the organization of the Board. In October 1983 it rebuilt itself into three categories: Honorary Governors were the Anglican Bishop of Ottawa and the Reeve of Rockcliffe; Life Governors — 19 of them, 15 of whom were alumni — were distinguished "elder statesmen" who were interested in the school and could be called on for advice and support; Term Governors, 16 in number, were effectively the Executive and held office for three years, and they alone could vote on Board matters. Ex officio, the Headmaster and the Presidents of the Ashbury Guild, the Alumni and the Parents' Committee were Term Governors. Eleven were parents; six were alumni; three were women; some were in two of these categories. The reorganization consolidated the gradual shift in influence and direction that had taken place over the years. Participation, continuity and renewal were now built in.

The character of the staff had been changing over the years and its numbers doubled since 1976. Around 60 percent now had no prior experience in independent education, and the great majority were Canadian. Tightened immigration early in the eighties sped the process. Out of 55 teachers in 1983-84, ten plus the Head were of British or Commonwealth origin, one came from France, five were French-Canadian.

With Tony Macoun at the helm, the staff had real expectations of change. He had proved himself as one of their most innovative and energetic working members; he had their undoubted respect professionally; and he was of their generation, open and approachable. Salaries were a matter of long-time concern. Teachers were still hired individually at the lowest rate the Headmaster could negotiate — or the most they could get. Salaries followed the rising trend but the gap yawned almost 20 percent below those of the Ottawa Board. Now the staff looked for some improvement.

Macoun, just up from the ranks and subject to the old individual salary negotiations, happily adopted a set scale. Now everyone knew what everyone else made. Some got substantial increases on the spot. When the celebration was over, some first-rate, long-service hands found they'd been short-changed for years. A great step ahead it was, but the inequities of the past left a bitter taste.

The Head had always been undisputed in firing as well as hiring. He decided, around March, whose contract to renew for the following year. Some decisions made in his office were viewed from the staff common room as pretty arbitrary. Dismissal for cause or professional inadequacy was one thing, a shortfall in personal qualities another. But personal qualities, bearing in mind what Ashbury sought to do, were vitally important. They were largely subjective, though, and could really only be judged by the one responsible for maintaining the tone of the school — the Head.

From the mid-seventies, with the Board taking a much more direct hand in matters like curriculum and school life, the staff had become much more involved in advising Board committees and working with the Parents' Committee. There'd even been suggestions in earlier years that a member of the staff should be on the Board. Now they proposed a formal Staff Advisory Committee to advise the Head on salaries, for instance, and contracts. Through the 1970s several independent schools had set up such bodies and many had adopted published salary scales. In the new Head's view, the Committee could seek to advise, but it would in no sense be a negotiating body.

Ross Varley, who represented the staff's views to the new Head, had brought an interesting background to Ashbury in 1976. Born and raised in Verdun, he went through teachers' college where he met and married Mary Ann Carter of Ottawa. Both taught in Quebec City for eight years. In the early seventies, the whole provincial public service locked horns with the government and strikes were epidemic. Varley saw it all at close quarters. As President of the Eastern Quebec Teachers' Association he organized three strikes himself. The English education system in Quebec City was shrinking and he began to look around. In 1976 he saw an Ashbury ad for a biology teacher. He wasn't going to apply but it happened that Graham Jackson was the guidance counsellor in the same Quebec school. He'd been Captain of the School at Ashbury in 1954, then had taught in the days of Ron Perry and suffered Arthur Brain's marathon staff meetings. Jackson urged Varley on, spoke highly of his talents to Bill Joyce, and the deal was done.

For one reared wholly in the public system, Ashbury was a culture shock. It was far more demanding of time and personal involvement, with after-hours sports and activities. It called for a definite standard of deportment among the staff. It was also run by an autocratic hand. Counter to Varley's earlier experience, school matters weren't hammered out by staff. There was no question of consensus, no challenging the system or the Head. Varley found satisfying academic freedom, though. He could explore and try new things. He liked the students, the small classes, the close involvement. He quickly came to believe firmly in the school's approach to education and what it was seeking to do.

Mary Ann Varley began to teach art, her specialized field, part-time. Then she came on staff full-time to build the outstanding programme that runs through the school today. Financially the Varleys were somewhat better off than they'd been in Quebec but they found they were well behind teachers in the Ottawa Boards. Ashbury was, though, a stimulating place to teach.

Varley and the Staff Advisory Committee did a lot of digging on salaries and benefits. In early 1984 they proposed that salaries be set at the mean of the Ottawa and Carleton School Board teachers' "level 3.5." That would put Ashbury teachers near the top of the Ontario four-tier definition of experience. The basic proposal wasn't accepted as school policy. Salaries did move closer to the Ottawa norms, though by 1985-86 there was still a disparity.

On other matters the staff felt less successful. Tony Macoun was analytical, with an active, questing mind, and he had a sure, firm hand. He was a man who made decisions and got on with school business very briskly. While his mind was always open to ideas and innovations — he produced many himself — he was a traditionalist. He maintained a deep regard for the essential values. And the Headmaster was unquestionably the one in charge. He was sometimes peremptory or selective in his consultation. For the teaching staff, a growing and increasingly long-service body, security was a rising concern. Many wanted to see formal recourse for dismissal and a staff evaluation process.

Macoun believed in a clear, well-defined structure within which staff and students could operate using common-sense and basic respect for others without a plethora of rules. Discipline was firm and fair. Corporal punishment had long since disappeared. Macoun was very clear on the matter of drugs: they were there in the city and they wouldn't be kept at bay by equivocating. In his first year as Head, he expelled eight students for using drugs at school. Smoking was finally banned. It had found its way into the school some 50 years back in the days when it was the fashionable thing to do. Somewhere in the nether regions there had always been a "butt-room" for addicts, replete with the reek of lung-destroying oils, tars and nicotine. Now such smokers as persisted had to huddle behind shrubbery or snowbanks for their surreptitious puff.

Macoun aimed at a senior school of 300: four classes averaging 15 in each of five grades. That would give the best selection of options and levels. The junior school had around a healthy 160 with a declining number of boarders. Macoun promoted energetically with External Affairs. Ashbury eventually got over half of the Canadian boarding school places that the Department subsidized for parents serving overseas. With the growing school a new gymnasium, on the wish-list for 30 years, was a sheer necessity.

Classes with Elmwood

Joint classes with Elmwood started with a few subjects in 1967. In 1973 Jane Kennedy came to teach business (above). The joint classes opened many more options to both schools and greatly improved teaching of French.   PHOTO: JOHN EVANS

W.A. Joyce with (from left): Donald Paterson, Captain of the School 1973-74, Peter Croal and Francisco Durazo of Mexico City looking over plans of the 1973 additions which greatly increased accommodation, lightened and brightened the old building and raised the spirits of all.   PHOTO: JOHN EVANS

Ashbury Day 1973

The Right Honourable Roland Michener, CC,CMM,CD, Governor General of Canada, presided at the biggest gathering in the school's history for the official opening of the new additions and renovations on 13 October, 1973. Chairman Ned Rhodes Jr. (1946-55) is with him.   PHOTO: JOHN EVANS

Canal Skating 1974

Friendly bus driver, Lorne Duberville, always joined in the junior school outings on the Rideau Canal. With him in February 1974 are (from left): D. Keith, M. Viets, J. Mitchell, R. Haslam, V. Rigby, J. Daniels, D. Farquhar, Lorne Duberville, C. Panneton, A. Nelson, J. Draper, K. Carter, P. Wright, T. Webb, L. Dunlop

Fighting in background: P. Griffiths and R. Bland

Outdoor Education 1975

High above Heney Lake in the Gatineau Hills, John Beedell leads a Grade 8 group opening a trail through to Mont Ste. Marie. They are (from left): B.E. Whitney, J.F. Turner, K.C. Mahoney, J.D. Fraser, D.M. Segall, D.W. Squires, I.R. Nicol, D.A. Farquhar.

Mary Boyce retired as junior school matron in 1974, after 11 years of sympathetic mothering and firm guidance for many young and often lonely boys. Her warmth, like so many in the unsung but essential positions at the school, won her a place in the hearts of all who knew her in her time.

In his 26 years at Ashbury, Chef Mark Tatichek cooked for many distinguished guests as well as hundreds upon hundreds of hungry young. Right Honourable John Diefenbaker joined the Forum for Young Canadians at Ashbury to celebrate July 1, 1976 and congratulated Mark on his splendid Canada Day Cake.

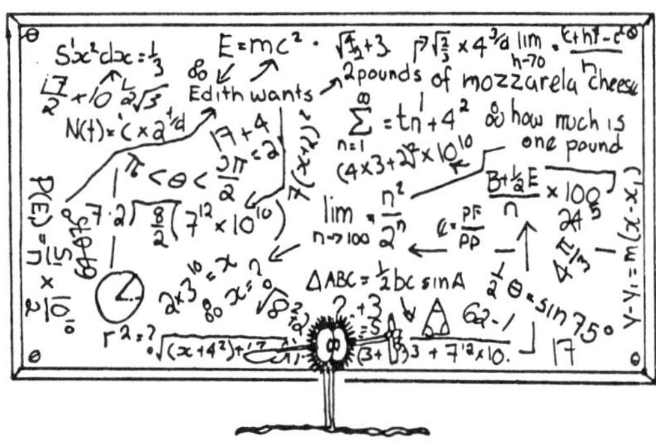

Ashbury eight on the Ottawa River in 1981. Rowing was revived in 1978 by Hugh Robertson helped by coaching from a national level oarsman, Dave Keeling, and the hospitality of the Ottawa Rowing Club. In 1986 Coach Bob Zettel took two teams to the Canadian Scholastic Championships in St. Catharines.

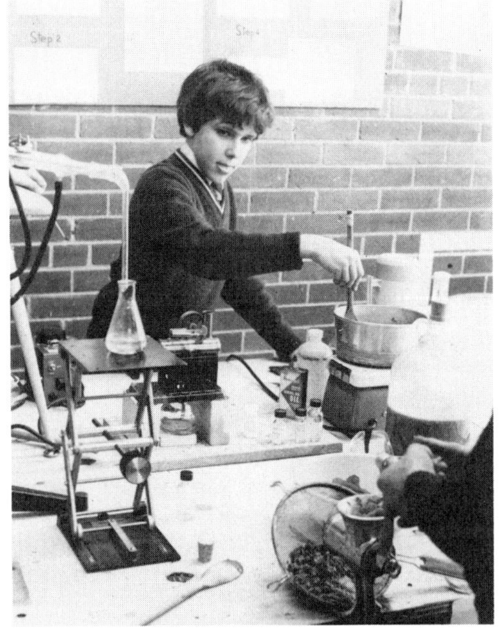

"Eye of Newt" – Robert Johnstone and helper mix up a witches' brew in the name of science at the Fair in 1981.

Tony Macoun, Headmaster 1981-86, at the Forum for Young Canadians' graduating banquet at the National Arts Centre. The Headmaster has been on the Forum Board since its founding in 1975.

Rev. E.E. "Jeep" Green (1969-87) was Ashbury's longest-serving Chaplain other than the Founder. He coached public speaking and the debaters – here in 1980. (from left) Fabrice Cadieux, Lauchlin Munro and David Owen.

At the Independent Junior Schools Boys Soccer Championships in Vancouver, 1979. Behind Coach John Valentine left to right: Phillip Kelly, Tony Rhodes, Ian Crockett, Patrick Bannister's head, Geoffrey Wilson, Josh Bates (Capt.). In front: "Alfie", Charlie Sezlik and Patrick Guglich. The first tournament was played at Ashbury in 1976. The trophy is a memorial to J. Scott Crockett.

Girls At Ashbury 1982

Back Row (from left): Nadine Jubb, Tina Reilly, Anna Childe, Sue Wurtele, Lisa Kelly
Front Row : Julia Rhodes, Elizabeth Wright, Lisa Mierins, Sheilagh White, Wendy Mutzeneek, Lisa Powell, Bari-Lee Myers, Caroline Martin
The first female students at Ashbury College were in fact G.P. Woolcombe's daughters Maithol and Phyllis, and next came Elizabeth Archdale. The first regular enrolment was in the fall of 1982.

Daffodil Day 1984

A rose in the buttonhole every day, a daffodil once a year. Prime Minister Pierre Trudeau (and Hon. Jean-Luc Pepin behind him) buy daffodils from (from left) Carola De La Guardia, Sean Cauldfield, Mr. Peter MacFarlane, Stuart Hensel and John Haffner.

The Class of 1990 in the new computer centre in 1983.
from left: David Hodgson, Ian Toth, Alasdair Stuart-Bell, Duncan Pound

Forum for Young Canadians 1988

Honourable John Fraser, Speaker of the House of Commons briefs the Forum for Young Canadians on the workings of the House. He and his predecessors have done so regularly since the Forum started at Ashbury in 1976.

After the formalities of Parliament Hill with the political leaders of the land the Forum students enjoy each other's company in the Ashbury common room.

Girls' Basketball Champs 1990

A first for Centennial year.
Back Row (from left): R.B. Napier, J. Napier, C. Freeman, A. Carruthers, T. Crombie, K. Wyatt, A.J. Sparks
Front Row: A. M. Baribeau, L. Edmison, G. Hahn, J. Rawlinson, M. Pound, A. Howard

The girls' basketball team celebrate winning the city high school championship. Coaches were Andy Sparks and Judi Ohlson.

Football 1990

Back Row (from left): I.H. Deakin (Coach), K. Guarisco (Coach), R.B. Napier, R. Tavel, A. Hageman, R.I. Gray (Coach)
4th Row: S. Desjardins, B. Valiquette, J. Stokes, J. Daugherty, M. Stevenson, C. Penton, R. Kenny, R. Lorrain, S. Fretwell
3rd Row: S. Grism, O. Tareen, B. Barber, A. Woodford, D. McNaughton, M. Burns, H. Bell, D. Cripps, M. Valiquette, A. Cole
2nd Row: Y. Massicotte, A. Movilla, M. Quamina, C. Gillen, J. Starr, A. Slawecki, M. Spratt, M. Maher
Front Row: D. Sheehan, W. Qirbi, A. Nichols, P. Bartlett, J. Hill, J. Robertson, J.P. Ostiguy, A. Zollinger, R. Dubras

The football team 1990 had an unbeaten season and won the Ottawa-Carleton Senior B championship to celebrate the Centennial year.

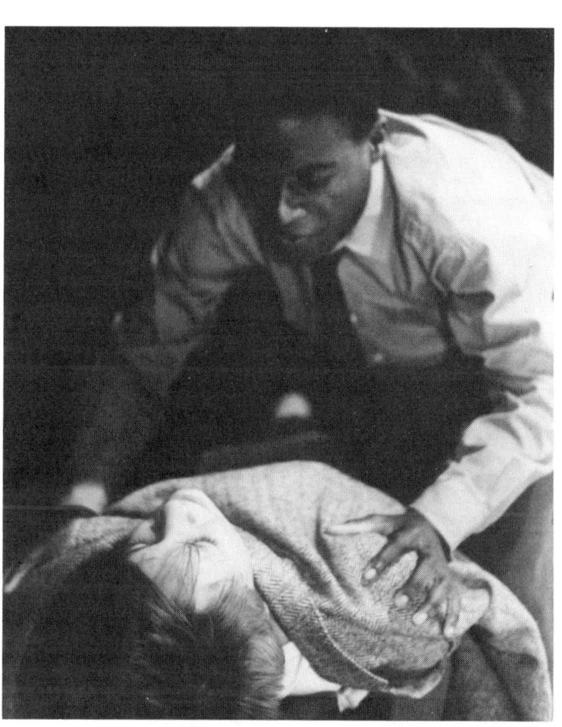

Theatre Ashbury 1988

Zaa Nkweta and Chris Stanton in Peter Shaffer's "Equus" in 1988. Theatre Ashbury chooses strong and difficult plays for its senior productions. Zaa went on to McGill and The National Theatre School in Montreal.

Junior Theatre 1988

"The Death and Life of Sneaky Fitch" by Theatre Ashbury junior players in 1988 with (seated) James Nambwangu, Tom Hyde and Josh Gibson (as Sneaky). Matthew Perry who played in the 1981 production went on to become a professional actor in Hollywood.

Canon George P. Woollcombe
B.A. Oxford
M.A. Bishops
LLD McGill
Founding Headmaster
1891 - 1933

Harry F. Wright
B.A. Sheffield
Cape University
South Africa
Headmaster, 1933 - 1936

Nicholas M. Archdale
M.A. Oxford
Headmaster, 1936 - 1945

C.L. Ogden Glass
B.A. Bishop's
M.A. Oxford
Headmaster, 1945 -1950

Ronald H. Perry
B.A. Toronto
M.A. Columbia
Headmaster, 1950 - 1966

William A. Joyce
DSO, E.D.
B.Sc. Manitoba
Headmaster, 1966 - 1981

Anthony M. Macoun
M.A. Oxford
Headmaster, 1981-1986

Robert B. Napier
B.Sc. Belfast
M. Ed. Bishops
Headmaster 1986-

From MacKay Lake in the foreground and the open space of Ashbury's grounds in the centre, the Nation's Capital of 1991 stretches away to the west. G.P. Woollcombe picked a dynamic and ultimately beautiful city for his school in 1891 and a fine location in 1910 to secure its future.

PHOTO: PETER WILSON

The plaque marking the site of the Victoria Chambers, Ashbury's first home in 1891, was unveiled on May 12, 1991 by Hon. Robert L. Stanfield 1929-32 and Dharini Woollcombe, great-grandaughter of the Founder.

Birthday Cake - Happy 100th Birthday!

Captain of the School Andrew Nichols, Roy Napier and Gabriela Hahn led the crowd singing "Happy Birthday." Julian deHoog cut the cake.

Chapter 21
The Challenge of Change

In 1983 parent Bill Teron, who had been on the Board in the early seventies, updated his 1973 concept that had included a future gym with the old one converted to a library. He also pledged to contribute the roof, which was a special Teron design. Later Chris Teron, 10 years out of Ashbury and a qualified architect, would supervise the construction of the roof, with younger brothers Willie and Bruce criticizing between classes. Topping off team Teron, their mother Jean had been a Governor since 1978.

As in 1973, Murray, Murray, Griffiths and Rankin were to be the architects. Tim Murray, who had been on the Board since 1978, was now Vice-Chairman and due to be Chairman in 1985. His partner-brother Patrick became an Honorary Governor in 1985 as Reeve of Rockcliffe. Creatively, architecturally, technically, and from the community and personal commitment viewpoint, the project would be in the best of hands.

That fall preliminary plans and estimates came in — minus the pool which was too big a bite. There was no spare money in the bank. But confidence was abroad. The school had been on a stable financial footing for years. It was debt-free, and the economy was taking an upward turn. Applicants were being turned away and fast-rising enrolment meant a projected surplus. The Headmaster pressed hard. Do it now, he said, or wait another 10 years.

The Board, encouraged by the Chairman, Lieutenant-General Bill Milroy, and by Finance Chairman John Graham, took the bull by the horns. The project would, to a considerable extent, be "user pay" — retiring a loan with future fees — with a fund-raising campaign to close the gap. Some neighbours on Glenwood petitioned the Village council against the new addition on the grounds of traffic flow. But all the bylaws were satisfied. On May 16, 1984, 52 years after he had graduated from Ashbury, the Honourable Robert L. Stanfield turned the first sod. Then he, as Honorary Chairman of "A Campaign for Ashbury," and an energetic committee set out to raise $1.5 million.

The new wing rose quickly. Its warm brick and architectural features blended quite beautifully with the old buildings and with the general surroundings. When it opened for business in 1985, it brought a stunning transformation to the school. The ripple effect was not just in space but in spirits.

For Ray Anderson and generations of coaches who had delivered such fine athletic and phys. ed. programmes for years with those meagre old facilities, it was a gift from heaven. With more and more students and the advent of girls, it gave Anderson, Bob Gray and the whole athletic programme new dimensions and a new lease on life. Gray, who had arrived in 1974, was director of physical education and an outstanding basketball coach. Now there was a real floor to play on.

It was quite extraordinary what had been done without the new facilities. In 1983-84, for example, in the whole school there were eight soccer teams, three each in football, hockey and rugger, two in basketball, plus teams in cross-country and downhill skiing, tennis, track and field, judo, curling, rowing and sailing. On top of all the competition with other schools there were interhouse games in just about everything, including cross-country running, swimming and softball, not forgetting regular phys. ed. All this with only three playing fields, including the Rockcliffe field by Mackay Lake, one outdoor rink, the undersized gym, a monster bus-shuttling operation to facilities around the city, coaching and management by teaching staff, and magical organization by Messrs Anderson and Gray.

In addition to the new gym, with the stage at the end and locker rooms and music rooms below, the old gym was freed up to become a library. This had been in the 1973 plan and it made space in Argyle for two more classrooms in the junior school. Librarian Bob Rice had come to Ashbury that same year. He was the first full-time professional to fill this role and he'd been patiently applying his thorough competence and engaging humour with very limited resources. It's people, of course, not bricks and mortar that really make a school.

A reminder of this came that year when David Polk Sr. retired. He had first come to Ashbury in 1940, left to serve at sea during the war and had come back in 1947. He was, very simply, the complete schoolmaster. He headed the junior school from 1953 to 1967 and went on to teach there until he retired. He devoted 42 years of his life to Ashbury boys. He taught superbly well, always; and to every one of his students he passed something of his own warm humanity. The fact that the junior school, through thick and thin, had such a friendly atmosphere and was a good place where youngsters *liked* school could be laid in large part at David Polk's door.

To keep alive the memory of one of those rare and unique characters who make places like Ashbury what they are, the Polk Award was established in the junior school. Polky, asked to set out the characteristics required of the winners, wrote: "Gentleness, friendliness, honesty and a conscience which allows only his best work to be presented." That, taken with his true sense of humour, his love of life and his joy in other people, sums up David L. Polk. His son, old boy David C. Polk, had started teaching at Ashbury in 1977 and kept on the family tradition.

Meanwhile, the campaign got a jump start with donations from a generous Board of Governors. The Ladies Guild organized a kick-off fund-raiser at the US Ambassador's residence courtesy of Ambassador and Mrs Paul Robinson, parents of student Virginia. Tim Newton and Tamir Sherif, with staff advisor Ross Varley, organized the raffling of a gleaming Thunderbird and brought in $21,000.

The Alumni Association was developing greater strength and interest with leadership from Bruce Hillary and John Rowan-Legg. An interesting sidelight came from the United States, where a non-profit corporation had been set up in the late sixties to receive donations from old Ashbury American citizens. So it could qualify for tax relief under new US laws, Ashbury itself formally adopted a non-discrimination policy. Now, inscribed in the record, was something that had been a fact at Ashbury since the latter half of the 1940s.

The gym cost $1,360,000 — the equivalent of 125 boarders' annual fees of $11,000. The gym was three times the size of the old Memorial Wing gym of 1924, which had cost $66,000, or 88 boarders' fees at the going rate of $750. In relative terms, not a bad deal for the 1980s. As in the past, fund-raising wasn't easy and it took a bank loan to tide things over. In the spring of 1986, two years after Bob Stanfield turned the sod, pledges topped $1.2 million. Interest had added to the load but now the balance could be managed out of the operating account.

Personal computers were everywhere by the early eighties and Ashbury was lagging behind the field — especially in a city with such a booming high-tech industry. There was the cost of hardware and software and the problem of space. Technical courses in computers weren't in Ashbury's scheme of things and they had to be intelligently integrated as tools in the existing curriculum. In 1982 parent Ross Tuddenham gave the school 14 Hyperion computers. Teachers took them home and got familiar with their potential for their own fields. Generous support from Ross and Michael Copeland made the first computer lab possible in 1983. The second was added in summer 1986.

The parting of the ways with Elmwood meant that Ashbury had to increase its own French department. The IB was a prime impulse for higher-level French because a second language in depth was required for a Diploma. Most boys who weren't going for the IB dropped French after Grade 11, but the majority of girls took it right through even if they weren't taking the IB. Overall the French classroom populations increased.

Cultural awareness became an important part of the French programme. Club Francophone met twice a week for lively discussions and got English mother-tongue students involved. A fun-packed annual event, La Semaine de Français, started in 1984. Food, music, posters, clothes, films and theatre performances — and at Ashbury a first-rate performance of *Antigone* directed by Marc-André Pelletier. That same year Chantal Jauvin of Grade 12 won first prize at Le Tournoi national de Débats held in Saskatoon. Benoit Hérique, in his first year teaching in the junior school, arranged a student exchange with a school in his native Nancy where he had taken his degrees in education, journalism and theatre. On another level, Robert Campeau, the Ottawa developer, made a strong contribution in this direction by donating the Campeau Family Scholarship for a francophone student with high scholastic achievement.

Music had come a long way in the 10 years since Alan Thomas arrived from England. Here was a man with true dedication to his discipline, with the patience, ingenuity and humour to persevere — and build — under pretty discouraging conditions. The "music room" then was below the old gym. The thumping of feet above, the clanging of the boiler next door and shrill cries from the junior locker room chased him and his classes to the Chapel. There, in turn, they bedevilled the English classes underneath until a portable classroom saved the day. The Ladies Guild produced a stereo and band instruments. Douglas Brookes, an excellent musician late of the Canadian Forces, had begun instrumental teaching in 1973. He formed and directed two bands.

Interest expanded with the school. Peter McLean, who'd arrived from England in 1980 as a housemaster in the junior school, brought the choir to new heights. It began raising money with local performances to help pay for tours in Canada and abroad. In the summer of 1984 the junior choir sang in Toronto, Winnipeg, Calgary and Vancouver. The junior play was always an annual treat. In 1984 Peter McLean wrote an original musical called *Piper*. Staff members Greg Simpson and Alex Menzies directed. With leads Alex Bright, Paul Macoun, Alejandro Colas, Gregor

Snedden and Peter McDonald, backed by 45 more juniors in the cast, it was a real dramatic and musical *tour de force*.

Building from the days of Irene Woodburn Wright, singing, recorder, wind and brass were now taught in all junior grades. Senior grades had full Ontario music credit options available, plus the rigorous IB courses in Grades 12 and 13. Concerts, house music competitions and an annual musical show were regular events. Most important to Alan Thomas, students now regarded musical knowledge and ability as useful, desirable elements of a rounded education. His was an outstanding contribution. In 1984, when he stepped down as department head, he'd made music part of the life of the school and laid a fine basis for his successor, Lionel Tanod.

For his first Closing Day Tony Macoun invited old boy Hon. John Turner as principal guest. He had been out of politics since 1975 and would be until he succeeded Pierre Trudeau as Liberal leader and Prime Minister in 1984. He didn't recall Closing Day pranks as being in vogue at Ashbury in the 1940s. No doubt they'd have been pretty heavily stamped on. But he ran straight into one on his way to the platform to deliver an inspiring and memorable speech in 1982. That morning, out to survey his immaculate campus prior to the great events of the day, the Headmaster had spied, in the middle of the playing field, the entire maintenance staff heaving roundly at . . . a brightly coloured Volkswagen. The graduating class, headed by School Captain Kevin Keenan, had unearthed the ancient and engineless bug, painted it in school colours and manhandled it out there in dead of night. The car was named, in large letters, "Woody's Duckmobile" — "Woody" for the popular Woody Stableford (who with his glasses on looked just like Woody Allen) and "Duckmobile" after Tony Macoun's obscure soubriquet "Ducky." Ducky stopped the frantic efforts of the staff. The Duckmobile stayed there for the day.

The following year Macoun's nickname was indelibly confirmed when, at Closing, the Founder's portrait in the hall was replaced by a fine likeness of Donald Duck signed by all the graduating class.

Next year, entering the main door one early morning a couple of days before Closing, the Head was stunned to find himself in a semi-tropical paradise. Wall-to-wall, overnight, the entire front hall and all the way down the main corridor had grown a lush green lawn. On the manicured grass were lawn chairs, beach umbrellas, barbecues and even pink flamingos. Pre-planning with meticulous care, the graduating class had underlaid it all with plastic sheeting. They moved the sod — top quality and a substantial investment — outside and laid it in an area that had needed attention. All was gorgeously groomed and ready for Closing. The speaker that year was Tommy Douglas. Remarkable, outstanding Canadian that he was, he captured the hearts of all.

With the best will in the world melding girls into the traditional, conservative boys' school wasn't without trauma. And maintaining a strong staff wasn't entirely without its mistakes. Carol Ann Theil, from Sault Ste. Marie, won a scholarship to Ashbury and was one of the first nine girls who came to board in 1983. She entered Grade 11, somewhat shy, the youngest of the lot and feeling a little on the outside. Outstanding as she proved — active, a first-rate student in the IB and a fine debater — she was appointed Captain of Woollcombe, the boarders' house, in her third and final year. It was a first in the school's history, of course. If any girl was to make the breakthrough, and indeed have the well-merited opportunity of such a leadership position, it would be Carol Ann. Even with her steely determination, dealing with boys on their own turf as the prefect in charge for the first time ever was a daunting task.

Ken Niles and Jane Kennedy were always there to help and advise. But with her house responsibilities the key person was, of course, the Woollcombe housemaster. Through her first two years it had been Hugh Penton, a wise and understanding man. But he then went on a leave of absence to teach in an international school in Europe. With a new housemaster, Carol Ann felt a lack of advice, guidance and support. What had promised to be a time of valuable experience and growth turned into a period of very heavy stress.

Lee Grainger was Captain of the School, in his seventh year at Ashbury and a young man of great capability. He lived in Ottawa but moved in to board and bear a hand. He in fact stabilized the situation, working with Carol Ann, not replacing her. Such time and energy dedicated to the school certainly cuts into studies and personal life, but that's what leaders are made of.

In a school like Ashbury, there's so much interweaving, most markedly so in the house functions. There's no doubt it takes special qualities, quite apart from academic qualifications or experience, to do the right job. This particular housemaster, who had come on the strength of outstanding credentials as an educator, wasn't on the required wavelength. He left at the end of the year.

Carol Ann didn't fail at her difficult task. Despite the problems she won the respect of her peers. She also won a scholarship to Bishop's University, became a University Scholar and won a prestigious prize for writing.

"Spirit Week," held each mid-winter since the mid-seventies, had always given plenty of scope for imagination. The prefects invariably pressed for various relaxations of routine. Having granted some pretty far-fetched proposals one year, "Ducky" was warmly thanked at a full school assembly by Brett Naisby, Captain of the School. Then, from behind a phalanx of prefects, leaped a sparsely clad lady decked in balloons. She writhed her way through a throatily sung, thank-you strip telegram, shedding her attire the while. As assembly turned to riot, she wound herself around the scarlet Headmaster, kissed him and oozed, "How in hell do I turn you on?" Maintaining headmasterly aplomb can be enough to tax the saints.

Programmes that had been going for years provided endless outlets for energy and resources for personal development — plays, science fair, outdoor education combining Duke of Edinburgh Awards, a growing programme of community service. The annual Ashbury contribution to the Cancer Society's Daffodil Day continued each April. Back in 1976 Bill Joyce had responded to a request from the Cancer Society for some boys for their tag day with "How many do you want? Three hundred?" Tony Macoun and Bill Babbitt organized what worked out to a couple of hundred juniors and seniors covering the centre of the city. Rain, snow, wind, sunshine, by the mid-

1980s the Daffodil Day sales force of 250 was bringing in something over $10,000 in the day's work. Boys and girls penetrated the inner sancta of the mighty with their flowers. Mitch Rosenberg, a high-powered salesman, leaving his shift, spotted Prime Minister Trudeau on Wellington Street, stopped the bus and leaped off to nail him. Mr. Trudeau had no money — or, as Mitch growled back aboard the bus, *said* he had no money. The P.M. got no daffodil from Mitch.

With the school in fine spirit, the International Baccalaureate firmly established, co-education in place and the new gym open, it was time to turn to the concept of Ashbury as "The School of the Commonwealth." In 1981 material had been sent to the Ottawa-based High Commissioners of Commonwealth countries. The idea of representative students coming from around the world on scholarships raised by their own countries to live and study together was very appealing. They would spend two years studying for the IB just as students from Pacific Rim countries came to Pearson College. Macoun promoted the idea very actively. The stumbling block basically was the scholarship money.

But that campaign went on hold in the fall of 1985 when Tony Macoun was appointed as the third Director of Pearson College, effective in the coming spring. It was a fine appointment, no question, and it had drawn applications from the very best in the profession. There's no doubt that the Pearson Board was well aware of Macoun and of Ashbury College and of his and the school's part in the IB. Cynthia Baxter and Bill Teron, both strongly and effectively committed to independent education, had been on the Pearson Board for some years. It wasn't a question of influence; wearing their Ashbury hats, both would have far preferred him to stay. But his achievements spoke for themselves; the school's record and reputation stood very high. It was a tribute to Ashbury in fact, the school where Macoun's philosophy, talents and energy had found full scope.

His leaving was certainly a bolt from the blue. He had done so much to set the school on the right course; he had promoted it so effectively and everything was going so well. The make-up of the student body was changing, of course. A lot of old boys' sons and daughters were coming to Ashbury now, but the "old Ottawa" stamp on the student body had faded considerably with the years. The city of the eighties was over four times the size of that of the twenties and so was the school. Parents, ever more strongly, were working professionals. Many were new Canadians and a lot came from Commonwealth and other countries where one traditionally looked to independent schooling for quality in education. Also, a lot of boarders came from foreign lands. Altogether quite a number had difficulty with English, but this was set right with regular classes in English as a second language.

The 1986 graduating class of 40 included 13 girls, three blacks, three Chinese, two from the Middle East, one European, one French-Canadian; half a dozen had lived in several different countries. It made a rich and stimulating mix, as diverse as the country itself was rapidly becoming.

More than anything, perhaps, Tony Macoun had realized the concept of education as the all-round development of each individual's capability through intelligent guidance by the staff and real endeavour by the students. At the same time he had fostered throughout the school a strong sense of community and true respect for the fundamental values it represented.

His portrait, painted and donated by Robert Hyndman, is one tangible reminder of his short and richly active regime; the Macoun Scholarship is another. His legacy to Ashbury College was dynamism — the willingness, indeed the eagerness, to meet the challenge of change.

CHAPTER 22

ROY NAPIER

Once again the selection committee, headed this time by past Chairman Bill Milroy, combed through a wealth of applications. They emphasized Ashbury's commitment to rounded, disciplined and challenging liberal education and to the idea of the School of the Commonwealth. Their choice from a large and highly qualified field was Robert B. Napier, known as Roy. He was Headmaster of Albert College in Belleville. By a long way he was the most widely experienced educator ever appointed as Headmaster of Ashbury College.

Roy Napier was born in Northern Ireland in 1942. Grammar school near Belfast's notorious Falls Road made him pretty quick on his young Protestant feet. After Queen's University, Belfast, with honours in physics, he taught in a secondary school in another tough part of the old city. In 1964, soon after he and Dorothy were married, the old Irish adaptability, sense of adventure and reaching out that had given Canada waves of pioneering immigrants prompted them to give it a try.

After a year's disenchantment teaching in a high school in St. Catharines, he went to Bishop's College School. It was very much more to his taste. He first encountered Ashbury in the person of Ray Anderson as an opposing soccer coach. Four years at Bishop's and another adventurous move: he became Principal of New Richmond High School in the Gaspé. Soon he became Assistant Principal and director of the English-speaking section of a big, brand-new, beautifully equipped *polyvalent*. Twelve hundred French students, 400 English, and a big contingent from a Micmac reservation made for a rich mix, a turbulent, political, fascinating — and ultimately successful — time, and a command of French.

By 1975, with the Parti Québecois in power and the future somewhat clouded, it seemed time to move. He spent six years as a housemaster at Ridley, which was now co-educational, taught math and physics and coached first team soccer. Most leading independent schools by this time were dropping the old individual dickering in favour of salary scales. Many had staff advisory committees. Ridley did and Napier chaired it.

A productive time at Ridley led to the Headmastership of Albert College, Belleville. Albert was an independent boarding and day school, co-educational for all its 125 years. An aging, inadequate plant, a quarter million dollar deficit, only 150 students and slim fund-raising potential made it a pretty daunting prospect. But Napier found strong support from a business-like Board. The principle was conservative fiscal management — "Don't spend money before you've got it." In five years Albert College was turned around. The handsome old stone building was restored, with a fine new wing fully paid for and in place. There were 245 students, a healthy operating budget and money in the bank.

When Ashbury advertised for a new Head in March 1986 Tony Macoun urged Napier to apply. He had set the course at Albert College and had a great attachment to the school, but age and stage of life come into such decisions. He was 44 and believed it was time for a move before reaching 50. A thriving Ashbury in the nation's capital with its first-rate reputation made an attractive and stimulating challenge.

Napier had firm, positive views on co-education. The major and most difficult hurdle, the initial move, had been achieved. But, he made clear to the selection committee, three top grades with 40 girls was less than half measure. He believed in full senior school co-education and he would bring more women on staff. As if to confirm the Ashbury commitment, in his first year as Headmaster Jean Teron — with eight years of service on the Board — became its first woman Chairman.

There were other Board changes that broadened involvement. The Presidents of the Alumni Association (Marc Dugay), the Ashbury Guild (Janet McLaine) and Parents Committee were ex officio members with full votes. In the continuing drive for scholarship and bursary funds $20,000 had been raised for the A.M. Macoun Scholarship. Cynthia Baxter proposed consolidating the various funds and memorials that had accumulated over the years. She achieved this in 1987 and took the chair of the newly incorporated Ashbury College Foundation with $270,000 to its account. It was the custodian of endowment and capital funds. The following year Mrs J.N. Maclaren, widow of old boy J. Norman Maclaren (1909-1916), donated $200,000 to the Foundation to support a full scholarship. It was the biggest donation in the history of the school.

After his first year settling in, Napier opened Grades 9 and 10 to girls. His target was at least one-third girls in the senior school to build a balanced community, especially among boarders, and a well-rounded girls' athletic programme. By the fall of 1990 there were 120 girls in the senior school out of 360 and they made up close to half the boarder population.

When Napier took the reins, finances were in sound shape, but some $800,000 was still owing for the gym. This was handled comfortably from the operating budget over the next two years. But the fact was that Ashbury had never in its history found the means to properly provide for depreciation, nor had it ever accumulated a long-range building and plant renewal fund. Napier was a conservative financial administrator but he saw the inevitability of change. He understood its dynamics and the need to plan for it. With the Board's Planning Committee he started to produce a planning document, "Towards the Year 2000." The imaginative School of the Commonwealth concept from 1980 hadn't developed further. Besides the problems of scholarship monies, more boarder quarters would be needed.

The school ceiling would be 520 students — 340 in the senior school, about a third of them girls. Boarding, an ongoing vital service and a strong dimension in the life of the school, should encourage a diversity of regional and national origins. Junior school boarding was declining and could drop, but ideally the senior school would have about 100 boarders — half of them boys, half girls. The basic thrust of the school, though, wouldn't change. The paper clearly spelled out the four essential elements — intellectual, physical, cultural and spiritual.

The aim was to ensure the optimum development of each student as a whole individual through the fundamental ideals of a good, liberal education. Academically it would follow the Ontario curriculum at the advanced level, with enriched courses designed by Ashbury staff — or faculty, as they were coming to be called —

complemented by the International Baccalaureate in the final two years. In athletics, all students must be involved. Opportunities would include individual and team "recreational" sports as well as competitive school teams. The idea, through athletics and outdoor education, was to foster healthy life-styles and life-long appreciation of physical activity. Culturally, everyone would have opportunities to develop in music, the arts, drama. Spiritually, the Anglican tradition would continue, taking into account the rich diversity of the school's religious and cultural mosaic. Each student would be challenged to think about the spiritual aspect of existence and apply the experience to his/her own life.

George Woollcombe's Chapel was outgrown by the far bigger school of the eighties, but it never lost the place he had made for it at the heart of the Ashbury ethos. Three services every morning, one for the junior school and two for the seniors, were now filled with a variety of religious affiliations. All attended except, for some time, the Jewish students who had their separate service. Most Ashburians, looking back, value Chapel, if not as a religious experience, as a few minutes of reflection, to dwell inwardly a little, to pull one's thoughts together for the start of another hectic day.

Reverend E.E. Jeep Green left the school in 1987. From its start in 1969 his chaplaincy left its mark and a lifelong debt of thanks with hundreds of Ashbury graduates. In his unstructured way, he was, right through his 18 Ashbury years, somewhat at odds with the school's administration. But through times of rebellion, questioning and rejection, of self over soul, Jeep Green made a profound contribution to keeping alive the warmth of unquestioning friendship. In his valedictory of 1978 Graeme Clark had paid a special tribute to the Chaplain. He did so again at the Easter-time Chapel service marking Jeep's retirement.

Graeme recalled arriving as a new boy in 1973. "I was paralysed with fear at the noise and smell of the locker-room, envious of the other boys who all seemed to know each other so well. As I walked out of the locker-room with a lump in my throat and my eyes glistening, I met a man who smiled at me and said Hello...."

The plant by now needed extensive renovation and improvement. Facilities were very tight. To properly meet the ideals that had been spelled out, some major new building would be needed — a new student residence, classrooms, student meeting places, improved library, an additional small gym, theatre/music auditorium. Nothing, though, should be built, in Napier's view, until at least half the money was in the bank; the rest could be covered by donations and to some extent from future operating budgets.

So the time to look after the future was now. Napier and Finance Chairman John Graham, then David McConomy, brought fiscal planning in line with reality. They started budgeting for annual capital renovations, plus earmarking something over a quarter million dollars a year to be used for building replacement.

What looked like a surplus, though, raised the hackles of some faculty members, still frustrated as they were in their campaign for salaries on a par with area school boards. Fees had to be kept within range of the other schools; and salaries, both Napier and the Board agreed, should be in the same ballpark as the public sector. It was still a juggling act, but serious salary consultations between the Head, the Finance

Committee and the Staff Advisory Committee in the winters of 1988 and 1989 hammered out scales that apparently satisfied both sides.

In any age parents look at fees and quail. In 1989-90 a senior day student's fee at Ashbury College reached $8100 per year; the next year, $8600. It didn't make them any happier to note that the Ottawa Board's cost per student in 1990 was $8440. They paid their share of that too. Compared with the public system alternative, the substantial fees bought over double the teacher/student attention in the classroom and out, athletic, outdoor and cultural programmes with places for every student, the opportunity to achieve an exceptional academic level following the International Baccalaureate, an atmosphere of achievement in which nearly every student went on to further education, a clear standard of civility and respect for others and a commitment to spiritual values as an essential element of life.

If donations couldn't realistically be the mainstay of plant development, the generosity of the Ashbury community provided wish-list items that couldn't be bought in tight times. The Ashbury College Guild had started as the Mothers' Guild in 1950. As well as generating interest and participation in school affairs, it became a faithful and substantial contributor. The Guild's annual fund-raiser, the Antique Fair, generated $36,000 in the fall of 1990. Guild donations over the years included hymn books and choir robes, musical instruments and microscopes, three tennis courts (in 1976), three school buses and recently a magnificent racing shell. Well over a quarter million dollars in 25 years represented a lot of dedicated hard work.

Resources of all kinds seemed to rise to the occasion. By 1987 AIDS was becoming a thorny issue across the country. In the absence of real understanding of the problem, some pretty hysterical reactions were cropping up especially in school boards. They were fuelled by the high statistical connection between AIDS and male homosexuals, Africans and Haitians.

That fall the conference of the Canadian Association of Independent Schools recommended that schools develop their own policy before they were suddenly faced with a problem. Ashbury had barely drawn a breath when an Ontario independent Christian college announced it would bar anyone from its staff or student body if they tested HIV positive. Queried by the press on Ashbury's position, Napier said a policy was under study and all aspects, including testing, would be considered. The *Citizen*'s interpretation was that Ashbury was planning to screen its people. Far from it.

An AIDS committee was formed. The Headmaster's position was that it mustn't wait and see what others did; it mustn't consider the best business approach or the easiest sell. It must concentrate on what *should* be done. The committee was chaired by Governor and parent Dr. Stuart Bell, and it reached right into the community: parents—physicians among them—a teacher and a phys. ed. specialist from the staff, students, a virus research specialist, the regional officer of health, his deputy, who was an AIDS specialist, and, of course, the school physician Dr. Bryan Boyd. A close friend, old boy Ian Rhodes, was in residency with Dr. Ralph Saginur, head of infectious diseases at the Civic Hospital. Saginur joined the committee.

When the Board accepted the AIDS report in February 1988, Ashbury was one of the first institutions in the community to have a policy. As student or faculty, an HIV positive carrier or AIDS sufferer was not considered a threat to the Ashbury community. The virus is transmitted almost exclusively by sexual intercourse which

Ashbury, like any responsible parent, did not countenance within its control. There would be no compulsory screening. Confidentiality would be respected. As far as physical capability allowed, sufferers would not be barred. It was a courageous and progressive policy and had a strong influence on decisions in a number of institutions in Ottawa and elsewhere.

Independent schools will always be different. Distinctive, private, accountable to themselves they certainly are. But for any kind of relevance or viability they have to live in the mainstream. They can never be protected from the pressures of society, and they can never think of themselves as having a reserved place with respect to society or the law.

In February 1988 parents of a junior school boy reported that they were most unhappy with the way Michael Sherwood, the Director of the junior school, had dealt with their son. Given the specific nature of the complaint, the Headmaster, as required by law, referred it to the Children's Aid Society (CAS). The CAS and the provincial police investigated and determined that, while "inappropriate" and "lacking in judgement," Sherwood's actions didn't constitute grounds for charges of sexual assault or sexual misconduct.

Clearly, though, this had to be dealt with in a forthright and open manner. The Head talked at length with the Board's senior echelons. After careful deliberation it was agreed that Sherwood had indeed shown lack of judgement and that he could no longer sustain the absolute confidence of parents and Board. On that basis it was decided that he should go, and that was announced by the Chairman at a special meeting of the Board.

It was a difficult issue. He couldn't be "tried" in the Boardroom. Certainly some members were sympathetic to his predicament after such long and productive service. However, the decision got the general support of the Board. While the matter was being considered, Sherwood was on leave of absence. He came back for the last month of school to largely administrative work and that summer he left the employ of Ashbury College. A reasonable settlement was arranged — well below the six figures later mentioned by news media — and so ended a career that had started in 1958.

He'd run the junior school since 1967 and it was first-rate. It was structured, disciplined and high-spirited. His predecessors, David Polk in particular, had laid a sound basis. Sherwood had the necessary ability, energy and commitment. By nature he was highly competitive. When the Hall-Dennis Report drained the competition from Ontario public classrooms, it didn't happen at Ashbury, and that proved a strong drawing card for a lot of parents. The sports programme, run for everyone with real gusto, was a major attraction. There were trips and special events, weekend outings for the boarders, an excellent choir, music, drama, science fair, outdoor education, lots to do and plenty of scope for young energies. Sherwood believed that boys learn best when they enjoy their school. It was a happy place.

He was very much his own boss. He had full control over his students within the overall school framework and dealt with their parents directly. W.A. Joyce was well satisfied with the way things ran and with the boys coming up to the senior school. So, too, was Tony Macoun. Junior numbers had climbed from 110 in 1967 (when there were 119 in the senior school) to 174 in 1988-89. That was Ashbury's biggest year, with a total of 516. The number of junior school boarders peaked at 40 in 1980, then tapered off to 16 in 1987-88; but day boy numbers more than compensated. Sherwood had had an outstandingly successful 22 years in charge.

At any other time his departure could well have been the end of it. But, starting that same year, the history of years of unchecked sexual abuse of boys by some Christian Brothers at Mount Cashel orphanage in St. John's, Newfoundland, was being exposed layer by dreadful layer. People who had been abused years before were coming forward with statements. The issue was sickeningly alive across the country. Spotlights turned on every possible corner.

In early summer 1989 an Ottawa television journalist started questioning Ashbury people about Michael Sherwood. A former student and his parents made statements about an incident in 1972 which ended in the boy being withdrawn from the school. A former teacher said he'd made complaints in 1984. The implications were that, with Sherwood's influence, everything had been swept under Ashbury's rug. That certainly couldn't be said of Napier's action. The OPP now began a widespread, lengthy investigation. Officers interviewed some 200 people as far away as California. They reported that many said Sherwood was the finest teacher they'd ever had.

In June 1990 the OPP laid five charges of assault alleged to have occurred between 1969 and 1981. In September they added three more. Of the eight, two were for assault causing bodily harm by caning in the late sixties, and the others concerned sexual assault. The court set a preliminary hearing for September 1991.

In the meantime over 200 allegations of sexual and physical abuse at the correctional schools at nearby Alfred and in Uxbridge had surfaced. In all such cases, along with natural revulsion goes an unfortunate public presumption of guilt. For Sherwood, innocent or guilty, another year's wait on top of a year's investigation was a terrible prospect to endure. The whole Ontario court system, inadequate for the times, was clogged with a huge backlog. Within three months, though, the Attorney General swept away thousands of lesser cases. That brought the Sherwood hearing ahead to April 1991.

There was a ban on publication of evidence at the preliminary hearing and the allotted days in court expired with only half the evidence examined. A date was set for resumption — in September 1991. The stress and pressure on Sherwood — and indeed the agony of everyone involved in such protracted circumstances — is a shocking indictment of our court system.

No Headmaster can expect affairs to run entirely according to plan. Minor crises go with the territory. But these events, alleged to have happened long before, were deeply disturbing. The publicity was negative to say the least, though the Ashbury community in no sense turned its back on the school. But just before the Sherwood case hit the press in 1989, a thunderbolt of another sort had struck. It was the nemesis of any independent school — a drive among the teaching staff to form a union.

CHAPTER 23
TERMS AND CONDITIONS

From the growth of the union movement among Ontario teachers just after World War I, the notion of a unionized staff at Ashbury College was about as improbable as the Canadian Labour Congress throwing its annual banquet at the Rideau Club. Thus, when a vote of Ashbury teaching staff in April 1989 fell one single vote shy of automatic certification of the Ontario Secondary School Teachers' Federation (OSSTF) as bargaining agent for Ashbury's faculty, a high-voltage shock surged through the school community.

Independent schools' Boards through the sixties and seventies took pride in the fact that their schools weren't affected by the strikes that plagued the public system. Their classes weren't disrupted. Their students weren't set in turmoil. School years weren't jeopardized. In their schools teachers' self-interest and the self-service of union leaders didn't take priority over the interests of their students.

In the bygone days when it was a gentleman's avocation to be a schoolmaster in a decent private school — the work "teacher" was almost perjorative — salaries and benefits weren't too bad and they were the last thing one talked about. As times went on and militant teachers' unions levered their members' financial status up from a fraction above the day labourer, a gap began to grow.

Independent school teachers had been chronically behind the public system in salaries and benefits and Ashbury's were always in the lower part of that bracket. From the fifties a master at Ashbury was getting substantially less than a high-school teacher in the Ottawa Board. The few women on staff did worse. W.A. Joyce turned down flat what could have been a financially helpful link with the Ottawa Board of Education when it became clear that all staff would have to join unions. Even more than the matter of salaries, though, Joyce was concerned about what the resulting loss of independence would mean.

The salary range at Ashbury was divined by the Head with one eye on the local school board, an ear on the telephone to his Headmaster colleagues, a finger on the economic pulse and the other eye — the one that counted most — on what his market would stand. Thus he would take on new staff, not in accordance with an established, published scale, but at the lowest figure each individual would accept. And that figure was invariably below the local board's. On the other side of the coin, as the public service became less disciplined through the sixties and seventies, Ashbury became a much more attractive place to teach.

Along with the decline in the public system, militant unions lofted teachers to the ranks of the very well paid. With a growing salary gap, Ashbury's Head sought not only good qualifications but special personal and social qualities plus experience, by preference, in independent schooling. He wanted people who were prepared to immerse themselves in their calling, to give more and — so be it — to take less.

In 1986, Roy Napier's first year as Head, he showed a more open, consultative style than his predecessors. He knew that territory — he'd chaired Ridley's Staff Advisory Committee in the early days of its salary scale. The Ashbury teachers' contract was a pretty thin document. Through 1987 he worked with the Staff Committee and a host of administrative matters, handled previously by custom or ad hoc decision, was gradually pulled together, formally or informally, into a "Teaching Personnel Policy."

Salaries were, of course, a regular topic. Parity was certainly an objective but the debt load from the gym was a worry. The scale favoured years of service rather than qualifications. As a result, the stable staff, built up over the years, with many first-rate, experienced long-termers, brought a paradoxical disadvantage. Any percentage increase in the scale meant a disproportionately larger total salary bill to balance off with fees. The annual salary increase for 1987-88 was held to little more than inflation.

By late 1987 the staff, feeling somewhat frustrated, was still pressing the 1984 policy proposal through the Advisory Committee. The Board wouldn't commit itself to a salary scale virtually fixed by the Ottawa and Carleton Boards over which it had no control. But by spring it had agreed to appropriate raises for the following year and recognized the need for cost-of-living and progressive upgrading. In the next two years the gap was closed to the point of general satisfaction.

That same year the Canadian Association of Independent Schools discussed at length the organizing methods of the Ontario Secondary School Teachers' Federation. The Toronto French School had had an in-house teachers' union for some three years. The Federation was actively recruiting in independent schools. Unions were on the march and the warning signals were out.

Why the OSSTF targetted independent schools was more likely financial than doctrinaire. When Ontario started funding Roman Catholic schools up to Grade 13, there was a significant shift of students and teachers from public schools — the Federation's territory — to Catholic schools. Union leaders draw their salaries from fees. With membership down they tried turning new turf.

They found fertile ground among poorly paid staff at old, established, hard-up Alma College in London. In the winter of 1988 Alma's newly certified faculty bargaining unit negotiated to a standstill with the Board and went on strike. Alma couldn't handle it and the senior school closed down and has not reopened since.

Through all this Peter MacFarlane chaired Ashbury's Staff Advisory Committee. He'd paid his way through Carleton University by driving Ashbury's school bus and had joined the staff in the fall of 1975 to teach geography and English. Next year he and his family had moved into a staff house on campus and stayed. He was involved from the early days of the Staff Advisory Committee and was Chairman (with Ross Varley as Secretary) in 1986 when he and some of the committee met local and headquarters officials of the OSSTF. It was exploratory, to collect information on benefits, contracts, research results, and to find out what the Federation might do for Ashbury staff. No one else at the school knew about it. But the lines were open.

In the fall of 1988 the visiting committee of the Canadian Education Standards Institute evaluated Ashbury College. Its detailed report summed up Ashbury as "a fine school." It noted that the Staff Advisory Committee appeared to be an "excellent forum" for staff relations. Its concerns were salaries, professional development, job security, financial planning, leaves, exchanges, early retirement and setting up a formal process for evaluation of the faculty.

The visitors recommended that department heads be periodically rotated. The Head had promoted that idea as there were some very capable people who had no chance otherwise of promotion. Around March break he announced that the positions of department heads would be reviewed, and responsibility could shift to another member of the department. What to the Headmaster was a normal management process no doubt stuck in the craw of some departmental heads. About the same time the level of bursaries for faculty's children was changed. The SAC felt that this should have been discussed as an employment benefit rather than an individual matter. Whatever it was that triggered the union drive, Roy Napier had inherited a legacy of something less than progressive staff relations.

In early April a group of half a dozen — including some of the Staff Advisory Committee — met again with the OSSTF. They had misgivings about the faculty voice in the existing system and felt their interests, salaries and security, especially, lay in forming a union. It was taken as read that Ashbury — Board, parents, Headmaster — would be dead against it, so they recruited secretly, selectively and carefully. Then, in mid-April, they called a general faculty meeting for a Friday evening in St. Alban's church hall.

Those outside the expanded circle arrived on a day's notice with little or no notion of what the meeting was about. They were stunned to find senior OSSTF organizers there from Toronto and a lawyer the group had retained to advise on labour law. There was one item on the agenda: forming an Ashbury College teachers' union affiliated with the OSSTF. Certification was automatic if 55 percent held union cards, and it appeared to be practically a fait accompli. The promoting group already had their numbers signed up, with union cards in hand. It was a cross-section of long-termers and newcomers. It would now just be a matter of applying to the Ontario Labour Relations Board for a hearing and a legal ruling.

It was an impassioned meeting. Battle lines were drawn with a sudden, bitter stroke — the strongly committed pro-union supporters versus those to whom the whole notion was completely incompatible with their principles. In no man's land was a sizeable group — those who were uncommitted or who might be swayed. They became the target for both sides.

News travels fast. Saturday morning found the Head in urgent conference with the Chairman, Jean Teron, and school lawyers. Roy Napier had two vital attributes for this crisis — experience as a high-school principal with unions and a level head. The situation was a potential minefield. Under labour law if there's any interference by management — in this case the Headmaster or Board — in the union-forming process, certification is automatic. The Board quickly retained a Toronto law firm which had acted for many public school boards, and for the hapless Alma College.

Alarms rang. In no time parents were on the phone. At a special parents meeting in May two points came across loud and clear. First, they had a very high regard for the Ashbury faculty. They wanted them to have appropriate salaries and conditions; some questioned the Board's alertness and sensitivity to faculty concerns. Second, they were overwhelmingly against a unionized teaching staff. The quality of education for which they paid substantial fees had everything to do with the teachers' dedication to the interests of their students. If a reminder was needed, Ottawa Board elementary teachers had been on strike for five weeks that very spring.

Ashbury's Board got the message. Quite apart from any personal views they had to resolve whatever the issues were, and they had to do it without a union solution or Ashbury College, as history had known it to date, would be no more.

The great potential allies, the anti-union faculty members, were strictly out of bounds. But they closed ranks themselves and hired their own lawyer. The union group applied for a Labour Board hearing and a date was set. As the school year drew to a close with all the pressure of exams and Closing Day, the faculty was split down the middle. Tension was high. Basic dedication to their students kept the strife out of the classrooms, but both sides recruited hard.

By the day of the hearing the no-union group had collected enough repudiations of union membership to make it a very close call. The three teachers in the "part-time unit" had signed cards and were automatically certified as a separate bargaining unit. Three other positions were in dispute: the Chaplain, a housemother and a teaching intern. With the part-time unit established and the dispute on the validity of the other three on hold, there were too few union cards for automatic certification — but only just.

The Labour Board then set a date for a supervised vote by ballot at the school. On voting day both sides agreed that the three in dispute could vote. When the count was done, it was 25 for the union, 26 against. A very near-run thing.

But it was by no means over. This was only the first step, and labour law allowed another vote in six months. Some, sticking staunchly to the traditional rule of authority, wouldn't countenance any formal body representing the faculty. The majority, though, agreed in June to form an independent Faculty Association of Ashbury College (FAAC). Its executive would negotiate with the Board. Peter MacFarlane who had led the union drive was elected President. Three others were pro-union. The fifth, Ross Varley, was all for negotiating from a common front, but with far more union experience than anyone else there he was against union affiliation.

The ultimate weapon under labour law was the right to strike (and to be locked out). The FAAC constitution stated that its members would never strike. Varley had led strikes in Quebec and never again wanted to stand on the picket line and see his students turned away from school. Labour law also provides grievance procedure on dismissals. That and other issues had to be resolved. But from his reading of the Ashbury community Varley believed the right vehicle, with which the Board could deal in good faith, was a strongly based independent faculty association.

The Association formally asked the Board to recognize it as the sole bargaining agent for all the faculty. That, though, would give the FAAC instant trade union status under the Labour Relations Act and it could later affiliate with the OSSTF if it chose. Further, it would leave dissenters with no voice and the faculty was far from unanimous on a great number of matters. The Board declined and appointed a Human Resources Committee. Its task: to develop a comprehensive teaching personnel policy with input from the Faculty Association.

The importance of the matter to Ashbury shows in the make-up of the Human Resources Committee. It was chaired by the Vice-Chairman of the Board, Peter Newcombe, a second-generation old boy and Governor who'd had a previous term on the Board in the sixties and whose father had done more than anyone else to keep

Ashbury afloat in the thirties and forties. Jim Smellie, another second-generation old boy and parent, was committee vice-chairman. Both were lawyers — a substantial asset. There were two Life Governors — Cynthia Baxter and Bill Milroy — and two current parent Term Governors, Elizabeth Waddell and Ann Coulson. Mrs Coulson chaired the Parents' Committee. Add the Chairman of the Board, Jean Teron, plus Finance Chairman David McConomy and the Headmaster, and this was a wise, experienced, indeed formidable committee whose recommendations would certainly warrant the support of the full Board.

In mid-July they met all the faculty and offered a draft Human Resources Policy for discussion. The Association tabled its "memorandum of agreement." Under a different name it was a standard form of collective agreement and, to the committee, inappropriate given the events of the past months. The committee recognized the FAAC executive as the body to negotiate on behalf of its members. It was prepared to discuss all the issues and fully consider faculty views. But signing an agreement could be a step towards recognizing a bargaining unit under labour law. That they would not do. The school's contract was to be with each individual teacher and not the Faculty Association. That was the mark of the independent school.

There was some heat. Ashbury's Board was dubbed at one point in the meeting "The Three R's" — Rockcliffe, Rideau Club and the Royal Ottawa Golf Club. Quite a few certainly did rank among the "R's". But Board membership was no sinecure. For years it had been made up of dedicated hard-working people who donated very substantial time, qualifications and talents to developing the school. The implication that they set themselves on some elevated plane and were on the Board because of who they were or what they had or to garner some social cachet was off the mark. The atmosphere augered rather ill.

Summer, fall, winter, meeting succeeded meeting with glacial progress. Boards and faculties of independent schools across Canada were rivetted. Ashbury was under siege. If this bastion fell, who'd be next? By Christmas the FAAC was still focusing on framework — the format of agreement. The committee wanted to get to the issues. By February 1990 the Board had agreed to the committee's proposed Human Resources Policy. The Association wouldn't discuss it without a dispute-settling mechanism including outside arbitration for all "grievances." That was the thin end of the labour law wedge and Ashbury wouldn't have it. There was still no agreement by the time teachers' contracts came up for renewal in March.

The Human Resources Committee now concluded that a faction of the Faculty Association wanted an agreement only under labour law and that some issues weren't getting through fully to the whole faculty. So, just before March break 1990, Jim Smellie (the chairman since Peter Newcombe had become Board Chairman in the fall) invited the whole faculty to air concerns and talk issues.

For the first time in many months the Human Resources Committee and the faculty had the opportunity to talk directly. It was a useful meeting and cleared up some misconceptions. But about the same time the prime supporters of the union option (who hadn't attended the meeting) recommended once again that the Association should seek union status.

A year had gone by without solution. The tension was palpable. The faculty was sapped, divided and distracted; energies were diverted. Still there was no classroom lobbying. Senior faculty had made it very clear that student demonstrations would be harmful and there were none. But the students knew what was up, who was on what side. They liked their teachers. They saw the divisions. It was a very disturbing time.

In April the Association executive was due for re-election. By now the ground had shifted. A number of members had concluded their leaders were aiming for a union rather than dealing substantively with their problems, and there were enough to make the vote a complete turn-around. Ross Varley became president, and this time all executive, save past president Peter MacFarlane, favoured the independent solution.

From mid-May the talks got down to substance with the Board's proposal and hammered it out clause by clause. In mid-June both sides agreed to a document called Terms and Conditions of Employment for Ashbury College — the TCE. It had a two-year life-span, provision for annual review, amendment by agreement and arbitration for particular issues. Dismissals or other disciplinary measures had due process, all agreed to by both parties. Contracts were still individual with all conditions, as fully spelled out in the TCE, applicable to each contract.

It was an Ashbury document, not a collective agreement, and it won the unanimous support of the Board and the majority support of the faculty. It was a landmark, the end result of a great deal of hard work and level-headed discussion. Many contributed to it. Key players were Roy Napier and Ross Varley. At such a critical point it was one of those fortunes of history that brought these two to the table. Patience, determination, endless hours and extraordinary forbearance had seen the matter through. In spite of the constant tension the students didn't suffer and that was to the credit of all. The other independent schools joined the mighty sigh of relief, and offered congratulations.

It had been a wrenching, exhausting, debilitating year. There were some deep scars. Nothing would ever be quite the same. But now the air was cleared and Ashbury College was a better place. Due process was defined. No one could be dealt with — or seen to be dealt with — in a cavalier way. This was a progressive solution and Ashbury was a leader among all Canadian independent schools. Most important, the interests of the essential parties, the students, the faculty and the institution — in that order — were preserved, and the basic tenets held — the independent integrity of Ashbury College, individual excellence versus the collective norm. Now it was up to everyone to make it work. Time alone would tell the final tale.

Ashbury opened at full strength in the fall of 1990. By April 1991 the Faculty Association executive and the Human Resources Committee had reviewed and amended the Terms and Conditions of Employment and agreed to the salary scale for 1991-92. The Board agreed unanimously. The Faculty Association membership accepted the documents by a vote of 41 to 3 (some of the faculty still, on principle, declined to join). Most significant, both sides agreed to extend the TCE for a further year and to discuss new items, like an early retirement scheme. Given the opportunity and the machinery to deal systematically with matters of substance to both sides, it was clear they could, and would, make progress.

In its 100th year Ashbury College had surmounted another challenge, possibly the greatest of its time.

CHAPTER **24**

A CHARACTER OF ITS OWN

The valedictorian at the Closing of Ashbury's 99th year was Jillian Napier, one of 24 girls in the graduating class of 84 and the first to be Captain of the School. The year before, the Governor General's Medalist had been Vivian Hill. Seventy students had taken International Baccalaureate subjects; 13 of them won full IB diplomas. By the fall of 1990, 80 of those graduates were studying at 29 different universities, seven of them in other countries. Most of the IB diploma students were in second year programmes. The standard of scholarship at the school stood very high.

In its day Ashbury had been called a shelter for a social elite, a refuge for rich kids, a reform school for problem children. Now, with its high standard, some growled that it had become the preserve of a scholastic elite. Most certainly the standards for entrance were firm, real effort by students was required and achievement was high. But the critic had only to look at the breadth of the place and the depth of students' involvement to realize that there was more to Ashbury than the academic.

There was no doubt about the importance of sports. The year before, the girls had won the Ottawa high-school soccer championship and come second in volleyball. Jillian Napier had been a miniature powerhouse. In her last two years she captained all five major teams on which she played. In rowing the girls had beaten three university crews to take "Head of the Rideau." Rowing coaches Bob Zettel and Fred Mueller had guided the boys to successes too, including first place in Ottawa-Carleton and fifth at the "Head of Trent" against 14 university crews. The boys had come third in the Ontario class A basketball championships; Noah Cantor, like his brother Mark the year before, led the team superbly. Rugby had really caught hold under Peter Ostrom's experienced hand and the team went to the city high-school semi-final and hosted a "first annual" tournament. Rugby up-and-comers in the junior school, coached by Jim Humphreys and Ben Hérique, were undefeated against Sedbergh, Bishop's and LCC.

Things change. Senior teams now competed mainly in the Ottawa high-school circuit. There were exceptions, like Elmwood's independent schools girls' volleyball tournament which Ashbury won in 1990, and other teams played occasional games against the old rivals. The junior school played soccer and hockey tournaments against independent schools. In soccer they topped the Ottawa Board in 1990. One down note — hockey had dropped from five teams to only one senior and one junior. Ice time, lack of competition in the middle years because of the intensely organized community leagues, the expense and the attractions of basketball and other sports all took a toll. For the time being at least, the long, strong 90-year tradition was being kept vigorously alive by a group of dedicated, and fun-loving, hockey-playing alumni.

As though to clinch the point on athletics and to celebrate Centennial year, the fall of 1990 brought three Ottawa high-school championships. The only previous ones in school history had been senior soccer in 1966 and senior B hockey in 1979. First team football had an unbeaten 1990 season to take the Ottawa-Carleton Senior B championship, and they beat TCS en route. Alfonso Movilla, Chris Gillin, Yannick Massicotte and Andy Cole were named to the *Ottawa Citizen*'s All-Star team. Next, the senior girls' basketball team won the city championship. Marie Baribeau and J.J. Rawlinson played for the Ottawa Board All-Stars and Ashbury coach Andy Sparks was picked to coach the team. Topping it off, the mixed tennis team broke a 20-year Lisgar stranglehold and won the high-school championship. Stephan, Peter, Michael and Phillip Mirsky saw the Pure Spring Trophy their family had presented in 1970 go to their old school.

Sports, though, were just part of the healthy whole. With their heavy workloads students in the top grades could drop out of them for a term. Like everyone they were in a multitude of other activities — outdoor education, serious pursuit of art and music. The 1990 fall concert directed by Lionel Tanod featured 50 musicians playing in various groups, including a jazz combo and a choir of 58 voices. It was a tribute to Douglas Brookes, retiring from the music department after 15 years. Groups and individuals were competing in music festivals and winning notable awards.

The Debating Society, guided by Ted Zrudlo, had revived public speaking after a lapse. It was active in every grade. In the winter of 1990 Antony Simpson, Stuart Hensel and Doug Cole went to Boston for the International Independent Schools Public Speaking Tournament. All made the individual finals and placed sixth out of more than 30 teams. Antony took high honours in the top-level tournament in England. Samir Chandan of Grade 11 won a $1000 scholarship as best debater in the *Ottawa Citizen*/University of Ottawa tournament.

Drama had reached a very high level of development and involvement guided by Greg Simpson. Challenging pieces of serious theatre, like *Equus, One Flew Over the Cuckoo's Nest* and *A Streetcar Named Desire*, certainly wouldn't have had approval as school plays in earlier times. They were performed with remarkable insight and won high praise from the *Citizen*'s and CBC Radio's critic Charles Haines, not as student performances but as dramatic productions in their own right.

The Ashbury Players were fed by juniors with experience in their own lively productions, and they'd become a real force in the school. In turn they fed the artistic community. Jay Ferguson started Second Stage Productions, an Ashbury alumni company. In June 1990 Jay directed Zaa Nkweta, Cindy Freeman and Stephanie Haffner in an emotionally intense production of *Agnes of God*. Melanie Quevillon and Simon Dawes, still at school, stage-managed and designed the lighting. Zaa was studying drama at the National Theatre School in Montreal. The production drew fine reviews.

Community service was put on a new track in 1990. Privilege carries responsibility and students had been involved in one way or another for some 15 years. But projects were hard to organize and rather random, and relatively few students had been really productively involved. Ann Coulson — parent, Governor, Guild President, professional social worker — had offered her advice and arranged financial help to start a systematic programme. On the purely practical side, community service was now required for an IB diploma, and leading universities were looking for involvement as well as marks on application forms. On the human side of the coin, there was a never-ending need in Ottawa.

Six IB students worked with Mrs Coulson, staff members and outside agencies, planning and preparing. A Montreal family foundation made a substantial gift to the Ashbury Foundation to help support an ongoing programme. At Closing 1990 the Coulson Trophy for community service was awarded, for the first time, to the student planners. From now on community service was to be a requirement for an Ashbury College Diploma. Michael Jansen was appointed as the school's first Director of Community Service. In the fall he worked with 80 Grade 12 and 13 students through their elected committee, nine parent volunteers and a dozen agencies. Student leaders rallied with enthusiasm and set the tone.

Hospitals, the Red Cross, the Ottawa Boys' and Girls' Club, homes for the elderly, the Humane Society and the Food Bank all had Ashbury students working hands-on in their own time. Some contributed over 100 hours, some just the first 15 of the minimum 30. Centennial year proved the programme's worth and it showed that the spirit was there. Community service wasn't only a requirement for a diploma; it was part of the life of the school.

Jansen had stepped down as IB coordinator after some very productive years. He and others on staff, like Hugh Robertson, Ken Niles and Ross Varley, had made major contributions, not only at Ashbury but in making the programme known across Canada. Robertson's book *The Research Essay* was in use by IB students around the world.

In the public sector, Ministries of Education in Alberta, BC, Manitoba, Quebec and Nova Scotia recognized the IB as ready-made enrichment for top students. A fair number of city high schools in all those provinces took it up; Calgary and Edmonton Boards had been involved since 1979. Ontario's Kingston Collegiate and some Toronto schools had actually joined on their own, but the Ministry under Bette Stephenson turned thumbs down.

The Ottawa Board of Education had set up an IB committee in 1982. Lisgar, Glebe and Nepean High Schools were keen to join and they got full benefit of Ashbury's knowledge and experience. But the answer from Queen's Park was a flat "No." Ontario's system, in the Ministry's eyes, was quite good enough. Taxpayers' money would not be spent on an elite programme. And an NDP government in Manitoba had said "Yes!"

Jansen's workshop in Toronto in 1987 had drawn a large group of Ontario high-school principals who badly wanted to join the programme. Of the 350 IB-accredited schools worldwide, some 45 were now Canadian. Ashbury had helped many of them get started and Jansen could certainly tell this Ontario group what the IB was about. Still, Queen's Park denied support. Victoria Park in North York was the lone Ontario public high school that finally offered the option of the IB. The principal raised funds himself from parents' groups and private foundations. Victoria Park produced its first IB diplomas in 1990.

In the meantime the Ontario Academic Credits had replaced Grade 13 courses as such in 1987. Some course requirements now diverged from the IB's and the Ministry withdrew Grade 13 credit status for Theory of Knowledge. Now it had to be taken in Grade 12. Diploma requirements by this time included athletics, the arts and community service, as well as Theory of Knowledge and the six core subject areas. Experience had proved that the IB wasn't solely a series of examinations; it was a system of education, truly scholastic with an intellectual approach that stimulated a broad world outlook and a thirst for knowledge. The pursuit of excellence is never without setbacks, but Ashbury's results year by year were consistently above the world average. The first three bilingual IB diplomas were awarded in 1990. In 1991 four students graduated with the first of the Ashbury bilingual diplomas.

When George Woollcombe founded Ashbury, Ontario's public education system was widely viewed as a model for the world. It's a tragic reflection on political leadership that this key to the future has failed to the extent that our country stands low in the civilized world in functional literacy, science literacy and high-school graduations and most students lack a significant understanding of their own country. The observations of educators, the studies and warnings of the fifties, sixties and seventies, the harsh evidence presented in the press during the soul-searching over national unity — all have had no obvious effect on the apparently closed minds of the educational bureaucracy.

While the Ontario Ministry will make commendable provision for disadvantaged children, for example, it won't lay hold of the IB as a ready means to challenge the brightest of our future citizens, the most committed to hard work and achievement. Neither will it make any financial concessions to parents who pay the full cost of an education they choose for their children and who still must pay their full share of the public system. Far from being mere enclaves of privilege, Ontario independent schools have made notable contributions to education. Back in the last century, Woodstock College pioneered manual training; in the twenties Pickering spearheaded progressive education and started psychological testing and counselling; outdoor education developed at Lakefield and elsewhere; the major movement in Canadian studies started with TCS; French immersion was tried and proved at the Toronto French School; Ashbury led the way in Canada with the International Baccalaureate and started the Forum for Young Canadians.

As Ashbury's Centennial approached there were heavy clouds looming over the future of the nation. They certainly weren't in the minds of the graduating class celebrating in the time-honoured way after Closing on June 9, 1990. Their memorable evening dinner dance at the National Arts Centre went as all such events should go. But from the balcony of the Arts Centre they could see, just across the Rideau Canal, the crowd outside the Conference Centre. Inside, the Prime Minister and the premiers of the provinces were locked in their closed-door conference on the Meech Lake Accord. They ended with apparent agreement: Quebec would be accommodated within the constitution at long last. But, as history shows, ratification failed. As 1990 closed and 1991 drew on, the next crop of graduates was tipped into a nation faced more and more starkly with the possibility of failure.

It was a burning topic, of course, for the 500 students who came from across the land in March and May 1991 for the Forum for Young Canadians. It was the Forum's 15th year. Laurier Lapierre, the principal animator with Keith Spicer's travelling Citizens' Forum, came to spark exchanges. By the end of their week the students were discussing things with far better-informed passion and a good deal more understanding than the great mass of people in the country.

They may not have agreed on solutions, but they had met, they had touched one another, they had felt the strength of common ties override the differences that divided.

It was hard to avoid the reflection that, had the Forum or its like been multiplied a few hundred times through the years, what a difference to the nation it would have made. Ashbury's key role in founding it was nicely underlined on Closing Day 1991 when the guest of honour was Honourable John Fraser, Speaker of the House of Commons.

There is always a light side, of course. Oliver Fisher, one of Ashbury's Forum scholarship winners, was a rare bird for 1991 — a genuine Brian Mulroney admirer. He was, in fact, a fan with a remarkable collection of Mulroney memorabilia and a birthday on the same day. What's more, it actually happened to fall during his Forum session. In the Centre Block on the day in question the group was in the right spot to see the Prime Minister en route to the caucus birthday party. They burst into "Happy Birthday." He stopped and shook hands — with Oliver — who blurted out, "It's my birthday too." At the closing banquet Oliver got two gems for his collection: a birthday greeting letter from the Prime Minister and a box of Kleenex from his group to stem his emotional tears!

Centennial Year, 1991, was a celebration: reunions, dinners, dances and galas, sports tournaments, concerts, art shows, international debating, a special edition of David Polk's selected poems to warm the memories. Old Ashburians came in droves. Hundreds said goodbye to Ray Anderson, retiring after 37 years. Jonathan Harrison came from England and brought back the voice of Abinger Hill to speak at the dinner for the First Half-Century Club. Justin Fogarty chaired a group that organized a series called Alumni Talks. Friends of the school packed the luncheon meetings to hear perspectives on Canada today by a brilliant slate of speakers: past parent and distinguished journalist Christopher Young; old boys Robert Stanfield and Robin MacNeil of the famed MacNeil-Lehrer News Hour; Donald Macdonald, returning after three years as Canadian High Commissioner in London.

Alumni interests and activities were extraordinarily widespread. David Berger had been Member of Parliament for St. Henri/Westmount since 1979. Ian Scott was a member of the Opposition at Queen's Park after a term as Attorney General of Ontario. In Ottawa Jamie Fisher was a busy Alderman, Bruce Firestone was embroiled in a mighty struggle to bring the Ottawa Senators and an NHL franchise back to the city. On his promotion team was Frank Finnigan, famed old Senators' right winger who had coached Charlie Stanfield, Peter Smellie et al. in the memorable Ashbury season of 1929. Bruce Hillary, who'd captained a championship football team in the fifties, was ending years of personal effort to keep the Rough Riders in the game. Overseas, Professor Georges Verhaegen, the double Governor General's Medal winner, was Rector of Université Libre de Bruxelles with an enrolment of 14,000 students. And Graeme Clark, a newly minted foreign service officer, found himself in conference with a cabinet minister prominent in the emerging democratic government of Nicaragua. It was Henri Dreyfus, recalling — after state affairs were done — Ashbury and cricket in the 1940s, with Buggy Brain and Robin MacNeil and other good friends, and Clog, and Duke, and the values he'd acquired then that had lasted through his life.

Alumni and friends flocked to the Birthday Party on a glorious, sunny May 12. It started where Ashbury had begun, at the corner of Wellington Street and O'Connor, with the dedication of a historic plaque to mark the site. Then back by bus to Princess Gate and a march up Mariposa to the pipes and drums of the Cameron Highlanders.

If Sergeant-Majors Carwardine and Stone stirred in their graves at the lack of military precision, their hearts would still have warmed to the spirit.

On the school grounds were music, singing, games, costumes, a huge birthday cake and a magnificent spread under seeming acres of marquee. And that splendid spectacle, eternally stirring to the hearts of Canadians — the traditional Musical Ride of the Royal Canadian Mounted Police. Fred Oliver certainly wouldn't have begrudged the hoofprints on his beloved playing fields — or the dollops of horse manure so familiar from his early days. Nor would Ted Marshall, or more lately Adam Morrison. And G.P. Woollcombe's heart would have swelled with pride.

Through his 42 years as Headmaster he had pursued his aim for his school steadfastly, heart and soul, and, in the long perspective of the times, very well. He ran it himself, of course, in the sure, confident Victorian tradition. But with G.P. retired, the Board focused little further than preserving a nice place for their sons to repeat their own experience. That Harry Wright, an outstanding schoolmaster, failed as Head was a deep disappointment. That circumstances and character — the Depression, Nicholas Archdale's neglect, the Board's lack of cohesion and corporate drive — conspired to run the school nearly into the ground must have come close to breaking G.P.'s heart. Then, before he died, he could see new hope, things on the rise, with Ogden Glass and the beginnings of Ronald Perry's time.

There were questions next of relevance, the place of Ashbury College in the social structure, the expanding city, the prospering country, and there was a wavering of aims. Tremendous pressures came to bear at that time on traditional institutions. But sagging confidence in public education after the upheaval of the late sixties brought a growing demand. To survive now, an independent school must provide not just personal attention and "polish" but a superior education. Freedom from provincial examinations had in fact given the scope to develop avenues of excellence. Ashbury's Board provided direction and support and the basic values which G.P. Woollcombe held so firmly were maintained by the strong and steady hand of William Joyce. Staff, students, Governors and parents were working to a purpose. Tony Macoun's vision, initiative and drive found the right base on which to build. To the school's new heights Roy Napier brought broad experience, a level head and sure touch, and the ability to carry forward G.P. Woollcombe's dream.

Values. The Ashbury Guild's gift of a fine stained-glass window for the Chapel was dedicated on October 28, 1990, by Chaplain Todd Meaker, Archdeacon Doug Christie and Bill and Peggy Joyce, she as longtime past Honorary President of the Guild. All the window spaces in this Chapel that G.P. had built nearly 80 years before were now complete. Each panel, each traditional symbol wrought in glass, had something of value to say. These spoke to the Ashbury family.

In the congregation were Captain George Woollcombe and his granddaugher, Dharini. Stephen Woollcombe and his wife had adopted Dharini as a little girl in India some years before during an External Affairs posting. Now they were in Europe and she was an Ashbury boarder. That in itself — a fourth generation Woollcombe in his school — would have given G.P. the most profound pleasure. A girl — how greatly his school had changed. Indian by birth — what changes had occurred in his country and the world. But wisdom, with such values as its base, rises to the challenges of change, adapts, rejoices, leads the way.

Ottawa is now a city matured and grown vastly over the past hundred years and it has become uniquely beautiful among the capitals of the modern world. And Ashbury has become one of its vibrant institutions. It has shown the true value of the independent school, not just in its ability to serve a somewhat privileged clientele but in the use it makes of its freedom to pursue the crucial matter of excellence in education. So it contributes, through its graduates and its programmes and the values it espouses, to the mainstream of the community and of the country in which it has been so fortunate to grow.

"A life of its own, a character of its own, a civilization of its own, and now 100 years of memories and traditions of its own." Mr. Woollcombe's school had been tempered by time and trial, had gathered strength, had overcome its own troubles along the way. Captain of the School Andrew Nichols, the 100th year's graduates and all of those to follow would step into a world ever more fraught with uncertainties and strife. Their knowledge, their intellects, their values and, as the Founder had visualized when he started the school, their "general culture, the all-round development that promises the highest type of character," would stand them, and their country, very well.

APPENDICES

APPENDIX A

PRESIDENTS AND CHAIRMEN OF THE BOARD OF ASHBURY COLLEGE

1900-1915 W.H. Rowley
1915-1931 Lieutenant Colonel J.W. Woods
1932-1934 G.E. Fauquier
1934-1938 Lieutenant Colonel E.F. Newcombe
1938-1945 S.E. Woods
1945-1949 Lieutenant Colonel E.F. Newcombe
1949-1951 Duncan MacTavish
1952-1954 E.N. Rhodes Sr.
1954-1956 R.W. Southam
1956-1958 J.S. Irvin Sr.
1958-1961 C.G. Gale
1961-1963 A.B.R. Lawrence

1963-1964 G.D. Hughson
1964-1966 Commodore W.G. Ross CD, RCN
1966-1968 D. MacLaren
1968-1970 M.E. Grant
1970-1972 C.K. Brown
1972-1975 E.N. Rhodes Jr.
1975-1978 F.S. Martin
1978-1982 J.R. Woods
1982-1984 Lieutenant-General W.A. Milroy DSO,CD
1984-1986 T.V. Murray
1986-1989 Jean Teron
1989-1991 E.P. Newcombe
1991-   James H. Smellie

APPENDIX B

THE HEADMASTERS

1891-1933
Canon George Penrose Woollcombe, B.A. (Oxford), M.A. (Bishops) LL.D. (McGill)
1933-1936
Harold F. Wright, B.A. (Cape University)
1936-1945
Nicholas M. Archdale, M.A. (Oxford)
1945-1950
C.L. Ogden Glass, B.A. (Bishops), M.A. (Oxford)

1950-1966
Ronald H. Perry, B.A. (Toronto) M.A. (Columbia)
1966-1981
William A. Joyce, D.S.O., E.D., B.Sc. (Manitoba)
1981-1986
Anthony M. Macoun, M.A. (Oxford)
1986-
Robert B. Napier, B.Sc. (Hon) (Queen's, Belfast), M. Ed. (Bishop's)

APPENDIX C

THE CAPTAINS OF THE SCHOOL

1910 M. O'Halloran
1911 M. O'Halloran
1912 A.M. Naismith
1913 H.W. Davis
1914 W.M. Irvin
1915 W.H.D. MacMahon
1916 A.E.D. Tremain
1917 P.S. Gault
1918 A.C. Evans

1919 C.L. Gault
1920 H.R. Hampson
1921 S.F.H. Lane
1922 J.J.B. Pemberton
1923 K.H. Tremain
1924 A.M. Irvine
1925 G.E. Fauquier
1926 T.G. Mayburry
1927 J.E. Fauquier

1928	J.S. Irvin	1960	J.G. Sarkis/C.W. Wilson
1929	K.R. MacKenzie	1961	P.C. Noel-Bentley/M.C. Spencer
1930	H.A. Fauquier	1962	A.F. Gill/S.G.R. Pottinger
1931	J.W.H. Rowley	1963	J.I. Bethune/R.N. Blackburn
1932	D.C. Southam	1964	D.B. McGaughey
1933	D. Fauquier	1965	W.J. Booth
1934	T.W. Beauclerk	1966	R.B. Southam
1935	M.D. MacBrien	1967	O.K. Lawson
1936	J.B. Kirkpatrick	1968	M.D. Wennberg
1937	A.C. Dunning	1969	W.B. Haughton
1938	J.C. Viets	1970	P.W. Barott
1939	W.A. Grant	1971	D.R. Hallett
1940	A.M. Wilson	1972	B.A. Boyd
1941	C.R. Burrows	1973	N.E. Macleod
1942	G.R. Goodwin	1974	D.C. Paterson
1943	R.G.R. Lawrence	1975	C. Pardo
1944	L.H. Chapman	1976	J.W. Beedell
1945	E.B. Pilgrim	1977	J.G. Mierins
1946	J.F. Smith	1978	G.C. Clark
1947	J.S. Pettigrew	1979	W. Chodikoff
1948	H.S. Clark/R.T. Kenny	1980	E. Abbott
1949	H.M. Dreyfus	1981	B.K. Keyes
1950	C.C. Hart	1982	K.M. Keenan
1951	R.E. Gill/B.A. Pritchard	1983	S.B. Naisby
1952	A.D. McCulloch	1984	J.E. Hill
1953	G.P. Jackson	1985	R.A. Spencer
1954	G.P. Jackson	1986	L.S. Grainger
1955	A.B. Wells	1987	O. Kitchlew
1956	L.M. Killaly	1988	I.J. MacRae
1957	G.S.M. Woollcombe	1989	A.J. Harewood
1958	M.W. Sutherland	1990	J.J. Napier
1959	R.D.F. Lackey	1991	A.L. Nichols

APPENDIX D

GOVERNOR GENERAL'S MEDAL WINNERS

For the highest academic standing in the school.

1912	L.E.L. Koelle	1923	C.L. Yuile
1913	P.E. Biggar	1924	H.B. MacCarthy
1914	P.E. Biggar	1925	J.M. Wilson
1915	A.R. MacLaren	1926	C. Craig
1916	A.E.D. Tremain	1927	G.S. Challies
1917	J.W. McLimont	1928	A.M. Clarke
1918	C.H. Hamilton	1929	P.H. Scott
1919	C.L. Gault	1930	D.F. Maccorquodale
1920	G.P. Sladen	1931	S. MacDonnell
1921	S.F.H. Lane	1932	R. Coristine
1922	L.H. Clayton	1933	G.E. Wodehouse

1934 W.F. Hadley	1963 G.C. Greenstone
1935 M.D. MacBrien	1964 G.R. Garton
1936 G.E. Brown	1965 J.A. Hunden
1937 H.M. Baker	1966 J.J. Read
1938 L.F. Burrows	1967 M.W. Evans
1939 W.A. Grant	1968 D.C. Thackray
1940 A.B. Lawrence	1969 R. Berger
1941 G.W. Green	1970 R.C. Woollam
1942 J.C. McLaren	1971 S.T. Whitwill
1943 G.D.M. Hooper	1972 B.A. Boyd
1944 G.D.M. Hooper	1973 P. Hope
1945 M. Shenstone	1974 F.L. Stoddard
1946 J.G.M. Hooper	1975 G. Yuen
1947 J.S. Pettigrew	1976 D. Singh
1948 C. Hampson	1977 A.I. Johnson
1949 W.G. Ross	1978 I.N. Rhodes
1950 D.F. Heney	1979 W.R. Brown
1951 J.M. Fraser	1980 M.T. Bravo
1952 D.R. Irwin	1981 R.M. Boyd
1953 L.W. Abbott	1982 A.K. Chan
1954 G. Verhaegen	1983 R.J.R. Mann
1955 G. Verhaegen	1984 C. John
1956 C.M.C. Calkoen	1985 A. Pang
1957 I.G. Cumming	1986 A.A. Bent
1958 V.B. Rivers	1987 P-D.G. Sarte/B. Teron
1959 V.J. Fascio	1988 P. Chan
1960 J.G. Sarkis	1989 V.E. Hill
1961 P.C. Noel-Bentley	1990 S.G. Hensel
1962 S.M.O. Parker	1991 K.S. McMillan

WINNERS OF THE SOUTHAM CUP

For the greatest achievement in athletics, while displaying academic competence in year five.

1922 F.G. Heney	1939 W.A. Grant
1923 F.G. Heney	1940 E.D. Wilgress
1924 L.G. Clarke	1941 G.D. Hughson
1925 C.E. Pacaud	1942 R.G.R. Lawrence
1926 D.R. McMaster	1943 R.G.R. Lawrence
1927 A.F. MacKenzie	1944 G.D. Hooper
1928 S.G. Gamble	1945 C.W.J. Eliot
1929 C.E. Stanfield	1946 J.F. Smith
1930 R.H. Craig	1947 J.S. Pettigrew
1931 E.C. Elwood	1948 F.G. Rose
1932 R.L. Stanfield	1949 W.G. Ross
1933 J.A. Caulder	1950 D.F. Heney
1934 J.A. Powell/G.D. Stanfield	1951 H.J. Hulsmann
1935 M.D. MacBrien	1952 J.H. Gill
1936 A.C. Dunning	1953 L.W. Abbott
1937 A.C. Dunning	1954 G.P. Jackson
1938 L.F. Burrows	1955 C. Nowakowski

1956	L.M. Killaly		1975	I.K. Bleackley
1957	G.S.M. Woollcombe		1976	J.W. Beedell
1958	V.B. Rivers		1977	C.P. Veilleux
1959	J.S. Rowan-Legg		1978	T.B. Murray
1960	P.K. Rowan-Legg/J.A. Tucker		1979	J.A. Sezlik
1961	M.A. Farrugia		1980	D.C. Beedell
1962	I.M. Ewing		1981	S.I. Mozer
1963	J.I. Bethune/J.G.A. Tyler		1982	B.F. Bossons/K.M. Keenan
1964	G.B. Keffer		1983	S.K.C. Grainger
1965	A.H. Rawley		1984	J.V. Smith
1966	R.B. Southam		1985	J. Binavince
1967	J.H. Smellie		1986	J.C. Hall
1968	D.J. Kelly		1987	O. Kitchlew
1969	P.C. Smith		1988	I.J. MacRae
1970	C.E.S. Barnes		1989	N.J. Cantor/A.J. Harewood
1971	D.R. Hallett		1990	Boys: M.R. Storey/J.R. Mikhael
1972	R.L. Bennett			Girls: S.A. Levesque/J.J. Napier
1973	M.L.W. Barnes		1991	Boys: J. Hill
1974	P.G. Copestake/P.S.T. Croal			Girls: L. Mrak

WINNERS OF THE WOODS SHIELD

The Junior School Award of Merit for academic, character and extra-curricular contribution.

1941	J.N.W. Turner		1967	B.A. Boyd
1942	A.M.C. Holmes		1968	N.E. Macleod
1943	A.E. Woodward		1969	R.H. Pitfield
1944	G.F.C. Plowden		1970	R.J. Henderson
1945	H.J. McCordick		1971	C.N. Teron
1946	D.M. Mansur		1972	A.I. Johnston
1947	J.D. Younger		1973	I.N. Rhodes
1948	C.R. Younger		1974	W.R. Brown
1949	E.N. Rhodes Jr.		1975	D.C. Beedell
1950	A.B. Wells		1976	A.M.S. Paterson
1951	E.T. Mulkins		1977	D.M. Alexander
1952	G.R. MacLaren		1978	S.K.C. Grainger
1953	F.A. Reid		1979	J.G. Booth
1954	J.R. Southam		1980	S.B. Matthews
1955	G.A. Malloy		1981	L.S. Grainger
1956	J.J. Powell		1982	J.D.S. Binnie
1957	A.F. Gill		1983	T.W. Zawidzki
1958	R.B. Logie		1984	A.J. Harewood
1959	M.R. Devlin		1985	J.R. Mikhael
1960	H.K. Reed		1986	J.E. Drouin
1961	P.K. Smith		1987	O.G. Fisher
1962	J.J.D. Read		1988	M. Weatherill
1963	S.B. Day		1989	M.J. Ryten
1964	A. Farrugia		1990	X. Fan
1965	D.A.H. MacFarlane		1991	B. Ritchie
1966	G.D. Blyth			

APPENDIX E

THE GUILD PRESIDENTS

ASHBURY MOTHERS GUILD

1950-51	Maryon Rhodes
1951-53	Glynne Heenan
1953-55	Anne Mulkins
1955-57	Dorothy Woollcombe
1957-58	Margaret Hiney
1958-60	Margaret Rowen-Legg
1960-61	Susan Hadley
1961-62	Rosemary Partridge
1962-64	Gladys Copeland
1964-65	Ethel Ewing
1965-67	Frances Smellie
1967-68	Dorothy Perley

ASHBURY LADIES GUILD (1969)

1968-70	Eileen Chick
1970-71	Joan Henderson
1971-72	Barbara Harcourt
1972-73	Eleanor Bates
1973-74	Mary-Elizabeth Mulock
1974-75	Mary-Lou Harris
1976-78	Mary Mahoney
1978-79	Fiona Morton
1979-80	Patricia Watson/Nancy Edmonds
1980-82	Janet Jones
1982-83	Jessie Naisby
1983-85	Penny Barr

THE ASHBURY COLLEGE GUILD (1985)

1985-86	Carol Henderson
1986-88	Janet McLaine
1988-90	JoAnn Thomas
1990-91	Margaret Bell

HONOURARY PRESIDENTS

1950-66	Mary Perry
1966-81	Margaret Joyce
1981-86	Ann Macoun
1986-	Dorothy Napier

APPENDIX F

FORUM FOR YOUNG CANADIANS CHAIRMEN

1975-77	Kenneth R. Lavery
1977-79	Ruth M. Bell
1979-81	Leo Cadieux P.C.
1981-83	Frederick Gall
1983-85	James R. Hurley
1985-87	Cynthia Baxter
1987-89	William R. Sloan
1989-91	David J. McConomy

APPENDIX G

ASHBURIANS ON ACTIVE SERVICE THE SOUTH AFRICAN WAR 1900-1902

Currier, E.D. '99 South African Mounted Irregular Force
Gilmour, A.U. '94 Private R.C.R.
Gilmour, J.F. '96 Private, Strathcona Horse
Ritchie, D.V. '93 Private, Strathcona Horse
Slater, N.J. '96 Private, Canadian Mounted Rifles

WORLD WAR I 1914-1918
ROLL OF HONOUR
These old boys and members of the staff gave their lives:

Armstrong, D.
Arnoldi, J.R.
Avery, F.G.
Billings, H.
Bostock, A.H.
Brooke, F.W.
Brown, G.B.
Carling, G.B.
Carling, J.B.
Chipman, G.C.C.
Cotton, C.P.
Currier, E.D.
Dickey, H.A.B.
Fraser, A.G.
Gilmour, A.U.
Godwin, C.R.M.
Godwin, J.L.
Gorman, C.F.O.
Hazen, J.M.
Henderson, A.A.

Heney, J.B.L.
Heron, G.R.
Barrington-Kennet, V.
Levievre, R.H.
Lemesurier, A.S.
Lowe, E.J.
MacLean, H
Masson, D.H.
Masson, R.G.
McLachlin, E.
Moore, A.W.
Pratt, A.C.
Read, E.H.
Ritchie, D.V.
Sladen, R.L.
Smart, D.A.B.
Smith, G.R.
Turriff, R.
Woods, J.R.
Wright, J.S.

ASHBURIANS ON ACTIVE SERVICE
1914-1919

Adams,J.W.'16 Lieutenant,R.N.A.S.
Allan,J.R.'08 Captain,R.F.C.
Anderson,A.A.'06 Major,6th Brigade
Engineers,m.i.d.,D.S.O.
Anderson,C.M.'11 Lieutenant,R.A.M.C.
Anderson,E.M.'95 Trooper,Cavalry.
Armstrong,D.'01 C.E.F. Killed in Action.
Arnoldi,J.R.'06 Corporal,C.F.A.,Killed in
Action.

Atkinson,R.E.B.'10 Corporal,C.F.A.
Aumond,C.deB.'02 Private,Borden Machine
Gun Battery.
Avery,F.G.'08 Captain,R.E.,M.C.,Killed in
Action.
Babington,F.C.'07 Air Mechanic,R.F.A.
Balfe,A.E.'15 Private,C.E.F.
Barwis,C.W.A.'11 Captain,Indian
Army,m.i.d.,Wounded Twice.

Barwis,G.D.G.'16 Lieutenant,C.F.A.
Bate,G.A.'16 Lieutenant,R.F.A.Wounded.
Bate,H.B.'08 2nd Lieutenant,Worcertershire Regiment,M.C.,Wounded.
Bate,H.N.'11 Lieutenant,R.C.D.,Wounded.
Bate,H.T.'08 Lieutenant,R.C.N.
Bate,S.C.'12 Lieutenant,Royal Canadian Regiment,Wounded.
Beard,C.T.'07 Lieutenant,R.C.N.
Beard,F.H.'13 Sapper,C.E.F.
Beddoe,A.B.'12 Corporal,Infantry, Wounded,P.O.W.
Belanger,J.B.'07 Private,R.A.M.C.,M.C.
Bell,G.G.'04 Lieutenant,Queen's Own Rifles,m.i.d.,D.F.C.
Bell,J.S.'17 Private,C.E.F.
Benoit,P.S.'01 Lieutenant-Colonel,R.C.R.
Benson,G.F.'15 Lieutenant,R.F.A.Wounded.
Benson,W.D.'16 Royal Garrison Artillery.
Biggar,P.E.'13 Lieutenant,R.F.C.,Two Foreign Decorations.
Billings,C.A.'12 Captain,C.E.F.Wounded.
Billings,Hugh'13 Lieutenant,R.F.C.,Killed in Action.
Birch,J.F.'12 Private,Victoria Rifles of Canada.
Birkett,E.W.'15 Sergeant,C.F.A.
Birkett,T.G.'15 Lieutenant,R.C.D.
Bishop,J.L.'08 Lieutenant,C.E.F.Wounded.
Blair,Donald'06 Lieutenant,Machine Gun Brigade.
Blakeney,T.L.'15 Lieutenant,R.N.A.S.
Bostock,A.H.'09 Lieutenant Strathcona Horse,m.i.d.,Killed in Action
Bourinot,S.P.'08 Private, C.A.S.C.
Bowie,G.G.'11 Lieutenant,C.E.F.,Wounded.
Boyce,C.D.'12 Captain,C.E.F.,Wounded.
Boyd,E.D.H.'12 Lieutenant,B.E.F.
Brooke,F.W.'09 Private,C.E.F.,P.O.W., died as P.O.W.
Brown,G.B.'16 Corporal,C.F.A.,M.C.,Killed in Action.
Bryson,K.C.'16 Gunner,C.F.A.
Burbidge,G.H.'07 Major,Strathcona Horse,M.C.
Burn,G.D.'08 Lieutenant,C.A.S.C.
Burns,M.C.'14 Flight Lieutenant,R.A.F.Wounded.
Burstall,J.W.H.'18 Sergeant,C.F.A.
Butterworth,C.H.'06 Lieutenant,C.A.S.C.
Caldwell,T.R.'08 Lieutenant-Colonel,21st Battalion.O.B.E.Wounded.
Campbell,A.T.'17 Lieutenant,C.F.A.
Campbell,B.B.S.'06 Major,C.E.F.

Campbell,F.R.L.'15 Lieutenant,Nova Scotia Highlanders.
Carling,G.B.'99 Captain,P.P.C.L.I.,Killed.
Carling,J.B.'17 Lieutenant,R.F.C. Died.
Carling,L.B.'15 Lieutenant,C.A.S.C.
Channonhouse,J.H.'14 Gunner,C.F.A.
Chipman,C.S.'08 Gunner,C.F.A.Killed in Action.
Chrysler,G.G.'98 Major,C.E.F.,M.C.,Wounded.
Chrysler, P.H. '99 Lieutenant, C.E.F
Cockburn,L.W.S.'02 Lieutenant-Colonel,R.C.H.A.
Code,A.L.'15 Lieutenant,R.F.C.,Wounded.
Codville,F.H.M.'08 Major,R.C.D.,M.C.
Colman,W.M.'16 Private,C.F.A.
Cory,W.M.'15 Lieutenant,C.F.A.
Cotton,C.P.'09 Lieutenant,C.F.A.Killed in Action.
Critchley,C.'09 R.N.
Critchley,T.S.'09 Lieutenant,Royal Navy.
Crocket,T.S.'16 Gunner,C.F.A.
Cunningham,F.deH.'09 Lieutenant,C.E.F.
Currier,E.D.'99 Lieutenant,C.E.F.Killed in Action.
Davidson,E.K.'16 Lieutenant,R.A.F.
Davis,H.W.'14 Lieutenant,R.C.R.,Wounded.
Dickey,H.A.B.'99 Captain, C.F.A.,Died of Wounds.
Dickey,O.B.'99 Major,R.A.S.C.,m.i.d.
Drummond,P.C.'17 Lieutenant,R.N.A.S.
Echlin,E.M.'14 Lieutenant,C.F.A.
Eddy,E.B.'02 Lieutenant,Flying Corps,U.S.A.
Edward,A.J.'15 Sergeant,Canadian Tank Corps.
Eliot,J.H.'07 Lieutenant,B.E.F.,M.C.,m.i.d.,Wounded.
Ellard,D.'08
Ellard,R.E.'08 Sergeant-Major,C.E.F.
Ferris,George'98 Gunner,C.F.A.
Fleming,A.M.'12 Lieutenant,Princess Louise Dragoon Guards,P.O.W.
Fleming,C.S.'08 Lieutenant,C.F.A.,m.i.d.
Fleming,N.S.'02 Lieutenant,C.E.F.
Forbes,D.S.'01 Major,P.P.C.L.I.,,M.C.,Wounded.
Forbes,N.B.'01 Lieutenant,R.C.H.A.,m.i.d.
Fowler,E.M.'01 Lieutenant,C.E.F.
Fraser,A.G.'07 Lieutenant,C.F.A.,Died of Wounds.
Fraser,H.N.'95 Captain,C.E.F.,P.O.W.
Fripp,H.D.'08 Captain,C.F.A.
Gault,P.S.'18 Gunner,C.F.A.

Gendron,J.F.E.'11 Major,C.E.F.,m.i.d.,Wounded Twice.
Gill,A.G.'05 Major,C.F.A.
Gilmour,A.U.'94 Private,C.E.F.,Died of Wounds.
Gilmour,H.L.'04 Lieutenant,C.E.F.
Gilmour,J.F.'96 Lieutenant B.E.F.,Wounded
Gilmour,S.B.'00 Captain,Canadian Forestry Corps.
Gisborne,F.H.'04 Lieutenant,C.E.F.,Wounded.
Gisborne,L.R.'14 Gunner,C.F.A.
Godfrey,V.S.'12 Lieutenant,R.C.N.
Godwin,C.R.M.'03 Lieutenant,C.F.A.,Killed in Action.
Godwin, J.L. '02 Killed.
Goldstein,C.H.'16 Gunner,C.F.A.
Gooch,H.C.'08 Sub-Lieutenant,R.F.C.
Gorman,C.F.O.'10 Gunner,Royal Horse Artillery,Died of Wounds.
Graham,F.D.'12 Captain,C.A.M.C.
Graham,H.E.'14 Private,C.E.F.
Graham,J.'08 Lieutenant,C.E.F.
Grant,D.A.'13 Lieutenant,R.C.D.,M.C.
Graves,G.R.'12 Lieutenant,B.E.F.
Graves,Philip'11 Lieutenant,B.E.F.
Greene,L.K.'08 Captain,Canadian Mounted Rifles.
Greene,M.K.'07 Lieutenant,R.C.R.,m.i.d.,Wounded.
Hale,Fred'03 Lieutenant,C.E.F.
Hallick,W.G.A.'13 Private,R.A.F.
Hanna,J.D.'12 C.E.F.
Harris,A.D.'96 Captain,R.E.
Harvey,L.E.L.'12 Lieutenant,P.P.C.L.I.,Wounded.
Hazen,J.M.'14 Captain,C.F.A.,Died Of Wounds.
Henderson,A.A.'01 Private,C.F.A.,Died of Wounds.
Heney,J.B.I.,'13 Lieutenant,R.F.C.,M.C.,Killed in Action.
Hennessy,A.B.B.'13 Lieutenant,R.A.F.
Hennessy,J.W.'13 Major,B.E.F.
Heron,G.R.'97 Major C.F.A.,Killed in Action.
Heron,V.W.S.'96 Lieutenant,R.C.R.,Wounded.
Heward,E.F.'12 Sapper,Canadian Engineers.
Higman,C.H.'11 Lieutenant,R.N.V.R.
Hill,K.M.'14 Gunner,C.F.A.
Hill,R.L.'14 Private,M.M.,Wounded.
Holland,H.L.'14 Lieutenant,R.F.C.,M.C.
Hughson,H.M.'12 Captain,C.F.A.,Wounded.
Hughson,J.W.'08 Captain,C.E.F.

Inderwick,C.C.'10 Lieutenant,R.N.V.R.
Irvin,W.M.'14 Private,United States Medical Corps.
Irwin,A.de la C.'01 Captain,C.F.A.
Irwin,R.H.'02 Major,R.C.E
Irwin,W.E.C.'06 Major,P.P.C.L.I.,m.i.d.,Wounded.
Jackson,L.W.'16 Lieutenant,R.F.A.
Keefer,T.G.'99 Major,R.C.E.
Lambert,M.L.B.H. Captain,C.E.F.
Lampman,A.O.'09 Lieutenant,R.C.D.
Lelievre,R.H.'13 Lieutenant,R.F.C.,Foreign Decorations.Wounded, Killed
Lemesurier,A.S.'05 Private,C.F.A.,Killed in Action.
Lethbridge,E.R.'12 Lieutenant,Strathcona Horse.Wounded.
Lewis,A.C.T.'01 Captain,R.C.E.
Lewis,J.T.jr.'03 Major,C.E.F.,Wounded
Lindsay,D.St.G.'12 Lieutenant,R.N.
Lindsay,John'10 Lieutenant,C.E.F.
Logan,W.S.'11 Private,C.E.F.
Lowe,E.J.'13 Sapper,Canadian Engineers, Killed.
MacDonnell,D.K.'11 Lieutenant,C.E.F.,Wounded.
MacIvor,R.S.P.'10 Captain,Indian Army.
Maclaren,A.R.'15 Lieutenant,C.E.F.,Wounded.
Maclaren,J.N.'16 Gunner,3rd Canadian Division.
MacMahon,W.H.D.'15 Lieutenant,R.F.A.,Wounded.
MacPhail,J.B.'08 Major,C.E.F.
MacPherson,J.A.C.'99 Major,Canadian Infantry.
MacPherson,K.C.'03 Lieutenant,Canadian Engineers.
Magrath,C.B.'00 Captain,C.F.A.,m.i.d.
Malcolm,Jack'16 Lieutenant,R.F.C.,M.C., R.A.F. Medal, Foreign Decorations,P.O.W.,Wounded.
Mansell,T.St.G.'12 Lieutenant R.C.E.
Marshall,Joseph'13 C.E.F.
Masson,D.H.'08 Lieutenant,R.N.A.S.,Killed in Action.
Masson,R.G.'12 Lieutenant,R.F.C.,Killed in Action.
Masson,W.G.'08 Lieutenant,C.F.A.
May,A.'09 Lieutenant,C.E.F.,M.C.,Wounded.
Maynard,Allan'08 R.F.C.
Maynard,G.'08 Sergeant,Sanitary Corps.

McCormack,P.M.'08 Private,C.E.F.,Wounded.
McGiverin,H.M.'13 Cadet,R.A.F.
McLachlin,E.H.'03 Lieutenant,C.F.A.
McLachlin,Ewen'05 Lieutenant,C.F.A.,Killed.
McLachlin,J.H.'00 Captain,C.E.F.
McLean,H.'94 B.E.F.,Killed in Action.
McLimont,J.W.'17 Lieutenant C.F.A.
Minto,Victor,Earl of '03 Lieutenant,Scots
Guards.
Montgomery,M.W.'14 Lieutenant,C.M.R.
Montgomery,R.S.'14 R.C.N.
Moon,C.O.'00 Lieutenant,Canadian
Engineers.
Moore,A.N.'08 Lieutenant,C.E.F.
Moore,A.W.'98Private,B.E.F.,Killed in Action
Moore,D.W.'98 Lieutenant,C.E.F.
Moore,K.W.'17 R.A.S.
Moore,P.R.'97 Lance-Corporal,C.E.F.
Morgan,H.R.'12 Gunner,R.C.H.A.
Morris,R.S.'15 Lieutenant,R.F.A.,Wounded.
Morse,C.O.'11 Sapper,Canadian Engineers.
Muirhead,W.P.'16 Gunner,C.F.A.,Wounded.
Mulkins,R G S '14 Gunner,C.F.A.
Naismith,A.N.'12
Lieutenant,C.F.A.,M.C.,m.i.d.,Wounded.
Nelson,H.M.'08 Sapper,Mechanical Transport
Engineers.
Newcombe,E.F.'07 Major,P.P.C.L.I.,Wounded.
Nutting,J.K.'05 Gunner,C.F.A.
O'Connor,Charles'16 Lieutenant,Signal
Corps.
O'Connor,H.Willis.'06
Major,C.E.F.,D.S.O.,m.i.d.,Wounded.
O'Halloran,Melbourne'11
Captain,C.F.A.,M.C.,Wounded.
Oliver,J.S.'11 Lieutenant,C.E.F.
Orde,R.J.'08 Lieutenant,R.F.A.
Palmer,A.Z.'98 Lieutenant-Colonel,C.M.G.
Palmer,L.C.D.'16 Lieutenant,R.A.F.
Panet,E.deB.'99 Brigadier-
General,C.E.F.,D.S.O.,C.M.G., m.i.d.
Parker,H.S.'11 Captain,C.F.A.
Patterson,R.B.'14 Lieutenant,B.E.F.
Perley,A.G.'12 Lieutenant,C.A.S.C.
Phillips,A.J.R.'08 Lieutenant,R.F.C.,Wounded.
Price,J.H.'11 2nd Lieutenant,R.F.A.,Wounded.
Prior,B.G.'01 Lieutenant,C.F.A.,Wounded.
Raphael,H.M.'04 Captain,C.M.C.
Read,C.E.'98 Major,Canadian Forestry
Corps,m.i.d.
Read,E.H.'16 Lieutenant,R.F.C.,Killed in
Action.

Reid,E.N.'11 Lieutenant,C.O.C.
Reid,H.E.'11 Lieutenant,R.C.N.,m.i.d.
Reiffenstein,J.C.'13 Gunner,C.F.A.,Wounded.
Renaud,E.J.'10 Major,C.O.C.
Richardson,H.R.F.'13 Lieutenant,R.N.A.S.
Ritchie,D.V.'93 Private,C.E.F.,Killed in Action.
Rivers,C.W.'15 Lieutenant,C.F.A.
Ross,G.LeB.'15 Lieutenant,R.C.A.
Ross,J.R.'04 Acting Captain,R.N.A.S.,m.i.d.
Rothwell,H '08
Russell,R.I.'11 Lieutenant,C.E.F.,Wounded.
St.Laurent,Adrian'13 Lieutenant,C.E.F.
Sample,L.E.'13
Scott,G.E.'17 R.A.F.
Shaw,A.L.'11 Segeant,C.F.A.
Sherwood,E.C.'12 Sub-Lieutenant,R.C.N.
Sherwood,H.L.'00 Major,Canadian Engineers.
Sherwood,L.P.'06 Major,R.C.D.,m.i.d.,Foreign
Decorations.
Simpson,J.A.'01 Private,C.F.A.
Sinclair,Colville'08
Lieutenant,C.E.F.,Wounded.
Skead,E.S.'11 Lieutenant,Canadian Remount
Division,P.O.W.,Wounded.
Sladen,C.St.B.'09 Lieutenant,B.E.F.
Sladen,J.D.'08 Captain,C.E.F.
Sladen,R.L.'15 Lieutenant,P.P.C.L.I.,Killed in
Action.
Slater,R.K.'04 Lieutenant,R.F.C.,P.O.W.
Smart,D.A.B.'12 Lieutenant,C.F.A.,Killed in
Action.
Smart,E.G.A.'04 Captain,Cameron
Highlanders,M.C.,Wounded.
Smart,G.A.R.'04 Lieutenant,R.F.C.
Smythe,A.E.'09 Sergeant,American Legion.
Smythe,H.C.'10 Corporal,Signal
Corps,Canadian Engineers.
Soper,E.N.'00 Captain,Canadian Forestry
Corps.
Spain,G.A.R.'07 Flight Commander,R.F.C.
Sparks,N.A.'11 Lieutenant,C.E.F.,Wounded.
Strubbe,G.A.'11 Captain,C.E.F.
Stewart,W.R.'16 Gunner,Canadian Field
Artillery.
Symes,A.W.'01 Sergeant,C.E.F.
Symes,J.A.'97 Lieutenant,C.E.F.
Taschereau,C.E.deM.'16 Lieutenant,C.E.F.
Taschereau,H.A.A.H.'15
Gunner,C.F.A.,Wounded.
Thackray,W.C.'14 Lieutenant,R.C.H.A.
Thorburn,W.C.'14 Lieutenant,C.O.T.C.
Thomas,J.V.'12 Field Artillery,U.S.A.

Thompson,A.T.'11
Lieutenant,C.E.F.,Wounded.
Thompson,V.W.'14 Lieutenant,R.F.C.
Thompson,W.H.'13 Lieutenant,C.E.F.
Tremain,A.E.'16 Lieutenant,R.F.A.
Trenholme,W.S.'08 Major,C.E.F.,m.i.d.
Tupper,Charles'96 Captain,C.E.F.
Tupper,C.W.jr.'16 Lieutenant,Canadian
Forestry Corps.
Tupper,J.M.'97 Lieutenant
Inspector,R.N.W.M.P.
Turriff,Robert'08 Private,P.P.C.L.I.,Killed in
Action.
Van Meter,Russell'17 Sergeant,Signal Corps.
Vernon,D.F.W.'13 Lieutenant,C.F.A.
White,A.'03 Lieutenant,C.E.F.
White,R.W.'11 Lieutenant,C.E.F.,P.O.W.
Wickware,W.H.'13 Driver Mechanical
Transport,C.A.S.C.
Williams,A.G.'03 Sergeant.
Wood,C.G.'15 Lieutenant,R.A.F.
Woods,J.R.'08 Captain,Govenor Generals Foot
Guards and Coldstream Guards,m.i.d.,Killed
in Action.

Woollcombe,P.H.P.'08 Captain,C.E.F.
Wright,F.S.'13 Gunner,C.F.A.
Wright,H.P.'06 Major,C.A.M.C.
Wright,J.S.'07 Major,C.F.A.,Killed in Action.
Wright,P.H.'05 Captain,Princess Louise
Dragoon Guards,Wounded.
Young,E.A.C.'16 Sapper,Canadian Engineers.

STAFF:
Barrington-Kennet, V. Major, R.F.C., Killed in
Action.
Creeth,N.A. Lieutenant,Canadian Engineers
Pratt,A.C. Lieutenant,Canadian Engineers,
Killed.
Sellwood,E.L. Lieutenant,C.E.F.,Wounded.
Smith,G.R. Lieutenant,43rd Rifles,Killed in
Action.
Weston,C.H.B. Major,B.E.F.,m.i.d.
Wiggins,A.B.H. Sergeant,Military Service
Clerk.
Wood,D.E.C. Captain,B.E.F.,Two Foreign
Decorations.

WORLD WAR II
1939-1945
ROLL OF HONOUR
These old boys and members of the staff gave their lives:

Angus, A.D.
Baker, H.M.
Beard, T.N.K.
Blue, D.A.
Critchley, J.
Emens, L.B.
Graham, R.M.
Hart, C.F.
Hart, F.J.
Hertzberg, P.H.A.
Hyman, G.H.
Jarvis, L.F.
Keefer, C.A.
Lambart, F.A.H.
Little, T.B.
MacBrien, M.D.

MacDonald, A.W.L.
MacDonald, I.A.
Millen, H.C.
Rowley, J.W.H.
Shuttleworth, R.U.P.K.
Smart, J.A.
Snell, A.E.
Soper, W.Y.J.
Symington, J.A.
Tudhope, W.F.
Wallace, J.K.C.
Waterfield, A.A.V.
Weldon, J.G.
Whinney, E.P.G.
Wood, J.E.R.

ASHBURIANS ON ACTIVE SERVICE
1939-1945

Abbott-Smith,K.B.'43 R.C.A.F.
Ahearn,Thomas,'22 Captain,Princess Louise Dragoon Guards.
Allan,J.A.R.'36 Lieutenant Commander,R.C.N.V.R.,D.S.C.
Allen,E.R.'34 Captain,Canadian Army.
Andrews,J.R.'41 Lieutenant,R.C.F.C.
Angus,A.D.'30 Pilot Officer,R.C.A.F.Killed in action.
Angus,F.W.R.'23 Commander, R.C.N.V.R.,O.B.E.
Arnold,J.S.H.'26 Captain,R.C.A.
Armstrong,J.S.P.'18 Major,48th Highlanders.
Baker,H.M.'37 Lieutenant,R.C.E,Killed in action.
Balders,A.H.'37 Corporal,R.C.E.
Barclay,I.'39 Lieutenant,R.C.N.V.R.
Baskerville,W.H.'35 Flight Lieutenant,R.A.F.
Bassett,J.W.H.'29 Major,Seaforth Highlanders of Canada.
Bates,T.L.'31 R.C.E.M.E.
Beard,T.N.K.'36 Midshipman,R.C.N.Killed in action 1941
Beard,C.T.'07 Commander,R.C.N.
Beardmore,E.'30 Wing Commander,R.C.A.F.
Beauclerk,T.W.'34 Major,Hastings & Prince Edward Regiment.
Beddoe,A.B.'12 Lieutenant,R.C.N.V.R.
Berry,P.C.'42 Sub-Lieutenant,R.C.N.V.R.
Biggar,H.W.'26 Flight Lieutenant,R.C.A.F.
Black,D.E.M.'35 R.C.A.F.
Blackburn,E.'25 Major,Princess Louise Dragoon Guards.
Blair,I.S.'18 Cameron Highlanders.
Blue,D.A.'32 Flight Sergeant,R.C.A.F.Killed.
Bogert,H.S.'18 Black Watch of Canada.
Bogert,J.R.'22 Captain R.C.A.M.C.
Bogert,M.P.'26 Brigadier,R.C.R.,D.S.O.,O.B.E.,Two Foreign Decorations.
Borden,R.A.'39 R.C.A.F.
Boutin,R.L.V.'44 R.C.N.V.R.
Boutilier,J.M.T.'34 R.C.A.F.
Bowman,R.T.'28 Broadcaster,C.A.S.F.
Brodie,A.B.'30 R.C.A.
Brodie,A.M.'31 R.N.
Brodie,J.C.'28 Black Watch of Canada.
Bronson,F.E.'41 Pilot Officer,R.C.A.F.

Brown,J.M.'38 R.C.A.F.
Burrows,C.R.'41 R.C.A.F.
Burrows,L.F.'38 R.C.A.F.
Calder,J.A.'34 Flight Lieutenant,R.C.A.F.
Caldwell,G.K.'40 R.C.A.F.,D.F.C.
Cann,H.W.J.'29 Captain,U.S.A.A.F.
Carrique,J.G.'27 Major,Victoria Rifles of Canada.
Carsley,Major,Canadian Army,O.B.E.
Carswell,H.B.'27 M.C. Wounded.
Challies,G.S.'27 Lieutenant-Colonel.
Chateauvert,P.R.B.'27 Corporal,Royal Montreal Regiment.
Chipman,W.W.'23 Lieutenant Commander,R.C.N.V.R.
Clark,G.C.'35 Lieutenant,R.C.N.V.R.
Clarke,L.G.'24 Brigadier,R.C.A.
Clayton,L.H.'22 Princess Louise Dragoon Guards.
Cole,I.F.C.'43 Coldstream Guards.
Colvil,J.H.C.'36 Canadian Army.
Coristine,C.F.'31 Leiutenant, Canloan,Wounded.
Coristine,R.W.'32 Lieutenant-Colonel,R.C.A.
Cowans,A.R.'39 Black Watch of Canada.
Cowans,Douglas,'31 Captain,R.C.A.C.
Cowans,H.A.'34 Black Watch of Canada.
Cowans,J.P.'32 Black Watch of Canada.
Cowans,P.P.'28 R.C.N.V.R.
Cowans,Russell,'35 Wing Commander,R.C.A.F.
Craig,Carleton,'26 Chief Civilian Ground Instructor,R.C.A.F.
Craig,R.H.'30 Captain,R.C.A.
Critchley,J.G.'09 Lieutenant,Scots Guards.Killed in action.
Croil,G.A.'42 R.C.A.F.
Currie,G.O.'29 Captain,Grenadier Guards.
Curry,A.M.M.'41 Flying Officer,R.C.A.F.
Davey,P.N.Lieutenant,R.C.A.
Davidson,R.K.'35 Flight Lieutenant,R.C.A.F.
Dewar,I.T.'28 Major,Wounded.
Drake,R.R.'42 Canadian Army
Drew,J.S.'39 R.C.A.F.
Duguid,G.H.T.'28 Lieutenant,Governor General's Foot Guards.
Dunn,R.W.A.Sub-Lieutenant,R.C.N.V.R.
Dunning,A.C.'37 Flight Lieutenant,R.C.A.F.

Eakin,W.R.'27 Major,Victoria Rifles of Canada.
Earle,J.B.'39 R.C.O.C.
Earnshaw,E.P.'38 Lieutenant,R.C.N.
Edwards,D.Kemp.'33 Lieutenant,R.C.N.V.R.
Edwards,J.C.'27 Lieutenant,Cameron Highlanders.
Ellis,W.H.'38 Captain,R.C.A.C., M.C.
Elwood,E.C.'31 Major, Canadian Army.
Emens,L.B.'33 Flying Officer,R.A.F.Killed in action.
Evans,A.C.'18 Black Watch of Canada.
Fauquier,David,'33 Lieutenant-Colonel, R.C.A.C.
Fauquier,E.B.'35 Lieutenant,R.C.N.V.R.
Fauquier,J.E.'27 Air-Commodore,R.C.A.F.,D.S.O.and bar,D.F.C.and two bars Canadian Airborne Forces.
Fauquier,H.A.'30 Lieutenant.
Fisher,G.S.'41 Flight Lieutenant,R.C.A.F.
Ferguson,J.'35 Lieutenant,Canadian Army.
Ferguson,G.W.'33 Lieutenant,R.C.N.V.R.
Forde,E.B.'40 Lieutenant,R.C.C.S.
Francis,Britton,Major,Canadian Army.
Fullerton,C.W.'34 Lieutenant,Queen's Own Rifles of Canada.
Gale,C.G.'34 Lieutenant,R.C.N.V.R.
Gamble,S.G.'28 Major,R.C.A.C.,M.C.,E.D.
Galt,N.'31 Lieutenant,R.C.N.V.R.
Gault,R.H.'27 Black Watch of Canada.
Ghent,D.J.'37 Captain,Canadian Army.
Gill,E.W.T.'19 Leiutenant Colonel.
Gill,F.E.T.'23 Captain,R.C.A.
Gillies,D.S. '30 Lieutenant-Colonel,O.B.E.
Gillies,N.B.'32 Captain,R.C.A.Wounded.
Gilmour,S.Blair '30 Captain, Stormont Dundas Glengarry Highlanders
Gobeil,F.M.'25 Squadron Leader,R.A.F.,A.F.C.
Godfrey,V.S.'12 Captain,R.C.N.
Goodwin,G.R.'42 Canadian Army.
Graham,R.M.'31 Pilot Officer,R.C.A.F.Killed in action.
Grant,J.F.'18 Squadron Leader,R.C.A.F.
Grant,M.E.'31 Squadron Leader, R.C.A.F.,A.F.C.
Grant,W.A.'39 Lieutenant,R.C.A.
Green,G.W.'41 Corporal,Field Artillery,U.S.Army
Gurd,D.S. '24 Captain,R.C.A.M.C.
Hadley,W.F.'34 Captain,R.C.A.
Hamilton,J.B.'25 R.C.R..
Hammond,H.C.'30 Lieutenant,R.C.E.

Hart,C.F.'28 Pilot Officer,R.C.A.F.Killed in action.
Hart,F.J.'31 Sergeant,R.C.A.F.Killed in action.
Hart,W.J.'22 Canadian Army.
Heath,H.B.'42 Pilot Officer,R.C.A.F.
Heaven,R.'43 Canadian Army.
Henderson,G.K.'22 Major,Wounded.
Hersey,C.A.'39 Lieutenant,R.C.A.C.
Hertzberg,P.H.A.'39 Captain,R.C.R.Killed in action.
Heubach,F.A.'32 R.C.A.F.
Higgins,H.H.'25 Canadian Army.
Holmes,R.T.'41 R.A.F.
Hose,W.J.F.'25 Commander,R.C.N.V.R.
Hughson,G.D.'41 Lieutenant,R.C.N.V.R.
Hughson,H.M.'41 Lieutenant,Canadian Army.
Hyman,G.J.'34 Lieutenant,Victoria Rifles of Canada,Killed in action.
Hyndman,R.S.'34 Flight Lieutenant,R.C.A.F.
Irvin,J.S.'28 Squadron Leader, R.C.A.F.
Irvine,A.M.'24 Major,Canadian Army.
Jarvis,L.F.'25 Flight Lieutenant,R.C.A.F.Killed in action.
Joseph,Henry,'28 Squadron Leader,R.C.A.F.
Keefer,C.A.'21 Lieutenant,R.C.N.V.R.,A.M.Killed in action.
King,H.W.'38 Lieutenant,Hastings and Prince Edward Regiment.
Kingsmill,W.J.'11 Lieutenant Commander,R.C.N.V.R.
Kirkpatrick,J.B.'36 Lieutenant,R.C.A.C.
Labatt,R.R.'21 Lieutenant-Colonel,Royal Hamilton Light Infantry.
Lambart,F.A.H.'25 Flying Officer,R.C.A.F.Killed in action.
Lane,R.L.'37 Lieutenant(E)R.C.N.
Lane,S.F.H.'21 Major,R.C.A.
Lawrence,A.B.R.'40 Captain,8th Canadian Reconnaisance Regiment M.C.
Lawrence,R.G.R.'43 Corporal, Stormont Dundas Glengarry Highlanders ,Canadian Army.
Leathem,R.M.'31 Captain,R.C.A.
Lee,A.P.'43 R.C.A.C.
Lewis,J.T.'35 Flying Officer,R.C.A.F.
Little,T.B.'32 Flight Lieutenant,R.C.A.F.Killed in action.
Lyman,W.F.S.'34 Captain,R.C.A.
MacBrien,W.R.'30 Group Captain,R.C.A.F.,O.B.E.
MacBrien,J.R.'28 Major,Royal Inniskilling Fusiliers.

MacBrien,M.D.'35 Flying Officer,R.C.A.F.Killed in action.
MacDonald,A.W.L.'30 Lieutenant,Nottinghamshire Yeomanry,Killed in action.
MacDonald,H.J.'42 Pilot Officer,R.C.A.F.
MacDonald,E.L.'35 Lieutenant,R.C.N.V.R.
MacDonald,I.A.'36 Sergeant,R.C.A.F.Killed in action.
MacGowan,J.A.'41 Black Watch of Canada,Wounded.
Mackenzie,D.W.'26 Lieutenant-Colonel,R.C.A.M.C.
Mackenzie,K.R.'29 Captain,R.C.A.M.C.
Maclaren,A.Roy,'15 Lieutenant-Colonel.
Maclaren,Donald,'39 R.C.A.
Macorquodale,I.D.'34 Lieutenant,R.C.O.C.
MacGuire,J.M. Lieutenant,R.C.N.V.R.
Magor,J.F.'32 Flight Lieutenant,R.C.A.F.
Magor,L.S.'34 Lieutenant,R.C.A.
Main,R.B.'39 R.C.A.F.
Marler,H.M.'27 Squadron Leader,R.C.A.F.
Mathias,F.D.'30 Captain,R C A
Mayburry,T.G.'26 Captain,Princess Louise Dragoon Guards.
McCallum,L.J.'39 R.C.A.F.
McCormick,G.A.'25 Captain,Canadian Army.
McGuckin,J.S.'32 R.C.A.F.
McMaster,D.R.'26 Major,R.C.A.,M.B.E.
McNeill,C.A.'25 Captain,Canadian Army.
McNutt,P.S.'34 Sergeant. Killed in action.
McKinley,J.C.'42 R.C.N.V.R.
McMahon,J.S.'21 Lieutenant-Colonel,R.C.A.C.,E.D.
Menzies,D.C.'31 Lieutenant,Black Watch of Canada.
Millen,H.C.'26 Pilot Officer,R.C.A.F.Killed in action.
Minnes,J.F.'27 Squadron Leader,R.C.A.F.
Molson,C.J.G.'18 Captain,Black Watch of Canada.
Mordy,B.P.'41 Trooper,R.C..A.C.
Nairn,M.'44 Canadian Army
Napier,C.E.'20 R.C.A.F.
Nation,G.H.'34 Lieutenant,R.C.N.V.R.
Neeld,J.H.'41 R.C.A.F.
O'Brien,J.B,'26 Lieutenant Commander,R.C.N.V.R.
Oppe,James S.'28 Lieutenant,R.C.N.V.R.
Oppe, J. Stephen, '28 Major, P.P.C.L.I.
Orde,E.T.C.'16 Captain,R.C.N.V.R.,O.B.E.
Pacaud,C.E.'25 Lieutenant Commander,R.C.N.V.R.
Palmer,H.Z.'30 Major,R.C.A.
Panet,E de B.'18 Major-General, D.S.O., C.M.G.
Panet,H.M. de L.'15 Lieutenant-Colonel,R.C.A.
Parker,Charles,'49 Lieutenant-Colonel.
Parker,V.S.'15 Group Captain,R.C.A.F.,D.F.C.,A.F.C.
Paterson,D.S.'36 Flight Lieutenant,R.C.A.F.
Perley-Robertson,A.'34 Lieutenant, R.C.A.
Perley-Robertson,G.'34 Lieutenant, R.C.A.
Perodeau,G.R.'31 Flight Lieutenant, R.C.A.F.
Phillips,A.'42 Lieutenant (E),R.C.N.
Phillips,D.P.'41 R.C.O.C.
Powell,J.A.'34 Lieutenant Commander,R.C.N.V.R.
Powell,R.M.'29 Commander,R.C.N.V.R.
Powell,W.H.'31 Lieutenant,Canadian Army.
Price,J.H.'11 Lieutenant-Colonel,P.O.W.Hong Kong.
Pugsley,W.H.'29 Lieutenant,R.C.N.V.R.
Read,T.H.W.'39 R.C.A.F.
Reid,H.E.'11 Rear-Admiral,R.C.N.,C.B.
Renaud,E.J.'10 Major-General,C.B.,Order of Orange-Nassau.
Rex,E.G.H.'32 R.C.A.F.
Reynolds,J.B.'36 U.S.Army
Riordon,J.E.B.'24 Lieutenant, R.C.N.V.R.
Ritchie,B.R.'30 Major,Black Watch of Canada.
Ritchie,J.W.'26 Lieutenant-Colonel,R.C.R.
Robinson,B.'31 Lieutenant Commander, R.C.N.V.R.
Ronalds,H.J.'35 Flight Lieutenant,R.C.A.F.
Ronalds,Leigh,'35 Pilot Officer,R.C.A.F.
Ross,W.G.'26 Lieutenant Commander,R.C.N.V.R.
Rowe,H.E.'23 Colonel.
Rowley,J.W.H.'31 Lieutenant-Colonel,North Shore New Brunswick Regiment,D.S.O.Killed in action.
Rowley,Roger,'33 Lieutenant-Colonel,Stormont Dundas and Glengarry Highlanders, D.S.O. and bar.
Schlemm,A.G.M.'34 Lieutenant,R.C.N.V.R.
Schlemm,L.G.W.'31 Lieutenant,R.C.N.V.R.
Sharp,J.W.'35 Black Watch of Canada,Wounded.
Sherwood,E.C.'11 Captain,R.C.N.
Sherwood,E.T.'31 Lieutenant,R.C.N.V.R.
Sherwood,F.H.'32 Lieutenant Commander,R.C.N.V.R.,D.S.C.

Sherwood,L.P.'06 Colonel.
Shuttleworth,R.U.P.K.'21 Flying Officer,R.A.F.Killed in action.
Simonds,G.G.'21 Lieutenant-General,C.B.,C.B.E.,D.S.O.and 7 foreign decorations.
Smart,J.A.'41 W.O.2,R.C.A.F.Killed in action.
Smellie,P.B.'31 Captain,Cameron Highlanders,M.C.
Snell,A.E.'26 Flying Officer,R.C.A.F.Killed on service.
Snell,D.M.'39 R.C.A.F.
Snell,D.I.'39 R.C.A.F.
Snelling,H.D.L.'37 Lieutenant,R.C.N.V.R.
Soper,R.W.'41 R.C.A.F.
Soper,W.Y.J.'41 Flying Officer,R.C.A.F.Killed in action.
Southam,G.T.'29 Lieutenant Commander,R.C.N.V.R.
Southam,G.H.'34 Captain,R.C.A.
Southam,J.D.'26 Lieutenant-Colonel,R.C.A.
Southam,R.W.'30 Lieutenant Commander,R.C.N.V.R.
Spafford,E.'40 Major,27th Canadian Armoured Regiment.
Spafford,T.'42 R.C.A.F.
Spence,N.'32 Pilot Officer,R.C.A.F.
Stairs,J.A.'35 Captain,R.C.A.S.C.
Stedman,R.W.'39 Captain,R.C.A.C., M.C.
Stevenson,A.G.'23 Lieutenant-Colonel,Black Watch of Canada.
Symington,J.A.'33 Captain,R.C.C.S., Killed in action.
Tamplet,H.'19 R.C.O.C
Thomas,R.'46 Canadian Army.
Tremain,A.E.D.'16 Brigadier,R.C.A.,O.B.E.
Tremain,K.H.'23 Colonel,R.C.A.,O.B.E.
Tudhope,W.F.'31 Pilot Officer,R.A.F.,D.F.C.Killed in action 1941.
Turner,Murray,'29 Captain,R.C.A.S.C.
Tyrer,J.C.'36 R.C.N.V.R.
Vickers,C.V.W.'34 Major,D.S.O.

Viets,J.C.(Peter)'38 Captain,R.C.A.,M.C.
Viets,R.D.'41 Flying Officer,R.C.A.F.
Vining,E.J.'44 R.C.N.V.R.
Wallace,J.K.C.'38 Lieutenant,R.C.A.C.Killed in action.
Wardrope,W.H.G.'41 R.C.A.F.
Weary,D.G.'39 Lieutenant,R.C.A.
Webster,R.C.'26 Flying Officer,R.C.A.F.
Weldon,J.G.'34 Pilot Officer,R.C.A.F.Killed in action 1943.
Whinney,E.P.G.'32 Sub-Lieutenant,R.N.Killed in action.
Wilgress,V.J.'39 Lieutenant,R.C.N.V.R.
Wilson,A.M.'40
Wilson,J.T.'25 Colonel,R.C.E.
Wilson,W.H.T.'35 Major,R.C.C.S.
Wilson,R.L.'40 R.C.A.F.
Wodehouse,G.E.'33 Major,R.C.A.M.C.
Wodehouse,R.F.'30 Canadian Intelligence Corps.
Wood,J.E.R.'32 Pilot Officer,R.C.A.F.Killed 1941.
Woods,D.M.'30 Captain,Royal Canadian Armoured Corps.
Wood,T.R.'39 Captain,R.C.A.S.C.
Woollcombe,G.A.'20 Lieutenant Commander,R.C.N.V.R.
Wright,G.K.'36 Lieutenant, Canadian Army,M.C.wounded.
Wurtele,D.B.'36 Squadron Leader,R.C.A.F.
Yuile,A.M.'34 Squadron Leader,R.C.A.F.

Johnson,J.W. Captain,Canadian Army.
McLeish,W.A.G. R.C.A.F.
Pratt, A.C. Killed.
Travers,R.F. Lieutenant,Canadian Army.
Waterfield,A.A.V. Flight Lieutenant,R.A.F.Killed in action.
Wood,A. Captain,Govenor General's Foot Guards.

ASHBURIANS ON ACTIVE SERVICE
THE KOREAN WAR
1950-1953

Bogert, M.P. '26 Brigadier, Commander, 25th Canadian Infantry Brigade, (previously D.S.O., O.B.E., two foreign decorations)

Forde, E.B. '40 Major, R.C.A.S.C.

Gault, M. '46 Counter Intelligence Corps, U.S. Army.

Woods, J.R. Lieutenant, R.C.R.

ABBREVIATIONS:

(These abbreviations apply to all lists).

A.F.C.   Air Force Cross
A.M.   Albert Medal
B.E.F.   British Expeditionary Force
C.A.S.F. Canadian Active Service Force
C.A.S.C. Canadian Army Service Corps
C.D.   Canadian Decoration
C.E.F.   Canadian Expeditionary Force
C.F.A.   Canadian Field Artillery
C.M.G.   Commander of St. Michael and St. George
C.O.C.   Canadian Ordnance Corps
D.F.C.   Distinguished Flying Cross
D.S.C.   Distinguished Service Cross
D.S.O.   Distinguished Sevice Order
E.D.   Efficiency Decoration
M.C.   Military Cross
m.i.d.   Mentioned in Dispatches
M.M.   Military Medal
O.B.E.   Order of the British Empire
P.O.W.   Prisoner of War
P.P.C.L.I. Princess Patricia's Canadian Light Infantry
R.A.F.   Royal Air Force
R.A.M.C. Royal Army Medical Corps
R.A.S.C. Royal Army Service Corps

R.C.A.   Royal Canadian Artillery
R.C.A.C. Royal Canadian Armoured Corps
R.C.A.F. Royal Canadian Air Force
R.C.A.M.C. Royal Canadian Army Medical Corps
R.C.C.S. Royal Canadian Corps of Signals
R.C.D.   Royal Canadian Dragoons
R.C.E.   Royal Canadian Engineers
R.C.E.M.E. Royal Canadian Electrical and Mechanical Engineers
R.C.F.C. Royal Canadian Forestry Corps
R.C.H.A. Royal Canadian Horse Artillery
R.C.N.   Royal Canadian Navy
R.C.N.V.R. Royal Canadian Naval Volunteer Reserves
R.C.O.C. Royal Canadian Ordnance Corps
R.C.R.   Royal Canadian Regiment
R.E.   Royal Engineers
R.F.A.   Royal Field Artillery
R.F.C.   Royal Flying Corps
R.N.   Royal Navy
R.N.A.S. Royal Naval Air Service
R.N.V.R. Royal Naval Volunteer Reserve
U.S.A.A.F. United States Army Air Force

APPENDIX H

ASHBURY COLLEGE TEACHING STAFF 1891-1991

Abel,F.L.   1964-1967 M.A. Oxford
Addison, A.H.   1973-1974
Alexander,P.   1967-1970 B.A.
Allan, Rev. James   1931-1934   Western (H) General TheologicalSem. N.Y.
Allen, Glenna B.Math WaterlooB.Ed. Western
Anderson, Raymond J.   1954- Dip. ASPT Army P.T. School
Angrave, Dr. James 1985-1986 B.A. Bishops DipEd M.Ed Bishops PhD University of Sheffield
Armstrong, Dr. G.R.   1971-1973 D.D.
Attwell, Rev. E.C.   1962-1965 B.A. Western L.Th Western
Atwood, H.W.   1942, 1965-1966 B.A. Queens B.Paed Toronto
Babbitt, Betty 1966-1981 Cert N.B. Teachers' College
Babbitt, G.W.   C.D.,1969-1981
Bacon, Dr. G.B.   1972-1973 B.A. New Brunswick Ph.D. New Brunswick
Bailey, J.A.   1975-1977 B.A. Carleton M.A. Carleton
Barrington-Kennet,V.   1910-1911   B.A.
Bates, Reginald 1902-1904
Batts, J.S.   1963-1965 B.A. Wales DipEd London
Baumann, Norbert 1926-1927 B.A. Cambridge
Beaulne, Claire 1983-1984
Beedell, John L.   1968- B.A. Carleton Ottawa Teachers College
Beetensen, B.R.   1960-1961 B.A. Bishops
Beique, B 1961-1962 B.A. McGill
Belcher, A.B.   1943-1963 Royal Military College
Belford, Rev. W.J.   1946-1951 B.A. Bishops B.Th. Bishops
Bellamy, B.A.   1971-1975 B.Sc. Carleton
Bellware, Federick T.   1973-1976 B.Sc. George Williams M.Sc Carleton
Benson,G.   1926-1930 B.A. Cambridge
Bercuson, Richard K.   1984-1988 B.A. Loyola B.Ed. McGill
Bernasconi, R.   1964-1964
Berry, Eva 1917-1921
Bewley, Rev. David 1987- 1990 B.Eng Technical University of N.S. M.Div. Toronto
Bickford - Smith, A.L.   1929-1930 M.A. Cambridge
Birch, J. Edgar 1904-1913, 1920-1931 L.C.O
Black, Larry J.   1961-1964 B.A. Mount Allison M.A. Boston
Black, Winnifred G.   1963-1966 ATCM Toronto NNEB Christopher's Coll., Kent
Blanchet, Miss A.   1904-1911 B.A. Mount Allison
Boettger, Constantin V.   1900-1902 M.A.. Leipsig University
Boon, Rev. T.C.   1941-1943 B.A. Manitoba
Boone, John C. 1953-1956 M.Ed. State University of New York
Booth, Ms. Leslie 1988- B.A. Toronto B.Ed. Toronto
Boswell, D.M.   1957-1960 B.Sc Dalhousie M.Sc Toronto
Bowley, R.W.   1951-1952 B.Sc. Queens

Brain, Arthur D. 1935-1966 B.A. Toronto Oxford
Brine, Mrs. E 1940-1950
Brine, Lt. Col. E.G. 1945-1950 R.M.A., Woolrich
Brodie, W.H.H. 1922-1937 B.A. London
Brookes, Douglas J., CD 1973-1991 BA Music Carleton
Burczak, Vic J. 1970-1972 B.A. Carleton
Burke, Rev. N.R. 1934-1935
Byford, William W. 1966-1976 B.Sc London
Cann, John O. 1973-1974 B.A. Guelph
Cardonnier, Mlle. M.A. 1962-1964 cert. Cambridge cert. Paris
Carleton, Patty 1989- BMath Waterloo B.Ed. Western
Carter, Harry H. 1982-1986 B.A. Toronto M.A. Toronto
Carter, K.R.F. 1966-1967 B.A. Acadia
Carver, Peter G. 1960-1961 B.A. Toronto B.J. Carleton
Cary-Elwes, Rev. H 1910-1913 B.A. Oxford
Cassels, K.C. 1922-1928 B.A. Cambridge
Castle, K.B. 1932-1935 B.A. Cambridge
Cattell, Keith M. 1981-1987 B.A. Carleton M.A. Carleton
Chappell, E.R. 1978-1979 B.A. St. Francis Xavier B.Ed. Ottawa M.A. Institute de
                              Filologia Hispani
Chester-Master, Rev. Harold 1922-1925 M.A. Durham
Chestnut, C.J. 1942-1943 M.A. Harvard
Clarabut, C.E. 1927-1929 B.A. Cambridge
Coles,Randall J. 1988- B.A. Carleton B.Ed. Queens
Comber, W.T. 1917-1918 M.A. Oxford
Conrad, D.L. 1983-1987 B.A. Ottawa M.A. McGill DipEd McGill
Copeland, I.D. 1965-1966 B.A. Western
Cordonnie, Marie-Aline 1969-1970
Corke, G. 1986-1988 B.A. Western BMath Waterloo M.A. Carleton
Cossar, K.B. 1931-1933 B.A. Cambridge
Coulter, F 1906-1907 B.A. Toronto
Cox, F.E. 1908-1910 Dublin
Cox, Sgt. M 1940-1941
Cranston, R.R. 1945-1946
Creeth, Norman A. 1913-1917 M.Sc. Manchester
Crockett, J.S. 1974-1981 B.A.Math Stanmillis College, Belfast
Currie, P.W. 1902-1915 B.A. Toronto B.Sc. Owens
Dalton, H.S. 1955-1964, 1966-1969 University of King's College
Dalton, Muriel 1954-1964 Toronto
Daratha, S.M. 1961-1963 Cert Saskatoon Teachers' College
Darby, Robert W. 1953-1954 B.A. Bishops
Dare, Capt. H 1943-1944
Darnill, A.W. 1917-1923 B.A. Durham
Davis, R 1950-1951 B.A. Duquesne
De Brisay, C.T. 1917-1918 B.A. Paris
De Corcuera, A. 1965-1969 B.A. Mexico

de Zela, Senora Pardo   1948-1950   B.A. Hunter College
Deakin, I. 1989-   B.A. Queens B.Ed. Queens M.B.A. Queens
de Corcuera, A.   1966-1970 B.A. Mexico
Denison, Christine   1988-   B.A. Lakehead
Denston, Mr.   1921-1922
Devine, R.G.   1950-1954   Ottawa
Discombe. N.J.   1981-1984   B.Sc. Sussex Cert.Ed. Sussex
Donald, D.   1988-1990
Donaldson, E.S.   1959-1961   B.A. Ottawa Trinity College, Dublin Ontario College of
Education
Douglas, Claire   1990-1991   B.A. Ottawa B. Ed.
Dowd, M.S.   1981-1982   B.A. Ed. Lakehead B.Out Lakehead
Drayton, C.G.   1948-1951   B.A. Canterbury
Dyson, P.   1986-1987   Royal Conservatory of Music.
Edge, W.A.   1948-1949   B.A. McGill
Edwards, E.C.N.   1923-1926, 1932-1938   M.A. Cambridge
Edwards, Miss Mary   1911-1924
Egan, Antony   1964-1971   B. Sc. London
Elder, D.M.   1939-1940   B.A. McMaster Cert Ontario College of Education
Emery, C.J.   1900-1912
Fair, R   1980-1981   B A   Western B Ed   Queens
Falstrup - Fischer, P.   1954-1956   M.A. Cambridge
Ferneyhough, F.C.   1973-1973
Fleming, Rev. M.   1983-1984   B.A. Carleton   M.Div Toronto
Fleuriau-Chateau, Mrs.Almut   1984-1990   B.A. Hons Leicester M.A. Germ Carleton
Fleury, Joseph-M.   1891-1908   M.A. Paris
Flynn, P.J.   1968-1973   Cert. Western Australian College
Ford, Dawn   1989-   B.A. Carleton
Fordyce, P.C.   1968-1970   M.A.
Fort, Karen   1978-1984   B.A. Toronto
Fortier, P.   1966-1968   B.Ped Montreal
Fox, D.M.   1976-1983   B.Math Waterloo B. Ed. Queens
Fronton, A.   1962-1963   B.A. Ottawa
Fudakowski, J.   1966-1968   B.A. Ottawa
Furnival, A.S.   1918-1919   B.A. Oxford
Galvin, M.J.   1959-1961   B.A. Ottawa
Gamble, D.G.   1958-1959
Gardner, Greer   1975-1976   B.A. Carleton
Gavel, Charlene A.   1983-1984   B.A. McMaster B.Ed. Queens
Gerrie, M.   1961-1962   B.Sc. Dubuque
Gibson, W.   1956-1956
Gilbert, Mr.   1911-1912   Toronto
Giles, Mrs. S   1970-1971
Gillean, P.   1955-1962   Cert. Ottawa Teachers College
Gillson, H.T.   1919-1920   London
Glover, J.   1968-1983   M.A. Oxford

Goldsmith, J.L.   1965-1968   Cert. Ottawa Teachers' College
Gosselin, P.H.   1977-1978   B.A. College de Saint Hyacinthe
Gounelle, Y.   1979-1981, 1982-1984   B.A. Carleton
Graham, F.K.   1970-1974   B.Mus FRCO Toronto FRCCO ARCT Toronto
Grainger, S.K.   1976-1983   B.A. Western
Gray, R.I.   1974-   B.P.E. Ottawa B.Ed. OTC   Queens
Green, Rev. E.E.   1969-1987   B.A. L.T.L Toronto B.D. Toronto
Groleau, G.   1988-1990   DipEd Trois-Rivières B.Ed. Quebec
Gwyn, Mrs. M.   1975-1976   B.A. Ottawa
Hancock, A.J.   1963-1966   B.Sc. Nottingham B.Sc. Nottingham
Harrison, E.D.   1940-1941   B.A. London
Harrison, J.G.   1940-1944   M.A. Oxford
Hartley-Stansfield, W.W.   1906-1907   B.A. Cambridge
Harwood-Jones, P.   1964-1965   B.A. McGill
Hastie, J.W.   1952-1953   Carleton College
Heaven, Rev. C.A.   1907-1908
Heffernan, A.   1978-1979   B.Ed. Sherbrooke
Heney, F.G.   1946-1951   B.Sc. McGill
Hepburn, W.W.   1920-1923   B.A. Bishops
Hérique, B.   1984-   M.A. Arts Nancy B.A. Sci. Nancy B.A. Nancy
Hewitt, W.H.   1912-1924
Heyd, G.   1974-1979   B.A. Toronto
Hichens, Mr.   1895-1896
Higgs, Capt.G.W.   1948-1953
Hillary, B.K.   1960-1961   B.A. Springfield College
Hincks, D.   B.Sc. British Columbia
Hinnell, R.A.   1975-1987   B.Sc. Bristol
Hinnell, Sally A.   1983-1984   B.Sc. Ed. Bristol Cert. London
Hoff, Dr. R.   1950-1951   Ph.D.
Hooper, C.H.   1910-1915   B.A. Queens
Hooper, J.G.   1946-1947   B.A. Toronto
Hopkins, Dr. D.E.   1975-   BSc. Sci. Hull Ph.D. Hull
Hopwood, P.   1954-1954
Howis, B.K.T.   1929-1935
Hughes, J.C.   1960-1962   B.A. Western
Humphreys, J.H.   1968-
Hunden, Sybil   1964-1965   Cert.
Hunt, Jaqueline P.   1983-1984   B.A. British Columbia   M.A. Carleton
Hunter, Elsie B.   1939-1964
Hyatt, G.E.   1972-1976   B.Sc. Bishops
Inns, C.J.   1970-1975   B.A. Wales
Jackson, G.P.   1957-1959   B.A. Bishops
Jacobsen, Nancy   1965-1966   Ottawa Teachers College
Jacombe, Miss G.   1951-1954   B.A. Queens
Jacques, G.W.   1966-1968   Ottawa Teachers College Toronto
James, Rev. H.G.   1968-1969   M.A. Theol Dip.

Jansen, M.E. 1976- B.A. Carleton M.Ed. Ottawa DipEd. London
Jobling, J.K. 1953-1959 B.A. Leeds DipEd Leeds
Johnson, E.R. 1981-1982 B.A. Victoria U. of Wellington
Johnson, J.W. 1931-1940 B.Sc. Toronto Dip Oxford
Johnson, L. 1941-1942 B.A. Durham M.A. Haverford
Joliffe, Miss M. 1917-1921
Jones, F.T. 1970-1972 B.Sc ACP Wales B.Ed. Wales FRGS London
Jones, P.F. 1964-1965 M.A. Oxford
Josselyn, P.H. 1969-1974 B.A. Nottingham DipEd. Nottingham
Jowett, Nancy 1985- B.A. Guelph B.Ed. Toronto
Kennedy, Jane 1973- B.A. Mount St. Vincent
Ker, E. 1923-1928 M.A. Oxford
Kettleborough, Rev. E.G. 1954-1959 B.A. McGill L.Th Montreal Theological
King, H. 1923-1927 B.A. Oxford
King, M 1989- B.Soc. Ottawa B.Ed. Toronto
Dr. Klein 1942-1942 Ph.D.
Knell, K. 1988-1989 B.A. Trent
Lahey, Mrs. L.M. 1978- B.A. Queens P.T.C. British Columbia Spec Ottawa
Laird, R. 1967-1970 Cert. Lakeshore Teachers College
Lancaster, R.L. 1961-1962 B.Sc. Wittenberg
Landry, M. 1983- B.A. Carleton B.Ed. Toronto
Lawson, T.W. 1951-1953 B.A. Toronto
Layton, Mr. 1921-1922
Lee,P.H. 1949-1951 B.A. Canterbury
Lemele, G.J. 1977- LicEs Lettr Paris M.A. Ottawa B.Ed. Queens
Lemele, Therese B. 1979-1990 B.A.C Lettr Ottawa D.E.C Ed. St. Jean Cert. Hull
Lewis, A.G. 1900-1902 B.A. Oxford
Linseman, M. 1987-1989 B.A. Queens B.Ed. Queens
Lister, D. 1974- M.A. York A.B. Princeton
Locke, R.R. 1953-1953
Lord, Rev. W.J. 1951-1954 Toronto
Lucas, L. 1937-1938 B.A. Queens
Lynn, Mrs.J.R. 1969-1977 B.A. Queens
MacFarlane, P. 1975- B.A. Carleton B.Ed. Carleton
MacIntyre, F. 1956-1958 B.Sc. Queens
Mack, G.S.B. 1940-1941 Trinity College, Dublin
MacKay, H. 1941-1942 B.A. Mount Allison
Macoun, A.M. 1974-1986 M.A. Oxford
MacPhail, Dr. M. 1937-1937 B.A. Queens M.A. McGill D.Phi. Oxford
MacSkimming, Suzette L. 1977-1982 B.A. Berkely
Marland, J.J. 1958-1976 DipEd. London
Marland, P.J. 1964-1966 B.A. Carleton
May,R. 1926-1928 B.A. Cambridge
McAdam, W.R. 1941-1942
McDougall, P.D. 1976-1977 B.A. Sir George Williams
McFarlane, P. 1946-1948 B.A. McGill

McGee, C.H.   1895-1897   B.A. Toronto
McGowan, H.   1967-1968   M.A. Edinburgh
McGuire, G.   1970-1978   B.A. Queens M.Sc. Bradley
McIntyre, W.   1964-1965   B.A. Vermont
McLaughlin, P.   1959-1960   B.A. London
McLean, Marian   1984-1985   B.Mus Western B.Ed. Western
McLean, P.   1980-   DipEd Music R.S.A.M.
McLeish, W.A.G.   1938-1940   B.A. McMaster Dip. Ontario College of Education
McMeekin, Dr. H.W.   1891-1906   L.L.D
Meaker, Rev. T.   1990-   B.A. Carleton B.Th. St. Paul
Meiklejohn, J.   1930-1931   B.Sc. St. Andrews
Menzies, T.A.   1979-   B.Sc. Hons. Dalhousie B.Ed. Mount St. Vincent
Mercer, E.   1938-1939   B.Sc. Dalhousie
Merritt, J.   1987-   B.Mus Ottawa
Michel, R.   1981-1983   B.A. PhysE Ottawa B.A. Educ. Ottawa
Monk, Mrs. C.   1974-1979   Dip Lyons B.A. Paris
Monks, Rev. K.B.   1930-1931, 1958-1965   B.Sc. Agr. McGill S. Th. Toronto
Montgomery, P.H.   1988-   B.A. Bishops PGCE London M.Ed. Saint Mary's
Montizambert, J.R.   1902-1910   M.A. Bishops
Morel, Lise   1991-   B.A. Hons Bishops B.Ed. Ottawa
Morgan, J.R.   1963-1965   B.Sc. FRSA Acadia
Morris, D.G.   1978-1989   B.A. Hons Toronto M.A. Essex M.A. Ottawa
Morris, G.   1931-1933   B.A. London L.L.B. Cambridge
Mortureux, Mlle.   1917-1919   Paris
Mousseau, M.R.   1986-   B.Sc. Hons Ottawa B.Ed. Ottawa
Moynihan, Mrs. G.   1981-1981   B.Sc. M.A. DePaul M.Ed. DePaul B.A. Carleton
Mueller, F.   1988-   B.Sc. Brock B.Ed. Brock M.B.A. Queens
Munson, R.J.   1965-1966   B.A. Manchester BPaed Manchester
Myers, Rev. H.N.   1925-1930   M.A. Oxford
Newton, J.S.   1944-1946   Cert
Nicol, R.H.   1918-1919   London
Niles, K.D.   1968-   B.A. Carleton
Novick, Mrs. Alyssa   1989-   B.A. Hons Queens M.A. York B.Ed. Brock
O'Keefe, B.J.   1974-1975   B.A. Carleton
Ostrom, P.   1982-   B.A. Queens B.PhE. Queens B.Ed. Queens
Parker, J.   1968-1970   B.A. Bishops
Parks, Rev. J.   1919-1921   M.A. Oxford
Parks, K.B.   1972-1974   BPaed. New Brunswick
Parlee, L.K.   1919-1922   B.A. Oxford
Parris, Mr.   1901-1902
Passy, C.W. O.B.E., D.F.C. 1948-1948   M.A. Cambridge
Pattison, J.R.   1924-1930   B.A. Oxford
Pelletier, M-A.   1981-   B.A. Laval L.Es Laval M.A. Quebec à Montreal
Pemberton, I.C.   1959-1964   B.A. Bishops Toronto
Penton, M.H.   1968-   B.A. Carleton
Pettigrew, J.   1947-1948
Petty, J.   1969-1970

Peyton, Rev. N.C. 1965-1966 B.A. Saskatchewan L.Th. Saskatchewan B.Ed. Saskatchewan

Phillips, D. 1928-1929 B.A. Wales

Philpott, H.S. 1915-1917 M.A. Oxford

Platt, Maj. P.L.W. 1962-1963 B.Eng. McGill

Plourde, Mme. Franz 1987-1989

Polk, D.L. 1940-1943, 1947-85 B.A. Dartmouth

Polk, D.C. 1977-1987, 1989-1990 B.A. Carleton B.Ed. Ottawa

Poole, Rev. A.J. 1943-1946 B.A. McGill L.Th. McGill

Porritt, H.M. 1932-1941 M.A. Bishops

Potter, R.M. 1977-1979 M.A. Oxford

Povey, J.F. 1958-1961 B.A. South Africa M.A. South Africa

Powell, A.J. 1946-1958 B.A. Toronto B.A. Cambridge

Pratt, A.C. 1903-1905, 1909-1911 B.Sc.

Price, C.L. 1928-1928 B.A. Cambridge

Price, E.A. 1951-1952 B.A. Bishops

Pritchard,Mrs. A. 1986-

Ratan, Mrs. K. 1975-1976

Redler, Dr. R. 1941-1941

Rees, J.M.P. 1954-1958 B.A. London Wales

Renny, Dr. A. 1943-1944 M.A. St. Andrews Ph.D. St. Andrews D.Sc. St. Andrews

Rhoades, H.G. 1913-1914

Rice, R. 1973- B.A. Trent

Robertson, H.J. 1968- B.A. South Africa Cert Ontario College of Education M.A. Ottawa

Rosen, L. 1985-1988 B.Sc. George Williams

Rossell, L. 1933-1935

Ruddick, C.T. 1956-1957 B.A. Haverford Yale

Sabourin, Judith 1977-1978 B.A. Ottawa

Sanders, Dr. H. 1916-1917

Schovanek, J.G. 1966-1968 B.A. St. Procopius

Sellwood, E.L. 1914-1917 B.A. Oxford Paris

Selman, Miss G. 1969-1970

Seyhun, Delia 1989-1991

Shaw, J.N.B. 1944-1945 B.Sc. McGill

Sherwood, M.H. 1958-1961, 1966-1988 B.A. Carleton M.Ed. Massachussetts

Sibley, L.H. 1945-1966 B.Sc. McGill

Sikora, H-U. 1990- B.A. McMaster M.A. Free University of Berlin

Simpson, G.H. 1982- B.A. Carleton B.Ed. Ottawa

Sinclair, A.C. 1963-1965 B.Sc. McGill B.P.A. Boston B.C.L. Montreal

Slattery, W.E. 1954-1961

Smith, Lt. G.R. 1905-1910 B.A. Cambridge

Smith, R.A. 1944-1944

Snelgrove, A.H.N. 1952-1966 Cert Mount Allison

Snell, J.G. 1964-1965 B.A. McGill M.A. Western

Somerville, W.H. 1967-1970 Middle Temple

Sparks, A.J. 1987- B.PE. Hons. Ottawa B.Ed. Ottawa

Speckert-Zettel, Helen   1986-   B.Sc. P.E. St. Francis Xavier B.Ed. Queens
Spencer, I.H.   1954-1964   B.A. Riverview College, Australia
Spencer, Dr. Katherine R.   1958-1961, 1965-1967, 1968-1969 DsCO Boston
Spencer, M.C.   1965-1967   B.A. Hist. Sophia Tokyo
Spenlove-Brown, T.   1987-1988
Stableford, W.E.   1976-   B.A. PhsEd Western DipEd. Western Cert. Western
Stewart, J.H.   1967-1968   BComm St. Patrick's College
Stone, Sgt-Major. F.W.   1924-1938
Storosko, B.   1985-1987 B.Sc. McMaster B.Ed. Western
Stout, R.L.   1983-1984 B.Sc. Temple DipEd. Alberta
Street, T.G.   1982- B.A. OTC Trent B.Ed. Ottawa
Sullivan, D.M.   1969-1970   B.A. Carleton
Swords, Janet   1991-   B.Soc Scien Ottawa
Sykes, R.A.   1940-1940
Tanner, A.L.   1933-1935   FRCO LRAM Royal Academy of Music, London
Tanod, L.A.   1984-   M.A. Hons McMaster B.Mus London
Thomas, Mr.   1911-1912   London
Thomas, A.C.   1974-1984   B.Mus Manchester University DipEd Reading, England
Thomas, G.G.   1979-   B.A. Hons Bishops M.A. O.T.C Bishops
Thomas, O.L.   1917-1918   B.Sc. London
Thompson, C.W.   1929-1933   M.A. Oxford
Thompson, L.K.   1930-1931
Thomson, G.W.   1967-1972   LRAM ARCM Royal College of Music
                                 ARCO LTCT Royal College of Music
Thorne, W.R.P.   1920-1923   B.A. Cambridge
Tigges, Rev. W.S.   1940-1942   B.Sc. Hvilan-Lund M.Sc. Ultuna-Upsala
                                 Ph.D. Halle-Wittenberg
Todd, Rosemary   1988-1989
Toft, Miss T.D.   1941-1941   Copenhagen
Tottenham, T   1968-1978   Cert Ottawa Teachers College
Travers, R.F.   1942-1943
Turcotte, Mrs. P.E.   1962-1963   B.A. Saskatchewan
Valentine, G.R.   1987-   B.A.   Manitoba
Valentine, J.N.   1977-   B.A. Manitoba M.Ed. Ottawa
Van Alstyne, Elizabeth   1989-1991   B.A. Queens B.Ed. Queens
Van der Byl, F.V.   1929-1930 Trinity College, Dublin
De Kerckhov Var, A.   1961-1964   B.A. Brussels B.Ed. Ottawa
Varley, G.R.   1976-   B.A. Concordia M.Ed. Queens
Varley, Mary Ann   1977-   B.A. Concordia
Vetter, F.A.   1956-1958   B.A. Carleton
Villarreal, O.   1991-   M.Spanish Ottawa
Vincent, B.B.   1963-1964   M.A. Oxford Toronto
Vincent, Rev. F.J.   1930-1931   L.Th C.F. Manitoba
Vincent, J.   1966-1968   A.Sc. Cambridge Carleton
Voorhis, Rev. E.1914-1919   M.A. Princeton Ph.D. New York University
Wakefield, Jennifer L.   1987-1989 B.A. Hons McGill DipEd. McGill M.A. McGill

Waldegger, Carmen   1985-1988   B.A. Western B.Ed. Saint Mary's
Wallin, B.   1970-1975   B.A. University of the Pacific M.A. Stanford
Walsh, C.J.   1942-1945
Wansborough, M.B.   1961-1963   B.A. Bishops
Waterfield, A.A.V.   1937-1939   B.A. Oxford
Watson, Rev. I.   1966-1968   M.A. Oxford
Wayland, J.W.   1952-1953   Vermont
Weatherall, T.L.   1953-1954   Dip. Army D.T. School Loughborough College
Weintrager, P.   1982-1988   B.A. Bishops Cert. Waterloo Toronto
Wells, A.B.   1956-1957   B.A.
Weston, W.H.J.   1928-1929   B.Sc. London
White, J.T.   1969-1970
Whitfield, F.E.B.   1927-1937   M.A. Durham
Whitwill, J.C.   1965-1968   B.A. Western
Wiggins, A.B.H.   1911-1917   M.A. Oxford
Williams, R.E.   1965-1967   Laval, Chicago
Williams, R.A.   1978-1981   B.Ed. Western B.Sc. McMaster
Williamson, L.E.   1964-1965, 1977-1984   B.P.A. Columbia M.A. Carleton   F.R.E.S.
Wilson, D.R.   1981-   B.Sc. Hons Belfast (Queens)
Wood, A.   1939-1940   B.A. Queens
Wood, D.E.C.   1910-1914, 1919-1921   Paris
Woodburn-Wright, Irene   1945-1967   B.Mus BAC Bishops
Woods, Maj. H.J., M.B.E.   1945-1948, 1956-1958, 1962-1964
Woollcombe, J.V.   1904-1906   B.A. Cambridge
Wright, Alison   1984-1985   B.A. Kingston Art College
Wright, H.F.   1919-1936   B.A. Cape University, South Africa Sheffield
Wright, W.R.   1946-1947   B.A. McGill
Zettel, R.J.   1986-   BMath Waterloo B.Ed. Queens BTheo Queens
Zrudlo, E.W.   1983-   B.A.Eng Carleton M.A. Carleton

BIBLIOGRAPHY

Annan, Noel. *Roxburgh of Stowe.* Longman Green, London 1965

Arlen, Michael J. *Exiles.* Farrar, Straus & Giroux, New York 1970

Cummings, H.R. *The Ottawa Public Schools: A Brief History.* 1971

Gossage, Carolyn. *A Question of Privilege: Canada's Independent Schools.* Peter Martin, Toronto 1977

Farson, Daniel. *Out of Step.* Michael Joseph, London 1974

Haig, Robert. *Ottawa, City of the Big Ears*

Harris, Andrew (ed). *Lakefield College School: The First Hundred Years.* 1979

Humble, A.H. *The School on the Hill: Trinity College School 1865-1965.* Port Hope 1965

MacNeil, Robert. *Wordstruck: A Memoir.* Viking Penguin 1989

Lynch, Charles. *Up From the Ashes. The History of the Rideau Club.* 1990

Moodey, E.C. & Spiers, R.A. *Veritas: A History of Selwyn House School, Montreal 1908-1978.* Montreal 1978

McMahon, J.S. *Professional Soldier: Guy Simonds — A Memoir.* Winnipeg 1985

Ottawa Collegiate Institute. *A History of the Ottawa Collegiate Institute.* Ottawa 1904

Patriquin, J.G. *B.C.S.: From Little Forks to Moulton Hill.* 1977

Penton, D.S. *Non Nobis Solum: The History of Lower Canada College.* Montreal 1972

Peterson, A.D.C. *Schools Across Frontiers: The Story of the International Baccalaureate and the United World Colleges.* Open Court, LaSalle, Illinois 1987

Shapiro, Bernard J. *Report of the Commission on Private Schools in Ontario* with Appendix, A History of Private Schools in Ontario, by Robert Stamp.

Stamp, Robert. *The Schools of Ontario.* University of Toronto Press, Toronto 1982

Walker, Dean. *Net Worth: The Memories of C.E. Pickering.* Yorkminister, Toronto 1973

Woods, Shirley E. *Ottawa: The Capital of Canada.* Doubleday 1980

INDEX

A

Abbott, Douglas, 124
Abinger Hill School, 107-121, 262
Acres, Julia (first Mrs. Woollcombe), 13
Action Ashbury, 183-184, 193
Acworth, Mrs, 109
Adams, F.J. ("Cruiser"), 27
Ahearn, Thomas, 11-12, 37, 40
Alexander, Angus, 122
Alexander, Brian, 136
Alexander, Earl, of Tunis, 136, 138, 203
Alexander, Shane, 136
Allan, J. Roberts, 30, 124
Anderson, Eve, 145, 148
Anderson, Montague, 192
Anderson, R.J., 145, 146, 148-149, 154, 175-177, 185, 210, 239-40, 246, 262
Archdale, Elizabeth, 120
Archdale, Nicholas, 78, 83-90, 107-108, 110, 113-124, 127, 147, 150, 212, 263
Archdale, Sheila, 83, 84, 115
Arlen, Michael, 111
Arlen, Michael J., 111, 112, 117
Armitage, Russell, 176
Armstrong, Jim, 72, 179
Art Levitt Trophy, 202
Ashburian, The, 19-20, 24, 26-29, 31, 34-38, 58, 63, 65, 70, 72, 81, 83, 86, 88, 110, 117, 126-127, 136-138, 140, 143, 146-147, 155-156, 187, 202, 209
Ashbury College Company Ltd., 17, 27, 30, 40
Ashbury College Debating Society, 37, 61
Ashbury College Development Fund, 181
Ashbury College Foundation, 247, 260
Ashbury College Guild, 247, 249, 263
Ashbury College Incorporated, 40
Ashbury College Literary and Dramatic Society, 66
Ashbury College Old Boys Association, 29, 72, 76, 78, 85, 124, 126, 127, 131, 135, 179, 181-182
Ashbury House School, 13-14
Ashbury News, 211
Ashbury Old Boys' Cup, 129
Ashbury Players, 259
Askwith, Charles, 208
Atwood, H.W., 175
Ault, Arthur, 155
Aylwin, Mrs., 29

B

D

G

H

I

J

K

L

M

N

O

R

U

V

W